KNOWLEDGE JUSTICE

KNOWLEDGE JUSTICE

DISRUPTING LIBRARY AND INFORMATION STUDIES
THROUGH CRITICAL RACE THEORY

EDITED BY
SOFIA Y. LEUNG AND JORGE R. LÓPEZ-MCKNIGHT

THE MIT PRESS   CAMBRIDGE, MASSACHUSETTS   LONDON, ENGLAND

The open access edition of this book was made possible by generous funding from Arcadia—a charitable fund of Lisbet Rausing and Peter Baldwin.

This book was set in Stone Serif and Stone Sans by Westchester Publishing Services. Printed and bound in the United States of America.

Library of Congress Cataloging-in-Publication Data

Names: Leung, Sofia Y., editor. | López-McKnight, Jorge R., editor.
Title: Knowledge justice : disrupting library and information studies through critical race theory / edited by Sofia Y. Leung and Jorge R. López-McKnight.
Description: Cambridge, Massachusetts : The MIT Press, [2021] | Includes bibliographical references and index.
Identifiers: LCCN 2020028167 | ISBN 9780262043502 (paperback)
Subjects: LCSH: Minorities in library science--United States. | Critical pedagogy--United States. | Social justice--United States. | Library science--Moral and ethical aspects--United States. | Information science--Moral and ethical aspects--United States. | United States--Race relations--Philosophy.
Classification: LCC Z682.4.M56 K58 2021 | DDC 020.89--dc23
LC record available at https://lccn.loc.gov/2020028167

10 9 8 7 6 5 4 3 2

Para Irlanda Estelí Jacinto
And for all the other Irlandas in LIS
The ones who left, the ones who stayed

CONTENTS

ACKNOWLEDGMENTS

There is a specific joy about looking back, about remembering how the collection has come together and is what it now is. But also for what it was before, and in between. It is hard to describe in words our deep gratitude for the care, support, and kindness we experienced on this path. A few kind, encouraging words at the end of an email or a sincere expression of thanks when connecting in person or, more often, online, felt more like a loving look from a familiar face, or a strong, meaningful laughter with dear friends. These moments and expressions provided light, affirmation, and strength, arriving just when they were needed. We are so profoundly grateful for our communities supporting this work. They will stay with us for a very long time, and are across all these pages.

Our loving thanks to Irlanda Jacinto for beginning this journey with us.

To Gita Devi Manaktala, our editor, a deep thank you for your advice, guidance, and belief in this project. To María Isela Garcia and Nhora Lucia Serrano for helping this collection become a collection. To Anne Davidson for copyediting the manuscript and Greg Hyman for guiding us through the production process. To Lori Salmon for indexing this collection and for her generosity in sharing her knowledge with two newer indexers.

Thank you to the anonymous reviewers, both at the proposal and manuscript stages, for their feedback and suggestions.

In the early stages of this project, when the proposal was still being formed, Nicholae Cline and Gina Schlesselman-Tarango offered valuable feedback, insight, and support. Thank you.

Rose L. Chou, Megan Cherewick, PhD, and Luis Poza, when the introduction was still in flight, your observations, ideas, and interpretations helped to push it further along in much-needed ways. Before it landed, Anne Cong-Huyen and Torie Quiño-nez provided comments, critiques, and editing that helped bring it to these pages. We are grateful to you all.

Dear Rae, sincere appreciation for holding and caring for our thinking and writing in the conclusion. Your generous, loving comments and suggestions made it better.

Thank you to Charlotte Roh and Katie Zimmerman for translating publishing contract language for us.

Special thanks to Sarah Kostelecky and Teresa Neely. Before this book was in full motion, when it was just a quiet dream, you both held space for this possibility. Eternally grateful for your belief in this project.

To Anthony Dunbar, Todd Honma, and Tonia Sutherland—it means something very heavy that you joined us; it is immensely special. We are so appreciative that you shared words with all of us. We hope this work makes you proud.

Along the way in the building of this collection, some truly wonderful thinkers and writers were not able to have their efforts included. Their words and ideas, especially Leslie's, were missed.

To the lovely, inspiring authors who are the heart of this collection, we are filled with a heavy sense of gratitude for your visions, energies, and efforts. You all made this project brighter, stronger, more alive. Thank you, Anastasia, Fobazi, Jenny, Myrna, Stacie, Jen, Nicholae, Marisa, Miranda, Sarah, Vani, Sujei, Shaundra, Harrison, Isabel, April, Maria, Torie, Lali, Antonia, Anne, Kush, Kafi, and Rae for sharing, for trusting us.

In these last lines of deep gratitude, we hold space for our loved ones, Sofia's and Jorge's partners and families. Thank you for holding space for us, for caring for us, for loving us.

INTRODUCTION: THIS IS ONLY THE BEGINNING

Sofia Y. Leung and Jorge R. López-McKnight

LAND ACKNOWLEDGMENT

Before we begin, we honor and offer gratitude to the Indigenous peoples who cared for the lands where the majority of this introductory chapter was written and the majority of the collection was edited. We acknowledge that the lands we inhabit are the unceded ancestral territory of the Massachusetts and Wampanoag peoples and of the Tonkawa, Lipan Apache, and Comanche peoples. As Chinese American and Mexican Black American settlers and guests, we acknowledge the history of violence, biological warfare, and genocide that led to the colonization of these lands and our eventual occupation of it. We cannot forget the loss of lives, culture, and knowledge that is a part of the US nation-state's history, and we work toward individual and collective action to combat the continued erasure of Indigenous land, life, stories, and experiences from our histories and institutions. We encourage you, reader, to do the same.

REFRAMING RACIAL POWER IN LIS THROUGH CRITICAL RACE THEORY

"Can't we get past race?" My response is, we've never gotten to race.
—David Stovall

For decades, in the United States, libraries and archives as professions have grappled with race and racism in terms of representation of people and ideas within the field, but with little concrete or meaningful success. Critical Race legal scholar Kimberlé

Crenshaw has stated that frames help us decide what kind of problem we want to deal with and who is most impacted by that problem. She emphasizes that the way a problem has been framed can tell us a lot about how it will be solved (2020). Like most other fields, library and information studies[1] (LIS) has framed the race problem as one of diverse representation of racialized bodies, rather than one of racial power, domination, and privilege. David James Hudson writes, "Diversity's preoccupation with demographic inclusion and individual behavior competence has…left little room in the field for substantive engagement with race as a historically contingent phenomenon" (2017). LIS as a whole understands the problem to be the supposed unintentional absence of racial diversity in librarianship and archives, by which they mean the lack of Black, Indigenous, and People of Color (BIPOC) in a field (librarianship) that is 88 percent white and has had only a 1 percent increase "in the percentage of racial and ethnic minorities working as credentialed librarians in the nation's public, academic and school libraries" over the last decade (American Library Association 2010).[2] This understanding lacks a *critical understanding* of racial power and how it operates in the field, which is unsurprising considering how radical justice efforts centered on race have materialized in the US society.

Historically and socially, we have observed this crucial misunderstanding and framing before. The Civil Rights movement of the 1950s and 1960s, part of a long tradition of BIPOC fighting for the right to be seen as human, opened doors that were previously closed to BIPOC, and it paved the way for us to continue the struggle for social justice. The liberal rhetoric of "color blindness"—as in, "I don't see race"— grew out of the mainstream Civil Rights movement, where noticing race became synonymous with racism and shifting away from its more deeply rooted critique of racial oppression.[3] So rather than using words like *racism* and *antiracism*, safer, diluted terms like *diversity* and *inclusion* became the normalized rhetoric, and demographic representation and cultural difference became the problem being framed rather than racial justice. Additionally, the incremental reforms of the Civil Rights movement are often used to indicate that the major issue of racism has been solved, that Black communities and other communities of color have been given the rights they demanded, so anything else we ask for is extra, too much, and how dare we ask for anything more. The movement is also sometimes used to demonstrate how slowly racial progress happens, that "these things take time" and everything cannot be changed at once. This is not to diminish the achievements of our ancestors in the Civil Rights movement, nor to belittle the sacrifices and pain they suffered. Instead, it is to show how racial justice movements have been co-opted by whiteness and liberal multicultural discourse,[4] and as a result, lost their commitment to lasting radical change.

Framing this problem as one of diversity (and/or inclusion) problematically allows LIS as a field to devise superficial solutions that maintain the racial hierarchy where whiteness is dominant. It provides people a way to talk *around* the endemic problem of racism while at the same time, signaling that the profession values diversity, social responsibility, and the public good. By claiming to care about diversity through the construction of a series of ineffectual strategies to solve the "diversity problem" (Hathcock 2015; Hudson 2017), the profession puts on a performance of virtuousness and benevolence that provides a false sense of racial progress. For example, term-limited diversity residencies, isolated diversity initiatives, and diversity committees or task forces are seen as transformative solutions that are accomplishing something. Instead, what they often end up doing is bringing in more BIPOC to replace the ones who have left (or been pushed out of) the profession. These so-called solutions perpetuate ongoing systems of oppression and cause harm and trauma to those they purport to help. The diversity framework is purely concerned with optics and how it can make an institution look "good." It is a great example of what Derrick Bell, the forefather of Critical Race Theory (CRT), would call interest convergence, where whites will only move the needle toward racial justice if it also benefits them. In this case, diversity is only interested in preserving white racial domination and therefore obscures the very real issue of racial justice with performative, futile gestures that make dominant white culture think, "If we're just welcoming and inclusive enough, then the problem of racism will be solved" or "I've been so welcoming, the problem must be with those people." It becomes another way to check a box and pretend that these stopgaps—a way to check off diversity as done or completed—will somehow solve racism (Ahmed 2012).

Consider diversity residencies, such as those endorsed by the Association of College and Research Libraries (ACRL) Diversity Alliance Program. These residencies, which are one of the dominant ideas of racial transformation for academic librarianship, often operate by hiring one to three new librarians or archivists from "underrepresented minority groups," dropping them into predominantly white institutions (PWIs) with majority-white staff and eventually forcing them to acquiesce to whiteness. As Hathcock puts it, "Our diversity programs do not work because they are themselves coded to promote whiteness as the norm in the profession and unduly burden those individuals they are most intended to help" (2015). The expectation is that having BIPOC working at libraries and archives, often in limited-term roles, will bring the diversity and inclusion the institutions so desperately want. This is not just true for diversity residencies but for BIPOC in the profession at large. However, in reality, BIPOC will be forced to assimilate and adhere to white cultural standards and behaviors, and as such, they are set up to fail (Brown and Leung 2018). Then, when they do fail, because those standards are framed as objective and neutral, the failures can be blamed on the individual BIPOC for not being able to "fit" in. Additional examples of this performative commitment to diversity are the requirements of academic search committees to ask applicants for diversity statements, the formation of offices for equity and inclusion that lack institutional power, and the hiring of diversity officers without the authority to make systemic change. Despite these administrative and organizational changes, there is still a distinct lack of critical, antiracist, anti-oppressive theorization and action. This is not a new critique of the profession's attempts to "fix" the demographic underrepresentation of BIPOC and/or to advance liberatory understandings of LIS as an institution. Over the past two decades, and arguably longer, this ground has been covered by many critical LIS scholars such as Tracie D. Hall, Todd Honma, Tonia Sutherland, Jarrett Drake, Anthony Dunbar, David James Hudson, and April Hathcock.

One of the other issues with the diversity framework is that it engages with racism at the individual level rather than at a systemic and institutional level. Cultural competency, as one of the approaches employed by the diversity framework, is a clear example of this. The ACRL "Diversity Standards: Cultural Competency for Academic Libraries" uses the National Association of Social Workers' definition of cultural competence: "a congruent set of behaviors, attitudes, and policies that enable a person or group to work effectively in cross-cultural situations" (Racial and Ethnic Diversity Committee of ACRL 2012). This framework appears to suggest that it is possible to reach a level of competency around other cultures that will result in fewer individual incidents of racism, that the problem we are facing is one of cultural difference, and that to fix it we must learn about other cultures. The diversity framework absorbs and builds on this idea by positing that racism can be fixed if we can just train white people to not be racist. Again, this ignores the intertwined structural and systemic issues of racism and White Supremacy that result in the oppression of BIPOC.[5]

More recently, cultural humility as a framework has entered the LIS lexicon, being advanced by BIPOC and non-BIPOC. Andrews, Kim, and Watanabe describe it as "an ongoing process that focuses on three things: self-evaluation of one's own background and expectations, committing to redress power imbalances, and building relationships" (2018, 20). This social justice framework, in its current artic-ulation, comes closest to addressing core issues of race and power but still seems overly focused on the behavior of individuals and the idea that culture difference is the problem, which will make it difficult to truly "redress power imbalances" at a structural level. We argue that cultural humility alone will be only a small stepping-stone and will not get us to the collective action needed to make real, radical, impact-ful change.

The profession tends to focus on demographics from a very particular liberal, mul-ticultural lens that is individualized and ahistorical, locating the problem not in the profession's history and current formation but in the bodies of BIPOC. Even within critical librarianship or #critlib, a growing movement that examines the structural oppression that librarianship perpetuates with a lens of critical theory, the focus is often on the practices and praxis of librarianship, without looking holistically, and specifically, at how interlocking systems of oppression intertwine to keep (and move) BIPOC out of the profession and therefore continue to perpetuate whiteness throughout the work of librarianship (Brown et al. 2018). Similarly, in archival criti-cal spaces, there have been calls to integrate social justice and critical theories more broadly into archival practice, theory, and scholarship, especially through the criti-cal archives studies movement (Punzalan and Caswell 2015; Caswell, Punzalan, and Sangwand 2017), and to move beyond the same cultural competence and diversity frameworks that hinder movement toward critical approaches in libraries. Yet, in our minds, given our profession's and field's (as well as nation-state's) history and unwillingness to (critically) engage structural racism, we worry that critical perspec-tives and social justice frameworks that do not attend to the specificity of White Supremacy allow for its perpetuation. We are not expressing that other critical left approaches and social justice frameworks are unimportant and unnecessary. We cer-tainly need some of them working in concert if we are going to destroy this struc-ture of domination. However, many of those engagements do not apply a structural understanding of how we arrived, and are still arriving, at this juncture.

CONFRONTING WHITE SUPREMACY

We demand that LIS directly acknowledge and address the root of the issue: White Supremacy was built into our structures and systems from the very beginning and continues to be an active destructive force. We use CRT scholar Frances Lee Ansley's definition to clarify what we mean throughout this book:

By "white supremacy" I do not mean to allude only to the self-conscious racism of white supremacist hate groups. I refer instead to a political, economic and cultural system in which whites overwhelmingly control power and material resources, conscious and unconscious ideas of white superiority and entitlement are widespread, and relations of white dominance and non-white subordination are daily reenacted across a broad array of institutions and social settings. (1989, 1024)

This definition employs a structural and systemic understanding of what White Supremacy is and how it operates. It considers the contextual elements that have led to white dominance over BIPOC and that continue to sustain and maintain that power structure. It also details exactly why it is so difficult to stop White Supremacy given its pervasiveness. Existing in a nation-state ruled by White Supremacy, we first have to determine what is taught to us that originates from White Supremacy and then consciously unlearn it. Without an understanding of the historical, social, economic, and political implications of structural racism and racialized power relations, LIS will never be able to move beyond superficial changes to the field and BIPOC will never be safe in LIS spaces. We need to go beyond diversifying the profession and being welcoming to all. Libraries and archives will need to reckon with how the field continues to harm BIPOC and other people with marginalized identities. The belief that the decisions we make, the policies we choose to enforce, and the people we choose to hire are based on objective and neutral standards is ~~complete bullshit~~ completely ignorant of the profession's history and the US nation-state's history. It is based on the fallacy that normalcy and objectiveness are synonymous with whiteness. As two People of Color, born racialized into this world, we have firsthand experience of the tense political climate that the Trump administration has fostered, which has intensified the need to go beyond mere discussion around race and diversity initiatives.

The current moment in history provides clear evidence of the fallacy of whiteness as our moral code. To contextualize and situate when and where we are writing this, it is 2019 in (what is currently known as) the United States. It is the time of white nationalists attempting to take away women's rights, immigrant rights, and the rights of anyone not white, cisgendered, heterosexual, Christian, and male. Climate disasters are disproportionately impacting low-income communities of color. Technologies, including machine learning and artificial intelligence, are being employed to continue the hypersurveillance of BIPOC and to "predict" who will be more likely to commit a crime. However, it is also the time of critical movements like Black Lives Matter, the Dakota Access Pipeline protests, #metoo, #SayHerName, and more—where people are taking collective action to fight White Supremacy, patriarchy, capitalism, sexism, and racism. The time for this type of critical engagement with the profession's adherence to White Supremacy is long past due. As Vincent Harding wrote about the Black student movement in 1970, "The only time we have is now" (1970, 100). A sea change is necessary and we contend that CRT will be a vital tool to get us there.

The purpose of this collection of chapters is to produce a volume that reenvisions what LIS could be with Critical Race Theory as a central philosophy, not only as a profession and academic field but also as a far-reaching institution with organizations, governing bodies, and professional standards and guidelines. We hope that this volume serves as a theoretical and methodological guide for placing CRT more firmly within LIS, and given the power and control of LIS, as an institution, in society, in—and over—our lives, that CRT becomes an important application toward making LIS structurally just. CRT, while not new to LIS, is not commonly employed in LIS except by a handful of scholars, and its presence in the field, which we unpack below, is marginal, at best. This book, as far as we, the editors, are aware, is the first to focus solely on applying CRT to LIS. The choice to use CRT as the main theoretical framework is a deliberate and significant one. While we recognize that there are many critical theories and social justice frameworks, CRT as a conceptual construct, and methodology, is about critically examining the structures and systems that maintain White Supremacy's chokehold on our society. It is about how we reconstruct our laws, our policies, and our systems so that change can happen at a broader, deeper level instead of at an individual level. Moreover, it provides opportunities to identify points of integration across dynamic and multifactoral forces that together work to re-create and sustain historical systems of racial power and oppression and provide new, actionable paths toward a liberatory future.

One of the problems CRT is seeking to remedy is the fact that BIPOC knowledge has never been considered valid knowledge, that it is effectively and purposefully missing from the knowledge that has shaped this country's governing structures and institutions, and that without it, we will not be able to break the oppressive cycle of White Supremacy. Part of why these systems of domination are so powerful is precisely because, beyond the control of BIPOC bodies, they rely on the erasure of BIPOC forms of knowledge and experience. Consider the significance that LIS as a field plays an enormous, active, and foundational role in determining what is and isn't regarded as knowledge and the unique positioning of archives and libraries as potential places of learning and support that can be accessed throughout one's life.

These institutions shape and (re)produce violence and harm but also have the capacity to build toward care, joy, and justice. In that direction, CRT can push LIS to ask critically important questions of race and power in distinctive, urgent ways that can create new social realities. This is a central focus and exploration of this collection, and it is absolutely necessary given how the institution primarily (mis)understands and frames race matters: through diversity, inclusion, and equity. Here, in this space, we are interested and focused on social justice projects that center race and its entanglements with other social positions, forces, and contexts.

We argue that as disseminators and centers of cultural knowledge that hold power in/over communities, libraries and archives have a deep ethical responsibility to create information institutions and systems that portray vantage points and life experiences that meaningfully attend to difference and social conditions. The application of CRT is needed to advance the development of holistic historical and cultural records, as well as to ensure the creation of spaces, programming, and practices, within instruction, reference, preservation, collections, and physical or virtual spaces in libraries and archives that are antiracist, humanizing, and equitable. This conceptual and methodological framework will help the profession name, understand, and act on the impact White Supremacy has—continues to have—on the various institutions and areas in LIS.

Before we get to this book's journey and what you can find in these pages, we must start with where and how CRT developed as a theory, its guiding tenets and methodologies, and its past and recent intersections within LIS.

BEGINNINGS AND FORMATIONS OF CRITICAL RACE THEORY

Critical Race Theory's genesis and development emerged from a particular place and time in legal scholarship when scholars, mostly People of Color (POC), recognized that mainstream legal studies firmly believed that color blindness was the opposite of racism.[6] As the introduction to *Critical Race Theory: The Key Writings That Formed the Movement* puts it, "Racism was identified only with the outright formal exclusion of people of color" (Crenshaw et al. 1995, xvi). Historically, law was seen as neutral, objective, and apolitical. In the 1970s, a group of legal scholars formed a movement, critical legal studies (CLS), to question this interpretation of the law and why it was institutionalized as part of the legal curriculum. However, many law students and scholars of color found that CLS still lacked an engagement with race and the impact of White Supremacy on BIPOC in the United States.

The Civil Rights movement paved the way for the emergence of CRT, but as mentioned earlier, its discourse became co-opted by the larger societal idea that racism is specific, concrete, and definite. In this interpretation, it was thought that by taking racist language out of the law, the law could no longer be racist. In fact, Crenshaw and colleagues argue that mainstream civil rights equated race consciousness with racism and saw color blindness as the answer to racism (1995, xv). This deeply problematic construction of civil rights and the law, which continues today, erases the lived experiences of BIPOC and does not take into account racism as a systematic and structural issue. At its root, CRT is about understanding how White Supremacy has oppressed and continues to oppress BIPOC in the United States through the legal system (Crenshaw et al. 1995, xiii) and how we might transform the law.

As CRT scholars themselves tell it, CRT as a movement crystallized over several formative events. The first occurred when Derrick Bell left the Harvard Law School to become dean of the University of Oregon Law School.[7] Bell was one of two African American professors in the entirety of Harvard's faculty at the time, and he taught a class called "Race, and Racism, and American Law." In 1981, student activists demanded that Harvard hire a professor of color to replace him and teach his course. They boycotted the performative "diversity" course with which Harvard administrators tried to placate them. Instead, they organized "The Alternative Course," their own student-led version of Bell's course, which taught law through the lens of racial consciousness. "The Alternative Course" helped to establish CRT as a movement by building a support network of legal academics of color, demonstrating that the creation, organization, and use of knowledge is political, and proving that a group of radical BIPOC operating within the confines of an institutional space was necessary and urgent, and that CRT scholarship stems from resistance to liberal mainstream ideas about race (Crenshaw et al. 1995).

The Critical Legal Studies National Conference meetings in 1986 and 1987 were where the differences between CRT and CLS became very clear. These distinctions helped CRT scholars further develop their critique of CLS and sharpen their own ideas that led to Critical Race Theory's formation. The conference in 1986 was organized by a group of majority-white feminist legal scholars who asked scholars of color to serve as facilitators in discussions of race. These discussions were framed with the question "'What is it about the Whiteness of CLS that discourages participation by people of color?' [and] revealed that CLS's hip, cutting edge irreverence toward establishment practices could easily disintegrate into hand-wringing hysteria when brought back 'home'" (Crenshaw et al. 1995 xxiii). While white CLS scholars were perfectly willing to critically deconstruct long-established legal practices, when the critical eye was focused on their own practices with race at the center, they dissolved into a state of defensiveness and denial.

CLS as a movement was unwilling to contend with race as a central part of the discourse around law. This divide spurred early CRT scholars to formulate their own theory and movement—"how law constructed race" (Crenshaw et al. 1995, xxv) through a series of informal and more formalized gatherings. Finally, in 1989, Kimberlé Crenshaw, Neil Gotanda, and Stephanie Phillips launched the first Critical Race Theory workshop. These organizers created the name "critical race theory" with "critical" marking the political and intellectual orientation, "race" being the focal point (it literally is centered in the project's name), and "theory" representing aspirations for explaining race and law meaningfully (Crenshaw 2001, 1361). The workshop helped form the foundation of this theory and the movement centering race in their interpretation and reformation of law.

As Critical Race Theory continues to evolve in legal scholarly activity, inclusion in the legal education curriculum, and an annual symposium hosted by UCLA School of Law's Critical Race Studies Program, the project has moved outside the legal field to the social sciences and humanities, notably ethnic studies, public health, sociology, and philosophy. These disciplines have found CRT to be a valuable project in investigating how (and why) race, power, and systems of domination operate in their particular areas of study, and, perhaps unintentionally, have illustrated the full ecology of racism in society (Delgado and Stefancic 2017; Ladson-Billings 1998). For example, in public health, a CRT framework has offered scholars important conceptual (e.g., race is socially constructed, racism as ordinary) and methodological tools to move the understanding of racism away from individual instances between people to conceive its structural nature and its relationship to health disparities and inequities, specifically in Black communities and HIV testing (Ford and Airhihenbuwa 2010, 2018).

Of particular relevance to the LIS profession, given that education, archives, and libraries are social institutions and their focus is on learning, is CRT's impact in the field of educational research, which has, arguably, transformed areas of the discipline, including policy, theory, and curriculum. Arriving in the educational literature just a few years after CRT's official emergence in law, CRT has become a visible, expansive, and sustained force in education with multiple book-length texts, an annual conference, a dedicated scholarly publication, as well as special issues of academic journals focusing on a CRT framework. Education scholars have centered race and racism in their analyses of educational inequities by drawing from CRT concepts, methods, and analytical and theoretical constructs. They have utilized the voices of parents, students, and faculty of color in various educational sites to disrupt the dominant conversation that places pathologies and deficits on and within these communities and used their knowledge and experiences to reveal the structures of racism in education. In analyzing teacher-education programs, scholars have explored interest convergence and critiquing of dominant ideologies (namely, color blindness and liberalism) to interrogate practices, curriculum, and policy. Some have argued that teacher-preparation programs continue to be sites that construct White Supremacy by their refusal to engage in a deep analysis of race, racism, power, and racial justice interests, inevitably benefiting whites (Dixson and Anderson 2017, 34–38; Howard and Navarro 2016).

As CRT in education continues to grow, explore, and assess its impact beyond its intellectual contributions, Marvin Lynn, the lead editor of the *Handbook of Critical Race Theory in Education,* points to one of the major issues facing critical race research in education: "We appear to be perpetually stuck in a 'problem-posing' pattern and, by and large, fail to see the importance of using CRT as a tool to frame solutions to these longstanding problems" (Decuir-Gunby, Chapman, and Schutz 2019, x). This will be a vital lesson for LIS to heed, as it can be an easy trap to fall into. While the first step is necessarily naming and understanding the problem, we must also develop solutions or we will be caught in an endless cycle of naming and understanding, never making progress toward measurable, concrete actions.

Additionally, in CRT's relatively short history, the theory has not just traveled to other disciplines, but also continued to evolve within some of those locations to address the specific legacies, realities, and needs of those racialized, oppressed communities. For example, Asian Critical Race Theory (AsianCrit), developed in law and transported to education, continues to explore the Asian American experience by problematizing the black-white binary, model-minority mythologies, and anti-Asian discrimination. Similarly, in both law and education, Latino Critical Race Theory (LatCrit) is a framework put forward to theorize racism and oppression and how its construction and deployment through immigration, human rights, language, and other social-identity markers impact Latinx[8] communities (Curammeng, Buenavista, and Cariaga 2017, 1–3; Iglesias 1996; Solórzano and Delgado Bernal 2001; Valdes 1997).

CRT, as an intellectual movement in its third decade, continues to move forward, especially in education, where CRT has branched out and prompted the development of group-specific and methodological frameworks (Decuir-Gunby, Chapman, and Schutz 2019). These theorizations aim to critique racial domination through specific racialized and intersectional experiences and oppression. For example, "racecrits" in education include Tribal Critical Race Theory (TribalCrit), which accounts for Indigenous peoples' distinctive experiences with colonization, the US government, and educational structures (Brayboy 2005). Likewise, Black Critical Theory (BlackCrit) specifically centers the Black experience and commits to "analyze how social and education policy are informed by anti-Blackness, and serve as forms of anti-Black violence" (Dumas and Ross 2016, 419). Other crit(s) formations, found in education and law, include Queer Critical Race Theory (QueerCrit), which pursues not only racial justice but also, simultaneously, social justice sexuality for racialized peoples and communities; QuantCrit, put forward by education researchers, grounds a quantitative methods approach in CRT in order to challenge dominant research method ideologies (objectivity, neutrality) while also pushing for quantitative methods to situate itself in relation to sociopolitical, historical forces, in hopes that these approaches can contribute to racial justice efforts; and dis/ability critical race studies (DisCrit), theorizing race and ability intersections, co-constructions, and their relationship to inequities in educational and societal contexts (Garcia, López, and Vélez 2017; Misawa 2012; Annamma, Connor, and Ferri 2013). These critical race projects seek to further our understandings of the entanglements of race, power, and racial domination in complex ways, and unveil the totality of White Supremacy.

CRT, and its various formations, we argue, have traveled well to, and within, other disciplines, including LIS, albeit inadequately. As CRT has been a mobilizing force in some areas, the movement and development of CRT in LIS and the majority of the profession's subfields has languished and largely been unsuccessful in coordinating an antiracist project and generating a coalition of critical race scholars employing CRT. Nevertheless, there has been and continues to be a CRT presence, however small, in LIS, and our hope is for CRT to occupy more space, create greater noise, and reposition itself from the margins to the forefront of the profession's discourse and actions, especially if LIS seeks to truly become antiracist, anti-oppressive, and equitable.

CRITICAL RACE THEORY TENETS AND METHODOLOGIES

The CRT framework consists of numerous tenets, and though there are not universal principles that all CRT theorists and practitioners believe or endorse, there are common themes that many in the movement would accept as foundational elements (Crenshaw 1991; Delgado and Stefancic 2017; Matsuda et al. 1993). CRT is deeply committed to social justice, having an activist element that is rooted in the erasure of racism and *all* types of oppression (Matsuda 1991). Ultimately, CRT strives for a number of goals that are underpinned by a specific tenet: *a commitment to social justice and to the elimination of racial oppression and all forms of oppression.*

Fundamental to these goals is an understanding that a gradual, liberal line of action toward justice is inadequate and that what is essential is a confrontation with a social hierarchy rooted in White Supremacy. This action-based construct of CRT is focused on empowerment and transformation for the oppressed, and should include, as Stovall (2013) suggests, "a dedication to the physical/material, social, and intellectual support of the efforts of historically marginalized groups to self-determine" (293). And though it is implied here, it is necessary to state directly that this dedication to relentlessly pursue justice happens in community and solidarity. CRT also uses a number of different methodologies and tools to operationalize its framework and progress toward social justice.

The tenets and methodologies, coming from seminal CRT scholars in both the law and education fields, are sketched out here to ground the reader in specific understandings, while opening space for further articulation in the chapters that await you.

TENETS

Race as a social construct   Race is a construction of our society, not one that exists biologically (Delgado and Stefancic 2017), and it carries significant, concrete meaning-shaping societal realities that have material, political, cultural, and psychological consequences. As the various iterations of the US census demonstrate, the category of "white" has been constructed and reconstructed to maintain White Supremacy. Definitions of who fits into what racial category are circumscribed by those in power (Ladson-Billings 1998), and white as the normative category is at the top of the racial hierarchy. However, it is important to note that we are not saying that racism exists only in people's behaviors and thoughts. The following tenet expands on this concept.

Racism is normal   Delgado and Stefancic (2017) state, "Racism is ordinary…the usual way *society* does business, the common, everyday experience of most people of color in this country" (8; emphasis added). One of the first and central tenets of CRT is the belief that racism is normal and deeply ingrained in American society through its systems and institutions. Racism is doing exactly what it is intended to do, which is to maintain a social structure rooted in White Supremacy.

Experiences and knowledge of BIPOC   Because the experiences and knowledge of BIPOC historically have been and continue to be ignored and erased, white people have little idea of what it's like to be Black, Indigenous, or a Person of Color, nor do they often understand the value of BIPOC experiences and knowledge. CRT contends that these experiences and knowledge are necessary and crucial to moving us to eradicating multiple oppressions (Matsuda et al. 1993; Yosso et al. 2009).

Intersectionality   Intersectionality is a lens through which we can locate overlapping oppressions in the intersecting social divisions of class, race, gender, sexuality, ability, ethnicity, and citizenship to better understand how power operates in a society and creates social inequality (Crenshaw 1991). It is a framework that provides a bridge between identity politics and coalition building through which change can be enacted (Collins and Bilge 2016).

Interdisciplinary   As legal scholars Matsuda and colleagues (1993) put forward in their original formation of CRT, and Yosso and colleagues (2009) include in the field of education, the framework pushes for the embracement of theories and methodologies from various academic disciplines and intellectual approaches. This flexibility allows for a more thorough examination of racial domination, both currently and historically, with the aim to more forcefully advance racial justice. It also implies that CRT is meant to be applied across disciplines, that the boundaries between disciplines are falsely constructed barriers.

Whiteness as property   Cheryl Harris (1993) put forward the concept of whiteness as property, which argues that in the construction of the US, the concepts and relationship of race and property took form together. The nascent nation was dependent on Black peoples being not peoples, but property (through chattel slavery), and the erasure of Indigenous peoples (through conquest and colonization) for their land (seen as property). In relation to these violent structures of domination (and while establishing a racial hierarchy), whiteness, legally as well as psychologically, became constructed as property, containing certain functions, including rights of disposition; rights to use and enjoyment; reputation and status property; and the absolute right to exclude (1731–1736).

Critique of dominant ideologies   Another central element of CRT is the challenging of dominant ideologies of color blindness, objectivity, neutrality, and meritocracy. These claims frequently are used as disguises for the dominant group (and their structures) to push forward their interests, thus (re)producing and extending their power and harmful systems of domination (Delgado and Stefancic 2017; Matsuda et al. 1993; Solórzano and Yosso 2002).

Focus on historical contexts   CRT scholars argue that in order to understand what is happening in the current moment, we must look to history and examine the particular historical, social, and economic contexts that led to this point. Those contexts are what allow us to identify and comprehend the underlying structural and systemic issues. Without that understanding, we will not be able to develop the necessary interventions (Delgado and Stefancic 2017).

Counterstorytelling and voice   Solórzano and Yosso (2002) define counterstorytelling as part of critical race methodology for the social sciences, and more specifically, within education. It is a way to communicate the experiences of people who are considered marginal and unvalued by society. "The counter-story is also a tool for exposing, analyzing, and challenging the [dominant white] stories of racial privilege" (Solórzano and Yosso 2002, 32). As Dixson and Anderson (2017) have noted, voice (counterstory, counternarrative) in CRT in education has been used in various forms, ranging from personal, direct experiences to fictionalized narratives rooted in the knowledge and realities of racialized peoples to counternarratives as units of analysis (35–38). Returning further back to CRT's legal roots to show the creative and imaginative form that voice can take, Derrick Bell's (1992) "The Space Traders," a story of speculative, allegorical fiction, provides incredible insight into racial oppression while incorporating other CRT elements.

Interest convergence   Derrick Bell presented this principle in his article "Brown v. Board of Education and the Interests-Convergence Dilemma," stating, "Interests of blacks in achieving racial equality will be accommodated only when it converges with the interests of whites" (1980, 523). Thus, whites' self-interests motivate their participation (or not) in racial justice and will not eliminate racism, or their dominance. That is to say, marginalized peoples' racial justice interests are considered only when they converge with the interests of powerful whites. Going further, Bell suggests that if a racial remedy does actually materialize, it "will be abrogated at the point that policymakers fear the remedial policy is threatening the superior societal status of whites, particularly those in the middle and upper classes" (Bell 1980, 523; 2004, 106).

In the following narrative, we will chronologically examine the application of these core CRT elements in the LIS discourse as a way to gain a deeper understanding of the work CRT has done in this field.

LOCATING AND EXCAVATING CRITICAL RACE THEORY
IN LIBRARY AND INFORMATION STUDIES

In 1991, Jean Stefancic, at the time an assistant librarian for technical services at the University of San Francisco School of Law, published an article in *Legal Reference Services Quarterly* titled "Listen to the Voices: An Essay on Legal Scholarship, Women, and Minorities." In the essay, Stefancic describes two revolutions: outsider jurisprudence, a new critical position in legal thought/scholarship that originated in CLS and expanded to include the two new movements of feminist legal theory and CRT; and the electronic (computer) revolution, a significant change in the amount of information accessible. The intersection of these two revolutions, according to Stefancic, has the possibility to (re)shape laws and social structures, and the article asks, "How can librarians respond to this new scholarship?" Though Stefancic does provide suggestions on what efforts information workers might undertake with this "new scholarship," they do not explicitly connect CRT concepts to LIS.[9] Rather, the question, an important one, and one we should consider, is a challenge to the profession to intellectually engage critically with race and gender. This brief essay is possibly the first published article in the LIS literature that connects CRT to information institutions, and it is where this story begins.

Even though CRT in LIS did not surface again until fifteen years later, critical scholarship from BIPOC and white scholars, including Isabel Espinal, Todd Honma, Lorna Peterson, Clara M. Chu, Teresa Y. Neely and Khafre K. Abif, and Christine Pawley, did speak to race and racism in their analyses of the LIS field that, while interrogating CRT concepts, did not formally locate their work within the specific scholarly lineage of CRT. They did, however, deepen and develop our understanding of race and power, and, arguably, pushed the conversation toward a more CRT-aligned direction. This direction has been in relation to the "diversity" paradigm in LIS that has driven and continues to drive the profession's and discipline's conversations and actions about race matters.[10] A critical point of departure, however, is that CRT rejects liberal frameworks as they do not examine and center critiques of power, race, and racism. We argue that current and past diversity frameworks continue to ignore these critiques. Further, the soft approach of diversity frameworks seeks a type of reconciliation that is not just misaligned with a CRT approach, but *incompatible* because a CRT perspective demands a fundamental shift of the racial power structure of the world, consequently transforming the profession and discipline.

In 2006, Anthony W. Dunbar published the foundational article "Introducing Critical Race Theory to Archival Discourse: Getting the Conversation Started," which as the title states, aimed to do just that for the archives community.[11] Dunbar, in bringing CRT to archives, explores how the framework conceptually and methodologically can help actors—practitioners, scholars, and institutions—create different, previously excluded epistemologies, while also uncovering racial biases in archival institutions. The CRT tenets that Dunbar argues can be used in the archival field—of record creation and of institutional and collective memory care—include counterstories, microaggressions, and social justice. Counterstories, as Dunbar conceives them, can be positioned in archives as a way to create different versions of narratives that are often hidden or silenced from the archive (given the social, political, and historical relationships between dominant and nondominant cultures), either by uncovering them in existing collections or by having, or creating, archives that are, in and of themselves, a counterstory to the deliberate absence of minoritized narratives, thus challenging official knowledge(s). Microaggressions, which can be part of counterstories, are understated acts of subjugation and can be present, specifically in the form of racial biases, in the assigning of value to records during the appraisal process if "frameworks that (re)enforce racial bias and the interests of dominant power structures" are used (Dunbar 2006, 116). Lastly, Dunbar suggests social justice principles that are rooted in an analysis of subjugation from the micro to macro level should be utilized when interrogating various elements of the archives as social institutions, professional practices, and scholarly discourse. At that time, concerned with the lack of theoretical, conceptual, and methodological constructs to examine racial oppression and the underdeveloped social consciousness in the profession, Dunbar positions CRT as a necessary intervention to confront race, both individually and structurally (Dunbar 2006).

Just the following year, Furner (2007) introduced CRT to the Dewey Decimal Classification (DDC) knowledge organization system as a framework that can be applied to assess how race is employed ideologically in the DDC's most recent (at the time, the 22nd) edition.[12] That edition had updated table 5 by removing "Racial" from its title (leaving "Ethnic and National Groups") as well as basic racial classifications, while largely conflating ethnicity with race (Furner 2007). Furner points out that through a CRT analysis, this change, or deracialization of Dewey, furthers the larger colonial project of White Supremacy by supporting the current racial hierarchy and its relations of power, control, and domination (2007). Unlike Dunbar, Furner does not neatly identify specific CRT tenets they are employing; however, multiple concepts—especially race as a social construct, challenge to dominant ideologies, and racism as endemic, among others—inform their analysis. Like Dunbar, Furner names and shows how racial biases operate within the profession's knowledge systems and institutional structures. Additionally, and similar to Dunbar, they connect CRT's social justice focus to LIS's (supposed) commitments and values, urging information workers to apply CRT and even proposing six concrete strategies to inform practice (provide antiracist service) and use it as a tool to examine, and ultimately transform, various LIS areas and institutions.

In looking at the racialized experiences of undergraduate students of color in an urban academic library and their sense of feeling welcome or unwelcome, Elteto, Jackson, and Lim, in 2008, extend the utility of CRT by analyzing their findings through the framework's concepts of race as a main component of US society and racism as ordinary (2008, 330). It is significant, and should not be understated, that they foreground the understanding of their academic library—its services and spaces—as already being impacted by structural racism, which will undoubtedly shape the experiences of students of color, as their findings indicated.

In 2009, CRT came to children's literature and school librarianship, with the important publication of "Promoting Equity in Children's Literacy Instruction: Using a Critical Race Theory Framework to Examine Transitional Books," by Hughes-Hassell, Barkley, and Koehler.[13] Like Furner and Elteto, Jackson, and Lim, the authors use CRT as an analytical tool to examine the absence of characters (and authors) of color in transitional books and how that exclusion impacts literacy and self-worth in children of color.[14] Hughes-Hassell, Barkely, and Koehler (2009) utilize numerous themes of CRT, especially racism as endemic, to address the pervasiveness of white racial subjugation in the children's literature industry. They argue that their findings illustrate whiteness as normalized and prized, and that children of color remain invisible in the literature, or when they do appear, they need to align with whiteness to be seen, understood, and valued. In pushing school librarians toward racial justice action, the authors attempt to operationalize CRT's social justice aspirations by offering nine direct actions, from collection building and programming to writing grants and conducting research, that resist inequitable literacy education for children and communities of color (Hughes-Hassell, Barkely, and Koehler 2009).

In the following years, 2010 to 2012, CRT further developed in the school librarianship discourse. Hughes-Hassell and Cox examined another area of children's literature, board books, to show (again) the lack of representation and misrepresentation of People of Color as well as the absence of authors and illustrators of color. They analyze their findings through a CRT lens and, similarly to Hughes-Hassell, Barkely, and Koehler's article, expose the white racial domination of the children's publishing industry and its destructive psychological effects on children of color (Hughes-Hassell and Cox 2010). Extending CRT's applicability to urban youth and school libraries, Kafi Kumasi (2012) calls for school libraries and school librarians to reenvision their practices through a CRT framing. This creates the possibility for transformation of deficit thinking and centering students' voices and experiences, in turn allowing for greater understanding of racism at a structural level, and pushes for interrogating whiteness in collections, spatially as well as ideologically. Further, Kurz (2012), building on this scholarship, provides a state-level context that had been missing from the discourse, with their examination of the nominated books for the South Carolina Picture Book Award. Using CRT as an analytical framework to interpret their findings, Kurz argues that the nominations, dominated by "White-centered books written and illustrated by Whites with casts of largely White characters," fail to represent the diversity of South Carolina and the US, thus reinforcing White Supremacy (136). Additionally, the author positions some of the literature that focuses on the Black American experience as counterstories disrupting majoritarian narratives that often do not confront racial oppression (Kurz 2012). Cumulatively, these articles utilize a CRT framework to center and analyze race and racism in children's literature and school librarianship and help us to understand unjust structures of racial power that subjugate children and communities of color. These articles also illuminate strategies to achieve racial justice in LIS.

Moving the discourse to Black librarianship, Tracie D. Hall's 2012 chapter, "The Black Body at the Reference Desk: Critical Race Theory and Black Librarianship," pushes for a racial analysis through a CRT framework by investigating interpersonal acts of racism and connecting those to institutional and structural racial oppression, and by a (re)examination of the history of libraries to Black communities. Further, Hall argues that given LIS's continued refusal to critically engage the relationship between race, racism, and power, the unchanging demographics of the profession, and ongoing unjust library services to People of Color, CRT becomes vital as a lens that can provide an understanding and language to challenge inequality in LIS. Responding to Hall's suggestion, Karin L. Griffin's 2013 "Pursuing Tenure and Promotion in the Academy: A Librarian's Cautionary Tale," narrates their Black, female, middle-class ascending path through the inequitable tenure process by grounding their analysis in Critical Race Feminism's (CRF) intersectional lens and CRT's concepts of racism as endemic and the valuing—and centering—of People of Color's experiences as legitimate sources of knowledge that provide insight into understanding interlocking systems of oppression. Significantly, Griffin's article provides the first in-depth, firsthand account deploying CRT and CRF to frame and analyze issues on their journey in the profession, such as the lack of racial diversity in the field, recruitment and retention, mentoring, and their relationship to the intersections of race, gender, and class.

Extending the CRT construct of POC's experiences as knowledge that challenges, and exposes, the dominance of white racial narratives over multicultural young adult literature, Hughes-Hassell (2013) argues counterstorytelling is articulated through the publication of (some) books by authors of color and (some) books that center youth of color by providing voice and visibility to marginalized youth. In this way, counterstorytelling disrupts the notion of only one type of narrative and showcases the intricacy of developing racial and ethnic identities. Lastly, Hughes-Hassell proposes that this CRT construct pushes readers belonging to the dominant culture to reckon with their own racial identities and privilege while gaining greater insight into social inequality (2013, 215). Though the author deeply examines counterstorytelling as a tool to expose and interrogate the permanent nature of racism (a core construct of CRT) and how it operates in society to oppress youth of color, they also advance counterstorytelling as acts of resistance. Kafi D. Kumasi (2013) uses voice, intersectionality, whiteness as property, and interest convergence to critically examine White Supremacy in school and public libraries, thus deepening our understanding of CRT's core ideas and applicability to youth of color and their relationship to libraries as a means to challenge LIS scholars and practitioners to imagine new possibilities and understandings of, and for, them. In particular, they reveal interest convergence operating when "a librarian holds a cultural deficit perspective toward Youth of Color and masks this belief system, but at the same time capitalizes on efforts to promote diversity with Youth of Color" and the property value of whiteness, demonstrated through the profession's positioning of youth of color literacy practices as abnormal and nonstandard in relation to whiteness (106–108).

Since 2015, as more critical approaches have materialized, CRT has seen an increase in its application in the LIS scholarly discourse. Building on the work of Karin L. Griffin (2013) and others, Shaundra Walker challenges the diversity paradigm and the absence of narratives from POC not participating in dominant diversity initiatives and programs. By providing a counterstory focusing on her recruitment, retention, and promotion as an African American, female librarian through a CRT lens, she importantly shares her experiences and connects them with specific CRT constructs—reexamining the US history of unequal educational access (revisionist history); critiquing LIS diversity efforts (critique of liberalism); and exposing LIS as racially structured (racism as endemic)—to provide a new perspective in the diversity demographic discourse and to position CRT as a much-needed framework to interrogate racial inequality (Walker 2015). In problematizing whiteness in academic libraries (spaces, library workers, and reference work) through their analysis of national professional library documents and LIS scholarship, Brook, Ellenwood, and Lazzaro focus on the CRT concepts of race as socially constructed, ending racial oppression, racism as pervasive, and voice to challenge and transform white hegemony in LIS. The authors contend that a CRT-based analysis offers antiracist approaches and understandings, situates racism at the structural level, and engages in deconstructing it. In that direction, they also put forward direct recommendations. Creatively, and similarly (in aim, though not in application) to how other scholars have used them, counterstorytelling and narratives of Peoples of Color in published scholarship are utilized to understand the architecture of inequities in libraries and the profession (2015, 247–251).

Extending CRT to the graduate curriculum in LIS, Nicole A. Cooke posits as a form of counterstorytelling the teaching of diversity and social justice courses focusing on race, racism, and justice from the perspectives of the vulnerable, oppressed, and dispossessed. This approach provides a disruption to majoritarian, normalized, liberal discourses on those topics and concepts, and it has the potential to inform future information workers' understandings of systems of oppression (2016). Returning to the archival field, and building on Dunbar's work, Kellee E. Warren utilizes CRT concepts to explore Black women's representation in the materials of French Antilles archives and connects their absence, oppression, and erasure in the record to the profession's low number of Black women archivists (2016). Grounding her understanding of Black women's oppression through an intersectional lens, Warren argues that archives still have power to control Black women's identities and narratives and influence multiple areas of their lives. However, Black women working in archive positions have the possibility to construct counternarratives that offer voice and agency to the marginalized and underrepresented. Warren advocates for critical frameworks, especially CRT's concepts, to be included in archive and LIS education, not only to provide students with theories and methods that inform their practice but also as a challenge to what constitutes knowledge in the curriculum.

In 2017, CRT made significant advances in the LIS discourse with the publication of two book collections, *Teaching for Justice: Implementing Social Justice in the LIS Classroom*, edited by Nicole A. Cooke and Miriam E. Sweeney (2017), and *Topographies of Whiteness: Mapping Whiteness in Library and Information Science*, edited by Gina Schlesselman-Tarango (2017). Writing in *Teaching for Justice*, Kurz (2017) shares their pedagogical and personal journey toward a social justice orientation utilizing CRT concepts—namely, its interdisciplinary flexibility that makes space for multiple perspectives that push racial justice forward; racism as ordinary and pervasive; and the entanglements of racism with other axes of oppression. Incorporating these core CRT elements allows for students of the author (an LIS educator) to critically examine race and racism in libraries and society, thus impacting future informational professionals' practices and understandings. Similarly, in the same collection, Hughes-Hassell and Vance provide a window into their youth services graduate LIS classroom, where they have constructed their course *around* CRT core concepts to ensure future librarians understand historical and contemporary structures of white racial domination and utilize a CRT approach regularly in their professional and personal lives to work toward abolishing racial oppression (2017, 114–119). Significantly, both chapters, especially Hughes-Hassell and Vance's, demonstrate the institutionalized possibilities of CRT.

Shaundra Walker's (2017) chapter in *Topographies of Whiteness*, a revisionist history— and counterstory—of Carnegie Library building grants to Black institutions of higher education, applies CRT concepts of whiteness as property and interest convergence to uncover and interrogate the operation of whiteness and its role in forming library spaces and access. In the South, Black colleges were shaped by White Supremacist law and the dispossession of Black folx;[15] the majority of those institutions were without buildings exclusively for academic libraries, and as Walker asserts, "at the turn of the century, the rights to grant access, use, enjoy and dispose of a freestanding academic library were enjoyed almost exclusively by Whites" (44), demonstrating that academic libraries were, in their origination, the property of whites. Also in *Topographies*, Joseph, Crowe, and Mackey (2017) apply the concept of whiteness as property (among other CRT themes), specifically its right to exclude in order to reveal how the beginnings of historically Black colleges and universities (HBCUs) and predominantly white institutions (PWIs) are based on this exclusion, domination, and privilege, which has undoubtedly shaped the construction of archives in higher education and continues to (re)produce white hegemony in archives and their records, practice, and theory (55–60). Lastly, in the same collection, similarly to Walkers' promotion and tenure narrative, though focusing specifically on teaching and learning experiences at PWIs, Jorge R. López-McKnight (2017) utilizes counterstorytelling to challenge and provide insight into the workings of whiteness.

Also in 2017, a special issue of the *Journal of Critical Library and Information Studies* signaled an important formation in the archival field: critical archives studies.[16] Writing in the introduction, Caswell, Punzalan, and Sangwand assert that by utilizing critical theories—in their many manifestations, one of them being CRT—critical archives studies "broadens the field's scope beyond an inward, practice-centered orientation and builds a critical stance regarding the role of archives in the production of knowledge and different types of narratives, as well as identity construction" (2017, 1–2). The authors further push the archive field to mobilize together under this term and its emancipatory approaches to examine, disrupt, and ultimately transform structures and systems of domination, whether they be archives as institutions or the field of the humanities. Though a few articles in the issue grapple with CRT concepts, Kim's (2017) article explicitly uses a CRT lens to interrogate whiteness as the norm and its function in constructing archival collections to exclude BIPOC records, which is made possible by a racial hierarchy that privileges and preserves White Supremacy. Though not writing, identifiably, under critical archives studies, but using a range of critical theories to inform their work on the digital life of records showing Black death, Tonia Sutherland's article, "Making a Killing: On Race, Ritual, and (Re)Membering in Digital Culture," employs CRT to account for the destructive force of race, racism, and power in US society that allows for the "conditional possibilities for people of color to be killed at the hands of police officers and armed citizens without also creating the space for restorative justice" (2017, 33). With a similar focus on archives and records, Bowers, Crowe, and Keeran (2017) engage a CRT framework to critique the intentional absence and silencing of Native voices and perspectives in the archival holdings of a private PWI, and the institution's intimate connection to the Sand Creek Massacre. Building on Dunbar's application of CRT to archives, and the work of other critical archives scholars, the authors put forward counternarratives to inform their path forward in developing collections that attend to difference, center Native peoples and communities, and ultimately reconstruct the historical record to contest archives hegemonic whiteness.

Since 2017, there has been an increasing push to elevate the LIS discourse around race, racism, and power through the utilization of critical frameworks such as intersectionality, decolonization, whiteness, and the interrogation of concepts like racial microaggressions, white racism, and unconscious racial bias to unveil and problematize the (continued) white racial domination and colonization of the field.[17] In this current critical discourse, CRT continues to move in similar and new directions. Building on the work of previous LIS scholars arguing for the LIS curriculum to center race, power, and social justice so that all students and faculty are part of the commitment to understanding and challenging structural racism and hegemonic whiteness, Gibson, Hughes-Hassell, and Threats (2018) examined the required readings in the core courses of the top twenty LIS programs for their inclusion of CRT. Applying a wide-ranging definition of CRT and its core ideas in their analysis, the authors still found that the "vast majority of the examined required foundational courses provided students with little to no exposure to CRT or critical theory" (64). In moving toward CRT's—and what should be LIS's—social justice aspirations, Gibson, Hughes-Hassell, and Threats advocate for LIS education to incorporate CRT's major concepts (intersectionality, race and racism) as a way to move the field toward a deeper engagement with racism as a structural phenomenon. Contributing to the emerging information behavior (IB) discourse that focuses on the ways in which youth are actively involved in making and distributing information, Kafi D. Kumasi (2018) utilizes CRT's counterstorytelling methodology to inform their InFLO-mation model. This new model, grounded in the foundations of hip hop, seeks to hold vital space for youth of color voice and expression that positions counterstorytelling as a method that not only challenges essentialized, dangerous, racialized dominant narratives but also illuminates their actual, active, rich, complex knowledges and information behaviors. In *Algorithms of Oppression*, Safiya Umoja Noble (2018) employs CRT to analyze algorithms, particularly Google's, to illustrate how racism is coded into those systems and how they continue to extend racism's hold on society to the detriment of BIPOC.

In 2019, Hines analyzed the curriculum, goals, evaluation, and costs of library leadership programs through a CRT lens, focusing on the conceptual elements of racism as normal, interests convergence, and structural determinism (6–8). In understanding the systemic issues of library leadership development, the author asserts that the leadership programs they examined set whiteness as the (desired) norm, reinforcing and furthering white racial power and control. Hines locates racism as normal in the programs' curricula or outcomes, which (unsurprisingly) do not include interrogating librarianship's race or gender inequities, and shows the role of interest convergence in the exclusiveness and individualized assessment of the programs' work toward benefiting the dominant white culture and maintaining its power. The way these elements interact in this particular issue in LIS shows the dynamic architecture of CRT's structural determinism, which the author describes as "the way academia is structured to educate library workers, the way libraries operate, and the way library leadership training works fundamentally reinforce [racial] societal biases" (2019, 7). Similar to Hines in both their application of CRT to a previously unexamined area of LIS—in this case, the *Framework for Information Literacy for Higher Education*—and their use of CRT's racism as ordinary element, Rapchak (2019) more forcefully, and appropriately, names White Supremacy as the structure of domination that shapes and produces relations of racialized power. Through a detailed analysis of the language of three critical adjacent frames—"Authority Is Constructed and Contextual," "Information Has Value," and "Scholarship as a Conversation,"—the author argues that the active avoidance of naming, and deeply examining, race and racism (contextually, historically, contemporarily) perpetuates White Supremacy in teaching and learning. The inability of the *Framework* to push learners' and educators toward an in-depth understanding of systems of oppression is not a coincidence; it is necessary to mask, and maintain, the operations of White Supremacy. In exposing and disrupting this operation, Rapchak asserts that centering the counterstories of students of color can provide an important and empowering insight into the workings and construction of structural racism (186–187). Similarly, Nicole A. Cooke (2019) offers counterstorytelling as an important strategy of resistance and truth-telling for BIPOC LIS faculty as they navigate the toxic, hostile, and violent spaces of academia. Counterstorytelling as strategy, Cooke argues, not only challenges the master narrative of race and power but also can be a significant psychological, emotional release, help show new LIS workers of color the professional spaces they will encounter, and contribute critical knowledge to the scholarly record (228). Lastly, we would be careless if we did not at least highlight the recent valuable effort by Ebony Elizabeth Thomas, *The Dark Fantastic: Race and the Imagination from Harry Potter to the Hunger Games* (2019). Grounding their analytic method in CRT, Thomas utilizes counterstories to address the imagination gap that whiteness in children's lit and media creates.

As we hope to have shown above, the migration of Critical Race Theory in library and information studies has crossed multiple facets of the discipline and profession. Scholars in the discipline employing CRT have sought to center race and racism in their analyses, challenge the multidimensions of White Supremacy, and reveal the inequities that are pervasive in our field. By no means is this an exhaustive, detailed examination and review of all CRT and LIS scholarship. The focus of this section is to sketch the lineage of CRT in LIS, making visible some of the critical intersections of our discipline and profession and the theoretical framework. We invite you to engage with the CRT in LIS literature that exists. It is on and with this scholarship, as well as previous generations' discourses around race and racism, that the voices in this collection humbly build, and we can look back to imagine forward.

COLLECTIVELY JOURNEYING

As editors, we decided to approach this work as an edited collection of pieces by a cross-section of BIPOC in US libraries and archives. This was a deliberate choice on our part to embody counterstorytelling, a CRT strategy, in order to collectively create a people's vision by the LIS community. This method allows for a wide range of BIPOC scholars, archivists, librarians, activists, students, and professionals in the field to examine race and racism and its relationship to inequities in the many areas of the LIS landscape. Our multidimensional approach crosses various professional boundaries—archives, public libraries, academic libraries, professional organizations, and more—and seeks to identify and closely examine the racial inequities that exist in those particular spaces. Concentrated on information institutions in the United States, the collective authors of this volume strive to provide steps and recommendations toward a new vision of the profession and field.

This book is intentionally a space created by BIPOC for a number of reasons. First, as previously stated, the field of library and information studies professionals is distinctly white. Seldom are voices of color heard or represented in the field's literature, and we want to provide a place for these voices to be lifted up. Second, the history/herstory of CRT has come out of the lives and experiences of BIPOC, and we want to reflect that in this academic scholarly space. Third, BIPOC are often asked to solve the problems of racism by themselves (although typically they are not listened to and or given any credit), which ignores how patriarchy, colonialism, and White Supremacy have historically led to these issues. This book will continue a legacy of BIPOC leading the struggle, as the people most impacted by White Supremacy. The justice movement cannot progress without the experience and knowledge that BIPOC have. Finally, BIPOC in this profession and field are constantly resisting and struggling with the implicit and explicit story of white superiority and BIPOC inferiority. White folx are always trying to contain us, not recognizing that we were never meant for white spaces. This book testifies to the fact that we do not need, seek, or desire white validation. We are the scholars of our own liberation.

At the beginning of this book's journey we were three editors, but our homie, Irlanda Jacinto, one of the brightest stars in the archival profession, decided to leave archives and this book project before we submitted our proposal. The loss of her presence, brilliance, and ferocity is deeply felt by us, the book's contributors, and the profession as a whole. One of the very reasons for this book was to address the profession's dangerous and toxic allegiance to White Supremacy and the impact of structural racism on the LIS workforce. It is not lost on us that Irlanda found it necessary to depart. She was not the first to go, nor will she be the last.

The genesis of this book grew out of conversations the editors had with one another and discovering that we shared a passion for Critical Race Theory and its application to libraries and archives. It was rare to find people in our field with these intersecting interests and a relentless curiosity to know more. In July of 2016, Jorge and Irlanda met during a job interview in Albuquerque, New Mexico, and stayed in touch because of this shared interest. A week later, Sofia and Jorge met in Minneapolis at the Minnesota Institute for Early Career Librarians (MIECL) from traditionally underrepresented groups. During a bicycle ride, Sofia and Jorge talked CRT and the possibilities of a collaboration, which led to a subsequent email between all three of us about this very book.

Each of the editors came to CRT on a different individual journey, but more importantly, we collectively arrived here with this book. As bell hooks (1991) says, we searched for theory because we were hurting and trying to understand in new ways what this world was trying to do to us and our communities. CRT gives us the language, framework, and tools to enact the type of transformational change we want to see in our field. We are also heavily influenced by adrienne maree brown's work on emergent strategy, where one of the principles states: "There is a conversation in the room that only these people at this moment can have. Find it" (brown 2017, 41). This is a concept that we experienced at MIECL with the rest of the participants; it is difficult to imagine how that particular time would have been with different people in the room. Our time at MIECL coincided with the state-sanctioned murder of Philando Castile (less than five miles from MIECL), the domestic terrorist attack at Pulse nightclub, and the run-up to the 2016 election. These overlapping events turned the institute into a crucible, where under intense stress, scrutiny, and pressure, *we*, not the institute, created a beautiful and transformative experience for ourselves. We took our time there into our own hands. In a space filled with archivists and librarians of color, we could see what the profession *could* be. The relationships we made have continued to this day, and many of those folx—Jennifer Brown, Nicholae Cline (Coharie), Fobazi M. Ettarh, and Rachel E. Winston—are in this book. We found many of our contributors through similar personal networks that were built by being the only BIPOC in a white space, particularly through We Here, a supportive online (and sometimes physical) gathering space for BIPOC working in archives and libraries.

One of the driving forces behind the formation of this book was the desire to create a community of CRT scholars in LIS to help move CRT into the center of the LIS field. We purposefully wanted to disrupt the dominant narrative of a scholar in isolation and the celebration of the sole genius whose work was his and his alone. We wanted to mirror the CRT principle of building knowledge through community and to recognize that this work happens collectively, intersectionally, and in tandem with many others. Our approach was to build intentional, generative spaces for shared efforts in a supportive environment where the individual chapter authors would have multiple opportunities to connect with us and each other. We organized large-group Google Hangouts, met one-on-one with the contributors of all the chapters, hosted drop-in virtual office hours, and created a Slack group and a shared Zotero library, all in hopes of creating coresistance possibilities and forming coalitions. We connected authors to others with whom we felt there was a relevant link—who had unknowingly signaled to each other, whether it was via the CRT tenets or methods they used or the LIS topic they were writing about—because we wanted people coming together to create. We asked each author to provide peer feedback on either a chapter, the introduction, or the conclusion, and tried to match up their expertise and skills with the needs of the chapter. Our hope is that these relationships strengthen the coherence and message of the book.

CRITICAL RACE THEORY PROJECTS IN THIS BOOK

We have arranged the collection in three parts and the chapters are organized by shared, though not necessarily matching, themes and principles. This arrangement of the collection is important and purposeful. Much care and thought went into the grouping and placement of each chapter as well as the concise, suggestive title for each part. The title of each part represents what we imagine the chapters in that location are trying to achieve. In other words, and this applies to all the chapters in each section, the chapters aim toward the goal stated with each section heading and taken all together mount a strong force in that purpose. But they also do so independently in different, nuanced ways, and each should be understood as its own world-building contribution, analyzed on its own terms, yet in conversation, engaging and exchanging across contradictions and tensions, with chapters that are close and others that are not. Lastly, one of the exciting elements of this collection is the invited contributions of the much-respected scholars Todd Honma, Anthony Dunbar, and Tonia Sutherland, who are all invested in a similar commitment to social and racial justice, particularly through LIS; they have written section introductions that provide context, framing, and analysis of the chapters and root the sections in a continuation of the work these scholars and many others have been engaged in.

PART I: DESTROY WHITE SUPREMACY
The first part, "Destroy White Supremacy," demonstrates important conceptual understandings and methodological approaches that work toward growing and understanding

CRT in LIS in ways that challenge and ultimately ruin White Supremacy. This part forms a strong foundation that illustrates a multidimensional approach and analysis that crosses institutional boundaries and professional duties and responsibilities, pushing information workers toward understanding and confronting the intersections of race, power, and domination. The authors here interrogate core values of libraries and librarianship; name and unveil a destructive organizing principle of society; problematize racialized and gendered labor expectations and realities of the white-dominated LIS landscape; and fight against colonial information authority and sharing. This section is introduced by Todd Honma, who wrote one of the foundational racial critiques of LIS, "Trippin' over the Color Line: The Invisibility of Race in Library and Information Science." In his insightful, attentive, and journeying section introduction, Honma urges us to consider the extraordinariness of racism and uses the title of the section as a liberatory destination to map the chapters' important contributions, guiding and teaching us along the way.

The collection opens with Anastasia Chiu, Fobazi M. Ettarh, and Jennifer A. Ferretti's "Not the Shark, but the Water: How Neutrality and Vocational Awe Intertwine to Uphold White Supremacy." The authors focus on CRT themes—racism as ordinary, critique of liberalism, and whiteness as property—to examine the deeply embedded, highly problematic values of neutrality and vocational awe and their toxic, necessary relationship to libraries and librarianship that White Supremacy undergirds. Weaving together professional documents, liberal delusions of libraries' histories and purposes, current realities of BIPOC library workers and users, and many of the primary services and spaces of libraries and librarianship, Chiu, Ettarh, and Ferretti show just how entangled and pervasive the values and concepts have been and still are. Going further, they challenge us to abandon these intimately connected (and held) destructive values so that we can then move away from this awful mess toward justice.

The next chapter is Myrna E. Morales and Stacie Williams's "Moving toward Transformative Librarianship: Naming and Identifying Epistemic Supremacy." They introduce the concept of epistemic supremacy and how it constructs, organizes, and facilitates racial and class domination in society and social institutions. Using CRT's storytelling method to center and critique two harmful, powerful figures who have profoundly influenced information structures, Morales and Williams provide insight into the workings of epistemic supremacy and libraries', and librarians', conformity to it, with careful attention to knowledge organization and scholarly communications that subjugate BIPOC. True to CRT's social justice roots, they offer a beautiful shape of praxis to fight this unjust system, which they call "transformative librarianship."

Jennifer Brown, Nicholae Cline (Coharie), and Marisa Méndez-Brady's chapter, "Leaning on our Labor: Whiteness and Hierarchies of Power in LIS Work," interrogates whiteness and diversity work by analyzing institutional documents that define diversity, equity, and inclusion efforts. Understanding that White Supremacy intricately shapes institutions, the authors highlight the immense weight (and devaluing) placed on BIPOC for this specific type of work and demonstrate that professional and institutional diversity efforts are a very specific thing—a commodity. By utilizing CRT themes of interest convergence (to show the relationship between race and power) and racism as normal (in its intentional omission from most diversity documents), and using their critically important counterstories, the authors direct us not only to understand and confront racialized labor inequities and the very institutions that (continue to) position us in asymmetrical work relations of power, but also to interrupt and dream new futures for collective efforts and ways of being.

Closing out part I is "Tribal Critical Race Theory in Zuni Pueblo: Information Access in a Cautious Community," by Miranda H. Belarde-Lewis (Zuni/Tlingit) and Sarah R. Kostelecky (Zuni Pueblo). Writing for, and toward, their home, they share three projects from their pueblo's cultural institutions that center Zuni voices and knowledge and rightfully shift the power of their information to their peoples. The authors put forward—for the very first time that we are aware of in LIS literature—Tribal Critical Race Theory (Tribal Crit), a formation of CRT in education that attends to the specificity of Indigenous peoples and which necessarily positions colonialism as the central structure of domination. In a very intimate, loving, and generous voice, Belarde-Lewis and Kostelecky share with us some of their stories to end their chapter and this section. It is a gift, and as settlers, guests, or visitors, we need to listen carefully and closely.

PART II: ILLUMINATE ERASURE

In the second section, "Illuminate Erasure," the authors challenge the profession and discipline, demanding a shift of realities and the elimination of racial domination, through voice and counterstorytelling. From a variety of perspectives, they collectively approach LIS issues of information access, scholarly communication, and exclusionary collection development, while also highlighting social justice in collection building as acts of change and resistance. By exposing oppressive institutional hierarchies and collections and centering the voices and bodies of communities of color that are experiencing injustice(s), the authors fearlessly disallow our erasure and instead raise us up and celebrate one another, while holding people, communities, and LIS accountable. Anthony W. Dunbar, a foremost CRT and LIS scholar who first introduced CRT to archives, opens this section with his own counterstory, "The Courage of Character and Commitment versus the Cowardliness of Comfortable Contentment." Before turning to his close description of the chapters, Dunbar, in an analytic, richly illustrative voice, reflects on his own critical race theorist becoming, examines the racialized social hierarchy of the US, and pushes for utilizing critical race theories in the LIS discipline to fight White Supremacy and contemporary segregation.

First, in "Counterstoried Spaces and Unknowns: A Queer South Asian Librarian Dreaming," Vani Natarajan uses several counterstories from their own life as entry points into exploring their praxis as a librarian, and by extension, the practices of libraries in general. They employ three CRT frameworks—community cultural wealth, intersectionality, and Queer of Color Critique—to analyze those stories and provide strategies for resistance. Community cultural wealth is a concept by Tara Yosso from the CRT in education realm, while Queer of Color Critique is a subcategory of CRT that centers the experiences of queer and trans People of Color (QTPOC). Natarajan substitutes the word *abundance* for *capital* to confront capitalism's desire for a false sense of scarcity to bolster competition rather than community. They end by weaving together the three frameworks to suggest ways to further develop their thinking and, by extension, the reader's.

Next, Shaundra Walker uses the counterstory of Ann Allen Shockley, a Black activist-librarian, to illustrate the importance of special collections in libraries at HBCUs in her chapter, "Ann Allen Shockley: An Activist-Librarian for Black Special Collections." Seen through the lens of CRT, Shockley's work toward racial justice for Black communities illustrates the ways in which the profession could further develop what she and other Black activist-librarians have already accomplished. Walker demonstrates through Shockley's accomplishments that the absence of special collections in HBCUs is a form of erasure that assists in the false stories of white superiority and as a tool of racial domination. Likewise, Sujei Lugo Vázquez highlights the work of several BIPOC librarians in her chapter, "The Development of US Children's Librarianship and Challenging White Dominant Narratives," to reimagine what children's librarianship can be when it centers the stories and experiences of BIPOC. She employs counterstorytelling and revisionist history to explore the permanence of racism in children's librarianship through Patricia Hill Collins's domains of power framework. Lugo Vázquez shares the counterstories of Augusta Braxston Baker, Pura T. Belpré, Charlemae Hill Rollins, Effie Lee Morris, and Lotsee Patterson to illustrate the social justice work BIPOC librarians have been doing throughout the history of libraries. Both Walker and Lugo Vázquez illuminate the historical context within which collections have perpetuated and continue to perpetuate the erasure of BIPOC stories and knowledge; they retell a necessary remembering of the ancestral library work of Black, Indigenous, and Afro–Puerto Rican women.

We end the section with Harrison W. Inefuku's "Relegated to the Margins: Faculty of Color, the Scholarly Record, and the Necessity of Antiracist Library Disruptions," where he interrogates the academic publishing apparatus and the professions—librarianship, publishing, academy—that shape it, to provide insight into the processes that (re)create racial domination. Grounded in CRT's racism as ordinary, Inefuku illuminates the ways in which knowledge in the academy has been constructed and naturalized by racial power and advances a number of racially just librarian interventions that can challenge the structural racism inherent in the scholarly communication system.

PART III: RADICAL COLLECTIVE IMAGINATIONS TOWARD LIBERATION

The third and final part, "Radical Collective Imaginations toward Liberation," offers radical solutions and charts new imaginative directions for structural transformations in LIS that interrupt the large colonial project of White Supremacy. The chapters in this part focus on interventions in the profession's demographic problem, challenging dominant Western archive practices, proposing new pedagogical and mentoring approaches, critically examining the labor practices in academic librarianship and digital humanities, and illustrating a variety of CRT tenets through a fictional counterstory, in the vein of Derrick Bell's "The Space Traders." These chapters put forward the care and love of self and community and the creation of sites of healing. They move us toward a radical collective imagination of future possibilities and transformations for the profession and, more importantly, ourselves and our communities. Beginning this final part of the book with their contribution "Freedom Stories" is Tonia Sutherland, a leading scholar in the intersections of race and digital and archival studies. In generous, graceful, and alive language, Sutherland foregrounds the full humanity of the chapters, then traces, with deep understanding, the nuanced ways the authors engage CRT's voice tenet in the particular areas of LIS under examination. With liberation on the horizon, Sutherland sets in motion the chapters to take flight.

We start this section with Isabel Espinal, April M. Hathcock, and Maria Rios's chapter, "Dewhitening Librarianship: A Policy Proposal for Libraries," in which they first put forth a new term, *dewhiten*, to replace the term *diversify*, as in "diversifying the profession," to make clear that whiteness is being decentered. They then delineate the economic history and policies of the United States to elucidate the structural inequities surrounding the fact that less than 12 percent of the LIS profession is made up of BIPOC. To address this issue, the authors present a plan to reallocate parts of library budgets toward increasing the number of BIPOC in the profession.

In "The Praxis of Relation, Validation, and Motivation: Articulating LIS Collegiality through a CRT Lens," Torie Quiñonez, Lalitha Nataraj, and Antonia Olivas gift us a new model of pedagogy, relationship growing, and critical race/gender praxis incorporating LatCrit, a relational-cultural mentoring framework, Yosso's community cultural wealth, and validation theory, that contest white-dominant ways of being and knowing. They use personal counterstories as examples of how epistemologies of whiteness work to isolate and otherize BIPOC. These highly racialized, gendered, and classed experiences informed and shaped their approach to their teaching, research, and each other.

Anne Cong-Huyen and Kush Patel begin their chapter, "Precarious Labor and Radical Care in Libraries and Digital Humanities," with an imaginative, deeply hopeful quote from Leah Lakshmi Piepzna-Samarasinha that shares important new ideas for building and sustaining relationships, which their chapter takes up. The authors push us to consider the practices, mechanisms, and conditions of an academic industrial complex rooted in White Supremacy, through their analysis of academic librarianship and digital humanities labor that is dependent on division, invisibility, uncertainty, and harm. In their opposition to this harmful, oppressive labor, Cong-Huyen and Patel highlight multiple critical movements within digital humanities and librarianship and put forward justice-focused approaches with radical care at the forefront.

Next, Rachel E. Winston's moving and engaging chapter, "Praxis for the People: Critical Race Theory and Archival Practice," directs us to consider—again, for the first time, to our knowledge, in archival and LIS scholarship—critical race praxis (CRP), a branch of CRT, in archival work. Responding to and extending both critical archives studies and CRT, Winston advances a CRP framework, consisting of five related yet independent elements—Disruptive, Responsive, Actionable, Informed, and Caring—that pushes toward relational and structural shifts in archives, which are critically necessary to change the relationship between race and power.

"'Getting InFLOmation': A Critical Race Theory Tale from the School Library," by Kafi Kumasi, closes this part and is the final chapter before the collection ends with a contribution from us. Kumasi displays CRT's imaginative underpinnings by offering a fictional story that centers the always already rich, deep, and nuanced information worlds of a Black family, community, and a Black male youth in an unnamed, contemporary US city and high school library. Kumasi presents a wide range of connected information formats—Black Twitter, text messages, college acceptance letters, conversations with family and friends—in the reality of her main character, Jamar. Through Jamar's understanding of CRT's whiteness as property and interest convergence concepts, college admissions, K–12 schooling enrollments, and Black-white relations are critiqued.

We hope that in reading this collection of some of the leading LIS scholars and practitioners utilizing CRT to reconstruct the field and profession, you too feel inspired, activated, and emboldened to engage with CRT in a transformative way.

We challenge you.

NOTES

1. Throughout the introduction and conclusion chapters, we intentionally use library and information studies, rather than library and information science, to move away from the idea that this discipline is scientific in any way. *Science* as a term is often used to imply that the thing we are talking about is neutral and objective when in reality it reflects the same racial hierarchy and structures of oppression that exist in the US nation-state. Contributors to this collection may still use library and information science as that is what the field is most commonly known as.

2. Throughout the introduction and conclusion chapters, we also intentionally use the term Black, Indigenous, and People of Color (BIPOC) not to rank oppressions but to call out the specific realities that exist for this group in the country now known as the United States.

3. "Color blindness" is intentionally enclosed in quotation marks to highlight the ableist nature of the term. Though the term is commonly used and has a long, significant tradition in Critical Race Theory scholarship, we believe it is necessary to move with DisCrit scholars who direct us toward the term *color evasiveness*, "which both refuses to position people who are blind as embodying deficit and recognizes the active evasion involved in people's refusing to discuss race in the face of racial inequities" (Annamma, Connor, and Ferri 2016, 6).

4. April Hathcock defines whiteness beyond its connection to individuals and racial identity and directs us to understand whiteness as not only "the socio-cultural differential of power and privilege that results from categories of race and ethnicity … [but] also … a marker for the privilege and power that acts to reinforce itself through hegemonic cultural practice that excludes all who are different" (2015, para. 3).

5. We capitalize White Supremacy throughout the book in order to call attention to its dominance and power, as it is often purposely hidden from view.

6. Here, we do not distinguish between BIPOC and POC because the leading scholars describing their own history do not do so and because it provides an example of how language around race continues to shift.

7. The late Bell is also recognized as one of CRT's leading intellectual figures. In a serendipitous closing of the loop, half of this introduction was written and revised one block from the Harvard Law School campus.

8. A challenged and still-evolving term, Latinx is used in the introduction and conclusion intentionally and politically to contest hetero/homonormativity and patriarchy, gesture our committed solidarity to queer, trans, lesbian, and gay justice movements, and imagine gender, sexuality, and subjectivity beyond binaries, boundaries, and borders.

9. Throughout this piece, and especially in this section, we default to the singular "they" in an effort to not misgender individuals.

10. As mentioned earlier in this introduction, the wonderfully thought-provoking 2017 article "On 'Diversity' as Anti-Racism in Library Information Studies: A Critique," by David James Hudson, incisively analyzes this phenomenon.

11. Building on the incredible work of the movement Cite Black Women, from here and throughout the rest of this section, when analyzing and describing singly authored and coauthored scholarship, we deliberately write out the full names of Black scholars as a way to honor, value, and elevate the intellectual contributions of Black thought.

12. It should be noted that the scholarship of critical, radical librarian Sanford Berman engaged CRT concepts, especially racial bias in the Library of Congress Subject Headings, long before the official emergence of the CRT movement.

13. This would turn out to be an important moment in the evolution of CRT in LIS scholarship, because it marked the beginning of CRT's presence in that particular area of librarianship, which, to date, has been the most prolific.

14. Transitional books are categorized as literature that moves children from an early reader stage to an independent one, which often takes place around the second or third grade.

15. Throughout the introduction, we use the term *folx*, rather than *folks*, as a gender-neutral term.

16. Though the term was introduced earlier, the intentional effort to organize scholars writing under this description took form in this issue.

17. Some of these efforts by mostly BIPOC that require mention include the edited collections *Pushing the Margins: Women of Color and Intersectionality in LIS* (2018); *In Our Own Voices, Redux: The Faces of Librarianship Today* (2018); *Asian American Librarians and Library Services: Activism, Collaborations, and Strategies* (2017); a *Collection Management* special issue, "Sharing Knowledge and Smashing Stereotypes: Representing Native American, First Nation, and Indigenous Realities in Library Collections" (2017); the *Library Trends* special issue "Race and Ethnicity in Library and Information Science: An Update" (2018); the *Journal of Radical Librarianship* special issue "Race and Power in Library and Information Studies" (2019); a special issue of *Archival Science*, "'To Go Beyond': Towards a Decolonial Archival Praxis" (2019); and the *Journal of Education for Library & Information Science* special issue "A Critical Dialogue: Faculty of Color in Library and Information Science" (2019).

BIBLIOGRAPHY

Ahmed, Sara. 2012. *On Being Included: Racism and Diversity in Institutional Life*. Durham NC: Duke University Press.

American Library Association. 2010. "Diversity Counts 2009–2010 Update." American Library Association. http://www.ala.org/aboutala/offices/diversity/diversitycounts/2009-2010update.

Andrews, Nicola, Sunny Kim, and Josie Watanabe. 2018. "Cultural Humility as a Transformative Framework for Librarians, Tutors, and Youth Volunteers." *Young Adult Library Services* 16 (2): 19–22.

Annamma, Subini Ancy, David Connor, and Beth Ferri. 2013. "Dis/ability Critical Race Studies (DisCrit): Theorizing at the Intersections of Race and Dis/ability." *Race Ethnicity and Education* 16 (1): 1–31. https://doi.org/10.1080/13613324.2012.730511.

Annamma, Subini Ancy, David Connor, and Beth Ferri. 2016. "Introduction: A Truncated Genealogy of DisCrit." In *DisCrit: Disability Studies and Critical Race Theory in Education*, edited by Subini Ancy Annamma, David Connor, and Beth Ferri, 1–8. New York: Teachers College Press.

Ansley, Frances Lee. 1989. "Stirring the Ashes: Race Class and the Future of Civil Rights Scholarship." *Cornell Law Review* 74 (6): 994–1077.

Bell, D. A. 1980. "Brown v. Board of Education and the Interest-Convergence Dilemma." *Harvard Law Review* 93 (3): 518–533.

Bell, Derrick. 1992. *Faces at the Bottom of the Well: The Permanence of Racism*. New York: Basic Books.

Bell, Derrick A. 2004. *Silent Covenants: Brown v. Board of Education and the Unfulfilled Hopes for Racial Reform*. Oxford: Oxford University Press.

Bowers, Jennifer, Katherine Crowe, and Peggy Keeran. 2017. "'If You Want the History of a White Man, You Go to the Library': Critiquing Our Legacy, Addressing Our Library Collections Gaps." *Collection Management* 42 (3–4): 159–179. https://doi.org/10.1080/01462679.2017.1329104.

Brayboy, Bryan McKinley Jones. 2005. "Toward a Tribal Critical Race Theory in Education." *Urban Review* 37 (5): 425–446. https://doi.org/10.1007/s11256-005-0018-y.

Brook, Freeda, Dave Ellenwood, and Althea E. Lazzaro. 2015. "In Pursuit of Antiracist Social Justice: Denaturalizing Whiteness in the Academic Library." *Library Trends* 64 (2): 246–284. https://doi.org/10.1353/lib.2015.0048.

brown, adrienne maree. 2017. *Emergent Strategy—Shaping Change, Changing Worlds*. Chico, CA: AK Press.

Brown, Jennifer, Jennifer A. Ferretti, Sofia Leung, and Marisa Méndez-Brady. 2018. "We Here: Speaking Our Truth." *Library Trends* 67 (1): 163–181. https://doi.org/10.1353/lib.2018.0031.

Brown, Jennifer, and Sofia Leung. 2018. "Authenticity vs. Professionalism: Being True to Ourselves at Work." In *Pushing the Margins: Women of Color and Intersectionality in LIS*, edited by Annie Pho and Rose L. Chou, 329–347. Sacramento, CA: Library Juice Press, 2018.

Caswell, Michelle, Ricardo Punzalan, and T-Kay Sangwand. 2017. "Critical Archival Studies: An Introduction." In "Critical Archival Studies," edited by Michelle Caswell, Ricardo Punzalan, and T-Kay Sangwand. Special issue, *Journal of Critical Library and Information Studies* 1 (2): 1–8. https://doi.org/10.24242/jclis.v1i2.50.

Chou, Rose L., and Annie Pho, eds. 2018. *Pushing the Margins: Women of Color and Intersectionality in LIS*. Sacramento, CA: Library Juice Press.

Clarke, Janet Hyunju, Raymond Pun, and Monnee Tong, eds. 2017. *Asian American Librarians and Library Services: Activism, Collaborations, and Strategies*. Lanham, MD: Rowman & Littlefield.

Collins, Patricia Hill, and Sirma Bilge. 2016. *Intersectionality*. Malden, MA: Polity Press.

Cooke, Nicole A. 2016. "Counter-storytelling in the LIS Curriculum." In *Perspectives on Libraries as Institutions of Human Rights and Social Justice,* edited by Ursula Gorham, Natalie G. Taylor, and Paul T. Jaeger, 331–348. Bingley, UK: Emerald Publishing.

Cooke, Nicole A., ed. 2018. "Race and Ethnicity in Library and Information Science: An Update." Special issue, *Library Trends* 67 (1): 1–181. http://muse.jhu.edu/issue/39275.

Cooke, Nicole A. 2019. "Impolite Hostilities and Vague Sympathies: Academia as a Site of Cyclical Abuse." *Journal of Education for Library and Information Science* 60 (3): 223–230. http://hdl.handle.net /2142/104218.

Cooke, Nicole A., and Joe O. Sánchez, eds. 2019. "A Critical Dialogue: Faculty of Color in Library and Information Science." Special issue, *Journal of Education for Library & Information Science* 60 (3): 169–238. https://www.utpjournals.press/toc/jelis/60/3.

Cooke, Nicole A., and Miriam E. Sweeney, eds. 2017. *Teaching for Justice: Implementing Social Justice in the LIS Classroom.* Sacramento, CA: Library Juice Press.

Crenshaw, Kimberlé. 1991. "Mapping the Margins: Intersectionality, Identity Politics, and Violence against Women of Color." *Stanford Law Review* 43 (6): 1241–1299. https://doi.org/10.2307/1229039.

Crenshaw, Kimberlé. 2020. CRT & Intersectionality Summer School. African American Policy Forum.

Crenshaw, Kimberlé Williams. 2001. "The First Decade: Critical Reflections, or a Foot in the Closing Door." *UCLA Law Review* 49 (5): 1343–1372.

Crenshaw, Kimberlé, Neil Gotanda, Gary Peller, and Kendall Thomas, eds. 1995. *Critical Race Theory: The Key Writings That Formed the Movement.* New York: The New Press.

Curammeng, Edward R., Tracy Lachica Buenavista, and Stephanie Cariaga. 2017. "Asian American Critical Race Theory: Origins, Directions, and Praxis." Center for Critical Race Studies at UCLA Research Briefs. June 1, 2017. https://issuu.com/almaiflores/docs/ec_tlb_sc_asianam_crt.

Decuir-Gunby, Jessica T., Thandeka K Chapman, and Paul Schutz. 2019. *Understanding Critical Race Research Methods and Methodologies: Lessons from the Field.* New York: Routledge.

Delgado, Richard, and Jean Stefancic. 2017. *Critical Race Theory: An Introduction.* 3rd ed. New York: New York University Press.

DiAngelo, Robin. 2011. "White Fragility." *International Journal of Critical Pedagogy* 3 (3): 54–70.

Dixson, Adrienne D., and Celia K. Rousseau Anderson. 2017. "And We Are Still Not Saved: 20 Years of CRT and Education." In *Critical Race Theory in Education: All God's Children Got a Song,* edited by Adrienne D. Dixson, Celia K. Rousseau Anderson, and Jamel K. Donnor, 34–38. 2nd ed. New York: Routledge.

Dumas, Michael J., and Kihana Miraya Ross. 2016. "'Be Real Black for Me' Imagining BlackCrit in Education." *Urban Education* 51 (4): 415–442. https://doi.org/10.1177%2F0042085916628611.

Dunbar, A. W. 2006. "Introducing Critical Race Theory to Archival Discourse: Getting the Conversation Started." *Archival Science* 6 (1): 109–129. https://doi.org/10.1007/s10502-006-9022-6.

Elteto, Sharon, Rose M. Jackson, and Adriene Lim. 2008. "Is the Library a 'Welcoming Space'?: An Urban Academic Library and Diverse Student Experiences." *portal: Libraries and the Academy* 8 (3): 325–337. https://doi:10.1353/pla.0.0008.

Ford, Chandra L., and Collins O. Airhihenbuwa. 2010. "Critical Race Theory, Race Equity, and Public Health: Toward Antiracism Praxis." *American Journal of Public Health* 100 (S1): S30–S35.

Ford, Chandra L., and Collins O. Airhihenbuwa. 2018. "Commentary: Just What Is Critical Race Theory and What's It Doing in a Progressive Field Like Public Health?" *Ethnicity and Disease* 28 (suppl. 1): 223–230. https://doi.org/10.18865/ed.28.S1.223.

Furner, J. 2007. "Dewey Deracialized: A Critical Race-Theoretic Perspective." *Knowledge Organization* 34 (3): 144–168.

Garcia, Nichole M., Nancy López, and Verónica N. Vélez. 2017. "QuantCrit: Rectifying Quantitative Methods through Critical Race Theory." *Race Ethnicity and Education* 21 (2): 149–157. https://doi.org/10.1080/13613324.2017.1377675.

Gibson, Amanda, Sandra Hughes-Hassell, and Megan Threats. 2018. "Critical Race Theory in the LIS Curriculum." In *Re-Envisioning the MLS: Perspectives on the Future of Library and Information Science Education*, edited by Johnna Percell, Lindsay C. Sarin, Paul T. Jaeger, and John Carlo Bertot, 49–70. Bingley, UK: Emerald Publishing.

Griffin, K. L. 2013. "Pursuing Tenure and Promotion in the Academy: A Librarian's Cautionary Tale." *Negro Educational Review* 64 (1–4): 77–96.

Hall, Tracie D. 2012. "The Black Body at the Reference Desk: Critical Race Theory and Black Librarianship." In *The 21st-Century Black Librarian in America: Issues and Challenges*, edited by Andrew P. Jackson, Julius C. Jefferson Jr. and Akilah K. Nosakhere, 197–202. Lanham, MD: Scarecrow Press.

Harding, Vincent. 1970. "Black Students and the Impossible Revolution." *Journal of Black Studies* 1 (1): 75–100.

Harris, Cheryl I. 1993. "Whiteness as Property." *Harvard Law Review* 106 (8): 1707–1791. https://doi.org/10.2307/1341787.

Hathcock, April. 2015. "White Librarianship in Blackface: Diversity Initiatives in LIS." *In the Library with the Lead Pipe*, October 7, 2015. http://www.inthelibrarywiththeleadpipe.org/2015/lis-diversity/.

Hines, Samantha. 2019. "Leadership Development for Academic Librarians: Maintaining the Status Quo?" *Canadian Journal of Academic Librarianship* 4 (February): 1–19. https://doi.org/10.33137/cjal-rcbu.v4.29311.

Honma, Todd. 2005. "Trippin' over the Color Line: The Invisibility of Race in Library and Information Science." *InterActions: UCLA Journal of Education and Information Studies* 1 (2): 1–24. http://www.escholarship.org/uc/item/4nj0w1mp.

hooks, bell. 1991. "Theory as Liberatory Practice." *Yale Journal of Law and Feminism* 4 (2): 1–12. https://digitalcommons.law.yale.edu/yjlf/vol4/iss1/2.

Howard, Tyrone C., and Oscar Navarro. 2016. "Critical Race Theory 20 Years Later: Where Do We Go from Here?" *Urban Education* 51 (3): 253–273.

Hudson, David James. 2017. "On 'Diversity' as Anti-Racism in Library and Information Studies: A Critique." *Journal of Critical Library and Information Studies* 1 (1). https://doi.org/10.24242/jclis .v1i1.6.

Hudson, David James, and Gina Schlesselman-Tarango, eds. 2019. "Race and Power in Library and Information Studies." Special issue, *Journal of Radical Librarianship* 5.

Hughes-Hassell, Sandra. 2013. "Multicultural Young Adult Literature as a Form of Counter-Storytelling." *Library Quarterly: Information, Community, Policy* 83 (3): 212–228. https://doi.org/10 .1086/670696.

Hughes-Hassell, Sandra, Heather A. Barkley, and Elizabeth Koehler. 2009. "Promoting Equity in Children's Literacy Instruction: Using a Critical Race Theory Framework to Examine Transitional Books." *School Library Media Research* 12:1–20. http://www.ala.org/aasl/slmr/volume12/hughes -hassell-barkley-koehler.

Hughes-Hassell, Sandra, and Ernie J. Cox. 2010. "Inside Board Books: Representations of People of Color." *Library Quarterly: Information, Community, Policy* 80 (3): 211–230. http://www.jstor.org /stable/10.1086/652873.

Hughes-Hassell, Sandra, and Katy J. Vance. 2017. "Examining Race, Power, and Privilege in the Youth Services LIS Classroom." In *Teaching for Justice: Implementing Social Justice in the LIS Classroom*, edited by Nicole A. Cooke and Miriam E. Sweeney, 103–138. Sacramento, CA: Library Juice Press.

Hurley, David A., Sarah R. Kostelecky, and Paulita Aguilar, eds. 2017. "Whose Knowledge? Repre-senting Indigenous Realities in Library and Archival Collections." *Collection Management* 42:3–4, 124–129.

Iglesias, Elizabeth M. 1996. "International Law, Human Rights, and LatCrit Theory." *University of Miami Inter-American Law Review* 28 (2): 177–213. https://repository.law.miami.edu/umialr/vol28 /iss2/2/.

Joseph, Nicole M., Katherine M. Crowe, and Janiece Mackey. 2017. "Interrogating Whiteness in College and University Archival Spaces." In *Topographies of Whiteness: Mapping Whiteness in Library and Information Science*, edited by Gina Schlesselman-Tarango, 55–78. Sacramento, CA: Library Juice Press.

Kim, Eunsong. 2017. "Appraising Newness: Whiteness, Neoliberalism, and the Building of the Archive for New Poetry." In "Critical Archival Studies," edited by Michelle Caswell, Ricardo Punzalan, and T-Kay Sangwand. Special issue, *Journal of Critical Library and Information Studies* 1 (2): 1–40. https://doi.org/10.24242/jclis.v1i2.38.

Kumasi, Kafi. 2012. "Roses in the Concrete: A Critical Race Perspective on Urban Youth and School Librarians." *Knowledge Quest* 40 (5): 32–37. http://digitalcommons.wayne.edu/slisfrp/71.

Kumasi, Kafi. 2013. "'The Library Is Like Her House': Reimagining Youth of Color in LIS Dis-courses." In *Transforming Young Adult Services: A Reader for Our Age*, edited by Anthony Bernier, 103–113. Chicago: ALA Neal-Schuman.

Kumasi, Kafi. 2018. "INFLO-mation: A Model for Exploring Information Behavior through Hip Hop." *Journal of Research on Libraries and Young Adults* 9 (1): 1–18. http://www.yalsa.ala.org/jrlya /wp-content/uploads/2018/11/INFLO-mation_Kumasi.pdf.

Kurz, Robin F. 2012. "Missing Faces, Beautiful Places: The Lack of Diversity in South Carolina Picture Book Award Nominees." *New Review of Children's Literature and Librarianship* 18 (2): 128–145. https://doi.org/10.1080/13614541.2012.716695.

Kurz, Robin F. 2017. "Transgressing LIS Education: A Continuing Journey toward Social Justice." In *Teaching for Justice: Implementing Social Justice in the LIS Classroom*, edited by Nicole A. Cooke and Miriam E. Sweeney, 77–99. Sacramento, CA: Library Juice Press.

Ladson-Billings, Gloria. 1998. "Just What Is Critical Race Theory and What's It Doing in a Nice Field Like Education?" *International Journal of Qualitative Studies in Education* 11 (1): 7–24. https:// doi.org/10.1080/095183998236863.

Matsuda, Mari. 1991. "Voices of America: Accent, Antidiscrimination Law, and a Jurisprudence for the Last Reconstruction." *Yale Law Journal* 100 (5): 1329–1407. https://doi.org/10.2307/796694.

Matsuda, Mari, Charles R. Lawrence III, Richard Delgado, and Kimberlé Williams Crenshaw, eds. 1993. *Words That Wound: Critical Race Theory, Assaultive Speech and the First Amendment*. Boulder, CO: Westview Press.

Misawa, Mitsunori. 2012. "Social Justice Narrative Inquiry: A Queer Crit Perspective." Paper presented at the Adult Education Research Conference, Saratoga Springs, NY, June 1–3, 2012. http:// newprairiepress.org/aerc/2012/papers/34.

Neely, Teresa Y., and Jorge R. López-McKnight, eds. 2018. *In Our Own Voices, Redux: The Faces of Librarianship Today*. Lanham, MD: Rowman & Littlefield.

Noble, Safiyah. 2018. *Algorithms of Oppression*. New York: New York University Press.

Punzalan, Ricardo L., and Michelle Caswell. 2015. "Critical Directions for Archival Approaches to Social Justice." *Library Quarterly* 86 (1): 25–42. https://doi.org/10.1086/684145.

Racial and Ethnic Diversity Committee of ACRL. 2012. "Diversity Standards: Cultural Competency for Academic Libraries (2012)." Association of College and Research Libraries (ACRL). May 4, 2012. http://www.ala.org/acrl/standards/diversity.

Rapchak, Marica. 2019. "That Which Cannot Be Named: The Absence of Race in the *Framework for Information Literacy for Higher Education*." *Journal of Radical Librarianship* 5 (October): 173–196. https://journal.radicallibrarianship.org/index.php/journal/article/view/33/51.

Schlesselman-Tarango, Gina, ed. 2017. *Topographies of Whiteness: Mapping Whiteness in Library and Information Science*. Sacramento, CA: Library Juice Press.

Solórzano, Daniel G., and Dolores Delgado Bernal. 2001. "Examining Transformational Resistance through a Critical Race and LatCrit Theory Framework: Chicana and Chicano Students in an Urban Context." *Urban Education* 36 (3): 308–342. https://doi.org/10.1177/0042085901363002.

Solórzano, Daniel G., and Tara Yosso. 2002. "Critical Race Methodology: Counter-storytelling as an Analytical Framework for Education Research." *Qualitative Inquiry* 8 (1): 23–44. https://doi.org /10.1177/107780040200800103.

Stefancic, Jean. 1991. "Listen to the Voices: An Essay on Legal Scholarship, Women, and Minorities." *Legal Reference Services Quarterly* 11 (3–4): 141–149.

Stovall, David O. 2013. "'Fightin' the Devil 24/7': Context, Community, and Critical Race Praxis in Education." In *Handbook of Critical Race Theory in Education*, edited by Marvin Lynn and Adrienne D. Dixson, 289–301. New York: Routledge.

Sutherland, Tonia. 2017. "Making a Killing: On Race, Ritual, and (Re)membering in Digital Culture." *Preservation, Digital Technology & Culture* 46 (1): 32–40.

Thomas, Ebony Elizabeth. 2019. *The Dark Fantastic: Race and the Imagination from Harry Potter to the Hunger Games*. New York: New York University Press.

Valdes, Francisco. 1997. "Under Construction—LatCrit Consciousness, Community, and Theory." *California Law Review* 85 (5): 1087–1142. https://doi.org/10.15779/Z38VX4J.

Walker, Shaundra. 2015. "Critical Race Theory and the Recruitment, Retention and Promotion of a Librarian of Color: A Counterstory." In *Where Are All the Librarians of Color? The Experiences of People of Color in Academia*, edited by Rebecca Hankins and Miguel Juárez, 135–160. Sacramento, CA: Library Juice Press.

Walker, Shaundra. 2017. "A Revisionist History of Andrew Carnegie's Library Grants to Black Colleges." In *Topographies of Whiteness: Mapping Whiteness in Library and Information Science*, edited by Gina Schlesselman-Tarango, 33–53. Sacramento, CA: Library Juice Press.

Warren, Kellee E. 2016. "We Need These Bodies, but Not Their Knowledge: Black Women in the Archival Science Professions and Their Connection to the Archives of Enslaved Black Women in the French Antilles." *Library Trends* 64 (4): 776–794. https://doi.org/10.1353/lib.2016.0012.

Yosso, Tara, William Smith, Miguel Ceja, and Daniel Solórzano. 2009. "Critical Race Theory, Racial Microaggressions, and Campus Racial Climate for Latina/o Undergraduates." *Harvard Educational Review* 79 (4): 659–691. https://doi.org/10.17763/haer.79.4.m6867014157m7071.

I

DESTROY WHITE SUPREMACY

With editing by contributors Anastasia Chiu, Myrna E. Morales, Lalitha Nataraj, Vani Natarajan, and Maria Rios, as well as Leslie Kuo

INTRODUCTION TO PART I

Todd Honma

"Racism is ordinary, not aberrational." So state Richard Delgado and Jean Stefancic (2001) in what is now a canonical formulation that functions as one of the key tenets of Critical Race Theory. Throughout the chapters in this book, we see this phrase invoked in many contexts and iterations to highlight the ways in which racism, and whiteness in particular, has come to structure the field of library and information studies (LIS). However, I'd like to pause for a moment and think about how racism is not just ordinary, but *extraordinary*. Extraordinary in its durability, in its capacity to be continually reanimated and recomposed, and in its insistent materialization in various sectors of LIS so easily seen and felt, yet its existence is still questioned and denied. Racism is extraordinary in the way it so centrally, yet so often invisibly, occupies the very "political unconscious" (Jameson 1981) of our field.

The editors of this book, Sofia Y. Leung and Jorge R. López-McKnight, have strategically assembled this cluster of chapters under the heading "Destroy White Supremacy" to confront "the intersections of race, power, and domination" in LIS institutions and practices. Critical race theory serves as the methodological tool kit to expose and dismantle the way that the current system is set up to reproduce a particular set of social relations, relations that embody and enact the structures of racial domination. Central to this investigation is a critique of whiteness. As Sharon Luk (2018) reminds us, whiteness functions as both an ontological position and an epistemological project. In order for us to mobilize toward a liberatory LIS, we need to confront how racial ontologies and epistemologies continue to (over)determine the shape and form of librarianship itself.

Each of the chapters in their own unique way gifts us with further insights into how these ontologies and epistemologies function. The chapter by Anastasia Chiu, Fobazi M. Ettarh, and Jennifer A. Ferretti, "Not the Shark, but the Water: How Neutrality and Vocational Awe Intertwine to Uphold White Supremacy," focuses on how the naturalization of professional values upholds racial regimes, particularly within a white liberal multiculturalist logic that reinscribes societal conceptions of the library as an institution of public good (despite histories that prove otherwise). This form of counterstorytelling unearths the contradictions inherent within American liberal democracy as a racial onto-epistemological project that has worked as much to exclude as it has to include—that is, as Alexander Weheliye (2014) has pointed out, the liberal state's strategic excising of alternative modes of being and knowing in reverence to what counts as the fully human (i.e., an onto-epistemology of whiteness). The authors here point out how "deep-seated fears of betraying the profession" mute the possibility of critical dialogue and function as a self-perpetuating disciplinary mechanism to maintain the status quo. If such is the case, then perhaps we, as a community dedicated to overthrowing this machinery, need to consider the possibility that betraying the profession is precisely the strategy that is necessary if we are serious about "destroying" White Supremacy.

Counterstorytelling again offers a productive method of critiquing the racial state's investments in White Supremacy and the systematic destruction of communities of color, as highlighted in Myrna Morales and Stacie Williams's chapter, "Moving toward Transformative Librarianship: Naming and Identifying Epistemic Supremacy." By renarrating and recontextualizing key moments and figures in the history of librarianship, the authors encourage a careful reexamination of the ways in which libraries have actively aided in and colluded with right-wing forces that promoted racial superiority, nativism, xenophobia, and anti-Communism. Learning from this history, the authors advance an alternative paradigm of transformative librarianship. Echoing Clara M. Chu's (1999) seminal work on transformative information services, the authors call for a librarianship predicated on "collective knowledge building and organizing" and redirecting its attention to the most vulnerable in our communities. In this way, librarianship can combat "epistemic supremacy" and begin to undo the lasting effects of White Supremacy.

At the center of any investigation into whiteness that uses the methodological tools of Critical Race Theory is Cheryl I. Harris's (1995) foundational work on whiteness as property and the "conscious selections regarding the structuring of social relations" (280). Harris's profound insights into the workings of whiteness compel us to recognize that the construction of racial meaning has historically emerged—and continuously reemerges—as a structural formation co-constitutive with US nation building, the territorial expansion of American empire, and racial capitalist development. The goal of destroying White Supremacy, then, routes us on a path to destroying the property relation itself—that is, destroying the system of ownership and control that reproduces relations of domination. In this vein, Jennifer Brown, Nicholae Cline, and Marisa Méndez-Brady's chapter, "Leaning on Our Labor: Whiteness and Hierarchies of Power in LIS Work," asks us to think carefully about the political economy of library services—in particular, how the commodification of information, the bureaucratization of diversity efforts, and inequitable distribution of labor seamlessly function to enact changes that don't actually change anything at all. This "stubborn resistance," as they call it, is, indeed, both ordinary and extraordinary, impeding the actual work of dismantling systems of oppression. Such a recognition forces us to consider whether a liberatory LIS is even possible within the very system of racial capitalism.

We are living in a particular historical moment in which it is becoming increasingly clear that our current system is failing. And so this is an opportune time to creatively (re)imagine other modes of embodying and enacting our collective ways of being in the world. In other words, we cannot be content with simply "destroying white supremacy." We must simultaneously be advancing alternative infrastructures and new ways of organizing information, an embrace of various ontologies and epistemologies within what Sandra Harding (2006) might call "a world of information sciences." Such a move would challenge and destabilize the Euro-American/ Western hegemony that has discredited other ways of practicing information services. Miranda Belarde-Lewis and Sarah R. Kostelecky's chapter, "Tribal Critical Race Theory in Zuni Pueblo: Information Access in a Cautious Community," provides a glimpse of what this reinvention could look like, as they guide us along a path to understanding specific Indigenous ways of knowing and practicing information services. As the authors make clear, prioritizing the ethics of Zuni information, particularly in regard to the curation and protection of Indigenous knowledge, can run counter to foundational principles of LIS, namely its insistence on access and discoverability. This paradigmatic shift in our understanding of information enacts a particular type of refusal—not simply a refusal to abide by white Western norms, but also a refusal to forget histories of colonial violence, displacement, and genocide that operate under the very logic of discoverability and access: the so-called discovery of

Indigenous lands and imperial access to land, people, and resources that have fueled white settler colonialism and racial capitalism.

Marx likes to remind us that capitalism forges the weapons of its own demise. It is within this context that we must understand racism as being both ordinary and extraordinary, normal and abnormal. Racism's creative capacities in service to systems of capitalism and White Supremacy should instigate those of us fighting for their mutual destruction to be equally creative, if not more so. Cedric Robinson (1996) opens up other vistas of our collective existence when he states, "We are not the subjects or the subject formations of the capitalist world-system. It is merely one condition of our being" (122). Insofar as capitalism and White Supremacy function as a conjoined system to dismantle and eviscerate other onto-epistemological possibilities, the work of critical LIS scholarship is to recover, illuminate, theorize, reenvision, and enact alternative possibilities for a liberatory librarianship, holding on to a utopian promise that the future is always already here in the present.

BIBLIOGRAPHY

Chu, Clara M. 1999. "Transformative Information Services: Uprooting Race Politics." *Proceedings of the Black Caucus of the American Library Association Conference*, Las Vegas, NV, July 19–22, 1999.

Delgado, Richard, and Jean Stefancic, eds. 2001. *Critical Race Theory: An Introduction*. New York: New York University Press.

Harding, Sandra. 2006. *Science and Social Inequality: Feminist and Postcolonial Issues*. Urbana: University of Illinois Press.

Harris, Cheryl I. 1995. "Whiteness as Property." In *Critical Race Theory: The Key Writings That Formed the Movement*, edited by Kimberlé Crenshaw, Neil Gotanda, Gary Peller, and Kendall Thomas, 276–291. New York: The New Press.

Jameson, Fredric. 1981. *The Political Unconscious: Narrative as a Socially Symbolic Act*. Ithaca, NY: Cornell University Press.

Luk, Sharon. 2018. "Ourselves at Stake: Social Reproduction in the Age of Prisons." *CR: The New Centennial Review* 18 (3): 225–253.

Marx, Karl, and Friedrich Engels. (1888) 1978. "Manifesto of the Communist Party." In *The Marx-Engels Reader*, 2nd ed., edited by Robert C. Tucker, 469–500. New York: W. W. Norton.

Robinson, Cedric. 1996. "Manichaeism and Multiculturalism." In *Mapping Multiculturalism*, edited by Avery F. Gordon and Christopher Newfield, 116–126. Minneapolis: University of Minnesota Press.

Weheliye, Alexander G. 2014. *Habeas Viscus: Racializing Assemblages, Biopolitics, and Black Feminist Theories of the Human*. Durham, NC: Duke University Press.

1

NOT THE SHARK, BUT THE WATER

How Neutrality and Vocational Awe Intertwine to Uphold
White Supremacy

Anastasia Chiu, Fobazi M. Ettarh, and Jennifer A. Ferretti

Libraries are beloved institutions both in practice and in the public imagination. Over half of the population in the United States used a public library in the year 2015 to 2016 (Horrigan 2016) and libraries are described by authors, philosophers, and intellectuals with lofty words such as *temples*, *sacred places*, and *sanctuaries*.

Similarly, professional library literature extends this belief that the very existence of libraries creates democracy, learning, and civilization, and it conflates librarians' work with the actual buildings themselves (Latimer 2011; Sweeney 2005). This conflation of profession and place creates a narrative that what librarians do must be "good," because libraries are "good," and "sacred places." This narrative results in vocational awe, a phenomenon traced and defined by Ettarh as "the set of ideas, values, and assumptions librarians have about themselves and the profession that result in notions that libraries as institutions are inherently good, sacred notions, and therefore beyond critique" (2018).

Both neutrality and vocational awe have been codified as values of librarianship, and rarely have these values been challenged in trade and professional literature, nor their ties to White Supremacy examined. Neutrality, defined as "the state of not supporting or helping either side in a conflict, disagreement, or war," has long been considered a library value.[1] For the purposes of this chapter, we will focus on what Charles Mills describes as the "present period of de facto White Supremacy, when whites' dominance is, for the most part, no longer constitutionally and juridically enshrined but rather a matter of social, political, cultural, and economic privilege based on the legacy of the European conquest, African slavery, and European colonialism" (1997).

This chapter examines these values and how they are embedded within librarianship, as well as the myriad ways they intersect to uphold White Supremacy throughout various types of work and service in librarianship.[2] Finally, the chapter will demonstrate how vocational awe and neutrality continue to disenfranchise librarians, particularly librarians of color. By deconstructing assumptions and values integrally woven into the field, the authors hope to posit how librarianship can potentially evolve into a field that not only supports the people who work in libraries, but also empowers marginalized communities and fosters librarians' avowed democratic values. We, the authors, identify individually as first-generation American and Black, first-generation American Latina/Mestiza, and first-generation Asian American, are deeply invested in seeing the profession grow in its capacity to critique and change itself, and will draw on Critical Race Theory (CRT), which examines the totality and embedded nature of racism.

THEORETICAL FRAMEWORK

The first CRT tenet that we rely on, "racism as ordinary," is defined by Delgado and Stefancic as the idea that "racism is an ingrained feature of our landscape, it looks ordinary and natural to persons in the culture" (2017, 8–9). Because White Supremacy culture underlies the landscape of librarianship, and vocational awe and *neutrality* are arguably two of its most important mainstays, the assumptions, beliefs, and policies born from these values are seen as the norm rather than things to be challenged and ultimately transformed.[3] Within this overarching tenet, we draw specifically on Alan Freeman's identification of a "perpetrator perspective" and a "victim perspective" in understanding White Supremacy, as well as Cheryl I. Harris's multifaceted approach to understanding whiteness as property. The second CRT tenet that we draw on to examine *neutrality* and vocational awe is "critique of liberalism," which pushes back against the idea that "equal treatment for all persons, regardless of their different histories or current situations," yields an equitable social structure, and that "with the election of Barack Obama, we arrived at a postracial stage of social development" (Delgado and Stefancic 2017, 26). Specifically because the value of *neutrality* in libraries relies on these misconceptions, we italicize this term throughout the rest of this chapter to highlight the fallacy in the goals of *neutrality*-framed library work.

Due to a prevalent idea that "libraries are for all," there is a misconception that racial inequity does not affect libraries and requires no real intervention in libraries because people from all races, creeds, and walks of life are treated equally in the space. This idea is a central defense of *neutrality*; proponents of *neutrality* state that since we serve everyone, we must allow materials, ideas, and values from everyone. It also bolsters vocational awe, in that it forestalls meaningful critique of the field, particularly critique of its racial dynamics. As three People of Color, we have experienced on the micro and macro levels how librarianship weaponizes vocational awe and *neutrality* to uphold White Supremacy and further marginalizes communities of color. However, our very marginality allows a clearer view of the disconnect between the espoused values of librarianship and the reality of the field. We use this view to examine the current narratives of library work and, in a CRT tradition, to revise the history that has so long comforted the white majority of our profession (Delgado and Stefancic 2017, 25).

Many of CRT's tenets overlap, particularly to relate the following ideas: that White Supremacy is purposefully maintained over time and is not happenstance and that the dismantling of White Supremacy is poorly served by incrementalism and similar liberal methods of achieving equality. Incrementalism, as defined by Lindblom, is the method of change by which many small policy changes are enacted over time in order to create a larger broad-based policy change (1980). Incrementalism, as a method, will not be limited to public policy in this analysis but will also encompass the larger implicit and explicit cultural rules that define the field of librarianship.

We argue that the predominant idea of racism, as discrete and easily identifiable acts of prejudice, creates a dangerous notion that racism is essentially so rare as to be almost mythical. Alan Freeman terms this mindset the "perpetrator perspective." In other words, the dominant ideology of racism holds that racism is merely discrete acts, visible as evil through intent. By contrast, the "victim perspective," a term that Freeman acknowledges is ironic, understands racism and White Supremacy not as acts, but as conditions of life (1995)—not as a shark, but as the very water (Blackwell 2018).

This analogy brings us to the first tenet we rely on in this chapter—racism as ordinary. As Freeman and many other CRT scholars posit, racism is ingrained in common, everyday experiences, as well as the larger systems that govern society. Due to its very ordinariness, and the dominance of the perpetrator perspective, racism is seen as a moral failing, and therefore it shouldn't be acknowledged lest it spread. This restrictive construction of racism also led to the idea that those who acknowledge race as important in any capacity were racist, and thus the true path toward racial equality is integration, assimilation, and "color blindness." Color blindness, or the belief that ending racial inequality requires treating everyone exactly the same, at its core, flattens all nuance. Eduardo Bonilla-Silva (2006) identifies four common "frames" of color blindness, including *abstract liberalism* and *naturalisation*. Abstract liberalism promotes abstract ideas such as "individual choice" and "equal opportunity" as cures for all social inequality. This results in common opinions like opposing affirmative action because it is seen as taking away equal opportunity and imposing preferential treatment. Through the frame of naturalisation, racial inequality is explained away as "just the way things are," rather than purposeful choices. Paradoxically, being biased toward one's own racial group is seen as being "natural."

According to John Gray, a political philosopher who identified common elements of liberal thought, liberalism is seen as the core of modernity; its distinctive features include individualism, universalism, and egalitarianism (Gray 1986). Liberalism sees color blindness, meritocracy, and equal opportunity as part of the dominant moral compass of racial enlightenment. Critical race theory counters this by "question[ing] the very foundations of the liberal order, including equality theory, legal reasoning, Enlightenment rationalism, and neutral principles of constitutional law" (Delgado and Stefancic 2017, 3), where traditional civil rights discourse stresses incremental step-by-step progress.

Critical race scholars challenge the idea that liberalism is the best framework for solving racial inequality. For example, while the idea of color blindness is admirable—"judging by the content of character rather than color" (King 1963)—more often its effects are both inherently harmful and detrimental to equity, and it disadvantages peoples and communities of color. Here, we are using the term *equity* to mean customs based on general principles of fairness rather than common or statutory law, unlike *equality*, which is to mean sameness (Hirsch, Kett, and Trefil 2002). Policies such as affirmative action, which has historically benefited white women most, are discounted on the belief that they grant race-based "preferential treatment" and therefore don't fulfill the liberal ideal of "equal opportunity" (Crenshaw 2006). Color blindness posits that taking race into account at all, even to acknowledge past wrongs, is wrong and that those who believe that race is important are in fact racist. This equates white supremacists and racial advocates, ignoring the *severe* underrepresentation of People of Color in systems and institutions and prioritizing abstract elements of liberalism above the reality of multiple nation-state–sponsored and systematic inequalities.

Prioritizing abstract liberal concepts like equal opportunity, meritocracy, individualism, and free choice above lived realities creates a skewed sense of scale for progress. Going back to Freeman's "perpetrator perspective," these abstractions of liberalism create an environment where racist acts are the results of discrete actions that are aberrations from a "normal" life. White people, who are unlikely to experience disadvantages due to race, can effectively ignore racism in American life, justify the current social order, and feel more comfortable with their relatively privileged standing in society (Fryberg 2010). Only the most heinous acts are seen as requiring justice or repair. People of color, who more regularly experience and witness racist acts and discrimination, are seen as "aggressive" or "sensitive" for pointing out the discrepancies between abstract liberal values and the messier nuances of reality (Ettarh 2014). The result of this is that the already always biased system is changed only incrementally, when what is needed, and what we are demanding from our profession, is a full paradigm shift.

"LIBRARIANSHIP IS A PUBLIC GOOD"

In order to fully grasp the ideology and methodology that maintains White Supremacy within librarianship, and its effects on patron/practitioner communities, it is necessary to examine the field of librarianship more closely. A fuller view of the narratives about the field, including its relationship to democracy, *neutrality*, and vocational awe, can situate librarianship fully within the nation-state–sponsored, systemic, and institutional racism prevalent in the United States of America. Exploring these issues requires a brief history of libraries and democratic values in the US.

At its most basic, a democracy is a system of government where the majority of the decisions are made by the people and for the people. There are few narratives so tightly woven into the American identity as that of democracy. Liberalism's mainstay interests, including equal opportunity, individual choice, liberty, and meritocracy, underpin the American identity, from the stories of the Puritans seeking religious freedoms to the Revolutionary War for legislative and economic freedoms. Therefore, tying an occupation or vocation to the narrative of democracy is ostensibly the highest honor and praise. And librarianship, without fail, is tied to democracy. Many, including authors, poets, and legislators, as well as librarians themselves, agree that the library is one of the few truly democratic institutions. Vartan Gregorian went so far as to say, "The library is central to our free society. It is a critical element in the free exchange of information at the heart of our democracy" (1989, 71). Because libraries espouse values such as equal access to all, dedication to lifelong learning, and acting as a sanctuary for diverse community needs, they are often touted as the last public noncommodified and inherently democratic public place. Libraries are not only built on the egalitarian promises of democracy; they exist to promote them.

One of the most ingrained values of American democracy that libraries work to uphold is the freedom of speech, as guaranteed in the First Amendment to the Constitution. However, the way that libraries do this perpetuates a common misapplication of the First Amendment. Mari Matsuda explicates this misapplication—because antiracists' right to protest and culturally foil racist speech is protected, the government assumes that it "must take affirmative steps to preserve" the right of racist speech (1993, 33). In this national context, where the state protects racist speech broadly and penalizes it narrowly, libraries use the assumption that the law is *neutral* and take on the same position. Library workers' vocational awe leads them to gloss over this fault of American conceptions of freedom of speech, because protecting the First Amendment is seen as right and democratic.

On the surface, it seems natural that libraries and librarians would embrace and celebrate these assumptions wholeheartedly. As many see it, not only do libraries and librarians work to save the democratic values of society, they also go above and beyond to serve the needs of their neighbors and communities. This can be seen as early as the dedication of the Boston Public Library McKim Building, one of the first public libraries in the United States, which was proclaimed "a palace for the people" (Wiegand 2015), with the walls themselves inscribed with phrases such as "Free to all," and which served as a model for many libraries that followed.[4] Speakers at the dedication discussed how the American library evolved from a pure temple of knowledge to a democratic and civic treasure—one open to "the rich and the poor...the high and the lowly born, the masses who wield the hammers of toil, and the unenvied few who are reared in affluence and ease" (Ditzion 1947, 22). As more time went by, the story of the democratic library grew more powerful.

Andrew Carnegie, a Scottish American steel tycoon and philanthropist, became the most famous library philanthropist.[5] Prohibited from using a local library as a young man because he couldn't afford its fee, he later went on to establish over 2,500 public and academic libraries; the very first was built in his hometown, Dunfermline, and has an inscription over the door, reading, "Let there be light." Arguably one of the most well-known biblical phrases, Genesis 1:3 refers not just to physical light, but rather to the mandate of all creation—that the Divine Light shine throughout the world. This Divine Light would be connected to truth and knowledge throughout the Bible (Daniel 5:14; 1 John 1–5). Plato and other philosophers would also use the metaphor of knowledge as light as an ascent from ignorance (darkness) to knowledge (light) (Lakoff and Johnson 1999). In both examples, the sacredness of the library is not just in the materials, but in its accessibility and public access to said knowledge.

As libraries and, by extension, librarianship continued to be venerated for their ties to democracy and library benefactors such as Carnegie became tantamount to "patron saints," what began as a good story became the *only* story about libraries and librarianship. This narrative grows with every allegorical reference to libraries as "temples of learning" and librarians as "generals in the war on ignorance" (Warren 2014; Nichols School 2017), until it essentially becomes mythology. Libraries become sacred spaces, and its workers become priests and missionaries. The job duties and values of librarianship are turned into work as a service to God and fellow men. Finally, vocational awe is born, and as these mythologies are perpetuated in trade and professional literature, they are accepted as truths. Most dangerously, the mythologies become more important than reality, especially if reality contradicts the mythology.

In the context of librarianship's self-perceived stake in democracy, which is deeply tied to vocational awe, it becomes extremely difficult to critique major precepts of the field, such as *equal access* and *neutrality*, without being seen as sacrilegious. To expose the discrepancies between rhetoric and reality is to challenge the very sacredness of librarianship, and in turn, to challenge democratic values. Okun defines this characteristic of White Supremacy culture as "only one right way" (Okun, n.d.), or the belief that there is one correct way to do things and once people are introduced to the correct way, they will see the light and adopt it. Vocational awe directly ties into White Supremacy culture by creating a narrative of librarianship as inherently good and sacred work while delegitimizing all other narratives as undemocratic and blasphemous. And through the codification of values into the trade and professional literature, vocational awe compounds the White Supremacy culture characteristic "worship of the written word," by valuing white documents and standards over the nuances and complexities of reality.

Just as early CRT scholars posited with regard to the legal profession, both vocational awe and *neutrality* shield the library profession from coming to terms with its racialized past and its integral part in the advent and growth of white supremacist systems in American society. Todd Honma refers to the American colonization process as a "whitening process whereby European ethnics possessed a particular ethnic mobility based on the color of their skin that allowed them membership to a white racial identity" (2005, 7). This racial project is the seat of power and privilege over racially marginalized communities. By virtue of their privileged position, librarians of the status quo can afford to remain neutral toward issues that don't affect them personally. The legacy of a homogenous profession has given power to this position. Oppression is seemingly overlooked for its lack of impact, whether direct or indirect, not only by the individuals who make up the profession, but also by the profession itself. *Neutrality* is seen as "fair" and therefore "good," playing into vocational awe.

NEUTRALITY AND VOCATIONAL AWE: THE SEAT
OF PRIVILEGE AND POWER

Neutrality as a framework for library work is used as a means to bypass all forms of implicit and explicit bias. As Brown and Jackson write, "The appearance of neutrality primarily operates to obscure the fact that the perspective of the white majority is embedded within this view" (2013, 14). *Neutrality* is not always the specific term that is used to invoke this framework; the terms *objective* and *unbiased* are also used interchangeably in the library context to describe a lack of bias. But because explicit and implicit bias is inherent to the human experience, this is not achievable. To argue for *neutrality* or objectivity as the framework for all library activities is to leave workers and institutions with the impossible task of providing a one-size-fits-all service to the public with subjective guidelines, which actually works to perpetuate harmful behavior.

This is not to say that those who believe in the *neutrality* framework are bad people. On the contrary, intentions may be good and yet yield harmful results that may not be immediately apparent to the white majority of the profession; good intentions with harmful impacts are a hallmark of Freeman's perpetrator perspective of White Supremacy. Delgado and Stefancic sum this up in their analysis of liberal preferences for color blindness, which is a form of *neutrality*: "Color blindness can be admirable, as when a governmental decision maker refuses to give in to local prejudices. But it can be perverse, for example, when it stands in the way of taking account of difference in order to help people in need" (2017, 27). The admirability of *neutrality* bolsters vocational awe by averting critique.

On the topic of objectivity in reference services, Brook, Ellenwood, and Lazzaro wrote, "Librarians are generally expected to take an objective or neutral approach to assisting patrons"; as detailed in the section that follows, this is codified as an expectation for service in key professional statements. This principle also helps to reinforce the "racialized power-dynamic status quo" (2016, 274). When the profession discusses *neutrality*, we believe that the profession actually seeks equity. However, *neutrality* will not yield equitable results and will always fall short because it relies on equity already existing in society. This is not the condition of our current society, nor is it true for the profession. Therefore, *neutrality* will actually work toward reinforcing bias and racism.

The definition of *neutrality* within the library context has, for some, become synonymous with intellectual freedom and antonymous to censorship. Those who believe it is the duty of the library to carry out policies and practices in a *neutral* manner also invoke the right to free speech as written in the First Amendment. *Neutrality* and vocational awe have intertwined deeply in such a way that disagreement with either is seemingly admission of being a "bad librarian" (Ettarh 2019). This was evident at the 2018 American Library Association (ALA) Midwinter Meeting President's Program titled "Are Libraries Neutral?" Formatted as a debate, this session focused on whether libraries *are neutral*, if they've ever *been neutral*, and if they *should be neutral*. Two speakers for *neutrality* and two speakers against *neutrality* read prepared perspectives on the subject and four commentators provided reactions to the debaters.

Framing *neutrality* as a "debate" works to polarize the profession, constructing the issue as black and white (for or against) and without nuance. The library worker is thus placed in the position of being either pro- or anti*neutrality*. The former works to obfuscate the experiences of the patrons we serve (as well as our workforce) and aids vocational awe. The unidentified gaps that result do the most harm to marginalized communities; only dominant communities benefit from *neutrality*. One could argue that an unintended consequence of this tactic works to further reinforce neutrality as a dominant professional ideology. Once this polarization is in play, we lose the intended purpose of the *neutral* ideology, which is equity.

CODIFICATION OF *NEUTRALITY* AND VOCATIONAL AWE AS PROFESSIONAL VALUES

As vehicles by which racism has been normalized in libraries, *neutrality* and vocational awe are codified in key symbolic documents by which library workers verbalize institutional and professional values. Though there are many examples, including longer-standing ones, two documents of ALA are preeminent—the Code of Ethics and the Library Bill of Rights. These documents are significant because ALA is the largest professional association for library workers in the United States, and these documents, both current and past versions, are expressions of professional ideals that are assumed to be common enough to organize around.

We argue that the codification and intertwining of *neutrality* and vocational awe in both documents makes them organizational fictions. *Organizational fictions*, a term brought to library and information science (LIS) literature by Pauline Wilson (1979) and Kaetrena Davis Kendrick (2017), was coined and defined by Robert Dubin as "fictions that are necessary in order that action within the formal organization may proceed" (1968, 341).

One example of *neutrality* as organizational fiction lies in the current ALA Code of Ethics statement, "We distinguish between our personal convictions and professional duties and do not allow our personal beliefs to interfere with fair representation of the aims of our institutions or the provision of access to their information resources" (American Library Association 2008). Like most *neutral* stances in librarianship, this principle assumes that American libraries function in a society that is already equitable—that all librarians' (and all people's) personal ethics are already equally represented in society and in libraries, and all that is needed to maintain this preexisting equity is to give equal weight and equal space to all viewpoints. The Code of Ethics also states, "We provide the highest level of service to all library users." Within context, this principle assumes *neutrality* to be a quality of "highest service," and furthermore, it acts to weaponize vocational awe in library workers attempting to live up to an aspirational code. It is entirely unclear how a "highest level of service" can be realized, and how library workers are to cope under constant capitalist pressure to expand and increase what can be considered a "highest" level of service.

Neutrality and vocational awe in the ALA Code of Ethics can be traced to its earliest 1939 version. For example, the 1939 code states, "Recommendations [for new hires] should be confidential and should be fair to the candidate and the prospective employer by presenting an unbiased statement of strong and weak points" (American Library Association 1939). Essentially, it presents the act of considering both "strong and weak points" as evidence of having overcome biases. Yet, bias manifests itself everywhere, not just in the selection of points to represent in deliberations or arguments. As librarians of color, we see that this root of *neutrality* as organizational fiction is particularly harmful because it remains pervasive in library hiring processes today. It is weaponized to uphold implicit biases in hiring, and the rhetoric of *neutrality* in hiring merely allows white supremacist ideologies to stand in as "unbiased" (Hathcock 2015). This is evidenced in demographic statistics of the profession, which indicate that librarianship is roughly 87 percent white (American Library Association 2012).

The 1939 code also states, "In view of the importance of ability and personality traits in library work, a librarian should encourage only those persons with suitable aptitudes to enter the library profession and should discourage the continuance in service of the unfit." Through this principle, the 1939 code allowed the reader to decide what characteristics were "suitable" for library work, without consideration of the impacts of racist, ableist, and classist biases on judgments of "suitability," and it entitled the dominantly white library profession to weaponize these biases through vocational awe. Excluding "unsuitable" library workers was posed as an act of protecting the purity of the profession from negative influence. This root of vocational awe was further built up by the 1939 code's invocation that library workers should have a "sincere belief and a critical interest in the library profession," and "criticism of library policies, service, and personnel should be offered only to the proper authority for the sole purpose of improvement of the library." The historical presence of these statements in the Code of Ethics indicates how rooted the rhetoric of *neutrality* and vocational awe is as a pillar of White Supremacy in the library profession, and their legacy remains in our professional culture today despite their removal from the code.

Vocational awe and *neutrality* also feature heavily in the Library Bill of Rights, another document adopted by the ALA in 1939 and continuing in modified form today. The Library Bill of Rights does not state whose rights it guarantees, and it largely reads as a bill of responsibilities for library workers; three of its seven articles begin with the phrase "Libraries should." Unlike the US Constitution's Bill of Rights or patients' bills of rights in the medical profession (some of which are passed as state or local law and thus enforceable), no part of the Library Bill of Rights or its official interpretations attempt to enforce or ensure support for libraries and library workers in upholding its principles. Because of this lack of infrastructure to uphold its highly aspirational principles, the entire document essentially acts as organizational fictions about library workers' ability to generate positive social outcomes in the dissemination and use of information. For example, library workers are often exhorted to protect free speech by resisting censorship; as stated above, this carries an implicit weight because protecting free speech is tacitly equated to protecting American democracy (American Library Association 2017). While positive in intent, the unfortunate fallout of this exhortation is a generalized professional inculcation of vocational awe, manifesting in library workers' performance and expectation of professional martyrdom (Ettarh 2018).

Many of the Library Bill of Rights' individual articles work to augment the way *neutrality* and vocational awe are upheld in libraries—for example, "Libraries should provide materials and information presenting all points of view on current and historical issues." This operates on an assumption that all points of view on all issues are equally fixed in formats that libraries collect and that publishers equally publish all points of view. Yet, research shows that authors of color, particularly Black and Indigenous authors, are published significantly less than white authors and that the publishing and library industries are similarly white (Roh 2016). Thus, this Library Bill of Rights article presents a farcically aspirational idea, that equal representation in library collections is a responsibility that librarians can and should take on alone; this organizational fiction feeds librarians' vocational awe by ignoring the fact that many of the barriers to fair representation in knowledge dissemination lie outside the domain of library work.

The ALA Code of Ethics and Library Bill of Rights are emblematic of the way *neutrality* and vocational awe thread through our professional values at a broad level. Their presence in profession-wide value statements ensure that they operate in institutional ones as well, including through institutional missions, policies, procedures, and common rhetoric behind specific library services. We encourage readers to reread their libraries' organizational documentation and consider the ways that *neutrality* and vocational awe are codified in them. We now turn to unveil and scrutinize *neutrality* and vocational awe in facilities access, collection development, public services, and resource discovery.

ACCESS TO FACILITIES

Providing equal access to library space is one of the more common ways the philosophical discussion of *neutrality* is pursued. At the 2018 ALA President's Program, it was discussed in the context of a public library allowing community members to book meeting spaces no matter the group's beliefs or agenda. Here again, *neutrality* works as a pillar of vocational awe. The argument in favor of *neutrality* in this procedural situation is that if you assent to everyone, you've treated everyone equally and are therefore inherently good. This is an example of what Delgado and Stefancic describe as a formal conception of equality, "expressed in rules that insist only on treatment that is the same across the board," and when in use can "thus remedy only the most blatant forms of discrimination, such as mortgage redlining or an immigration dragnet in a food-processing plant that targets Latino workers or the refusal to hire a black Ph.D. rather than a white college dropout, which stand out and attract our attention" (2017, 9). The library space itself is seen and treated as *neutral* ground, but as Charles Mills describes it, "Space is just *there*, taken for granted, and the individual is tacitly posited as the white adult male, so that all individuals are obviously equal" (1997, 41).

Libraries as institutions and the LIS profession have a historical legacy of complicity and participation in racism and segregation, but to attribute that solely to our history leads us to believe we are postdiscrimination. On the contrary, we are closely aligned with racism in the US, past and present. We may not have separate restrooms for People of Color and whites, but there are now other structural means of discrimination. We convince ourselves that because we have a *policy* and because we believe in *neutrality*, we are protected from being accused of discrimination. Yet, those very policies, written for subjective interpretation, give staff, library security, and police the opportunity to decide whether or not someone *appears* as if they are utilizing the library properly and the way it was *intended* to be used.

Stories in which Black and Latinx students and members of the community are asked to leave library spaces, or in some cases are removed forcibly by police, are not uncommon. Unfortunately, this is on trend with US statistics. It's so common for the Black community, in fact, that a hashtag is associated with these instances, #studyingwhileblack. For example, in 2018, a Black library and information science student at Catholic University of America in Washington, DC, was told he could not use the university's law library (untrue, according to the policy) and the law school student who was staffing the desk that day called campus safety to remove him. Seven officers showed up before he left the library (Harriot 2018). Similarly (and worse), in April 2019 at Barnard College's library, a Columbia University student went to the Barnard library as all Columbia University students are permitted to do and was physically detained by campus police officers. As Scott Jaschik reported, "Barnard has a policy of checking IDs as people enter various facilities after 11 p.m., and this incident took place close to midnight. But many students said that the policy is inconsistently enforced, and that applying it to a black person—particularly in this way—constitutes racial profiling" (2019).

These incidents show that there is a pervasive belief among many library workers that Black and Latinx patrons do not belong in library spaces and that the library space needs to be returned to its default or *neutral* state. Unconsciously, many see this *neutral* state as whiteness, which leads to a belief that Black and Latinx patrons should be removed. Much as the ALA's original Code of Ethics indicated a pervasive belief that "unsuitable" people should be prevented from entering the profession and it used vocational awe as a justification for upholding racial bias, these incidents show a general belief that library spaces are elevated spaces and that those considered "unworthy" should be prevented from accessing them.

In building a key CRT concept, whiteness as property, Cheryl I. Harris points out that the right to use and enjoy anything that could be considered "property" throughout history has been either exclusively or disproportionately enjoyed by white people, and the systematic dispossession of People of Color's right to use and enjoy property is a means by which White Supremacy is normalized (1995, 282). Harris further points out that property itself tends to be governed by "custom," or social norms; the process of dispossessing people of their right to use and enjoy something is rarely recognized as anything other than a *neutral* act because it upholds what the dispossessors see as just, normal, and right. Thus, inconsistencies in enforcement of policies about who can access library spaces are commonly justified as *neutral*. We argue that subjective policies loosely followed in a racialized space are neither *neutral* nor equitable. Claiming that the profession provides unbiased service using the *neutrality* framework is false and prevents the profession from doing actual equity-based work.

COLLECTION DEVELOPMENT

When selection of materials is based on subjective policies, how does one remain *neutral*? How does one select library materials using the *neutral* framework when the materials aren't *neutral*? According to "Diverse Collections: An Interpretation of the Library Bill of Rights," library workers have a "professional and ethical responsibility to be fair and just" in "defending" the user's right to read, view, or listen to material protected by the First Amendment, regardless of the creator's views or personal history. Furthermore, "library workers must not permit their personal biases, opinions, or preferences to unduly influence collection development decisions" (American Library Association 2019). The methods by which to work *neutrally* in collection development are unclear, particularly because contrary to public belief, libraries are not mandated to collect and keep all materials in perpetuity.

The constant framing of *neutrality* as a for-or-against "debate" prevents any substantive discussion about equity in collection development. It also magnifies vocational awe in a number of ways. First, it sets up an argument that the written word is sacred. Worship of the written word is a characteristic of white supremacist culture and a form of epistemic supremacy, defined by Morales and Williams in chapter 2 as the "set of social systems, infrastructures, and knowledge pathways" that facilitate and uphold the destruction of any system of knowledge not controlled by the ruling class. It is a primary means by which the knowledge of many nonwhite cultures, and the traditions by which that knowledge is passed down, is suppressed (Okun, n.d.). Because the written word is considered sacred, librarians who organize and bring together printed works are sacred by extension, and furthermore, any assumptions that they make about which materials are good for the library's community are seen to be true. Very rarely do librarians discuss the problem that library patrons gener-ally have no democratic outlet by which to have a unified and organized voice in the selection and deselection processes. The profession has not properly differentiated between depository and library. A depository may keep unused material of historical value, but a library serving the needs of its community properly must have an up-to-date collection that changes consistently (Slote 1997).

Similar to policies that address who may use library space and for what purposes, many libraries have collection development policies to help guide their collecting and discarding of materials. Historically, it is in collection development that morality conflates with *neutrality*. In describing the early years of libraries, Jaeger and colleagues explain, "From the beginning of the American republic, some leaders saw the library as a social institution that could simultaneously diffuse knowledge to members of society and prevent the wealthy and socially elite from having hegemonic domina-tion over learning and education—although it was those elite who selected materials for library patrons" (2013, 167). Before young adult (YA) fiction was popularized, it was under intellectual scrutiny by libraries (Freedman and Johnson 2000). Similarly, romance novels were morally scrutinized (Speer 2001).

Today, these genres are regularly held in library collections. Yet, their acceptance in libraries was hard-won, and it served only to bolster the free-speech argument that *banning is always bad because it isn't* neutral. A *neutrally* framed response holds that *all* viewpoints deserve equal weight and space in collections, when, as mentioned in a previous section, authors of color are published significantly less than white counterparts. This response is underpinned by a lie—that all viewpoints are equal and valid, including viewpoints that compromise the safety of People of Color. Providing a platform for those viewpoints with shared community resources tells patrons of color that their safety in the library's community is not as important as the appear-ance of humoring all perspectives equally. It also causes harm to library workers of color, who are required to disembody from their lived experiences in order to perform purchasing, cataloging, shelving, and checkouts of these materials in order to be seen as "professional" by employers and a profession that is unconcerned with their safety.

LIBRARY PUBLIC SERVICES

When discussing the *neutral* framework for library services, many people might first think about reference work. At the 2018 ALA Midwinter President's Program, James LaRue, then-director of the Office for Intellectual Freedom, made the point that words on a T-shirt are not the same as action, and he went on to say, "We claim that just by listening or reading we have been injured. So my safety requires someone else's silence. This view is the foundation of censorship and tyranny" (American Library Association 2018). Psychologically, this is a powerful statement and it evokes feelings with which it is difficult to argue. Stripped of positionality or context, the slogan on a T-shirt should not "injure" individuals. The social reality LaRue ignores is that T-shirt slogans about your marginalized identity *can be* traumatic. As Matsuda points out, victims of hate messages and hate crimes experience both psychic violence (usually resulting in physiological symptoms that can accumulate to produce negative health impacts over time) as well as material restrictions on their personal freedom (1993, 24–25). We are safe from immediate bodily harm when reading a T-shirt, but is that standard enough to support, retain, and value People of Color in this profession? As Matsuda also points out, hate speech commonly correlates to increases in hate crimes and violence against those targeted by the hate speech.

As Alan Freeman points out, much like the US and its antidiscrimination laws, libraries have policies on only the most blatant forms of racist attack, in which perpetrators clearly intend harm. There are no policies that support a library's only person of color working at a reference desk when a person wearing a T-shirt promoting a hate group comes to the desk. Vocational awe leads many librarians in this situation to believe that societal equity depends on their willingness to serve. There is no room in *neutrality* and vocational awe frames for the danger that the librarian of color faces in this situation.

While the word *neutral* is not found in the "Guidelines for Behavioral Performance of Reference and Information Service Providers" developed by the Reference and User Services Association (RUSA), a division of the ALA, *objective* is included. Under "Listening/Inquiring," the guidelines state that the librarian "maintains objectivity; does not interject value judgments about the subject matter or the nature of the question into the transaction" (2013). Again, utilizing the *neutral* framework for reference services is an attempt to provide equal service to all. However, as Brook, Ellenwood, and Lazzaro describe, "to develop an understanding of how to build antiracist solidarity through reference practices and to better respond to marginalized groups in ways that are culturally responsive, but not essentializing, it is important to analyze the ways in which reference librarians' professional guidelines reinforce Whiteness and limit solidarity" (2016). In other words, there can be no solidarity without understanding how whiteness marginalizes, and objectivity is not achievable if whiteness is actively trying to marginalize you.

METADATA AND DISCOVERY OF RESOURCES

As services that are not generally performed in communication with library users, library catalogs and metadata are easily presumed to be *neutral*, but they are anything but. For many years, metadata workflows in libraries have emphasized metadata automation, reusability by other library institutions, and centralization of controlled vocabularies. Over time, these have become such fixtures of metadata workers' vocational awe that almost all cataloging or metadata operations rely on at least one centralized controlled vocabulary or organization system, such as Library of Congress Subject Headings (LCSH), despite a growing body of literature and a growing awareness regarding the ways in which these standards uphold White Supremacy in their structure and content (de la Tierra 2008; Webster and Doyle 2008; Hoffman 2015).

A well-publicized example is the attempted change to the subject heading "Illegal aliens," which gained national attention in 2016. A group of student activists and librarians at Dartmouth College collaborated to propose that the heading be changed in 2014; from 2014 to 2016 (Baron, Gross, and Cornejo Cásares 2016) the proposal passed through an arduous, but typical, process. It was rejected at first, and when revised and proposed again, underwent a compromise decision to be split into two headings, neither of which emphasized well the experiences and rights of racialized undocumented immigrants.

At that point, conservative members of Congress itself intervened through two actions. A report accompanying the 2017 funding bill for legislative agencies (including the Library of Congress) directed the Library of Congress to "maintain certain subject headings that reflect terminology used in title 8, United States Code" (US House. Committee on Appropriations 2016), and Republican congressperson Diane Black (TN-6) introduced a stand-alone bill specifically ordering the acting librarian of Congress to retain the "Illegal aliens" heading (US House 2016). While the former bill is not specific, and the latter never moved to a vote, these tactics had the impact of intimidating the library community; as of August 2020, the announced change to the heading has yet to be made, though the decision has not been formally reversed. In the meantime, the heading remains present in many catalogs; many cataloging workflows deploy LCSH in such an automated way that it takes significant labor and creativity to make local deviations (Fox et al. 2020).

While Congress's intervention in this example is unusual (notably, it occurred as anti-Latinx and xenophobic rhetoric during the 2016 presidential campaign rose to a fever pitch), it reminded library workers of the fact that the proposal process for LCSH has never been *neutral* or apolitical. White supremacist terminology is deeply entrenched in LCSH and many other universal cataloging mainstays, and it echoes and reinforces the White Supremacy in library spaces, collection development, and public services. The process that the Dartmouth students and librarians went through returns us to Harris's concept of whiteness as property and the way "custom," or social norms, governs legal property. A crux of Harris's analysis is that, in many ways, whiteness as an identity has many of the characteristics of legal property. She refers to the example of European colonization of the "New World," experienced as violence and obliteration of custom by Native American people but viewed as "common sense" by the European colonizers because it "confirmed and ratified their experience" (Harris 1995, 280).

Seen through this lens, the crucible that the Dartmouth LCSH proposers underwent is clearly seen as a struggle in which they worked to reassert the customary language of racialized undocumented immigrants in the vast property of LCSH, and they were refused because this language did not confirm and ratify the custom that built the system. As a vocabulary built by, for, and about white people, LCSH essentially acts as the primary extension of the property of whiteness in library structures. Although considered an incremental improvement upon previous systems, the proposal process is nevertheless still designed to restrict approval where proposals do not conform to white supremacist custom, and, as is traditional in White Supremacy, it acts as that custom's mechanism to accept or refuse the social norms represented in it.

CONCLUSION

In locating *neutrality* and vocational awe in professional codes and tracing their impacts across library facility access, public reference services, collection development, and metadata and discovery, we find that no part of the library work cycle benefits from the intertwining of *neutrality* and vocational awe. Although well intentioned, these values work together to normalize and uphold racism and White Supremacy in libraries, even where they are espoused with the intent of working toward equity. They function to justify libraries' demonstrably harmful impacts on workers of color and patrons of color, and to erase their experiences. Because the entire framework of *neutrality* assumes that equity already exists in all social systems, it functions in our inequitable culture to obfuscate the myriad experiences of library patrons and workers. It aids vocational awe in creating a professional culture that assumes and relies on its own perceived goodness and curtails meaningful criticism and dialogue, particularly about the ways that libraries perpetuate oppression. Together, these two precepts create a culture in which white norms for recognizing racism are allowed to predominate; only egregious attacks or acts are recognized as "racist," and the underlying culture and systems that produced the egregious attacks go unchallenged.

We demand a paradigm shift, to begin to dismantle racism and live up to the values that libraries espouse. This requires a commitment to let go of vocational awe and *neutrality* as professional values. Because vocational awe functions to quash critique or dissent toward librarianship and library institutions and prevents us from reimagining our future, relinquishing it will enable full and rational discussions based on criticisms of the profession, without repression from deep-seated fears of betraying the profession. Rejecting *neutrality* while acknowledging that inequity is endemic in current and common LIS praxis will help library workers to meet patron communities (and each other) where they are, rather than forcing marginalized people further to the margins.

Furthermore, because White Supremacy is naturalized within library professional culture through these values, we believe that full relinquishment, rather than partial and incremental, of *neutrality* and vocational awe is needed for library workers and institutions to actualize our espoused values of equitable and inclusive service for all. We demand that libraries finally change, not only to meet the world that we currently live in but to meet the world that we are striving for.

NOTES

1. *Dictionary.com*, s.v. "neutrality," accessed July 4, 2019, https://www.dictionary.com/browse/neutrality.

2. The authors use "librarianship" here very broadly. It is not limited to those with the degree, but rather includes all people that work in libraries.

3. Italicizing *neutrality* is essential to our thesis, as it provides a visual, stylistic cue for the reader to critically identify elements of domination.

4. Augst and Carpenter point out that, although the idea of equal access is now considered foundational, it encountered significant class- and race-based resistance at first. When Boston Public Library began accommodating working-class and affluent people in a single building, "the fear of outsiders in the temple of culture—children and immigrants, the homeless and tourists—became outright fear of physical and moral contamination, as with the idea that books circulated in the slums would spread cholera to the suburbs, like pathogens of class breakdown" (2007, 172).

5. Significantly, Carnegie's library-as-enlightenment ideal was never intended to uplift all equally; Shaundra Walker connects his investments in historically Black colleges and universities to an interest in keeping Black Americans in manual and industrial labor, and highlights his disinterest in HBCUs that did not adhere to "industrial-vocational" curricula (2017, 37–38).

BIBLIOGRAPHY

American Library Association. 1939. "History of the Code of Ethics: 1939 Code of Ethics for Librarians." American Library Association. http://www.ala.org/Template.cfm?Section=coehistory &Template=/ContentManagement/ContentDisplay.cfm&ContentID=8875.

American Library Association. 2008. "Code of Ethics of the American Library Association." American Library Association. January 22, 2008. http://www.ala.org/advocacy/sites/ala.org.advocacy /files/content/proethics/codeofethics/Code%20of%20Ethics%20of%20the%20American%20 Library%20Association.pdf.

American Library Association. 2012. "Diversity Counts." American Library Association. http:// www.ala.org/aboutala/sites/ala.org.aboutala/files/content/diversity/diversitycounts/diversitycount stables2012.pdf.

American Library Association. 2013. "Guidelines for Behavioral Performance of Reference and Information Service Providers." American Library Association. May 28, 2013. http://www.ala.org /rusa/resources/guidelines/guidelinesbehavioral.

American Library Association. 2017. "First Amendment and Censorship." American Library Association. http://www.ala.org/advocacy/intfreedom/censorship.

American Library Association. 2018. "Are Libraries Neutral?" President's Program, American Library Association Midwinter Meeting, Denver, CO, February 11. https://www.eventscribe.com /2018/ALA-Midwinter/fsPopup.asp?Mode=presInfo&PresentationID=336430.

American Library Association. 2019. "Diverse Collections: An Interpretation of the Library Bill of Rights." American Library Association. June 25, 2019. http://www.ala.org/advocacy/intfreedom /librarybill/interpretations/diversecollections.

Augst, Thomas, and Kenneth Carpenter. 2007. *Institutions of Reading: The Social Life of Libraries in the United States*. Amherst: University of Massachusetts Press. https://muse.jhu.edu/book/4295.

Baron, Jill, Tina Gross, and Óscar Rubén Cornejo Cásares. 2016. "Cataloging News: Timeline of 'Illegal Aliens' Subject Heading Change Petition." *Cataloging and Classification Quarterly* 54 (7): 506–520. https://doi.org/10.1080/01639374.2016.1218707.

Blackwell, Kelsey. 2018. "Why People of Color Need Spaces without White People." *The Arrow: A Journal of Wakeful Society, Culture, and Politics*, August 9, 2018. https://arrow-journal.org/why -people-of-color-need-spaces-without-white-people/.

Bonilla-Silva, Eduardo. 2006. *Racism without Racists: Color-Blind Racism and the Persistence of Racial Inequality in the United States*. 2nd ed. Lanham, MD: Rowman & Littlefield.

Brook, Freeda, Dave Ellenwood, and Althea Eannace Lazzaro. 2016. "In Pursuit of Antiracist Social Justice: Denaturalizing Whiteness in the Academic Library." *Library Trends* 64 (2): 246–284. https://doi.org/10.1353/lib.2015.0048.

Brown, Kevin, and Darrell D. Jackson. 2013. "The History and Conceptual Elements of Critical Race Theory." In *Handbook of Critical Race Theory in Education*, edited by Marvin Lynn and Adrienne D. Dixson, 9–22. New York: Routledge.

Crenshaw, Kimberlé. 2006. "Framing Affirmative Action." *University of Michigan Law Review First Impressions* 105 (1): 123–133.

Delgado, Richard, and Jean Stefancic. 2017. *Critical Race Theory: An Introduction*. 3rd ed. New York: New York University Press.

Ditzion, Sidney Herbert. 1947. *Arsenals of Democratic Culture: A Social History of the American Public Library Movement in New England and the Middle States from 1850 to 1900*. Chicago: American Library Association.

Dubin, Robert. 1968. "Organization Fictions." In *Human Relations in Administration*, 493–498. 3rd ed. Englewood Cliffs, NJ: Prentice-Hall.

Ettarh, Fobazi. 2014. "Making a New Table: Intersectional Librarianship." *In the Library with the Lead Pipe*, July 2, 2014. http://www.inthelibrarywiththeleadpipe.org/2014/making-a-new-table -intersectional-librarianship-3/.

Ettarh, Fobazi. 2018. "Vocational Awe and Librarianship: The Lies We Tell Ourselves." *In the Library with the Lead Pipe*, January 10, 2018. http://www.inthelibrarywiththeleadpipe.org/2018 /vocational-awe/.

Ettarh, Fobazi. 2019. "Becoming a Proud 'Bad Librarian': Dismantling Vocational Awe in Librarianship." Invited presentation at the Association of College and Research Libraries Conference, Cleveland, OH, April 13, 2019.

Fox, Violet B., Nick Bennyhoff, Kelsey George, Erin Grant, Tina Gross, Cate Kellett, Arden Kirkland, et al. 2020. "Report of the SAC Working Group on Alternatives to LCSH 'Illegal Aliens.'" Working group report. Philadelphia, PA: Association for Library Collections and Technical Services. https://alair.ala.org/bitstream/handle/11213/14582/SAC20-AC_report_SAC-Working-Group-on -Alternatives-to-LCSH-Illegal-aliens.pdf.

Freedman, Lauren, and Holly Johnson. 2000. "Who's Protecting Whom? 'I Hadn't Meant to Tell You This': A Case in Point in Confronting Self-Censorship in the Choice of Young Adult Literature." *Journal of Adolescent and Adult Literacy* 44 (4): 356–369.

Freeman, Alan. 1995. "Legitimizing Racial Discrimination through Antidiscrimination Law: A Critical Review of Supreme Court Doctrine." In *Critical Race Theory: The Key Writings That Formed the Movement*, edited by Kimberlé Crenshaw, Neil Gotanda, Gary Peller, and Kendall Thomas, 29–46. New York: The New Press.

Fryberg, S. M. 2010. "When the World Is Colorblind, American Indians Are Invisible: A Diversity Science Approach." *Psychological Inquiry* 21 (2): 115–119.

Gray, John. 1986. *Liberalism*. Milton Keynes, UK: Open University Press.

Gregorian, Vartan. 1989. "Vartan Gregorian on the New York Public Library." In *In Praise of Libraries*, edited by Carlton C. Rochell, 57–76. New York: New York University Press.

Harriot, Michael. 2018. "Video: Librarian Calls Cops on Student for Brazen Attempt at #StudyingWhileBlack [Updated]." *The Root* (blog), October 23, 2018. https://www.theroot.com/video -librarian-calls-cops-on-student-for-brazen-attem-1829940301.

Harris, Cheryl I. 1995. "Whiteness as Property." In *Critical Race Theory: The Key Writings That Formed the Movement*, edited by Kimberlé Crenshaw, Neil Gotanda, Gary Peller, and Kendall Thomas, 276–292. New York: The New Press.

Hathcock, April. 2015. "White Librarianship in Blackface: Diversity Initiatives in LIS." *In the Library with the Lead Pipe*, October 7, 2015. http://www.inthelibrarywiththeleadpipe.org/2015/lis -diversity/.

Hirsch, E. D., Joseph F. Kett, and James S. Trefil. 2002. "Equity." In *The New Dictionary of Cultural Literacy*, 316. 3rd ed. Boston: Houghton Mifflin.

Hoffman, Gretchen. 2015. "What's the Difference between Soul Food and Southern Cooking? The Classification of Cookbooks in American Libraries." In *Dethroning the Deceitful Pork Chop: Rethinking African American Foodways from Slavery to Obama*, edited by Jennifer Jensen Wallach, 61–78. Fayetteville: University of Arkansas Press.

Honma, Todd. 2005. "Trippin' over the Color Line: The Invisibility of Race in Library and Information Studies." *InterActions: UCLA Journal of Education and Information Studies* 1 (2): 1–24. http:// escholarship.org/uc/item/4nj0w1mp.

Horrigan, John. 2016. "Libraries 2016." Pew Research Center. September 9, 2016. https://www .pewinternet.org/wp-content/uploads/sites/9/2016/09/PI_2016.09.09_Libraries-2016_FINAL.pdf.

Jaeger, Paul T., Ursula Gorham, Lindsay C. Sarin, and John Carlo Bertot. 2013. "Libraries, Policy, and Politics in a Democracy: Four Historical Epochs." *Library Quarterly: Information, Community, Policy* 83 (2): 166–181.

Jaschik, Scott. 2019. "Entering Campus Building While Black." *Inside Higher Ed* (blog), April 15, 2019. https://www.insidehighered.com/news/2019/04/15/barnard-suspends-police-officers-after -incident-black-student.

Kendrick, Kaetrena Davis. 2017. "ShoutOut: Pauline Wilson (Ret.)." The Ink on the Page (blog). November 20, 2017. https://theinkonthepageblog.wordpress.com/2017/11/20/shoutout-pauline -wilson-ret/.

King, Martin Luther, Jr. 1963. "I Have a Dream." Speech delivered at the March on Washington for Jobs and Freedom, Washington, DC, August 28, 1963. The Avalon Project, Yale Law School. https://avalon.law.yale.edu/20th_century/mlk01.asp.

Lakoff, George, and Mark Johnson. 1999. *Philosophy in the Flesh: The Embodied Mind and Its Challenge to Western Thought*. New York: Basic Books.

Latimer, Karen. 2011. "Collections to Connections: Changing Spaces and New Challenges in Academic Library Buildings." *Library Trends* 60 (1): 112–133.

Lindblom, Charles. 1980. *The Policy-Making Process*. 2nd ed. Englewood Cliffs, NJ: Prentice Hall.

Matsuda, Mari J. 1993. "Public Response to Racist Speech: Considering the Victim's Story." In *Words That Wound: Critical Race Theory, Assaultive Speech, and the First Amendment*, edited by Mari J. Matsuda, Charles R. Lawrence III, Richard Delgado, and Kimberlé Williams Crenshaw, 17–51. Boulder, CO: Westview Press.

Mills, Charles. 1997. *The Racial Contract*. Ithaca, NY: Cornell University Press.

Nichols School. 2017. "Faculty Friday Features: Ms. Britt White!" *Faculty Friday* (blog). April 21, 2017. https://www.nicholsschool.org/news-events/story-details/~post/faculty-friday-ms-britt-white -20170421.

Okun, Tema. n.d. "White Supremacy Culture." Dismantling Racism Works. Accessed June 1, 2019. http://dismantlingracism.org/uploads/4/3/5/7/43579015/whitesupcul13.pdf.

Roh, Charlotte. 2016. "Inequalities in Publishing." *Urban Library Journal* 22 (2): 17.

Slote, Stanley J. 1997. *Weeding Library Collections: Library Weeding Methods*. 4th ed. Englewood, CO: Libraries Unlimited.

Speer, Lisa. 2001. "Paperback Pornography: Mass Market Novels and Censorship in Post-War America." *Journal of American Culture* 24 (3/4): 153–160.

Sweeney, Richard T. 2005. "Reinventing Library Buildings and Services for the Millennial Generation." *Library Administration and Management* 19 (4): 165–176.

de la Tierra, Tatiana. 2008. "Latina Lesbian Subject Headings: The Power of Naming." In *Radical Cataloging: Essays at the Front*, edited by K. R. Roberto, 93–102. Jefferson, NC: McFarland.

US House. 2016. 114th Cong. 2d Session. *H.R. 4926. Stopping Partisan Policy at the Library of Congress Act*. Washington, DC: Government Printing Office. https://www.congress.gov/bill/114th -congress/house-bill/4926/text.

US House. Committee on Appropriations. 2016. *Report Together with Minority Views to Accompany H.R. 5325*. H. Rept. 114–594. Washington, DC: Government Printing Office. https://www .congress.gov/congressional-report/114th-congress/house-report/594/1.

Walker, Shaundra. 2017. "A Revisionist History of Andrew Carnegie's Library Grants to Black Colleges." In *Topographies of Whiteness: Mapping Whiteness in Library and Information Science*, edited by Gina Schlesselman-Tarango, 33–53. Sacramento, CA: Library Juice Press. https://kb.gcsu.edu/cgi /viewcontent.cgi?article=1003&context=lib.

Warren, Roz. 2014. "In the Age of Information Overload, What Are Librarians?" WHYY.org, December 18, 2014. https://whyy.org/articles/in-the-age-of-information-overload-what-are-librarians/.

Webster, Kelly, and Anne Doyle. 2008. "Don't Class Me in Antiquities! Giving Voice to Native American Materials." In *Radical Cataloging: Essays at the Front*, edited by K. R. Roberto, 189–197. Jefferson, NC: McFarland.

Wiegand, Wayne. 2015. *Part of Our Lives: A People's History of the American Public Library*. Oxford: Oxford University Press.

Wilson, Pauline. 1979. "Librarians as Teachers: The Study of an Organization Fiction." *Library Quarterly* 49 (2): 146–162. https://doi.org/10.1086/630131.

2

MOVING TOWARD TRANSFORMATIVE LIBRARIANSHIP
Naming and Identifying Epistemic Supremacy

Myrna E. Morales and Stacie Williams

As Chiu, Ferretti, and Ettarh explore in chapter 1, librarianship is not neutral. In fact, it is riddled with biases and oppressive acts that have gone unexamined by the profession. By extension, we argue in this chapter that information is not neutral. The biases we hold as human individuals affect every aspect of library work. They affect whom we allow to enter, whom we allow to stay on the premises, the programs and services we offer, the collections we organize, curate, and archive, and most importantly, they affect our colleagues and the people we choose to serve. It is not an accident that librarianship remains predominantly white and gender- and middle class–oppressed, or that its relevance is being questioned in this current moment. As the chapters in this book show, the profession has been undergoing an identity crisis for the past fifty years—using equity, diversity, and inclusion programs to fill the gaps of demographic disparity, as well as expanding the notion of librarianship to include data management and digital scholarship once the bricks-and-mortar model of libraries was perceived to be outdated.

Using Critical Race Theory, this chapter questions the biases that contribute to how scholarly communications work in the profession is executed and how information organization methodologies are weaponized against working-class and poor communities of color. As Matsuda and colleagues (1993) write, "Critical Race Theory is grounded in the particulars of a social reality that is defined by our experiences and the collective historical experience of our communities of origins" (3). CRT was a response to the conditions precipitated by neoliberalism, an economic school of thought that seeks to erase the collective responsibility to the individual. CRT borrows from other frameworks such as Marxism and feminism, which is necessary because, to paraphrase black womanist writer and former librarian Audre Lorde, nothing is a single-issue struggle because we do not live single-issue lives. Though the term *intersectionality* was coined by law professor Kimberlé Williams-Crenshaw, the notion was explored as far back as 1919 in black feminist organizing spaces where race intersected with class, gender, and sexuality, with groups such as the US Communist Party, Chicago's Alpha Suffrage Club, and the Combahee River Collective (Matsuda et al. 1993; McDuffie 2011; Smith 1983).

A CRT scholar seeks to understand the truth of their condition, and through that journey to come to identify all the mechanisms, including *systems of knowledge*, that make systemic oppression function. It behooves us to understand that history is told from the "winning" side (in this case, all those who gain materially from White Supremacy); that forces us to challenge ahistoricism and examine the conditions that we live in thoroughly and unapologetically. Some who embraced a critical race framework for approaching librarianship, such as Lorde and Dorothy Porter (Nunes 2018), offer examples over time of social justice work that allows us to reimagine what librarianship could look like if we addressed the needs of those who are most impacted by the tyranny and fascist conditions of our times: working-class and poor communities of color.

Similarly, we, two class-straddling scholars of color—Black and Puerto Rican women, respectively—with strong ties to working-class communities, introduce to the library and information science profession the concept of epistemic supremacy: a political ideology that facilitates, enables, and upholds the conditions that lead to the destruction of communities of color, particularly working-class and poor Black and Indigenous communities. Utilizing CRT as an important intervention to combat epistemic supremacy, we will discuss ways that librarian methodologies have facilitated community destruction via a lack of the epistemological conversations and training that form librarians' foundational education. Two use cases that provide insight on how library science theories and methodologies are applied to the detriment and destruction of Black and Indigenous communities in the US involve former Federal Bureau of Investigation director J. Edgar Hoover and Mellon family heiress Cordelia Scaife May.

Hoover credited librarianship and its processes to his "success" as the director of the FBI in disrupting or dismantling civil rights organizations and leadership throughout the twentieth century. May used scholarly communication channels and content to facilitate epistemic supremacy by funding and supporting biased and racist research about immigrants. We will examine the ways that Hoover's repression of communities of color mirrors the ways that librarianship reinforces White Supremacy—an output of epistemic supremacy that uses information to privilege whiteness, heteropatriarchy, and capitalism. From there, we will examine the ways that May's money has supported and sustained the far-right and white nationalist organizations that use epistemically privileged scholarship to manipulate the research life cycle and public opinion. We will close this chapter by defining *transformative librarianship* that can help combat epistemic supremacy.

EPISTEMIC SUPREMACY MEETS CRITICAL RACE THEORY

Epistemology is the study of knowledge. For librarians, epistemology is the *business of information gathering* that helps construct individual and shared knowledge. For example, what assumptions do librarians make about their primary audiences or users when determining programs and collections? How does that programming or collection development inform that community? For instance, if a public library is situated in a neighborhood with a large immigrant population, are there resources available specific to the needs of that community on citizenship processes or social service agencies? Are library staff having or facilitating honest conversations about the dangers that exist for undocumented immigrants in this country, including labor exploitation, physical assault, and state-sanctioned concentration camps for children and infants? Who makes decisions about programming or resources, and how transparent are those decision-making processes to library staff and users? Additionally, what *information* is used to make those decisions? In what ways do libraries facilitate either destruction or healing in communities through their information-as-business model?

These questions outline the concept of epistemic supremacy. For the purposes of this chapter, epistemic supremacy is defined as *societal systems, infrastructures, and knowledge pathways that facilitate and uphold the conditions for tyranny and fascism by destroying any system of knowledge* (epistemicide) *not controlled by the ruling class as a means of facilitating racial monopoly capitalism.* Epistemic supremacy obscures the best question to be asked in this current cultural moment, which is, "Can (or will) I trust your information?" When the pathways that lead to understanding information are severed, damaged, or corrupted via epistemic supremacy, it stops us from being able to fulfill a central tenet of librarianship: to provide access to accurate, relevant information that creates an informed citizenry to further uphold democratic ideals of freedom.

Epistemic supremacy is like a root, one planted in the base of phenomena such as "sundown towns" and events such as the Wounded Knee Massacre, the Trail of

Tears, and the Great Depression and Great Recession. Those events were triggered by information tainted by epistemic supremacy. Manifest Destiny, a Jacksonian concept and practice grounded in the notion of settler colonialism, destroyed communities of color because settlers' "right" to westward expansion was seen as an objective truth. Epistemic supremacy has roots in the current family separation crisis in the border-lands; the climate crisis; the gentrification and displacement crisis; the disproportion-ate killings and disappearances of Black and Indigenous people, especially women; and the assault on gender-oppressed bodies. Epistemic supremacy is facilitated through programs such as the US Counter Intelligence Program (COINTELPRO), started by Hoover, and more recently, TigerSwan, where Standing Rock water protectors were surveilled by the US government (Brown, Parrish, and Speri 2017; Goodman 2017). Both of these programs have specifically surveilled Black and Indigenous people who have protested against state infringement on their collective rights. Surveillance pro-grams employed by the government are not a new phenomenon, or even uncom-mon in the Black community (Browne 2015; Ford 2018; Maxwell 2015; Washington 2015). The harmful impact of these programs on communities of color is still being unraveled today.

The first step to solving a problem is to name it. In Critical Race Theory (CRT), the power to name a problem is essential to solving it. Naming it allows us to offer political analysis or perspective grounded in our experiences of this moment. CRT allows us to identify and isolate epistemic supremacy, because when we actively politicize the LIS field through a recontextualization of history, we see our complicity in enabling the conditions of our current moment.

Critical race theorists and some social scientists hold that racism is pervasive, systemic, and deeply ingrained. Indeed, one aspect of whiteness, according to some Critical Race Theorists, is its ability to seem perspectiveless, or transparent. White people do not see themselves as having a race, but as being, simply, human. They do not believe that they think and reason from a white viewpoint, but from a univer-sally valid one—"the truth"—that everyone knows. We argue that that vantage point is what creates epistemic supremacy (ES), which historically bred and continues to breed pain, destruction, and disequilibrium in our society.

Naming and identifying epistemic supremacy pushes librarian theory and praxis into the spotlight for necessary interrogation across our areas of practice, including collection development, access policies, metadata and description, and physical and digital infrastructure. For instance, in 2015, technical services and metadata librar-ians, in collaboration with student activists at Dartmouth College, advocated for the

Library of Congress to change the subject heading "Illegal alien" to reflect people-first language that points to a lack of state documentation, replacing a phrase that questions the legitimacy of a human being's existence. In that instance, college students were the ones interrogating the epistemic supremacy found in Library of Congress Subject Headings—our primary means of making collections discoverable—and worked on behalf of racialized working-class immigrants nationwide to advocate for making the changes that will eventually determine how librarians describe related items or collections. The Policy and Standards Division of the Library changed the heading to "Noncitizen"—a term that does nothing to make visible the humanity of the individual it describes—and changed the heading for the act of residing to "Undocumented immigration."

Language is at the heart of epistemic supremacy. Jamaican philosopher Sylvia Wynter argues that the language we use to describe ourselves as human has been inextricably linked to Western European notions of "self" as white bourgeois/affluent capitalist. "Self" is defined only in contrast to an existing "Other" who couldn't possibly be human for lack of being able to express or perform Western bourgeois expectations of what it means to be human. If Self only exists in contrast to an Other, then language is what builds the walls between us before anyone even utters those words (Wynter 2003).

As a profession, we could have taken the opportunity from the LCSH example above to learn more about how librarians use language to support epistemic supremacy and build a workforce that is grounded in solving the political crises of capitalism and fascism. Instead, we are facing a professional endangerment in many ways, none more urgent than the ideas that objective facts are irrelevant; that proven science could be subject to "devil's advocate" claims by op-ed broadcasters in our media platforms; and that people have learned how to create, use, and manipulate information using the same frameworks that we currently use to organize and free information.

We respectfully engage a redistribution analysis offered by critical race and education theorist Gloria Ladson-Billings, wherein without a redistribution of resources spread across public school systems, inequality will remain and reproduce (Ladson-Billings 1998). Without a commitment to design, or in some cases, redesign, or to redistribute physical and virtual spaces that facilitate epistemological discourse and training for librarians, workers in the GLAM sector (galleries, libraries, archives, and museums) will continue to perpetuate the basic inequalities of society and virtually guarantee a white, heteropatriarchal, ableist, capitalist status quo, not just for our users, but for library staff as well.

Information isn't neutral; it is created and shared by human individuals who remain imperfect and hold both implicitly and explicitly biased viewpoints. As librarians, we need to ask how we can respond to our users, who are increasingly being faced with information that cannot be trusted at any point in the creation or dissemination life cycle. Librarians who operate with liberatory methodologies like the ones created by Critical Race Theorists have learned not to trust structures that maintain the status quo, and as a result, they interrogate the roles that librarians play in maintaining epistemic supremacy. If one is not a member of the ruling class, epistemic supremacy creates an ontological crisis that forces them to either assimilate and reproduce negative conditions in society or to go in search of liberatory frameworks found in CRT, to help co-construct their place in this society.

J. EDGAR HOOVER, KNOWLEDGE ORGANIZATION, PRODUCTION, AND APPLICATION

J. Edgar Hoover was a librarian clerk who became one of the most powerful men in the history of the United States, having accumulated so much power through information gathering and surveillance that he was able to influence US presidents and foreign and domestic policy throughout much of the twentieth century. One of his first jobs, while attending George Washington School of Law, was an entry-level position at the Library of Congress. After college, he was hired at the Justice Department at age twenty-two. In 1919, at age twenty-four, he rose to the head of the FBI's new General Intelligence Division, also known as the "Radical Division," which sought to surveil and disrupt Black nationalist movements and leaders, self-described socialists and feminists, reproductive justice organizers, and anarchists. President Woodrow Wilson's 1919 to 1920 Palmer Raids were a direct result of the Radical Division's surveillance and destabilization measures, and part of a concerted effort to capture and deport Eastern European communists, anarchists, socialists, and leftist labor activists, to stop them from sharing with others concepts that did not align with ruling-class ideologies.

As part of this work, he immediately started building a working library that would be his personal ready reference collection on radicalism and radical movements. During his time at the Library of Congress, one of his first tasks was replacing handwritten catalogs with mechanically reproducible printed cards with the aforementioned Library of Congress Subject Headings. Hoover also borrowed from aspects of the Library of Congress cataloging system to create a filing system that he boasted was unparalleled by any other system of organizing. Features such as "multidirectional cataloguing,…each item receiving a unique code, a generic classification and all pertinent cross references" helped build an early, analog type of algorithm for systematic extraction of "radical texts" (Maxwell 2015). For Hoover, "literary language in and of itself performed political action," and as a result, the Bureau needed tools for a working library and librarians (50).

LIS scholarship has yet to examine the impact of J. Edgar Hoover's use of library and information classification skills on democracy in this country, though considerable evidence exists of the ways that he applied systems and cataloging knowledge to developing the FBI's extensive surveillance operations and practice of civil rights and privacy violation. In a 1951 letter referencing his former position, Hoover wrote, "This job…trained me in the value of collating material. It gave me an excellent foundation for my work in the FBI where it has been necessary to collate information and evidence" (FBI 2012). Library science curriculum around the time that Hoover received it had just shifted emphasis from types of libraries (academic vs. public vs. government) to specific library services or tasks such as "abstracting and indexing…cataloging and classification" (Richardson 2010, 3). This would prove to be invaluable to Hoover's job at the FBI, as he used this library science foundation to create filing and archiving systems designed to destroy and destabilize Black and Indigenous communities and all those deemed to be "radical"—those who are considered part of the revolutionary Left today (Maxwell 2015).

One of Hoover's first programs was hiring FBI "ghostreaders" to monitor the literature created in various Black communities for information about radical organizers (Maxwell 2015). Because Hoover saw the written word as equal to direct political action, he saw his responsibility as protecting the US from the radical Left. This system created and targeted Black literary, entertainment, and activist figures such as Marcus Garvey, Lorraine Hansberry, and Paul Robeson. Under Hoover, the FBI also targeted numerous rights- or identity-based organizations during the Civil Rights movement from the 1920s through the 1970s, infiltrating groups as varied as the US Communist Party, the American Indian Movement, the Black Panther Party, the Puerto Rican Young Lords, La Raza, and the Weathermen, in order to stop them from sharing radical and liberatory ideas with others. The disruption of the Panthers was especially damaging, because it disrupted an intergenerational exchange of liberatory theories and praxis via works such as the Panthers' free breakfast program for children (Taylor 2017).

The ghostreaders were joined by ghostwriters in Hoover's Crime Records and Communication Division, who were responsible for writing personal correspondence to US journalists throughout the 1940s and signing Hoover's name, in hopes of swaying the media toward favorable coverage of the Bureau and its practices. Hoover was so successful with this ruse that in 1950, the American Civil Liberties Union's own general counsel Morris Ernst defended the FBI in *Reader's Digest*, a widely read mainstream publication that went into homes across America. That a lawyer for the ACLU would write that the FBI has a "magnificent record of respect for individual freedom" (1950), based on what he believed to be a personal friendship with Hoover, and then document that conflict of interest in his article, would be shocking if we didn't understand as librarians how easily biased information can alter public opinion, which is the point of epistemic supremacy. It seeks to establish biased, racialized information as fact and gains legitimacy through widespread dissemination across all media platforms.

By the time Hoover enacted COINTELPRO in 1956, he had amassed more than thirty years of surveillance literature to target and abuse communities considered a threat to the capitalist status quo, including clergy who were civil rights organizers, as well as members of the LGBTQIA community. It wasn't just the existence of these organizations that made them dangerous to Hoover's FBI; they were producing their own knowledge, sharing it widely, and altering public opinion. Hoover also had his ghostwriters create and send surveillance literature or correspondence to undermine civil rights organizers and their interpersonal relationships, as with the anonymous letters and phone calls to Martin Luther King Jr. and his wife, Coretta Scott King, detailing the former's extramarital affairs (Gage 2014; Maxwell 2015). Hoover also targeted Black independent bookstores across the country in order to identify Black "extremists." Librarians need to interrogate the fact that someone trained in their methodologies and processes used those same methodologies and processes to violate individuals' civil rights and destabilize marginalized communities through a surveillance and disruption program.

Hoover's actions are an example of the damage that can be wrought when individuals who are invested in epistemic supremacy have access to bureaucratic infrastructure, finances, and policies to scale up harm in a way that has been devastating to working-class and poor communities of color. For instance, Holy Week Uprisings immediately following the assassination of Martin Luther King Jr. in places such as Chicago's West Side, Newark, Detroit, Memphis, Pittsburgh, and more than 100 other cities caused damages of nearly $81 million (adjusted for 2015 inflation; Levy 2018). Over the past forty years those communities have lost billions of dollars in resources and development, which impacted property values and public schools, leading to population losses of People of Color when those blighted neighborhoods began gentrifying in the 1990s; this has continued through to the present (Levy 2018).

Critical race theorist Audre Lorde, who worked for a time as a librarian at Barnard College, described the concept of *vulnerability theory* in *The Cancer Journals* (1990), which identifies all people as "embodied creatures" who are susceptible to harm and notes that people with marginal identities are especially vulnerable to institutional harms. Much of her argument was situated in the context of the health-care system, but it is relevant across other US institutions. Harm is compounded in working-class and low-income communities of color because of our disproportionate involvement with institutions (legal, education, health care, social services, among others), all of which subject those communities to pervasive and long-term surveillance.

Surveillance and privacy pose unique threats to both library staff and users, and while the profession's governing bodies have made statements or signed letters of support, our inconsistencies leave vulnerable populations at considerable risk of harm.

The last major initiative advocating for patron privacy and antisurveillance measures was updated on September 30, 2004, when the American Library Association (ALA) took a position against the Patriot Act and any related policies that explicitly or implicitly placed libraries in a position to violate patron privacy. However, the organization, which purports to represent the largest number of information professionals in the country, did not take a hard position on bills such as the Anti-Terrorism Intelligence Tools Improvement Act, which would have allowed secret surveillance and searches of individuals without any evidence of connection to a foreign government or terrorist group; and the Civil Liberties Restoration Act of 2004, which would have mandated reports of data-mining activities conducted by the government, ensured due process for detained individuals, and ended secret deportation hearings.

In this example, we see how librarians and our professional organizations or governing/legislative bodies can make decisions that uphold frameworks of White Supremacy instead of facilitating healing for those being harmed. And to the world outside of librarianship or other GLAM spaces, our governing or professional association bodies purport to speak on our behalf or express our collective values. Our words—that we value privacy, intellectual freedom, and individual and collective civil rights—are frequently inconsistent with our actions (Yousefi 2017). Our professional organizations across GLAM spaces encourage diversity and inclusion, yet continue to hold space for groups who perpetuate harm, such as transphobic lecturers or white nationalists who wish to use public library space for organizing. We purport to care deeply about special collections, rare books, and archives, yet we have buttressed archives/rare book/special collections professions with internships, term jobs, and soft money. We build spaces where some of our users and staff can't even access collections because stacks in our legacy buildings do not accommodate wheelchairs or lack ADA-compliant doors and doorways.

In what ways does our silence uplift the whiteness of information? In what ways does our silence facilitate White Supremacy in word and deed?

CORDELIA SCAIFE MAY: MANIPULATING THE RESEARCH LIFE CYCLE

Cordelia Scaife May was a private individual who initially had few solid connections in government but who also understood how to use scholarly publishing to create and share incredibly harmful information about immigrant communities of color. That information has had a direct and catastrophic impact on current immigration and deportation policies. In our second case study, we bear witness to her work and understand that how we legitimize information as librarians and information management professionals is in large part responsible for the wide dissemination of the research she funded.

May was a member of the Mellon family—the same philanthropic family that built public libraries all over the country and which continues to fund libraries, archives, and other cultural heritage programs across the country. May utilized her enormous wealth—estimated at around $800 million during the mid-twentieth century—to fund scholarly research that supported anti-immigration, eugenics, racism, xenophobia, forced sterilization, and white nativism in the form of white papers, funded studies, and op-eds in both scholarly and mainstream media publications. An August 2019 article by the *New York Times* detailed how the incredibly secretive heiress identified organizations that supported her positions, drawing clear links between that financial support and the work those organizations continue to do to create research that overwhelmingly supports a white-only America (Kulish and McIntire 2019).

May was originally a supporter of Planned Parenthood and Margaret Sanger, specifically Sanger's goal of helping women prevent unwanted pregnancies. By 1973, her interest in abortion access had turned toward using abortion as immigrant "population control," to which she felt incoming immigrants should be subjected to help keep immigration numbers down. According to Kulish and McIntire, May resigned from the Planned Parenthood board at the end of that year, surprising her fellow board members and Planned Parenthood leadership. Her obsession with immigration numbers revealed more xenophobic roots. "The U.S. should seal its border" with Mexico, she had her top aide write to the head of the US Population Council that same year (Kulich and MacIntire 2019).

With her fortune hidden behind her philanthropic arm, Colcom Foundation, May bankrolled three organizations that later became central to current anti-immigration platforms and policies: the Federation for American Immigration Reform (FAIR), NumbersUSA, and the Center for Immigration Studies (CIS). According to Kulish and McIntire, FAIR alone received $56.7 million between 2005 and 2017. A data visualization that accompanied the *Times* article showed that Trump administration advisor Stephen Miller and former Trump administration attorney general Jeff Sessions (2017–2018) are longtime FAIR supporters. From the investigation:

Restrictionist groups she financed have blocked attempts at amnesties and immigration reform bills in Congress over the years. They fought for Proposition 187 in California to deny education, routine health care and other public services to undocumented immigrants; they argued against in-state tuition for the children of undocumented workers in Utah. They supported "show me your papers" laws in Arizona and Georgia and draconian local ordinances in Hazleton, Pa., and Farmers Branch, Tex. (Kulish and McIntire 2019)

Each of these organizations—FAIR, CIS, and NumbersUSA—is listed as being a legitimate source of information in numerous academic library LibGuides found on the library websites of public universities, private universities, Ivy League schools, R1 schools, small liberal arts colleges, universities with a focus on STEM, schools that are part of the Big Ten Academic Alliance (which shares collections and resources), and community colleges. A cursory web search using the DuckDuckGo search engine and the terms *FAIR + immigration + LibGuide* returned hundreds of results of LibGuides identifying these organizations as "independent" or "nonpartisan" sources of information.

The causes May supported created media and communication that exemplify epistemic supremacy—that is, the work and organizations support a vision of our world where white people have the only lives that matter. The policies enacted under that specific vision mean that epistemic supremacy can be directly linked to ICE raids in immigrant communities that separate children from parents, or borderland concentration camps housing weeks-old babies. These are policies borne of epistemic supremacy as it appeared in administration policy briefings, comprised of information gathered from conspiracy theory racists' websites like Alex Jones's *InfoWars* and *Breitbart News*, and prepared for the current presidential administration to bolster many of its immigration policies.

ES AND SCHOLARLY PUBLISHING

The scholarly communication channels May exploited have been a part of academic librarianship nearly from the beginning, when the first peer-reviewed journal was published in 1731 by the Royal Society of Edinburgh. Over the decades, as services evolved, academic libraries have created full-time positions whose sole job is to address scholarly communication topics such as open access, journal publishing, copyright, dissertation work, and research dissemination. Librarians create programming that introduces faculty and students to institutional repositories where their published journal articles can live free outside of vendor paywalls. This work is usually grounded in both a university's and a library's respective missions to provide access to scholarly research and pedagogy that will help create informed citizens of the future. But librarians should interrogate a model of creation and dissemination of scholarly output that can be so easily co-opted by someone with an agenda that runs on the marginalization, sterilization, and displacement of working-class Black and Brown immigrants.

May's continued support of organizations that held particularly noxious views on immigration absolutely created institutional harms for vulnerable populations. FAIR, CIS, and NumbersUSA have had staff over the years whose scholarly work (e.g., white papers, data collection and analysis, peer-reviewed journal articles) has led lawmakers to create policies that determine how immigrants are received, where they can work, live, send their children to school, receive further education, and receive government funding for food and housing. These organizations are not subtle about how they feel about immigrants, especially those from countries and continents in the Global South. The rhetoric against them has been cited as inspirational by people who have committed violent acts against People of Color, people experiencing homelessness, and people who may simply share an ethnic group, religion, or sexual identity with those identified through ES as an Other, a not-human.

At the time of this writing, the most recent mass shooting tied to White Supremacy or White Supremacist rhetoric involved a gunman who killed twenty-two people and wounded twenty-six others at a Walmart in August 2019. His manifesto declared that he was "targeting Mexicans." Trump and his administration used language that was degrading and racially charged from the start of his candidacy, likely emboldened by public support for his bigotry. And in 2018, while reconsidering countries that could retain temporary protected status, Trump referred to Haiti, El Salvador, and African countries as "shitholes," and then asked why the US doesn't have more immigrants coming from Norway. The language is the wall. The language that *others* immigrants of color and other marginalized communities is the same language found in white papers produced by FAIR and NumbersUSA. It's the same language that likely helped draw May to her conclusions that the US would be a better place if there were fewer immigrants, or that the ones who were here should be forcibly sterilized.

May also funded book publishing that espoused epistemic supremacy. A second philanthropic arm that she administered funded the Institute for Western Values to translate a French novel, *The Camp of the Saints* by Jean Raspail. The novel about

European immigration is used by white nationalists as a key foundational text for their views, and it was frequently cited by Trump's former advisor Steve Bannon as the seed for many of the policies that came out of the Trump administration in 2017, such as the travel ban and trade tariffs (Kulich and MacIntire 2019).

Bannon himself was formerly the executive director of *Breitbart News*, a website featuring far-right or openly racist views, which frequently published misleading or inaccurate stories, or conspiracy theories that paint working-class and poor People of Color as inherently criminal and undeserving of civil rights or policies that affirm their humanity and dignity. An October 5, 2017, *Buzzfeed* investigation revealed a cache of emails between Bannon and one of his most influential employees, Milo Yiannopoulos, who worked to intentionally thread White Supremacist rhetoric and ideals into *Breitbart*.

As an editor, Yiannopoulos published pieces such as "Birth Control Makes Women Unattractive and Crazy" and breaking news such as "Satanic Temple Joins Planned Parenthood in Pro-Abortion Crusade." He leveraged deep connections between online alt-right and white nationalist writers to keep *Breitbart* trending, making money and also headlines in mainstream media for their incendiary content. *Buzzfeed*'s investigation revealed that Yiannopoulos had allies in more traditional and even left-leaning media such as *Broadly*—a Vice Media vertical that promised a feminist exploration of news items relevant to and inclusive of all women—and *Slate.com* (owned by the Washington Post Company). Digital media thrives on content; Yiannopoulos's *Breitbart* stories would get picked up by mainstream publications that reported them as jokes or carnival curiosities, which distributed those stories even further via the "clickbait" articles that *Breitbart* sought to legitimize.

These connections illuminate a broken research life cycle with horrific implications—one that begins with the policy papers supported by May's philanthropy and that continues to flourish, assisted by media outlets that tend to cover such ideas and individuals with a mix of fascination and subtle allegiance, or that choose to repeat or reprint inaccuracies or biases without challenging them. Librarians then must wade through even more bad information in order to best serve patrons, as these ideas become amplified across digital platforms.

LIMITATIONS OF CONTEMPORARY LIBRARIANSHIP

Critical Race Theory is not needed to decode the work of openly racist or nativist anti-immigration groups, but it provides useful solutions to figuring out how to keep it out of mainstream discourse. Lorde, in one of her most often quoted speeches, published in *Sister Outsider*, said that using "the master's tools will never dismantle the master's house" (1984). The spirit of intellectual rigor in academia, and in academic libraries, encourages the idea that *everything* is subject to debate, even people's humanity, civil rights, and freedom.

Librarians committed to interrogating epistemic supremacy or mitigating its presence in our collections, services, and staff can't look to academia as the place where those biases will be debunked. If anything, because higher education is an institution with its own set of generally conservative values, working-class BIPOC information professionals are at risk of great institutional harm for speaking out about racist or offensive materials. *The Scholarly Kitchen*, a peer-moderated blog for people involved in scholarly publishing, published in 2018 a series of comments by People of Color in scholarly publishing. Employees who work in book or journal publishing spoke of low morale, targeted workplace bullying, microaggressions, and racialized disrespect.

Considering the ways that these two persons, J. Edgar Hoover and Cordelia Scaife May, were able to affect the lives of millions of working-class and poor communities of color, sexual minorities, clergy, and radical activists who supported movements of equality, we understand that readers may be ready to throw their hands up at the possibility of confronting institutions where epistemic supremacy is embedded in the very fabric of its work and policies. Both use cases also offer instructive observations for how we have created or reproduced oppressive conditions for our users in both public and academic libraries. Librarians are grappling with pervasive surveillance, not just from our government but also from our vendors—those who wish to extract our data and those who want to sell to us based on our data, our lived experiences. Increased use of technology in our profession in turn increases the privacy risks for staff and patrons, as people who design technology seek to capture more of our offline worlds for profit. Users may experience institutional harm, sometimes through interaction with a vendor's profit-seeking paywall, which denies users access to important scientific information. Our information-seeking processes mean that we as staff may have to submit to those potential harms while interrogating the provenance of our data; for instance, archivists have to process collections that include or document details of traumatic harm to marginalized individuals or communities in order to simply conduct the basic functions of their jobs (Sloan, Vanderfluit, and Douglas 2019). Librarians have to submit to the harms of epistemic supremacy in the form of literature reviews to determine if we indeed can or will trust the information being given to us.

To librarians who wish to counteract the propaganda that undergirds our culture and democratic institutions, we offer the solution of transformative librarianship, with examples that explore how we can create the conditions for political resistance to epistemic supremacy across the profession.

TRANSFORMATIVE LIBRARIANSHIP AS PRAXIS

We have named our problem. Epistemic supremacy, as expressed across our staff, services, and collections, serves to uphold the white ruling class and White Supremacy as status quo. While we can use CRT as a tool to identify this content or the channels through which the information flows, the next step to making meaningful change must be aligning our LIS methodology with working-class or poor Black or Indigenous communities of color—knowing that in centering that group, we could create the conditions for radical change.

Critical race theorists encourage education and communication with each other. The Combahee River Collective coalesced as a study group that together explored feminist, communist, and other radical texts, challenging ideas found inside and then coming to a collective understanding of politics that centered around Black working-class and poor women, or women in the Global South. However, that collective understanding was not a fixed, static notion of justice. Combahee's statement committed the group to a "collective process and a nonhierarchical distribution of power within our own group and in our vision of a revolutionary society. We are committed to a continual examination of our politics as they develop through criticism and self-criticism as an essential aspect of our practice" (Smith 1983).

Library workers, especially those in academia, have to embrace collective knowledge building and organizing in order to change their conditions and create the conditions for those they work with to organize around information and concepts that are accurate and relevant and that challenge or negate epistemic supremacy. Beyond group chats, social media platforms have become organizing and information-sharing spaces among librarians of color. The Libraries We Here group, for example, started by Jennifer Ferretti, Jennifer Brown, and Charlotte Rock, notably offers specific job support around best practices for library résumés and interviews, and answers questions around professional development and technical skilling up. This is critical assistance because "the current librarian job market solicits performance" of whiteness "and creates barriers to entry in three ways: cultural negotiation, conspicuous leisure, and access to wealth" (Galvan 2015).

Labor and union organizing in library and other cultural heritage spaces reflects an acknowledgement that the field excludes far more people than it includes by structuring employment around modes of privilege and mobility: unreimbursed travel to distant cities for interviews; unpaid internships; jobs where the entry-level salaries rarely cover the nearly six-figure price tag of obtaining a master's degree in library and information science. By supporting GLAM sector unions, we create the conditions that allow more low-income and working-class People of Color to participate in those fields. Jobs that allow everyone equal opportunities for professional development and continuing education and that might center the material needs of working-class or poor BIPOC help create a workforce that can respond forcefully to epistemic supremacy. For example, could we create alternatives to the invoice/reimbursement model of most professional development opportunities, where workers are shouldering the burdens of costs that their institutions can usually cover upfront? These are ways that librarians can transform the work of librarianship and the business of information toward one that is centered in equitable labor practices and services and away from one that centers privilege and precarity.

Seeding those individuals in jobs all over the library, such as in cataloging or technical services, digital infrastructure, and collection development—not just in an ethnic studies collecting area or on a temporary grant project focused on "hidden collections" of underrepresented materials—-means that there are more people bringing different ways of knowing to our interactions with vendors who don't understand or respect privacy; to our physical spaces, where we can interrogate the unique institutional harms we perpetuate on underrepresented or unaffiliated researchers when they access our spaces and electronic collections, especially, while also asking, open access, but for whom?; and to our service models, where we can create programming that is inclusive of humanity but that does not further harm, erase, or diminish working-class communities of color. And to be clear, there are some initiatives that do center our most vulnerable communities. Large public library systems in Chicago, Los Angeles, St. Louis, Cleveland, and Washington, DC, to name a few, have gone fine-free or created automatic renewals to remove barriers to access that would have disproportionately hit working-class or poor communities of color harder, but now the *entire* community of library users benefits.

Access to information is a basic human right. The role of library workers has been to help patrons access the information they desire. While technology has altered how that is accomplished, the basic function of a librarian remains the same, and understanding that role is critical in this era of mis/disinformation, no matter if you are working in technical services, facilitating instructional workshops, or providing reference assistance. But we still do not show collective solidarity for those who are most affected by epistemic supremacy: working-class and poor communities of color. The profession makes little room to learn with and from those communities in ways that are actually meaningful and useful to them. Professional library workers who understand what is happening in this current moment may be protecting themselves from racism, sexism, or other oppression in the workplace, or they may show apathy derived from exhaustion or privilege toward their colleagues. As a result, our profession is slow to rise to the challenge that our country has always faced, which is to *acknowledge* the true pain and destruction of colonialism and White Supremacy.

Transformative librarianship seeks to understand how information fosters our self-awareness while at the same time holding an awareness of the community to which we belong. These librarians lean into discomfort, sometimes running toward it, because they see pain and know that within their grasp lies information that may be able to help alleviate it. These librarians go where the problems are and serve the people who are most affected by the harms created by cisheteropatriarchy, White Supremacy, xenophobia, ableism, and capitalism. They go there because that's where real information and real solutions can be unearthed. These librarians understand that democracy is praxis. These librarians are political actors. They work every day to engage with truth and facilitate trust.

Transformative librarianship is a pathway that could allow us to fully lean into our purpose of transforming and upholding libraries as the cornerstone of democracy. But it can only be achieved by recognizing epistemic supremacy as a framework being used to dismantle working-class and poor communities of color. We need a commitment to dismantling that epistemic supremacy, and to challenging it and ourselves at every turn.

BIBLIOGRAPHY

Accardi, Maria T., Emily Drabinski, and Alana Kumbier. 2010. *Critical Library Instruction: Theories and Methods.* Sacramento, CA: Library Juice Press.

Adam, Alison. 2002. "Exploring the Gender Question in Critical Information Systems." *Journal of Information Technology* 17 (2): 59–67.

Alberti, Fay Bound. 2018. "Loneliness Is a Modern Illness of the Body, Not Just the Mind." *The Guardian*, November 1, 2018. https://www.theguardian.com/commentisfree/2018/nov/01/loneliness-illness-body-mind-epidemic.

American Library Association. 2017. "Cybersecurity and Information Sharing (CISA/CISPA)." American Library Association. December 29, 2017. http://www.ala.org/advocacy/advleg/federallegislation/cisa.

Barnes, Luke. 2018. "Exclusive: Leaks Show How Boston 'Free Speech' Group Acts as a Front for Far-Right Organizing." *ThinkProgress*, May 18, 2018. https://thinkprogress.org/resist-marxism -front-for-far-right-organizing-9bd959325ae1/.

Bernstein, Joseph. 2017. "Here's How Breitbart and Milo Smuggled White Nationalism into the Mainstream." *Buzzfeed*, October 5, 2017. https://www.buzzfeednews.com/article/josephbernstein /heres-how-breitbart-and-milo-smuggled-white-nationalism.

Birdsall, William F. 2006. "A Progressive Librarianship for the Twenty-First Century." *Progressive Librarian* 28:49–63.

Brown, Alleen, Will Parrish, and Alice Speri. 2017. "Leaked Documents Reveal Counterterrorism Tactics Used at Standing Rock to 'Defeat Pipeline Insurgencies.'" *The Intercept*, May 27, 2017. https://theintercept.com/2017/05/27/leaked-documents-reveal-security-firms-counterterrorism -tactics-at-standing-rock-to-defeat-pipeline-insurgencies/.

Browne, Simone. 2015. *Dark Matters: On the Surveillance of Blackness*. Durham, NC: Duke University Press.

Cecil, Matthew. 2011. "Friends of the Bureau: Personal Correspondence and the Cultivation of Journalist-Adjuncts by J. Edgar Hoover's FBI." *Journalism and Mass Communication Quarterly* 88 (2): 267–284.

Cesar-Chavez, Julio. 2019. "El Paso Mass Murder Suspect Pleads Not Guilty, Accused of Targeting Mexicans." Reuters, October 10, 2019. https://www.reuters.com/article/us-texas-shooting/el-paso -mass-murder-suspect-pleads-not-guilty-accused-of-targeting-mexicans-idUSKBN1WP1CN.

Collins, Patricia Hill. 2012. *On Intellectual Activism*. Philadelphia: Temple University Press.

Coppins, McKay. 2017. "The Far Right's Day in Boston." *The Atlantic*, August 19, 2017. https:// www.theatlantic.com/politics/archive/2017/08/boston-free-speech-rally/537435/.

Croft, Stuart. 2012. "Constructing Ontological Insecurity: The Insecuritization of Britain's Muslims." *Contemporary Security Policy* 33 (ii): 219–235. Restricted access.

Davis, Joshua Clark. 2018. "The FBI's War on Black-Owned Bookstores." *The Atlantic*, February 19, 2018. https://www.theatlantic.com/politics/archive/2018/02/fbi-black-bookstores/553598/.

Delgado, Richard, Jean Stefancic, and Angela Harris. 2012a. "Legal Storytelling and Narrative Analysis." In *Critical Race Theory: An Introduction*, 2nd ed., edited by Richard Delgado and Jean Stefancic, 43–56. New York: New York University Press. http://www.jstor.org/stable/j.ctt9qg9h2.8.

Delgado, Richard, Jean Stefancic, and Angela Harris. 2012b. "Looking Inward." In *Critical Race Theory: An Introduction*, 2nd ed., edited by Richard Delgado and Jean Stefancic, 57–74. New York: New York University Press. http://www.jstor.org/stable/j.ctt9qg9h2.9.

Delgado, Richard, Jean Stefancic, and Angela Harris. 2012c. "Power and the Shape of Knowledge." In *Critical Race Theory: An Introduction*, 2nd ed., edited by Richard Delgado and Jean Stefancic, 75–98. New York: New York University Press. http://www.jstor.org/stable/j.ctt9qg9h2.10.

Doherty, John. 2005. "Towards Self-reflection in Librarianship: What Is Praxis?" *Progressive Librarian* 26 (1): 11–17.

Du Bois, W. E. B. 1903. *The Souls of Black Folk: Essays and Sketches*. Chicago: A. C. McClurg.

Ernst, Morris L. 1950. "Why I No Longer Fear the FBI." *Reader's Digest*, December 1950. Herbert H. Lehman Papers, Special Correspondence Files, Rare Book and Manuscript Library, Columbia University Library. http://www.columbia.edu/cu/lweb/digital/collections/rbml/lehman/pdfs/0279/ldpd_leh_0279_0040.pdf.

Fanon, Frantz. 1952. *Black Skin, White Masks*. New York: Grove Press.

FBI. 2012. "The Hoover Legacy, 40 Years After. Part 2: His First Job and the FBI Files." FBI. June 28, 2012. https://web.archive.org/web/20160314092138/https://www.fbi.gov/news/stories/2012/june/j-edgar-hoovers-first-job-and-the-fbi-files/j.-edgar-hoovers-first-job-and-the-fbi-files.

Ford, Anne. 2018. "Bringing Harassment out of the History Books: Addressing the Troubling Aspects of Melvil Dewey's Legacy." American Libraries. June 1, 2018. https://americanlibrariesmagazine.org/2018/06/01/melvil-dewey-bringing-harassment-out-of-the-history-books/.

Gage, Beverly. 2014. "What an Uncensored Letter to MLK Reveals." *New York Times Magazine*, November 11, 2014. https://www.nytimes.com/2014/11/16/magazine/what-an-uncensored-letter-to-mlk-reveals.html?auth=login-google&login=google.

Galvan, Angela. 2015. "Soliciting Performance, Hiding Bias: Whiteness and Librarianship." *In the Library with the Lead Pipe*, June 3, 2015. http://www.inthelibrarywiththeleadpipe.org/2015/soliciting-performance-hiding-bias-whiteness-and-librarianship/.

Gangadharan, Seeta Pena. 2013. "From COINTELPRO to PRISM, Spying on Communities of Color." *Bay State Banner*, July 10, 2013. https://www.baystatebanner.com/2013/07/10/from-cointelpro-to-prism-spying-on-communities-of-color/.

Giddens, Anthony. 1991. *Modernity and Self-Identity: Self and Society in the Late Modern Age*. Stanford, CA: Stanford University Press.

Goodman, Amy. 2017. "COINTELPRO 2? FBI Targets 'Black Identity Extremists' Despite Surge in White Supremacist Violence." *Democracy Now!*, October 16, 2017. https://www.democracynow.org/2017/10/16/cointelpro_2_fbi_targets_Black_identity.

Grosfoguel, Ramón. 2013. "The Structure of Knowledge in Westernized Universities: Epistemic Racism/Sexism and the Four Genocides/Epistemicides of the Long 16th Century." *Human Architecture: Journal of the Sociology of Self-Knowledge* 11 (1). https://scholarworks.umb.edu/humanarchitecture/vol11/iss1/8.

Kulish, Nicholas, and Mike McIntire. 2019. "Why an Heiress Spent Her Fortune Trying to Keep Immigrants Out." *New York Times*, August 14, 2019. https://www.nytimes.com/2019/08/14/us/anti-immigration-cordelia-scaife-may.html.

Ladson-Billings, Gloria. 1998. "Just What Is Critical Race Theory and What's It Doing in a Nice Field Like Education?" *International Journal of Qualitative Studies in Education* 11 (1): 7–24. https://doi.org/10.1080/095183998236863.

Laing, R. D. 1969. *The Divided Self*. New York: Pantheon Books.

Levy, Peter B. 2011. "The Dream Deferred: The Assassination of Martin Luther King Jr. and the Holy Week Uprisings of 1968." In *Baltimore '68: Riots and Rebirth in an American City*, edited by

Jessica I. Elfenbein, Thomas L. Hollowak, and Elizabeth M. Nix, 153–188. Philadelphia: Temple University Press. https://doi.org/10.1017/9781108381659.006.

Levy, Peter B. 2018. *The Great Uprising: Race Riots in Urban America during the 1960s*. New York Cambridge University Press.

Lorde, Audre. 1982. *Zami: A New Spelling of My Name—A Biomythography*. Trumansburg, NY: Crossing Press.

Lorde, Audre. 1984. *Sister Outsider*. Trumansburg, NY: Crossing Press.

Matsuda, Mari J., Charles R. Lawrence III, Richard Delgado, and Kimberlè Williams Crenshaw, eds. 1993. *Words That Wound: Critical Race Theory, Assaultive Speech, and the First Amendment*. Boulder, CO: Westview Press.

Matthews, David. 2019. "Capitalism and Mental Health." *Monthly Review*, January 1, 2019. https://monthlyreview.org/2019/01/01/capitalism-and-mental-health/.

Maxwell, William J. 2015. *F.B. Eyes: How J. Edgar Hoover's Ghostreaders Framed African American Literature*. Princeton, NJ: Princeton University Press.

Maxwell, William J. n.d.-a. "Claude McKay." *F.B. Eyes Digital Archive: FBI Files on African American Authors and Literary Institutions Obtained through the U.S. Freedom of Information Act (FOIA)*. Accessed August 20, 2019. http://omeka.wustl.edu/omeka/exhibits/show/fbeyes/mckay.

Maxwell, William J. n.d.-b. "Lorraine Hansberry." *F.B. Eyes Digital Archive: FBI Files on African American Authors and Literary Institutions Obtained through the U.S. Freedom of Information Act (FOIA)*. Accessed August 20, 2019. http://omeka.wustl.edu/omeka/exhibits/show/fbeyes/hansberry.

Maxwell, William J. n.d.-c. "W. E. B. Du Bois." *F.B. Eyes Digital Archive: FBI Files on African American Authors and Literary Institutions Obtained through the U.S. Freedom of Information Act (FOIA)*. Accessed August 20, 2019. http://omeka.wustl.edu/omeka/exhibits/show/fbeyes/duboisweb.

Noble, Safiyah U. 2018. *Algorithms of Oppression: How Search Engines Reinforce Racism*. New York: New York University Press.

Nunes, Zita C. 2018. "Cataloging Black Knowledge: How Dorothy Porter Assembled and Organized a Premier Africana Research Collection." American Historical Association Perspectives on History, December 18, 2018. https://www.historians.org/publications-and-directories/perspectives -on-history/december-2018/cataloging-black-knowledge-how-dorothy-porter-assembled-and -organized-a-premier-africana-research-collection.

Ransby, Barbara. 2005. *Ella Baker and the Black Freedom Movement: A Radical Democratic Vision*. New ed. Chapel Hill: University of North Carolina Press.

Richardson, John V. Jr. 2010. "History of American Library Science: Its Origins and Early Development." In *Encyclopedia of Library and Information Science*, 3rd ed., edited by Marcia J. Bates and Mary Niles Maack, 1–9. Abingdon, UK: Taylor and Francis. https://pages.gseis.ucla.edu/faculty /richardson/ALS.pdf.

Shani, Giorgio. 2017. "Human Security as Ontological Security: A Post-colonial Approach." *Postcolonial Studies* 20 (3): 275–293. https://doi.org/10.1080/13688790.2017.1378062.

Shor, Ira. 1987. *Freire for the Classroom: A Sourcebook for Liberatory Teaching*. Portsmouth, NH: Heinemann.

Sloan, Katie, Jennifer Vanderfluit, and Jennifer Douglas. 2019. "Not 'Just My Problem to Handle': Emerging Themes on Secondary Trauma and Archivists." *Journal of Contemporary Archival Studies* 6 (20).

Smith, Barbara, ed. 1983. *Home Girls: A Black Feminist Anthology*. New York: Kitchen Table: Women of Color Press.

Steele, Brent J. 2008. *Ontological Security in International Relations: Self-Identity and the IR State*. London: Routledge.

Taylor, Keeanga-Yamahtta. 2017. *How We Get Free: Black Feminism and the Combahee River Collective*. Chicago: Haymarket Books.

Trosow, Samuel E. 2001. "Standpoint Epistemology as an Alternative Methodology for Library and Information Science." *Library Quarterly* 71 (3): 360–382.

Washington, Mary. 2015. *The Other Blacklist: The African American Literary and Cultural Left of the 1950s*. New York: Columbia University Press.

Watts, Duncan, and David Rothschild. 2017. "Don't Blame the Election on Fake News, Blame It on the Media." *Columbia Journalism Review*, December 5, 2017. https://www.cjr.org/analysis/fake-news-media-election-trump.php.

Woodhouse, Leighton A. 2018. "Trump's 'Shithole Countries' Remark Is at the Center of a Lawsuit to Reinstate Protections for Immigrants." *The Intercept*, June 28, 2018. https://theintercept.com/2018/06/28/trump-tps-shithole-countries-lawsuit/.

Wynter, Sylvia. 2003. "Unsettling the Coloniality of Being/Power/Truth/Freedom: Towards the Human, after Man, Its Overrepresentation—An Argument." *New Centennial Review* 3 (3): 257–357. https://muse.jhu.edu/article/51630/pdf.

Yousefi, Baharak. 2017. "On the Disparity between What We Say and What We Do in Libraries." In *Feminists among Us: Resistance and Advocacy in Library Leadership*, edited by Shirley Lew and Baharak Yousefi. Sacramento, CA: Library Juice Press.

3

LEANING ON OUR LABOR
Whiteness and Hierarchies of Power in LIS Work

Jennifer Brown, Nicholae Cline (Coharie), and Marisa Méndez-Brady

FRAMING LIBRARY DIVERSITY WORK USING CRITICAL RACE THEORY

It's no myth that labor inequity in academia disproportionately affects marginalized faculty, students, and staff. Critical race theory (CRT), and the scholars who undertake this research, continually affirm this phenomenon as fact. But where these inequalities are most keenly felt is in institutional efforts around diversity, equity, and inclusion—often referred to as "diversity work." Here, Black, Indigenous, and People of Color (BIPOC) scholars are disproportionately leaned on for emotional and physical labor; this typically translates into us having to chair diversity and inclusion committees, informally teach privileged peers about "cultural competence," navigate white fragility, and more (Chou and Pho 2018).

We (the authors of this chapter) posit that such labor inequities don't simply begin at the individual level—they are first embedded in the collective documents that shape an organization's public persona and define its institutional legacy. To that end, this chapter will analyze examples of written materials that frame what institutional diversity efforts typically look like, while employing CRT frameworks to demonstrate how these ephemera commodify institutional diversity efforts and devalue the labor of BIPOC scholars. Then, we'll utilize CRT's theme of valuing the voices and counternarratives of communities of color to share our lived experiences around inequitable labor expectations relating to our own diversity, equity, and inclusion work.

In the spirit of Delgado and Stefancic's seminal work (2001), which introduced critical CRT questions into the fabric of each chapter, we'll also explore the following queries to deepen our engagement with this topic:

- How do critical scholars define "diversity work" and whiteness, and how do these two concepts interplay with one another throughout the academy?
- How do institutions commoditize diversity? Further, when considering inequitable distributions of labor around "diversity work," how do institutions communicate its value?
- How do our lived labor experiences around "diversity work" intersect with career advancement and performance/tenure review? What have those labor inequities cost us?

But it's not enough to simply critique current systems of labor inequity. After all, CRT aims to "not only understand our social situation, but transform it for the better" (Delgado and Stefancic 2001, 3). Therefore, we'll draw inspiration from the work of visionary fiction writers (Imarisha 2015) and allow ourselves to do something marginalized scholars are rarely afforded the opportunity to do: radically imagine scenarios wherein our labor, energy, and spirits aren't weighed down by White Supremacist, imperial work structures. The following question will be our guide:

- Given our positionalities and lived experiences, what might just, equitable labor around diversity work in libraries look like in practice?

WHITENESS AND DIVERSITY WORK

Before diving into our document analyses we must first till the soil on which our analysis rests. Whiteness and "diversity work" aren't new concepts, but there are many manifestations of these terms throughout the literature. For reference, we are particularly interested in "whiteness" as defined by LIS scholar April Hathcock, who asserts:

Whiteness refers not only to racial and ethnic categorizations but a complete system of exclusion based on hegemony. [It] refer[s] not only to the socio-cultural differential of power and privilege that results from categories of race and ethnicity; it also stands as a marker for the privilege and power that acts to reinforce itself through hegemonic cultural practice that excludes all who are different. (Hathcock 2015)

"Whiteness," then, is more than skin color or cultural origin—it's systematic. It's a set of practices and norms that define societies by exclusion, and in particular, by what whiteness strives *not* to be. CRT scholars who engage in whiteness studies have also reflected that it's based on a kind of "social distance from blackness and a cultural practice that constructs race-based hierarchies" (Rogers and Mosley 2006). This is particularly important to consider in our analysis within the library context, given the legacy of White Supremacy in US libraries (cf. Mississippi Civil Rights Project, n.d.).

"Diversity work" serves as shorthand, typically referring to the stuff (physical or otherwise) that makes up an institution's attempt to address systemic inequalities around race, gender, ability, class, sexuality, religion, and other identities represented (or not represented) by their staff. Brown and Leung further discuss it as "librarianship [having] its own set of top-down, hierarchically organized documents that frame acceptable ways for diversity work to be thought of, articulated, and performed across institutions" (2018, 326). In this way, diversity work can be thought of as a set of hierarchically defined values that institutions perform to achieve some kind of socially acceptable rightness. It's seen as the thing institutions do; the ways in which they perform wokeness for the benefit of public-facing websites, media, and more— *instead* of acknowledging the complexity of interconnected -isms in their institution and working to dismantle these through action and robust accountability.

Critical Race Theory (CRT) helps us make sense of the connections between systemic oppressions, "whiteness" as a set of professional and social norms, and diversity work. The CRT theorists who posed frameworks for understanding the *how* and *why* behind racialized inequality are at the core of our comparisons of institutional documentation versus lived experiences.

DOCUMENTARY APPROACHES: WHAT AND WHO ARE WE EXAMINING?

For the purposes of this chapter, the institutional documents that we've chosen to analyze represent the "stuff" of diversity initiatives in an academic library context. We found these documents by conducting web searches for paperwork that's typically cited by library leadership and diversity committees as evidence that they are "doing" diversity work, included in new employee packets, and devised during large-scale strategic planning efforts. The overarching framework guiding our selection process centered on the question, can the circulation of these documents in and of themselves be considered "diversity work"? We were able to answer in the affirmative for the following document types: diversity statements (value statements), diversity action plans (typically associated with a timeline), and diversity initiatives (broad approaches intended to diversify institutional demographics).

Ahmed's seminal work around performativity and diversity documents helps to illustrate our documentary approaches. She argues that the emphasis on documents over action allows institutions to perform being "good"' at diversity. Thus, "diversity and equality become 'things' that can be measured" (2007, 596). That performance can then be measured against those documented standards, suggesting that the institutions "doing well" at diversity are simply the ones most skilled in creating auditable structures. In Ahmed's words, "[Diversity documents'] very existence is taken as evidence that the institutional world documented by the document (racism, inequality, injustice) has been overcome" (597). In turning to documents, we can unpack latent connections between diversity work and labor inequity. Further, "worshipping the written word" is a well-studied marker of White Supremacist workplace culture, positioning the diversity documents themselves as more legitimate than the actual lived experiences of the BIPOC in predominantly white institutions (PWI) (Jones and Okun 2001).

Since we're also concerned with *who* is disproportionately leaned on to author and act on these documents (i.e., serve as representatives for "diversity work"), our documentary analysis includes examining job ads that contain the word *diversity* in the position title itself. We chose to juxtapose diversity positions typical for early career librarians of color and for more senior positions, limiting our analysis to "diversity resident" roles and "diversity officer" positions. The Association of College and Research Libraries' (ACRL) Diversity Residency Alliance defines a residency as a post-MLIS/MLS degree work experience designed for entry-level librarians, and purports that residencies increase the pipeline of "underrepresented racial and ethnic groups" into the profession (American Library Association 2017). Diversity officer positions are more varied and nuanced, but are typically situated in administrative roles (Williams and Wade-Golden 2008).

DIVERSITY AS COMMODITY IN ACADEMIC LIBRARIES

Once diversity initiatives are given a value based on documents rather than actions, the groundwork has been laid for labor inequities. This is because when whiteness is the de facto standard against which the success of diversity work is measured, racialized social hierarchies are inevitably reproduced, demoting everyone outside those boundaries to the metaphorical bottom of labor systems.

Building on Ladson-Billings and Tate's groundbreaking work introducing CRT to education (1995), Iverson has written at length about how diversity policies reproduce whiteness by centering dominant discourses while simultaneously failing to name whiteness as a barrier to inclusion (2007). This creates a kind of measurable standard of whiteness, positioning white people as the primary beneficiaries of diversity initiatives that purportedly support marginalized staff. Iverson's earlier discourse analysis supports this claim, as they found that institutions they studied utilized "diversity as a resource for an enriched and engaged academic environment" (2005, 53). When diversity is treated as a resource, institutional conversations focus on how a more diverse population might improve the quality of the institutional experience, and as a result, institutions can measure their success based on quantifiable metrics rather than critical self-reflection. So, wherever white people dominate the demographics, diversity initiatives offer them a multicultural experience rather than avenues toward institutional change. They're absolved from having to examine their role in institutional racism, because the standard for excellence was devised using Western Eurocentric ways of thinking, learning, and being and is rooted in (white) Western history. What's more, the institution at-large ignores whiteness because of its obsession with "race-neutral bureaucratic structures" (Ray 2019, 26). Ignoring whiteness paves the way for diversity to become a commodity. Diversity becomes commoditized when it becomes measured, assessed, and used to justify racist structures and behaviors. Diversity work literally becomes valuable to the white institutions so they can avoid things like lawsuits and public outcries.

ACRL not only participates in the commoditization of diversity but also explicitly names their diversity document as an assessable standard that can be ascribed a value. The "Diversity Standards: Cultural Competency for Academic Libraries" is designed to present academic librarians with a framework for both interacting with patrons from diverse backgrounds and recruiting diverse librarians (American Library Association 2012). Published by the Racial and Ethnic Diversity Committee, this document does the very thing Iverson critiques: it positions white people as the primary beneficiary of diversity. In fact, the document explicitly states, "Everyone can benefit from diversity." Due to the overwhelming whiteness across library spaces, in our context, "everyone" is generally white people. If a majority white population benefits from diversity, then diverse individuals become a trafficable good that can add value to a primarily white institution or organization. Later in this chapter we will explore the role of diversity residencies, but it's worth noting here that using a revolving door of temporarily employed nonwhite bodies (i.e., diversity residents) as a mechanism for diversifying explicitly treats diverse individuals as a (replaceable) trafficable good. In this light, it is unsurprising that diversity documents proliferate while the profession stays stubbornly white.

We looked at ten diversity documents from academic libraries in large and midsized public and private doctoral-granting universities, ranging from lengthy strategic plans to outreach-friendly bullet points on institutional websites. Evidence of commoditization was apparent throughout our documentary analysis. Take one example of a diversity statement that states that the institution "benefits from broad perspectives and depths of insight derived from working collaboratively with [diverse] individuals" (Columbia University Libraries, n.d.). Because we *know* that the labor around diversity work typically falls to BIPOC staff, this language suggests a kind of transaction between "diverse" individuals and staff members from dominant identity groups, wherein the latter receive enrichment and insight. But what BIPOC and other marginalized communities receive from this collaboration (besides more emotionally draining labor) is unclear.

It's especially telling that mentions of race and racism were completely absent from these documents. The absence of race points to the basic tenet of CRT that racism is such a normal, ordinary occurrence that even people writing diversity documents think it doesn't even need to be made explicit (i.e., "color blindness"). And racism cannot truly be addressed unless its ordinariness is disavowed and race is explicitly named (Delgado and Stefancic 2001, 8). In one diversity statement, the authors put forth a plan where they sought simply "respect and appreciation for all" (University of North Carolina Libraries, n.d.). Even the most comprehensive plans stubbornly refused to name whiteness (though we did sometimes notice race or ethnicity mentioned—but in reference to library users exclusively). Refusing to name whiteness disadvantages everyone outside of the white hegemonic heteronormative ableist paradigm, but does the most damage to those who have been racialized, because these power structures are rooted in categories of race and ethnicity. So, how does the commodification of diversity, and refusal to name whiteness, affect the labor around diversity work?

Aguirre gives us a clear framework for understanding what he calls "the diversity rationale in academia" through the CRT tenet of interest convergence (2010). *Interest convergence* is a term introduced to the CRT literature by Derrick Bell. It refers to the theory that racial justice work is tolerated only when it benefits the majority group (Delgado and Stefancic 2001, 177). Through an interest convergence lens, diversity initiatives are established to restore the social order that has been disrupted when nonwhites are introduced into a racially homogenous environment. Making the explicit connection between interest convergence and diversity work, Aguirre further notes that the language of diversity (instead of whiteness) allows white academics to capitalize on diversity work, in some cases even positioning *themselves* as the experts on diversity (2010, 769). To provide the "diversity value," minority librarians have no choice but to participate in their own commoditization—to participate in this exchange of our bodies, narratives, and voices in order to survive organizational cultures rooted in whiteness.

If BIPOC reject institutional pathways for diversity work, we may be viewed as "liabilities to organizational culture" (Aguirre 2010, 770). With interest convergence in mind, white academic librarians and administrators will respond only to diversity documents that don't threaten their dominance. Thus, it's unsurprising that such policies buy into the narrative of diversity as white-centered pluralism—so much so that one university's diversity statement defined diversity work as "fostering an environment of inclusion, equity, non-discrimination, and pluralism" (University of North Carolina Libraries, n.d.). Diversity work can mask discriminatory practices and even become discriminatory itself, especially considering the absence of CRT strategies in the diversity documents we examined, such as creating counterspaces for BIPOC and fostering community building (Solorzano, Ceja, and Yosso 2000). Considering the enforcement of whiteness in diversity work in higher education, Aguirre notes, "The challenge for academia is how to mask those [interest-convergent] practices so that their purpose is not readily apparent" (2010, 769).

We can further dissect how interest convergence works to create labor inequities around diversity by looking at who is doing the work—namely, diversity resident and diversity officer positions, which are held largely by BIPOC librarians. In fact, one of the diversity statements we looked at laid out an entire diversity plan centered on one labor contract: the diversity resident position their library nascently developed (University of Notre Dame, Hesburgh Libraries, n.d.). The same is true for diversity officer positions, which are often tasked with tackling unachievable goals using minimal resources, which also makes for a convenient scapegoat if these goals are not achieved. The mere existence of these positions allows universities to claim they are assessing and measuring how well they're performing diversity work, and to pat themselves on the back for the "good" they're doing, as opposed to challenging the institutional *structures* established to commoditize the labor output of these individuals. Both types of positions give PWIs the ability to check the proverbial box without having to make meaningful shifts in power. This is yet another example of interest convergence, as these positions reinforce the fact that BIPOC are permitted the space to address their concerns only when their interests converge with white interests (Bell 1980; Alemán and Alemán 2010).

INEQUITABLE LABOR DISTRIBUTIONS: ON OFFICERS, COMMITTEES, AND RESIDENTS

The apportionment of labor in any organization is always political, and this is especially true around diversity work. Libraries routinely rely on the skills, expertise, and experience of BIPOC in order to further institutional diversity, equity, and inclusion (DEI) goals. This not only plays out at the level of practice and expectation, but can also be evinced in the language used to promote those goals in the responsibilities that structure diversity-related position descriptions. Victor Ray, who joins CRT with organizational theory to address this phenomenon, aptly notes, "Once racial structures are in place, a racial ideology—or racism—arises to justify the unequal distribution of resources along racial lines" (2019, 32). This is critical to the unequal distribution of labor throughout academia and points toward the ways in which diversity work, inequitable labor practices, and the commodification of racialized labor are imbricated and mutually reinforcing. In looking at job advertisements and position descriptions, we hope to create space for dialogue around how institutions value and understand diversity work as a job responsibility and to shed light on how diversity is indexed and measured.

Few diversity officer positions exist in the library field today, even as chief diversity officer positions have proliferated in the administrative body of universities and governments. Few libraries have (or are willing to invest) the money needed to create such dedicated internal positions, and so this work and the oversight of DEI in libraries is often given to diversity committees (typically comprised of faculty members and other academic staff) and nonpermanent academic positions (such as diversity residencies). In looking at three of the few diversity officer positions that do exist (at two academic libraries and one public library), however, we noticed several things: they are routinely hired to administer strategic plans, they typically are required to coordinate training and outreach activities (University of Michigan Library, n.d.-b), and they are expected to collaborate and cross interdepartmental boundaries without necessarily having dedicated resources for doing so (such as permanent teams or assistants). Additionally, many diversity workers in both types of positions have other areas of responsibility and oversight as part of their portfolio.

The labor that constitutes DEI work, whether equitably distributed or holistically supported at the institutional level, is coherent and surprisingly (if accidentally) standardized across institutions, though there are local variations on certain themes. The primary responsibility of most library diversity officers and diversity committees is the actualization, assessment, and maintenance of internal diversity strategic plans (while also facilitating cultural competency programming and performing a variety of outreach), and their work is primarily guided by the goals and vision outlined in the plans they administer and oversee (Williams and Wade-Golden 2008). Many institutions have maintained long-standing diversity groups of one kind or another, historically focused on multicultural objectives and programming and discussion, and these groups eventually saw their responsibilities include the drafting or management of strategic plans relevant to DEI. Others created diversity councils and committees as part of their putative commitment to diversity. Frequently, the existence of such committees (as well as that of officer positions or residencies) is the extent of investment required of an institution, with the creation of a strategic plan as an end in itself.

Our analysis of strategic plan documents, position descriptions, and job ads for diversity officers and library residents (as well as diversity committee charges) suggests a stubborn resistance to recognizing the necessity of dismantling oppression (viz. whiteness) as part of DEI work. These documents further support the commodification of diversity in higher education in general and libraries in particular, focusing on DEI work's benefit to the institution itself. The University of Michigan (UM) Library Diversity Alliance Resident Librarian program description makes this process of racial commodification (of diversity itself, as well as of resident librarians) clear: as one of their key program objectives, they include "Enhance UM's reputation as an institution that supports, trains and mentors diverse librarians" (University of Michigan Library, n.d.-a)

Library residency programs are contested terrain in the landscape of institutional progressivism, and the librarians who move through these programs are burdened not only by the responsibilities that characterize their work and roles, but also by the beliefs and projections that structure their existence in the organization (Dankowski 2018). Even if they are not given responsibilities that are explicitly relevant to DEI, by their very nature these positions are meant to perform and complete/further diversity objectives. In other words, many residents will do diversity work as an official part of their area of responsibility, and many more will find themselves expected to fulfill those obligations in addition to a full workload (Galvan 2015). Nearly all of them, however, will provide labor for and benefit to their institutions (in terms of reputation, identity, sometimes even funding) that is not fully valued, compensated, or acknowledged. As we reviewed position descriptions and job ads, it was consistently unclear how these roles were, or would be, resourced to complete complicated work that necessarily requires support and collective engagement. The problem of residencies with respect to labor is also a function of their relative precarity (and brevity, given most residencies last between one and three years) compared to permanent positions (Hathcock 2019).

Whether or not diversity work is written into their positions, it is frequently an expectation of library residents that they will provide the bulk of support for diversity initiatives, and this responsibility is difficult to resist or challenge, as a result of white fragility and institutional racism. If they are to progress in the field, or even just find another job, they need positive reviews and recommendations or a narrative that is amenable and intelligible to other institutions—and ideally, both. By creating residency positions and programs, whether directly in support of diversity objectives or as an act that itself is meant to fulfill diversity-related commitments, institutions are able to offset and offload a complicated array of responsibilities and expectations onto racially marginalized librarians, which enables other, nonmarginalized librarians to not have to do or engage with this work. Further, though these initiatives and programs nominally benefit everyone, in a profession in which whiteness clearly predominates, the voices that create and structure these programs are mostly (often, only) white; library diversity residents are frequently, even if inadvertently, put into a position in which they and their labor are commoditized for and evaluated by whiteness as a result. As a result of the ways in which their efforts are directed toward and structured by white objectives, and because their positions are temporary, marginalized people in library diversity residencies may never see the benefits of the time, energy, and labor they invest in this work or in supporting institutional goals they so rarely have a voice in creating.

LIVED LABOR EXPERIENCES

For us, this chapter wouldn't be complete without utilizing CRT to tell our counterstories, to centrally position the ways in which our labor has been exploited and devalued. For "experiential knowledge that directly names race and racism…create[s] counterstories to the dominant ideology," promoting a kind of "collective empowerment and knowledge reconstruction" (Sleeter 2012, 492). First, we acknowledge our positionalities. We write this from myriad perspectives—Blackness, queerness, Latinidad, femme, indigeneity, nonbinary; from a perspective of living with chronic pain, chronic illness, and mental illness. We each also work, and have previously worked, in dramatically different academic library and campus environments, with a variety of professional expectations, and more. The ways in which we experience labor inequity, as it relates to diversity work and beyond, vary just as widely as our identities do.

For one of us, inequitable labor began while they worked at a large, private research university, where diversity and equity work was publicly embraced by higher administrative staff but never propagated downward to counter structural microaggressions occurring at the departmental level. Because this author constantly navigated misogynoir (a particular type of misogyny directed at Black women and Black femmes), they had a strong interest in engaging in diversity work at the library and campus levels. But this translated into that work becoming hypervisible and seen as a valuable commodity capable of being monetized through websites and other public-facing material meant to entice donors. In fact, anyone who publicly engaged in diversity work was then tapped for participation on associated initiatives. It was no wonder that this author spent the bulk of their time working with other BIPOC library staff on behalf of the institution, while white peers and colleagues did no more than perform the correct responses (or often the correct silences) in departmental meetings, rarely contributing to the labor around diversity work. Since they moved on, commodified diversity initiatives have continued to define this author's professional experiences.

For another, the labor inequities around diversity have played out through both formal and informal structures. In one instance, they were placed on an institutional diversity committee almost immediately after starting a new position, without ever being formally asked. The assumption was that due to the dearth of diverse faculty, there was no question about whether this extra labor was voluntary, despite being well above and beyond an already full workload. Intersectional oppression in the diversity committee itself became apparent in a committee meeting where we reviewed an institution-wide inclusive pedagogy training program. This online training explicitly mentioned gender, sexuality, and disabilities, but nowhere did it mention race or ethnicity. In fact, the text read as though race wasn't a barrier that needed to be considered. But rather than rethink the training program approaches when this was brought up, the chair of the committee tasked a subcommittee with coming up with additional frameworks that addressed race and ethnicity. Whom did they ask? A team of Black women and women of color.

Beyond these formal structures for diversity work, the informal diversity work expectations often take the form of recruitment and mentoring. And there is rarely any choice in the matter; we must do this to prove our value to the institutions and administrators that see us as a commodity. For one of the authors, this value manifests in the form of serving on search committee after search committee as the token representative of their race. In another expression, informal expectations around relationship building with marginalized and nondominant campus communities often results in a labor tax that is not recognized in promotional and tenure documents.

ERADICATING INEQUITY: WHAT MIGHT "JUST" LABOR PRACTICES LOOK LIKE?

Doing the work to radically and responsibly dismantle inequality is hard. In many cases, it's also emotionally and mentally draining. But doing the work can also be liberating. It can free and inspire; it can connect marginalized folks dispersed across the institution, for the betterment of all. In the spirit of CRT theorists and speculative writers, who allow themselves to postulate futures and imagine directions, in this section we explore what systemic change might look like. We embody the practice of adrienne maree brown's *Emergent Strategy*, and the radical, awe-inspiring work of visionary writers such as Octavia Butler, where imagining just futures provides an arable beginning. Here, we allow ourselves to dream.

For us in this moment, equitable labor practices look like:

• **Shifting the labor of managing dominant fragilities away from marginalized folks.** In the same way that white fragility is draining, other fragilities are just as bad. When you fuck up, misgender someone, lead with cultural biases and assumptions, or perform any kind of micro- or macroaggression, and someone calls you out and you start to lash out at them, work on that fragility away from the person(s) you've harmed. Do the self-work, then come back to collective efforts later.

• **Compensating staff well, and increasing transparency around salary.** In librarianship, everything functions around an ethos of service linked to vocational awe (Ettarh 2017), but the prestige of our institutions, or the (unrealistic) expectation that our efforts might actually shift institutional climates, **will not feed us.** Equitable labor means reassessing the pay gaps between marginalized staff and those who fit into white hegemonic standards (while also acknowledging the credentialed divide that often relegates BIPOC to library assistant roles with lesser pay), bumping the salaries of existing staff accordingly, and being transparent about salary at every step in our careers—*especially* when expecting us to lead the lion's share of your diversity efforts. In particular, post salaries in your job ads (especially if those roles are resident positions or require a heavy amount diversity and equity work).

• Having **fearless library leadership without platitudes.** We're talking about executive administrators—library deans and directors, associate university librarians, and university librarians—whose ethos involves passionately and fearlessly defending its staff, conducting thorough reviews around organizationally and departmentally intensive projects to see who's had to carry efforts alone, and advocating at executive campus-wide levels for better pay and treatment of its staff. Yes, higher education is a business; that means the buck may stop with an institution's trustees, or its donor base, but there is no reason for any leader to tell a staff member to expect poor compensation and overburdening because that's how it's always been. Do better.

- Having **expansive views on leadership that include critical perspectives.** Often we have found ourselves overburdened not just by executive administrators but also by the inequitable labor practices of white peers who lead committees, task forces, or departmental projects. Because these forms of leadership aren't formally recognized in strict academic library hierarchies and organizational charts, it is all too easy for labor inequities to be swept under the rug. As a profession, we must reckon with how power is distributed outside of formal leadership positions, which starts with **everyone** recognizing the ways in which they lead in library workplaces. Further, library leadership should hold all staff accountable for their actions. Otherwise, nothing changes.

- **Majority groups volunteering on collective diversity efforts, in ways both large and small.** If you are white, or otherwise privileged, be the one to take notes and distribute them after meetings; be the one to send out information regarding upcoming diversity training(s), so that when your colleagues want to complain, it's not directed at the BIPOC organizers who've likely been roped into organizing it.

- Having **values-based professional review systems** that credit the labor of this work, making space for it by giving folks dedicated time during the workday to take on such projects. For example, one author wrote the majority of this chapter using research days, which allowed them to write from home and compose thoughts in an environment that was conducive to doing the work and didn't add extra stress. Libraries, at large, should consider adopting such policies, or explore adjacent benefits, given that the "research days" terminology may exclude those working in public, school, or special libraries. Other examples include more highly valuing diversity work in tenure review processes or, frankly, any performance review process; meaningfully incorporating diversity work into job descriptions; and considering review processes that allow staff to review their management for competency in this and other areas of work.

- Having **equal standards for engagement in diversity work across the board.** It's the work of everyone, including deans and department heads. And it's not work that should exist "in addition to" one's full workload.

- Having **transparency in institutional documentation.** Specifically name "racism" in your diversity statements. In job ads, frame your institution's current challenges and areas for growth alongside the general blurb that details the size of your collections and other celebratory tidbits. How radical would it be to read, "We've recently begun a series of internal conversations around tone policing in meetings and committees here," next to "We're proud of the size and depth of our library collection"? Let folks know what they're really getting into when considering your institution as a place of work.

- **Learning to value the complexity of diversity work, and giving properly resourced opportunities for leading it to those willing and capable of taking it on.** It's not only done in contained, controlled environments and committees; it's part of the daily fabric of interacting and existing in academia and society. Therefore, what the "work" looks like is going to vary on any given day, and thus burnout happens that much faster. Resourcing to dismantle burnout altogether should be the goal. Diversity workers need to be given proper staff, authority, and space to work through the nuances of the interactions that lead to discrimination and racism within the white hegemonic systems that comprise our academic library institutions.
- **Reflecting critically on how Westernized, capitalist labor practices disproportionately affect staff of color.** When institutions fail to support students of color, it's minoritized staff and faculty who are expected to mentor, guide, and emotionally support these students. Consider that these same staff take that (and other) work home with them, often leading to heavy bouts of emotional labor and being overworked to the point of sickness. Equitable, just labor practices mean moving beyond current framings and critiques and applying CRT to better understand how race intersects with the system's ableist, sexist, and White Supremacist underpinnings. And then, be prepared to adjust schedules accordingly; understand that without flextime and boundaries between work and life, we cannot exist as our full and healthy selves because hegemonic whiteness deeply affects our physical and emotional wellness.

If all that wasn't enough, consider looking at the speculated futures that a group of library workers brainstormed at "Moving Beyond Race 101: Speculative Futuring for Equity" (Brown et al. 2019), a panel/workshop presented the 2019 ACRL Conference. We invite our readers to engage with the question, what do equitable labor practices look like for you? Collectively, we hope to ideate a future in which we liberate ourselves from top-down institutional diversity schemas—which both limit how BIPOC library workers engage with diversity and exploit our labor—so we can truly work toward racial justice.

BIBLIOGRAPHY

Aguirre, Adalberto, Jr. 2010. "Diversity as Interest-Convergence in Academia: A Critical Race Theory Story." *Social Identities* 16 (6): 763–774. https://doi.org/10.1080/13504630.2010.524782.

Ahmed, Sara. 2007. "'You End Up Doing the Document Rather than Doing the Doing': Diversity, Race Equality and the Politics of Documentation." *Ethnic and Racial Studies* 30 (4): 590–609. https://doi.org/10.1080/01419870701356015.

Alemán, Enrique, Jr., and Sonya M. Alemán. 2010. "'Do Latin@ Interests Always Have to 'Converge' with White Interests?': (Re)Claiming Racial Realism and Interest-Convergence in Critical Race Theory Praxis." *Race Ethnicity and Education* 13 (1): 1–21. https://doi.org/10.1080/13613320903549644.

American Library Association. 2017. "ACRL Diversity Alliance FAQ." Association of College and Research Libraries (ACRL). March 6, 2017. http://www.ala.org/acrl/issues/alliancefaq.

Bell, Derrick A. 1980. "Brown v. Board of Education and the Interest-Convergence Dilemma." *Harvard Law Review* 93 (3): 518–533. https://doi.org/10.2307/1340546.

Brown, Jennifer, and Sofia Leung. 2018. "Authenticity vs. Professionalism: Being True to Ourselves at Work." In *Pushing the Margins: Women of Color and Intersectionality in LIS*, edited by Rose L. Chou and Annie Pho, 329–348. Sacramento, CA: Library Juice Press.

Chou, Rose L., and Annie Pho, eds. 2018. *Pushing the Margins: Women of Color and Intersectionality in LIS*. Sacramento, CA: Library Juice Press.

Columbia University Libraries. n.d. "Commit to Inclusion | Strategic Directions." Columbia University Libraries. Accessed May 10, 2019. https://strategicdirections.library.columbia.edu/seek-difference.

Dankowski, Terra. 2018. "The Reality of Residency Programs." *American Libraries Magazine*, September 30, 2018. https://americanlibrariesmagazine.org/blogs/the-scoop/jclc2018-reality-residency-programs/.

Delgado, Richard, and Jean Stefancic, eds. 2001. *Critical Race Theory: An Introduction*. New York: New York University Press.

Ettarh, Fobazi. 2017. "Vocational Awe?" *WTF Is a Radical Librarian, Anyway?* (blog), May 30, 2017. https://fobaziettarh.wordpress.com/2017/05/30/vocational-awe/.

Ferretti, Jennifer. 2019. "Libraries We Here: Resources." We Here. April 16, 2019.

Galvan, Angela. 2015. "Soliciting Performance, Hiding Bias: Whiteness and Librarianship." *In the Library with the Lead Pipe*, June 3. http://www.inthelibrarywiththeleadpipe.org/2015/soliciting-performance-hiding-bias-whiteness-and-librarianship/.

Hathcock, April. 2015. "White Librarianship in Blackface: Diversity Initiatives in LIS." *In the Library with the Lead Pipe*, October 7, 2015. http://www.inthelibrarywiththeleadpipe.org/2015/lis-diversity/.

Hathcock, April. 2019. "Why Don't You Want to Keep Us?" *At the Intersection* (blog), January 18, 2019. https://aprilhathcock.wordpress.com/2019/01/18/why-dont-you-want-to-keep-us/.

Imarisha, Walidah. 2019. "How Science Fiction Can Re-envision Justice." *Bitch Media*, February 11, 2015. https://www.bitchmedia.org/article/rewriting-the-future-prison-abolition-science-fiction.

Iverson, Susan Van Deventer. 2005. "A Policy Discourse Analysis of U.S. Land-Grant University Diversity Action Plans." EdD diss., University of Maine. https://digitalcommons.library.umaine.edu/etd/1769.

Iverson, Susan Van Deventer. 2007. "Camouflaging Power and Privilege: A Critical Race Analysis of University Diversity Policies." *Educational Administration Quarterly* 43 (5): 586–611. https://doi.org/10.1177/0013161X07307794.

Jones, Kenneth, and Tema Okun. 2001. "White Supremacy Culture." *Dismantling Racism: A Workbook for Social Change Groups*, presented at Changework 2001. http://www.cwsworkshop.org/PARC_site_B/dr-culture.html.

Ladson-Billings, Gloria, and William F. Tate. 1995. "Toward a Critical Race Theory of Education." *Teachers College Record* 97 (1): 47–68.

Mississippi Civil Rights Project. n.d. "The Tougaloo Nine." Mississippi Civil Rights Project. Accessed June 2, 2019. https://mscivilrightsproject.org/hinds/organization-hinds/the-tougaloo-nine/.

Ray, Victor. 2019. "A Theory of Racialized Organizations." *American Sociological Review* 84 (1): 26–53. https://doi.org/10.1177/0003122418822335.

Rogers, Rebecca, and Melissa Mosley. 2006. "Racial Literacy in a Second-Grade Classroom: Critical Race Theory, Whiteness Studies, and Literacy Research." *Reading Research Quarterly* 41 (4): 462–495. https://doi.org/10.1598/RRQ.41.4.3.

Sleeter, Christine E. 2012. "Critical Race Theory and Education." In *Encyclopedia of Diversity in Education*, edited by James Banks, 491–494. Thousand Oaks, CA: Sage. https://doi.org/10.4135/9781452218533.n154.

Solorzano, Daniel, Miguel Ceja, and Tara Yosso. 2000. "Critical Race Theory, Racial Microaggressions, and Campus Racial Climate: The Experiences of African American College Students." *Journal of Negro Education* 69 (1/2): 60–73.

University of Michigan Library. n.d.-a. "Diversity Alliance Resident Librarian." University of Michigan Library. Accessed June 2, 2019. https://www.lib.umich.edu/diversity-equity-inclusion-accessibility/diversity-alliance-resident-librarian.

University of Michigan Library. n.d.-b. "Jeffery Witt." University of Michigan Library. Accessed June 2, 2019. https://www.lib.umich.edu/users/wittjef.

University of North Carolina Libraries. 2019. "Diversity Statement—UNC Chapel Hill Libraries." University of North Carolina Libraries. Accessed April 6. https://library.unc.edu/about/diversity/.

University of Notre Dame, Hesburgh Libraries. n.d. "Diversity and Inclusion | Hesburgh Libraries." Hesburgh Libraries. Accessed May 26, 2019. https://library.nd.edu/diversity-inclusion.

Williams, Damon A., and Katrina C. Wade-Golden. 2008. "The Complex Mandate of a Chief Diversity Officer." *Chronicle of Higher Education*, September 26, 2008. https://www.chronicle.com/article/The-Complex-Mandate-of-a-Chief/9952.

4

TRIBAL CRITICAL RACE THEORY IN ZUNI PUEBLO
Information Access in a Cautious Community

Miranda H. Belarde-Lewis (Zuni/Tlingit) and Sarah R. Kostelecky (Zuni Pueblo)

If I had to characterize the Zuni or their Pueblo neighbors in one word the word would be *silent*.
—Larry McMurtry

Despite many attempts by Zuni Pueblo people to remain private about our culture, a continuous stream of colonizers, anthropologists, settlers, and tourists have never respected our privacy. Since the late 1800s, Zuni people have been under intense research scrutiny by ethnographers and anthropologists (Colwell 2017; McFeely 2001). Research by outsiders has resulted in the publication and dissemination of ancient sacred knowledge, esoteric traditions, and religious practices—without free, prior, and informed consent of Zunis. The information and knowledge collected was not the author's information to share or the readers' to know. In addition, subsequent publications build on this unethical work and continue to depict us only as historic people, ignoring our contemporary lives, which are a mix of our traditional culture and modern conveniences. All of these factors have resulted in a community-wide distrust of research, common in many Native and Indigenous communities (Smith 2012).

We are members of Zuni Pueblo. We are also library and information science/studies (LIS) professionals. We are part of a steadily growing number of Native scholars actively engaged in responsible research practices that privilege and center tribal sovereignty with regard to each tribe's information resources. We recognize that the cultural desire to remain private about our knowledge systems can clash with foundational purposes of libraries, which primarily support full access to any and all information. We also recognize that a fraught history of the representation of our people embedded in Western collecting practices means that the information available does not adequately serve Zuni people seeking information about Zuni subject areas. As researchers and tribal members, we realize there is a distinct need for accurate and appropriate information about Zunis, particularly for Zuni people.

Such accurate and appropriate information should be created by Zuni people, sharing our voices and perspectives on who we are, where we came from, and how we will continue. Many information sources already exist; some are written, but some are documented in other forms such as stories, songs, artwork, and ceremonies. Considering the importance of this information, accessing the content from any of these forms should be done respectfully and in accordance with Zuni epistemologies.

To that purpose, the Pueblo has created its own cultural institutions, and has initiated a number of information-sharing projects in an effort to retain authority over what information gets shared and for what purpose, for both tribal members and nonmembers. Our institutions include the archeology program, the archives office, and the Zuni Cultural Resources Advisory Team (ZCRAT), comprising the leaders of various religious groups in Zuni. One of the projects, discussed later, is the Zuni Map Art Project, initiated by the A:shiwi A:wan Museum and Heritage Center (AAMHC). The formation of Zuni institutions centering Zuni voices are examples of counternarratives or counterstories, "a method of telling the stories of people whose experiences are not often told" (Solórzano and Yosso 2002, 32) and a tool often used by Critical Race Theorists (Parsons, Rhodes, and Brown 2011). Native peoples' efforts to challenge erroneous misinformation circulated about us, without our knowledge or consent, serve as a response to the long history of exploitation of our culture by outsiders. Counternarratives reinforce sovereignty and self-determination by allowing us to shape the output of information regarding us to be based on our sociopolitical, lived realities, realities virtually ignored by non-Natives.

In this chapter we engage Tribal Critical Race Theory (TribalCrit) to examine three projects that share Zuni cultural information and knowledge. This theory provides a relevant framework, as it is based on the acknowledgment that "colonization is endemic to society" (Brayboy 2005, 428), and for Indigenous people, this reality affects all aspects of our experience: personal, professional, historical, and contemporary. TribalCrit empowers us as Native women in academia as it recognizes stories as data and provides space to discuss our tribal knowledge practices while also thoughtfully critiquing how our LIS field often disregards Indigenous knowledge and Indigenous experts.

The projects discussed here place TribalCrit into practice and illustrate strategies Zunis have used to access tribal knowledge in our own community while being respectful of sensitive and privileged information. Finally, we include a dialogue between us about a current project to digitize Zuni language materials and our thoughts about balancing roles as academics and tribal members. Our goal is to highlight projects that are contributing to the continuance of our culture, traditions, and lifeways. These projects are not replacing, but are complementing the millennia-old methods Shiwis (our name for ourselves) have developed to document and pass on our various ways of knowing. While we primarily focus on our specific tribal community, the themes of information taking and importance of tribal philosophies as guiding principles likely characterize other Native American experiences. Non-Indigenous LIS practitioners should consider these concepts in relation to their local tribal communities, Native collections, and outreach services.

To this end, we will not begin our discussion with the linear layout typically found in the field of Native and Indigenous studies by first providing a background of who and where our community is located. Instead, we choose to begin by addressing the possible uses of TribalCrit for Indigenous LIS scholars and practitioners. Our goal is to examine the relevance and applicability of TribalCrit for our fellow Indigenous LIS professionals, tribal community members, and non-Indigenous allies before highlighting the potentials of applying the TribalCrit framework to projects and information institutions at work in our home community of Zuni Pueblo.

TRIBAL CRITICAL RACE THEORY

Developed by Lumbee scholar Bryan McKinley Jones Brayboy in 2005, Tribal Critical Race Theory, or TribalCrit, draws inspiration and guidance from the fields of Critical Race Theory (CRT), anthropology, political/legal theory, political science, American Indian literatures, education, and American Indian studies to provide a framework that acknowledges the complicated and complex history of Native peoples existing and resisting in the United States. Brayboy posits that TribalCrit, while influenced greatly by CRT, "is rooted in the multiple, nuanced, and historically and geographically-located epistemologies and ontologies found in Indigenous communities" (Brayboy 2005, 427).

While CRT is a useful theoretical lens to examine issues of power, law, and race, its limitations when applied to Native communities in the US context are, ironically, *because* of "race." American Indians and Alaska Natives, as we are federally identified and subsequently labeled, are not just an ethnic and racial category of minoritized peoples; we hold *a different political status* from other US citizens (US Department of the Interior, Bureau of Indian Affairs, n.d.). Our political status as political entities, complete with our sovereign rights as governments, was acknowledged with treaties signed between government agents and tribal leaders and has been affirmed through an entire canon of state, federal, and Supreme Court cases (US Department of the Interior, Bureau of Indian Affairs, n.d.). The complicated and complex history Brayboy references is different for every Native community, even as we share many of the same struggles under the weight of colonialism. While CRT identifies racism and various systems of oppression meant to limit access to education for People of Color, it lacks a widespread acknowledgment that the entirety of Native ways of knowing—including, but certainly not limited to, our conceptions of what constitutes information and knowledge, and our specific protocols regarding the sharing of our information resources—has been specifically targeted for eradication and erasure. While the methods of elimination of Native culture and communities have morphed from the blatant (outright genocide, containment through the reservation systems, forced assimilation through the cruelty of the board and residential schools) to the quietly insidious (continued land theft, predatory economics, and broken treaties) (Fixico 2008; Simpson 2014), the challenges specific to Native communities are not central to CRT. TribalCrit was born out of this gap and this need within the CRT space, and thus it has at its core the needs of Native communities.

The nine basic tenets of TribalCrit are listed below; bolded tenets are directly referenced throughout the chapter:

1. **Colonization is endemic to society.**
2. US policies toward Indigenous peoples are rooted in imperialism, White Supremacy, and a desire for material gain.
3. Indigenous peoples occupy a liminal space that accounts for both the political and racialized natures of our identities.
4. **Indigenous peoples have a desire to obtain and forge tribal sovereignty, tribal autonomy, self-determination, and self-identification.**
5. The concepts of culture, knowledge, and power take on new meaning when examined through an Indigenous lens.
6. **Governmental policies and educational policies toward Indigenous peoples are intimately linked around the problematic goal of assimilation.**
7. **Tribal philosophies, beliefs, customs, traditions, and visions for the future are central to understanding the lived realities of Indigenous peoples, but**

they also illustrate the differences and adaptability among individuals and groups.

8. Stories are not separate from theory; they make up theory and are, therefore, real and legitimate sources of data and ways of being.

9. Theory and practice are connected in deep and explicit ways such that scholars must work toward social change. (Brayboy 2005, 429–430)

Tribal Critical Race Theory is a tool that should be broadly utilized in library and information science (LIS) to recognize the problematic processes in the field that serve to marginalize and even erase the Indigenous experience. While strides have been taken by some to acknowledge Indigenous systems of organizing information and knowledge in mainstream information institutions (Webster and Doyle 2008) and the pervasive colonialism in the subfield of knowledge organization (Littletree, Belarde-Lewis, and Duarte 2020), there is ample room for critique of the LIS profession when it comes to incorporating Indigenous ways of knowing into the field. TribalCrit has thus far not been utilized by the LIS field, and we use it here to discuss three Zuni Pueblo information resources created and shared in ways that respect tribal knowledge structures and for the purpose of strengthening our culture and traditions.

COLONIZATION IS ENDEMIC TO SOCIETY

A discussion of the history of any Indigenous community must include an acknowledgment and analysis of the destructive nature of colonization on the bodies, languages, spiritual practices, and homelands of Native peoples. The pervasive and long-standing nature of colonialism and the actions that uphold and maintain colonization are numerous and include the privileging of written sources over all other forms of documentation. American Indian communities in the US who adopted a constitutional system with public elections in the early twentieth century (Wyaco 1998, 67–70) began keeping records about tribal meetings, documenting policies and tribal resolutions. While easier from a bureaucratic standpoint, these records conflicted with millennia-old formats of transferring knowledge, which in Zuni Pueblo include the oral tradition, ceremonies, and art. Similar to nearly all Native communities, Zuni people have experienced a diminished reliance on the oral tradition as our governance model has shifted from a theocracy to public elections (Isaac 2007, 17). While the religious leadership in the community is highly respected and the ceremonial calendar determines a large part of the community's social structure, we acknowledge that our elected governance replicates Western political structure; this is further confirmation that colonization is endemic to us all (TribalCrit tenet 1) and impels Native people to address colonization within our own systems.

Indigenous peoples have a desire to obtain and forge tribal sovereignty, tribal autonomy, self-determination, and self-identification.

In 1978, Lakota scholar Vine Deloria Jr. wrote "The Right to Know," a paper that outlined what he saw as an "imperative need" of Native communities—the need to know. He wrote that Indian communities need "to know the past, to know the traditional alternatives advocated by their ancestors, to know the specific experiences of their communities, and to know about the world that surrounds them in the same intimate manner they once knew the plains, mountains, deserts, rivers and woods" (Deloria 1978, 13). The paper was prepared for the 1978 White House Preconference on Indian Library and Information Services on or near Reservations. In addition to asserting that Native peoples should be able to know the specifics of legislation regarding them and their lands, Deloria stated that Native peoples specifically negotiated for education provisions in their treaties. He argued that if libraries had been as much of a public right at the time of treaty signings, they certainly would have been specifically negotiated for at the time. Bringing libraries into a present-day context, Deloria called for "direct funding *from the federal government to tribes for library, information and archival services* and [said] every effort should be made in joint planning to transmit the major bulk of records dealing with tribal histories to modern and adequate facilities on the reservations" (Deloria 1978, 13; emphasis added).

As Native communities continue to create and sustain their own libraries, archives, and museums, these tribal information institutions are uniquely positioned to forge and strengthen tribal sovereignty. As tribes assert our positions in defense of our treaty rights and our abilities to self-determine the future of Native communities, tribal information institutions will continue to play a pivotal role. Granted, the relationship between Indigenous peoples and the information field, specifically libraries and museums, is a complicated one, one discussed briefly in the next section.

LIBRARIES AND INDIGENOUS PEOPLES

Libraries have a complex history in relation to Indigenous peoples, considering the fact that governmental policies have an assimilationist agenda, which privileges the written word and ignores the many manifestations of Indigenous knowledge (TribalCrit tenet 6). Often the materials in libraries reflect the stereotypes of tribal communities, rarely including our voices (Bowers, Crowe, and Keeran 2017). The privileging of non-Native perspectives and consideration of outsiders as "experts"—instead of the Indigenous people who embody their cultures and worldviews—has often led to weariness and skepticism from Native people in considering libraries as resources (Burke 2007). Perhaps not surprisingly, less than 1 percent of academic librarians in the United States identify as Native American (American Library Association 2012); therefore, these embedded colonial practices in libraries are rarely acknowledged by information institutions.

Unfortunately, there are a multitude of examples illustrating ways in which the library enacts colonial practice. Standard cataloging, description, and metadata used in libraries ignores Indigenous place-names, utilizes inconsistent spelling and nam-ing of peoples, and uses terms meant to erase the abuse and violence enacted on Indigenous peoples (Webster and Doyle 2008; Cooper et al. 2019). These practices are known barriers to Indigenous studies researchers, both Native and non-Native (Cooper et al. 2019), ultimately counteracting the stated aim of libraries, which is to enable knowledge access.

These factors (mistrust of Western cultural institutions, few Indigenous librarians in the profession, inaccurate descriptive metadata) lead to the common occurrence of Indigenous researchers inadvertently discovering tribal knowledge they are not meant to access, or do not want to access. Information-sharing practices in Zuni are based on a variety of factors including gender, clan group, religious initiation, family group, and age, but libraries have often disregarded our protocols for access-ing knowledge, either through ignorance or indifference. We have both experienced reading a description of a ceremony or sacred being, or viewing a photograph of an item we think might have ceremonial purposes—and only then realizing we should not be accessing this information due to our community role. Based on our con-versations with other Zuni people who regularly conduct research for education or professional purposes, we know these disturbing situations are common.

Yet there are models for improvement in cultural institutions, developed either in collaboration with or solely by and for Indigenous people. For example, The Mashan-tucket Pequot Thesaurus of American Indian Terminology is a controlled vocabu-lary developed to better reflect Indigenous knowledge classification, for use in the Mashantucket Pequot Museum (Littletree and Metoyer 2015). The Makah Culture and Research Center in Neah Bay, Washington, houses an extensive archeological collec-tion and community interviews documenting the community's millennia-old history of whaling (Bowechop and Erikson 2005). There is also Sípnuuk, the Karuk tribe's digi-tal repository, built on the Mukurtu content management system (Karuk Tribe et al. 2007). Mukurtu is an open-source content management system (CMS) developed for

Indigenous community use, as it allows a variety of levels of access to cultural materials, recognizing and allowing for traditional knowledge system organization (Center for Digital Scholarship and Curation, n.d.). These successful projects illustrate the possibilities for truly representative libraries that reflect Indigenous worldviews rather than obfuscate the history and contemporary lives lived by Indigenous people today.

HOME: ZUNI PUEBLO

Now we shift focus to Zuni Pueblo, first describing the people and the place.

Zuni Pueblo is located on the Zuni Reservation about twenty minutes from the eastern Arizona border. Zuni is the largest of the nineteen pueblos in New Mexico, with a population of about 12,000 residents (Zuni Pueblo Census Office, in conversation with the author, 2018). The Pueblos have common elements of lifestyles and philosophies while maintaining their unique identities (Sando and All Indian Pueblo Council 1976, 4). Like the other pueblo communities, Zuni is rich in culture, language, and ceremonial practices that have existed for thousands of years. The Zuni leadership moved from a theocracy to an elected council structure in the 1930s (Wyaco 1998, 67–68), although it is still the religious leaders of the community who confer authority on the incoming elected leader every four years. The spiritual obligations of the Zuni people guide the social calendar, with residents contributing in both direct and tangential ways. Zuni traditions would not continue without the Zuni language, which is a linguistic isolate, completely different from the language families of the nineteen other pueblos (Sando and All Indian Pueblo Council 1976, 4–5).

While such description gives the facts about Zuni, we also want to share what it is like to be a Zuni tribal member. Spirituality and humor are the threads that run throughout Zuni life. Shiwis like to laugh and enjoy spending time with our families, often cooking and eating together, which is especially important around times of ceremony. Though it is common to hear the Zuni language being spoken at home and in school, many of us are not fluent; however, most of us can greet, joke, and pray in our language. Art has always been a way for us to share Zuni stories and culture within our community. Zuni is known for our artists, who create jewelry, pottery, and 2-D art grounded in traditional symbols and imagery.

Zuni people know the stories of why we live at Halona I'diwana (the Middle Place), how we survived attacks by Spanish conquistadors and other tribes, and why we have to value and cherish our culture by continuing our traditional ways. Our ancestors and our children are counting on us. They guide us in our daily lives, and we engage in library/archive/museum work always thinking of them.

INFORMATION PRACTICES IN ZUNI

With the religious cycles guiding daily life, information about the ceremonies shared orally in the Zuni language is powerful and valuable. We grew up knowing that information is shared with individuals based on one's clan group, specific roles a male family member may have in a religious group, life-altering events, and other factors. Zuni people understand that information and knowledge are powerful; we understand and accept that there is some information that is known by only a select few in our village (Enote 2011, 4). This tacit knowledge is also recognized by outsiders. Described by a non-Zuni researcher, Zuni knowledge is shared in both the familial realm (everyday use) and the differentially privileged realm (with others in the same religious society) (Isaac 2007, 35). Information about all aspects of Zuni lifeways is vital to our continued existence; therefore, we have developed unique systems of knowledge organization, sharing, and access (TribalCrit tenet 5). However, these systems are consistently disregarded by non-Native outsiders, including researchers from across the academic spectrum.

ZUNI PEOPLE AS SUBJECTS OF RESEARCH

Former Zuni Pueblo governor Malcolm Bowekaty is straightforward in his judgment of outsider research with our people as the subjects: "Research can be dangerous and divisive for our people" (2002, 148). He mentions the harmful history of ethnographic research done in the pueblo as a direct reason for the creation of a tribal council review process for potential research to be conducted today. While Bowekaty focused on harm related to health and biological research, he conversely recognizes that some research can be useful. His point is that research *about* Zunis needs to *benefit* Zuni people. As tribal members who are also part of the LIS profession, we are acutely aware of the contradictions between these conflicting worldviews and exercise great care when working with our community or advocating for Native peoples in the LIS field.

The following section discusses how the application of a TribalCrit lens can be used as a methodological and epistemological tool when analyzing Native projects, particularly when the Native community initiating these projects has a century-long distrust of information-gathering institutions.

APPLYING TRIBALCRIT TO A CAUTIOUS COMMUNITY

Although Western cultural institutions are often problematic for Indigenous people, we have also seen promising examples of how these organizations can be decolonized and Indigenized. As Native peoples develop our own institutions and center our ways of knowing, we create counternarratives that focus on what we envision for, and how we will continue in, the future (Sumida Huaman and Brayboy 2017). Next, we review examples of such counterstories that Zuni cultural institutions have created to share Zuni knowledge within the community, illustrating TribalCrit tenets in practice.

TOOLS OF ART, HUMOR, AND HISTORY

The A:shiwi A:wan Museum and Heritage Center (AAMHC) was founded in 1992 (Isaac 2007). Its purpose since the beginning has been to reflect the living culture, language, and *ways of knowing of the Zuni people, for the Zuni people*. The AAMHC is an eco-museum, not focused on building a collection of objects to care for but instead primarily focused on community outreach and long-term projects that center Zuni history (Isaac 2007). The AAMHC has actively worked to correct misinformation about Zuni people documented through the work of outsiders. Two examples of the tribe retelling history through projects centering the Zuni perspective are the book *A Zuni Artist Looks at Frank Hamilton Cushing*, with cartoons drawn by tribal member Phil Hughte, and the Zuni Map Art Project. *A Zuni Artist* was published by the A:shiwi A:wan Museum and Heritage Center in 1994. Cushing was one of the first ethnographers to come to Zuni, in 1879 (McFeely 2001), and he published extensively about Zuni culture. Many of his writings are still referenced today, with outsiders recognizing him as an expert on our community. He was well known in his time because he came to be regarded as a member of the pueblo: he was initiated into a religious society, learned the language, and generally lived like a Zuni. However, Cushing, as the Zuni artist Hughte notes, "dug too far" and violated the trust bestowed on him by the community (Hughte, Sneddon, and Ruiz 2003). Appallingly, Cushing created and sold replicas of religious items when he returned to his post at the Smithsonian (Colwell 2017, 25), had portraits taken while wearing the replica (Hughte 1994, 96, 105), and continued to act unethically by publishing what he had learned in confidence while living as a citizen of the community (Hughte 1994, 112–113). While Cushing did advocate on the tribe's behalf in Washington, D.C., and helped protect some Zuni traditional lands, he is a derided figure in Zuni even today.

Considered a master Zuni painter during his lifetime, Phil Hughte was interested in Frank Cushing's experience in Zuni and challenged himself in an unconventional art form to draw a series of one-panel cartoons depicting how Zuni people may have perceived Cushing during that time (Hughte 1994, 107–108). Hughte captioned each image, giving some context for what historic A:shiwi may have thought of Cushing's actions and what Cushing was doing, based on his own accounts and letters. Depicting and revisiting this historical moment, which ultimately brought continuous outsider scrutiny to Zuni, helps the community remember events that created our current reality while incorporating specific Zuni humor and voice into this reflection. The cartoons contribute a critical—and hilarious—commentary and are fondly regarded in Zuni.

Hughte's creation of the cartoons exemplifies the TribalCrit tenet 4, Native peoples' need to forge self-identity, telling our own stories of what it feels like to be ourselves. People around the world likely became aware of Zuni Pueblo through Cushing's writing, but his vision was clouded by his Western ideology, by his need to appropriate and exploit Zuni culture and knowledge, and it was skewed by his own ambition. Hughte's representations of Cushing turns the narrative inward and speaks directly to Zuni people, depicting a fuller picture of these historic events in a way that makes sense to *us*.

The Zuni Map Art Project is a series of fine art paintings that depict the migration history of our ancestors, the ancient A:shiwi, creating a visual representation of knowledge historically shared through stories (TribalCrit tenet 8). The process, developed and stewarded by the AAMHC, engaged language teachers, religious and tribal officials, and artists in a series of conversations about the need for Zuni people to know their own history. The community advisory board conferred for over a year about the Shiwi migration/creation story, landmarks, and historical sites, as well as how to facilitate the communication of that knowledge while still respecting the various levels of access to information at work in our community (Enote and McLerran 2011). The result is nearly forty large-scale fine art paintings that have been exhibited as *A:shiwi A:wan Uhlonnone: The Zuni World*, in Zuni, Flagstaff, Albuquerque, Los Angeles, and New York City, with an accompanying catalog. Three maps depict the middle village, the reservation boundaries, and the waterways that define our traditional territories. Printed as posters with a select number of locations labeled in the Zuni language, the maps are available only to Zuni households and available for pickup at the AAMHC, adding a level of control over the posters, now considered a valuable information resource in the pueblo (Belarde-Lewis 2013). The notion of taking control of access to our information and knowledge is not new, but the *enactment of control* in this manner has been a challenge when there are thousands of records, publications, and objects that originated in our community and are now in the care of non-Zuni institutions.

These two creative endeavors are not merely visually pleasing, artistic representations of Zuni Pueblo history and cultural knowledge; these are tools to dismantle outside misrepresentations of A:shiwi people. These works were produced to talk back to narratives and depictions that place our knowledge as secondary to the outsider who uses our knowledge for their own gain. The Zuni Map Art Project and Hughte's artwork make sense to Zuni people, build on Zuni knowledge, and reinforce tribal methods of information sharing.

The two projects exemplify multiple TribalCrit foundations. Their existence shows the need for Indigenous people to tell our own stories and self-identify, as in tenet 4. Tenet 2 recognizes material gain and imperialism are the foundation of US policies to regulate Indigenous people; researchers such as Frank Cushing take Native information and knowledge for institutions (cultural and educational) to tell us our lands are not as large as we know, to tell us which places we do or do not have ancestral connections to, all in support of removing us from existence. Researchers have taken and published for material gain Native creation stories, which libraries generally classify as myths; these are not myths, but histories of our migration. The Zuni Map Art pushes against this imperialism to show outsiders we are connected to these sacred spaces and always have been.

ZUNI LANGUAGE DIGITIZATION WITH UNIVERSITY OF NEW MEXICO (UNM)

We recognize Native stories as legitimate sources of data, and we exercise TribalCrit tenet 8 by including a conversation between us to share our experiences in our own voices. We specifically discuss a hybrid project that respects and acknowledges Zuni knowledge systems, yet was created in a Western library: the Zuni Language Materials Collection. Additional TribalCrit tenets surface as themes in our discussion, including a desire to forge tribal sovereignty and self-identification (tenet 4); US policies—and arguably library practices—rooted in imperialism and desire for personal and institutional gain (tenet 2); and tribal traditions and visions for the future that are central to the understanding of the lived realities of Indigenous peoples (tenet 7). These concepts are embedded in the inspiration for the language project, the purpose of the collection, and the tension that comes from working with our community while also navigating academic spaces as Native women.

Miranda Belarde-Lewis (MBL): In your 2018 article [Wise and Kostelecky 2018], you outlined the process of digitizing Zuni language materials in the UNM library collection. How did you become involved with that project?

Sarah Kostelecky (SK): UNM had a branch campus in Zuni, and some students there were taking classes and working as educators in the Zuni Public Schools. Many of them wanted more resources about our Zuni history and culture. But the branch didn't have dedicated library space or library support. As both the UNM education librarian and a tribal member, I knew I had to help.

And I was angry that UNM--Zuni did not have the same basic services as other branches, but the university had no problem taking their tuition money. I could not ignore this, and I decided I would provide library services there that they should have had all along.

MBL: How did you help provide these services?

SK: We worked with students and brainstormed with UNM faculty and Zuni educators. It was suggested that digital Zuni language materials—which were only available in print from the Zuni Public School District's bilingual department—would be a welcome resource. I volunteered to work within UNM Libraries to get the items scanned and published online.

When planning to digitize these cultural materials, I worked to center Zuni values in every decision. From the start, I made clear that the top priority was what was best for Zuni. I was aware that as a librarian, I would have the agency to develop a project that was respectful of the tribe, more so than if I were involved as an individual tribal member. I wanted this digitization project to be useful to Zuni people and still in accordance with our tribal worldview. I put a lot of pressure on myself to ensure this was done in a good way. And I think it was successful.

MBL: I agree! From the social media posts I've seen of the link, folks back home seem excited about the collection. We've both worked in mainstream institutions, and just like others who are from underrepresented groups, we often find ourselves in the position of being the "institutional contact person" or "point person" for our communities, even as we recognize personal, organizational, and structural inequities around us. What has your experience been being the "point person" for folks back home?

SK: Doing research within and about my/our own community is rewarding and stressful. I work with Zuni people to keep myself grounded in the academic space or else I would leave, because it is a challenging environment for me. But living with the potential to have Zunis view my work negatively or to be perceived as acting in a way that is not in accordance with tribal values, despite my intentions to do the opposite, leaves me feeling very vulnerable. My tribe defines the core of who I am, and I value my relationship with my culture and people more than my career. This description by Dr. Kim TallBear of her own research resonated with me: "I do not simply study indigenous communities, but I inhabit them, both local and virtual, within and without the academy" [2014, 3].

MBL: Dr. TallBear is amazing. Thinking more about this specific project, can you describe how you see this digitization project? Does it help to control Zuni information and knowledge? How does this project of Shiwi language materials contribute to the narrative of community-held language knowledge? How are we controlling/contributing to the narrative of community knowledge?

SK: These materials are available in a publicly accessible digital collection space, without password protection. But I believe these digital materials share Zuni information while still being in Zuni control. First, the language materials were selected by knowledgeable bilingual department educators who had the discretion to donate only materials they thought were appropriate to be digitized. Zuni people would have final say on the project, not the library.

Second, because the collection does not require authentication to access, I believe this represents tribal recognition of new strategies to share community knowledge. Developing this project through the lens of librarian and tribal member, I thought of relatives who don't live in the pueblo because they are in the military, have moved for jobs, or did not grow up there because of the choices their parents made. You and I are living away because of our careers. By digitizing Zuni language materials, I hope we help those relatives feel connected to home.

MBL: I think about that a lot, especially for my son. He doesn't have the luxury of growing up at home like we did. It's not as easy for him to learn about our language, history, and ceremonies, so I have to work harder at it. It would be best to be at home, but like you said, we are working on our careers away from home.

SK: Of course it would be ideal to learn or relearn the Zuni language from a grandparent or relative in the pueblo, but that is hard to make happen. Providing access to these materials helps our own community "see" Shiwis who are not home but are trying hard to live and teach the values and stories important to us, in our own language. Reaching out to Zuni people away from home is a counternarrative to colonization as we are recognizing that there is no "one way" to be Zuni or "one" Zuni experience.

MBL: Exactly. And once we find ourselves working in large libraries, in "mainstream" museums, we realize that it's not just Zuni people we're serving. It's Native people from all over. Even though sometimes I do feel that vulnerability of being judged by people at home, I try to keep in mind that our presence and voices in these spaces means a lot to students wondering if they made the right decision to be here in the academy, or in the field doing research. And when it comes to the research process at home, I feel like our community should do what former governor Bowekaty was advocating for—to develop an IRB [institutional review board] process to monitor what research is being done about us.

SK: That is definitely needed. What would be a bigger goal? Developing a record center from the archives at the former archaeology program?

MBL: Or to have a consolidated building and department like the Ziibiwing Center of Anishinaabe Culture and Lifeways in Mount Pleasant, Michigan. They have a museum, library, research and archive area, and a meeting space all in one location.

SK: Great idea, though that requires skilled staff, space, money, partnership with other information resources in Zuni. But a central office could support community research, K–12 education, people at home and away at school, lawyers working for the Pueblo....If our community got together to imagine the possibilities like you and Marisa encouraged [Duarte and Belarde-Lewis 2015], we would have the beginnings of an amazing resource to support traditional knowledge sharing that really utilizes all of the rich information resources that already exist at home.

CONCLUSION

Though the Zuni people desire privacy and have dealt with a long history of exploitation and disrespect of our cultural practices, we continue to persevere and grow. We have always recognized that knowledge is sacred. Zuni knowledge continues to be shared through systems thousands of years old.

This counternarrative is our recognition of TribalCrit tenet 9, where theory and practice are deeply connected and therefore push us as scholars to support social change. The example projects and stories we shared respect and follow specific Shiwi knowledge theory and structures. By examining tribal projects that respectfully share information about Zuni culture and lifeways, we have presented counternarratives and illustrated how specific practices utilized by our people have pushed against endemic colonization in Western institutions. These stories are also a way to give voice to the variety of A:shiwi experiences today.

As Zuni people in the information field, we endeavor to be part of current efforts by Zuni Pueblo organizations to create more opportunities to share cultural knowledge and history to ultimately strengthen our community now and in the future. In utilizing some tenets of the TribalCrit theoretical framework to analyze Zuni Pueblo knowledge sharing for our own uses as Zuni people, we see where the tribe has been forward-thinking and note opportunities to build on these successes. To share knowledge with Zuni tribal members in a cohesive way, we argue that a record center for the tribe would be ideal. Rather than having piecemeal efforts by various tribal organizations, resources can be leveraged by one entity. However, we are only two individuals, and larger community conversations about these concepts should happen before any action can be taken. We have to consider where we are today as a Native community and the many ways colonization is embedded in our lives.

Tribal Critical Race Theory is a tool that must be utilized in library and information science broadly to recognize the problematic processes in the field that serve to marginalize and even erase the Indigenous experience. This theory allows us, as Zuni women and LIS faculty, to create a framework to share stories of our people's experiences. The stories range from when we did not have control of our knowledge that was shared by outsiders to how our communities can create counternarratives to correct the record.

Brayboy developed TribalCrit as an intervention in the education field. He hopes that TribalCrit might improve "the ways that both schools and educational researchers think about American Indian students" (2005, 442). We hope TribalCrit is used to help Indigenous information professionals advocate for the value and strength in their local practices to non-Native colleagues. We strongly encourage librarians, archivists, and museum professionals to acknowledge and respect Indigenous ways of knowing and put in the work toward making these cultural institutions more reflective of Indigenous values. TribalCrit can compel non-Zuni outsiders to finally accept our "silence" as our answer to their constant questioning. For our own efforts, we hope to empower the generations following us. Elahkwa.

BIBLIOGRAPHY

American Library Association. 2012. "Diversity Counts 2009–2010 Update." http://www.ala.org/aboutala/offices/diversity/diversitycounts/2009-2010update.

A:shiwi A:wan Museum and Heritage Center. n.d. Facebook. Accessed December 28, 2019. https://www.facebook.com/Ashiwi-Awan-Museum-Heritage-Center-332821340826833/.

Belarde-Lewis, Miranda Hayes. 2013. "From Six Directions: Documenting and Protecting Zuni Knowledge in Multiple Environments." PhD diss., University of Washington. ResearchWorks Archive. http://hdl.handle.net/1773/24191.

Bowechop, Janine, and Patricia Pierce Erikson. 2005. "Forging Indigenous Methodologies on Cape Flattery: The Makah Museum as a Center of Collaborative Research." *American Indian Quarterly* 29 (1/2): 263–273.

Bowekaty, Malcolm B. 2002. "Perspectives on Research in American Indian Communities." *Jurimetrics* 42 (2): 145–148.

Bowers, Jennifer, Katherine Crowe, and Peggy Keeran. 2017. "'If You Want the History of a White Man, You Go to the Library': Critiquing Our Legacy, Addressing Our Library Collections Gaps." *Collection Management* 42 (3–4): 159–179.

Brayboy, Bryan McKinley Jones. 2005. "Toward a Tribal Critical Race Theory in Education." *Urban Review* 37 (5): 425–446. https://doi.org/10.1007/s11256-005-0018-y.

Burke, Susan K. 2007. "The Use of Public Libraries by Native Americans." *Library Quarterly* 77 (4): 429–461.

Center for Digital Scholarship and Curation. n.d. "Welcome to Mukurtu CMS." Mukurtu CMS. Accessed May 30, 2019. http://mukurtu.org/.

Colwell, Chip. 2017. *Plundered Skulls and Stolen Spirits: Inside the Fight to Reclaim Native America's Culture*. Chicago: University of Chicago Press.

Cooper, Danielle, Tanya Ball, Michelle Nicole Boyer-Kelly, Anne Carr-Wiggin, Carrie Cornelius, J. Wendel Cox, Sarah Dupont, Cody Fullerton, MaryLynn Gagné, Scott Garton, Ridie Wilson Ghezzi, Michelle Guittar, Kawena Komeiji, Sheila Laroque, Kayla Lar-Son, Kim Lawson, Deborah Lee, Janice Linton, Julia Logan, Keahiahi Long, Lorisia MacLeod, Shavonn Matsuda, Sara E. Morris, Lisa O'Hara, Rebecca Orozco, Annemarie Paikai, Michael Peper, Michael Perry, Gina Petersen, Verónica Reyes-Escudero, Anthony Sanchez, Kapena Shim, David Smith, Jennifer Sylvester, Jennifer Toews, Niamh Wallace, Amy Witzel, and Desmond Wong. 2019. *When Research Is Relational: Supporting the Research Practices of Indigenous Studies Scholars.* Ithaka S+R Research Report. April 11, 2019. https://sr.ithaka.org/publications/supporting-the-research-practices-of-indigenous -studies-scholars/.

Deloria, Vine, Jr. 1978. "The Right to Know: A Paper." Report for the White House Preconference on Indian Library and Information Services on or near Reservations. Washington, DC: Office of Library and Information Services, US Dept. of the Interior.

Duarte, Marisa Elena, and Miranda Belarde-Lewis. 2015. "Imagining: Creating Spaces for Indigenous Ontologies." *Cataloging and Classification Quarterly* 53 (5–6): 677–702. https://doi.org/10 .1080/01639374.2015.1018396.

Enote, Jim. 2011. "A:Shiwi on A:Shiwi: Zuni on Zuni." In *A:Shiwi A:Wan Ulohnonne: The Zuni World*, edited by Jim Enote and Jennifer McLerran, 4–9. Zuni, NM: A:shiwi A:wan Museum and Heritage Center, Museum of Northern Arizona.

Enote, Jim, and Jennifer McLerran, eds. 2011. *A:Shiwi A:Wan Ulohnanne: The Zuni World.* Zuni, NM: A:shiwi A:wan Museum and Heritage Center, Museum of Northern Arizona.

Fixico, Donald Lee, ed. 2008. *Treaties with American Indians: An Encyclopedia of Rights, Conflicts, and Sovereignty.* Santa Barbara, CA: ABC-CLIO.

Hughte, Phil. 1994. *A Zuni Artist Looks at Frank Hamilton Cushing: Cartoons by Phil Hughte.* Limited ed. Zuni, NM: Pueblo of Zuni Arts & Crafts, A:Shiwi A:wan Museum and Heritage Center.

Hughte, Phil, Matthew Sneddon, and Mario Ruiz. 2003. *The Other Side of the Story. Colores!* Albuquerque: KNME-TV. DVD.

Isaac, Gwyneira. 2007. *Mediating Knowledges: Origins of a Zuni Tribal Museum.* Tucson: University of Arizona Press.

Karuk Tribe, Lisa Hillman, Leaf Hillman, Adrienne R. S. Harling, Bari Talley, and Angela McLaughlin. 2007. "Building Sípnuuk: A Digital Library, Archives, and Museum for Indigenous Peoples." *Collection Management* 42 (3–4): 294–316. https://doi.org/10.1080/01462679.2017.1331870.

Littletree, Sandra, Miranda Belarde-Lewis, and Marisa Duarte. 2020. "Centering Relationality: A Conceptual Model to Advance Indigenous Knowledge Organization Practices." *Knowledge Organization* 47 (forthcoming).

Littletree, Sandra, and Cheryl A. Metoyer. 2015. "Knowledge Organization from an Indigenous Perspective: The Mashantucket Pequot Thesaurus of American Indian Terminology Project." *Cataloging & Classification Quarterly* 53 (5–6): 640–657. https://doi.org/10.1080/01639374.2015 .1010113.

McFeely, Eliza. 2001. *Zuni and the American Imagination*. New York: Hill & Wang.

McMurtry, Larry. 2001. "Zuni Tunes." *New York Review of Books*, August 9, 2001. http://www .nybooks.com/articles/2001/08/09/zuni-tunes/.

Parsons, Eileen R. Carlton, Billye Rhodes, and Corliss Brown. 2011. "Unpacking the CRT in *Negotiating White Science*." *Cultural Studies of Science Education* 6:951. https://doi.org/10.1007/s11422 -011-9349-z.

Sando, Joe S., and All Indian Pueblo Council. 1976. *The Pueblo Indians*. San Francisco: Indian Historian Press.

Simpson, Audra. 2014. *Mohawk Interruptus: Political Life across the Borders of Settler States*. Durham, NC: Duke University Press.

Smith, Linda Tuhiwai. 2012. *Decolonizing Methodologies Research and Indigenous Peoples*. Kindle ed. London: Zed Books.

Solórzano, Daniel G., and Tara J. Yosso. 2002. "Critical Race Methodology: Counter-Storytelling as an Analytical Framework for Education Research." *Qualitative Inquiry* 8 (1): 23–44. https://doi .org/10.1177/107780040200800103.

Sumida Huaman, Elizabeth, and Bryan McKinley Jones Brayboy, eds. 2017. *Indigenous Innovations in Higher Education*. Rotterdam: Sense Publishers.

TallBear, Kim. 2014. "Standing with and Speaking as Faith: A Feminist-Indigenous Approach to Inquiry." *Journal of Research Practice* 10 (2): 17.

US Department of the Interior, Bureau of Indian Affairs. n.d. "Frequently Asked Questions." US Department of the Interior, Bureau of Indian Affairs. Accessed December 28, 2019. https://www .bia.gov/frequently-asked-questions.

Webster, Kelly, and Ann Doyle. 2008. "Don't Class Me in Antiquities! Giving Voice to Native American Materials." In *Radical Cataloging: Essays at the Front*, edited by Keller R. Roberto and Sanford Berman, 189–196. Jefferson, NC: McFarland.

Wise, Mary, and Sarah R. Kostelecky. 2018. "Respecting the Language: Digitizing Native American Language Materials." *Digital Library Perspectives* 34 (3): 200–214. https://doi.org/10.1108/DLP -02-2018-0006.

Wyaco, Virgil. 1998. *A Zuni Life: A Pueblo Indian in Two Worlds*. Albuquerque: University of New Mexico Press.

ILLUMINATE ERASURE

With editing by contributors Nicholae Cline and April M. Hathcock

INTRODUCTION TO PART II: THE COURAGE OF CHARACTER AND COMMITMENT VERSUS THE COWARDLINESS OF COMFORTABLE CONTENTMENT

Anthony W. Dunbar

The nonviolent approach does not immediately change the heart of the oppressor. It first does something to the hearts and souls of those committed to it. It gives them new self-respect; it calls up resources of strength and courage they did not know they had.
—Martin Luther King Jr.

THOUGHTFULNESS

Let me open this brief introductory essay for "Part II: Illuminating Erasure," with acknowledgement and appreciation. To create and operate outside the comfort zones of conventional acceptance takes an uncommon level of strength, courage, and conviction. To then organize and collaborate with others to _center_ a much-needed discourse from a historically consistent starting point too often existing at the outer margins of inclusive participatory discourse is more than activism or intellectual contribution. It more certainly is a highly spiritual journey. In organizing this endeavor, the volume's editors, Sofia Leung and Jorge López-McKnight, exemplify the relentless courage and tenacity to be the type of advocates and academic warriors necessary to lead a Critical Race Theory (CRT) endeavor in library and information science (LIS) and archival studies.

As the subjects and terminology of equity, privilege, inclusion, whiteness, social justice, and, yes, Critical Race Theory become less exotic, gradually more normative, and make their way into the LIS and archival nomenclature, it is clear this volume of collected critical works is destined to become the foundational seminal primer for those seeking illumination and inspiration regarding the application of CRT. In these pages the editors initiate the critical-cultural communication essential in forming an academic solidarity, which, in turn, can challenge and substantively disrupt White Supremacy and hypersegregation in LIS and archival studies (Rodino-Colocino 2016).

People who are truly strong lift others up. People who are truly powerful bring others together.
—Michelle Obama

REFLECTION

While humbled to participate, I am also led to be a bit reflective about my personal journey and evolution in becoming a critical race theorist in LIS and archival studies. Reading the chapters of this collective volume is an emotionally conflicted experience. Best stated, it is a Frankie Beverly experience—an experience captured in the lyrics of the R&B classic "Joy and Pain" (Beverly 1981).[1]

In pursuit of my master's of education at the University of Utah, I was able to engage with both scholars of color and white scholars whose work is grounded in critical social consciousness. However, it was the "Joy and Pain" experiences of pursuing and ultimately attaining my MLIS and PhD at the University of California Los Angeles that led me to author the first CRT article in a peer-reviewed information science journal (Dunbar 2006).

Being blessed to have CRT icons Daniel Solórzano and Kimberlé Crenshaw on my dissertation committee is a clear moment of academic joy, which is juxtaposed to the very real emotional pain of being personally targeted with institutional racism at both the departmental and university levels. Reading this groundbreaking volume brings me back to the conflicting sentiments I stated in the acknowledgements of my dissertation over a decade ago (Dunbar 2008). It is my UCLA experiences along with subsequent higher education and professional librarianship experiences inundated with White Supremacy, nonetheless, which make the creation of and contribution to CRT work in LIS and archival studies a form of post-traumatic growth (Tedeschi and Calhoun 2004).[2]

PERSPECTIVE AT THE LEVEL OF SOCIETY

Let me offer some perspective. Any phenomenon that is deeply rooted, sustained, transcending, and unyielding at the meta level of society inevitably permeates throughout most, if not all, human interactions at the subcultural level of society (Landman and Carvalho 2016, 24–25; Roberts 2020). Such is the case when examining the societal realities of White Supremacy and premeditated segregation in the United States. The threads of White Supremacy and segregation are interwoven in the entire fabric of American life and culture (Christian 2002; Rothstein 2017). In fact, the current American racial climate can quite possibly be characterized as a unique iteration of apartheid—in this instance, forming a twenty-first-century version of what is often discussed as neo-apartheid. That said, the more accurate truth of the matter is that the realities of economic, health, political, and educational disparities along racial lines, coupled with hypergeographic segregation, have a centuries-long legacy in the United States of America (Krysan and Crowder 2017; Massey and Fischer 2003; Rashid 2011).

Obviously, there is very little that is new when there are constants that have held true over centuries. In the traditional model of apartheid, the systems of oppression are control mechanisms when the white population is the overwhelming minority group, as in South Africa. Madlingozi frames neo-apartheid as a means to call attention to the post-1994 constitutional rearrangements, which offer minimal departure from the inherited and bifurcated social configuration of the past (Madlingozi 2017).[3]

In applying the neo-apartheid framework to the US, one could easily argue that the structural tenets of apartheid have either been at the point of development and emergence or have been well in place over the last 400 years (Malcom 2019). The "neo," or divergence from traditional apartheid model of South Africa, is that US neo-apartheid has the legacy with all the "bifurcated social configuration of the past"—namely, White Supremacy and hypersegregation—while whites have been the majority population.

It is projected that at some point close to 2040, there will be no racial majority in the country (Frey 2015). Without a substantive shift in the bifurcated economic, educational, political, and social configurations of the United States over the next couple of decades, the possibility of an authentic form of diversity will disappointingly give way to America's legacy of White Supremacy and hypersegregation, enabling the removal of the "neo" in neo-apartheid and leaving the US less than twenty-five years away from being simply an apartheid nation. It would be well beyond naïve to consider that as White Supremacy and segregation are interwoven into the entire fabric of American life and culture, that accordingly the very same fabric is not also clothing the professional practices and intellectual expressions in LIS and archival studies.

PERSPECTIVE AT THE DISCIPLINARY LEVEL

Thoroughly articulating the full infiltration of White Supremacy and apartheid-level segregation at the societal level allows for the discussion of the existence and impact of the destructive dynamic duo of White Supremacy and segregation in information-based discourses. Moreover, the need for critical race frameworks as a deconstruction tool of White Supremacy and segregation in LIS and archival studies becomes apparent, if not obvious. The over thirty-five-year legacy and success of CRT in challenging multiple forms of oppression like White Supremacy and segregation in disciplines such as education, ethnic studies, gender studies, law, queer studies, and sociology bodes well for the ability of critical race frameworks to assist in confronting White Supremacy and segregation in information-based discourses. If CRT is to be used as a tool to deliver on the possibilities and opportunities for equity, inclusion, and social justice in LIS, then we need the professors, practitioners, and professionals of the field to follow the example of courage of character and commitment set by the authors of this section and strive for knowledge justice by disrupting LIS through CRT.

No person is your friend who demands your silence, or denies your right to grow.
—Alice Walker

THE WORK

The authors in this section, Natarajan, Walker, Lugo Vázquez, and Inefuku, honorably uphold the CRT legacy by creating lenses that make apparent the very nuanced micro- and systemic macroaggressions that are too often ignored and thus reduced to virtual invisibility against the backdrop of whiteness and White Supremacy.[4] The contributions in this section utilize well some of the now iconic CRT tools, such as Crenshaw's intersectionality, Delgado's counternarrative/counterstory as expressed through the work of Yosso and Solórzano, Pierce's microaggression, the deconstruction of white privilege and White Supremacy, and Collins's domains of -power framework and the idea that value neutrality actually exists. There certainly will be inspirations and future aspirations that manifest from the scholarship in this section, based on the authors' rigorous and responsible use of the CRT tools that, in most cases, have already been introduced to LIS. Moreover, the contributions of Natarajan, Lugo Vázquez, and Inefuku also present opportunities to introduce to the CRT in LIS discourse additional CRT tools that have not been as substantively present in previous LIS literature.

In "Counterstoried Spaces and Unknowns: A Queer South Asian Librarian Dreaming," Natarajan shares an essay of personal reflection through a lens constructed with the CRT frameworks of community cultural wealth, intersectionality, and Queer of Color Critique. Through Vani's lens—featuring the intersectionalities of second-generation South Asian American, queer, femme, nonbinary, and person of color marginalization; sexual oppression; misrepresentation; homophobia; transphobia; and racism—we clearly see the multilayers of exclusions ranging from micro-moments of relatively naïve expressions of racism by library professionals and professors to the accumulative macro power of a society *ignoring* the actual viable cultural aspects of a community *into near invisibility*. Natarajan deconstructs the whiteness of their personal experiences.

That said, the author also breathes life into understanding White Supremacy as a neo-apartheid experience, one fraught with near-debilitating segregation of them as an individual and the identities they represent. We can also consider this contribution's added value in its ability to illustrate post-traumatic growth as a CRT tool (Tedeschi and Calhoun 2004).[5] Vani successfully administers a self-therapeutic process of resilience and locating community to move beyond the moments of traumatic segregation to a vibrant expression and experience of post-traumatic growth, thus snatching victory from the jaws of victimization.

I'm writing my story so that others might see fragments of themselves.
—Lena Waithe

In "Ann Allen Shockley: An Activist-Librarian for Black Special Collections," Shaundra Walker powerfully delivers what CRT counterstories should be expected to deliver—that is, a glimpse into the strength and struggle of the protagonist. Walker, in this instance, offers the story of Ann Shockley, a Black activist-librarian who while unique in her advocacy for special collections in libraries serving historically Black colleges and universities, was also representative of "a continuum of Black activist-librarians." If we consider equity as one the primary goals of CRT scholarship and activism, then intellectual acceptance and acknowledgement should certainly be the gold standard for pursuits of equity. As Walker clearly states, Black special collections, particularly those developed at and through institutions of higher learning, are viable and vibrant expression of "Black intellectual legacies." Shaundra's presentation of Ann Shockley's story stands as a considerable contribution to CRT work in LIS and will most certainly lead to additional opportunities, which bring equity to the intellectual work conducted by People of Color. In turn, the social justice possibilities inspired by this work move from substantial to exponential.

We need, in every community, a group of angelic troublemakers.

—Bayard Rustin

The architecture of Sujei Lugo Vázquez's contribution is grounded in Patricia Hill Collins's notion of racism having four domains of power, as articulated in *Another Kind of Public Education: Race, Schools, the Media and Democratic Possibilities* (Collins 2009). What Lugo Vázquez builds on Collins's infrastructure of the structural, disciplinary, cultural, and interpersonal domains is an authentic challenge to LIS broadly and to children's librarianship more specifically. The challenge is to address the often-ignored permanence of racism embedded in the institution of librarianship, expressed by the absence of People of Color as a topic in children's collections, as well as People of Color as authors. The fine craftsmanship of Sujei's scholarship is showcased in the detailed historical reflections, which include both the history of exclusion and the legacy (1921–1972) of counterstorytelling library activists, including Augusta Braxston Baker, Pura T. Belpré, Charlemae Hill Rollins, Effie Lee Morris, and Lotsee Patterson. Lugo Vázquez's CRT contribution moves beyond merely problematizing the dynamics in children's literature; she also offers a seven-point plan to "reimagine the past." The plan presents distinct actions that can and should be taken to "decenter whiteness," with a goal of creating a standard of critical-cultural literacy in children's librarianship.

There is still more potential CRT depth that can be drawn from Lugo Vázquez's contribution. What if we suggest Derrick Bell's CRT tool of interest convergence as a possible addendum to this counternarrative? Interest convergence, as defined by Bell, is the idea that "the interest of blacks in achieving racial equality will be accommodated only when it converges with the interests of whites" (1980, 523). When applied more broadly in the context of Lugo Vázquez's contribution, we can expand on Bell's notion to understand that the interest of subordinated groups is accommodated only when it serves some clear benefit for dominant groups. As a contribution to the CRT in LIS tool kit, interest convergence is a complementary tool that assists in locating existing points of interest, identifying interested parties, further contextualizing possible counterstories, and revealing situations where multiple identities exist but are underdiscussed.

In fact, in Lugo Vázquez's seven-point plan to reimagine the past we can see the development of interest convergence as endeavors of equity building versus conflicts for dominance. For example, the author's first point, "Acknowledge the humanity of ALL children," can and should be a point of interest convergence that transcends race or any other context of identity politics. An application of Bell's interest convergence as an analytical tool to Lugo Vázquez's text, along with future CRT in LIS research, can certainly add to efforts of equity and social justice in the field.

It is easier to build strong children than to repair broken men.
—Frederick Douglass

Harrison W. Inefuku adeptly does what all CRT work should do—that is, describe in detail the nuances and micro-nuances of racism and or other forms of bias and discrimination. In "Relegated to the Margins: Faculty of Color, the Scholarly Record, and the Necessity of Antiracist Library Disruptions," Inefuku shines a light on many of the hiding places of institutional racism as it plays out in the hiring, retention, and promotion of faculty of color.

Inefuku's work presents an opportunity to introduce another CRT tool to the LIS discourse—namely, Smith's concept of racial battle fatigue (Smith, Allen, and Danley 2007).[6] Racial battle fatigue is a theoretical framework for examining social-psychological stress responses (e.g., frustration; anger; exhaustion; physical avoidance; psychological or emotional withdrawal; escapism; acceptance of racist attributions; resistance; verbally, nonverbally, or physically fighting back; and coping strategies) associated with the experiences of People of Color, including both students and faculty at historically white campuses (552). Examining together the works of Inefuku and Smith and colleagues enables us to bring in a model from equity and inclusion work, the intention and impact paradigm. While in most cases the intention of nuanced, semisubtle expressions of White Supremacy and white privilege *may* not be to inflict trauma, the impact of institutional racism on college campuses and in LIS certainly and perhaps consistently results in the trauma of racial battle fatigue.

It is never too late to give up your prejudices.
—Henry David Thoreau

Given the contributions in this section as well as the overall collected work in this book, I am proud to state that Critical Race Theory work in library and information science and archival studies is courageous, committed, intelligent, articulate, relevant, and evolving.

Change will not come if we wait for some other person, or if we wait for some other time. We are the ones we've been waiting for. We are the change that we seek.
—Barack Obama

NOTES

1. The quintessence I am expressing, that metaphorically joy and pain are indeed like sunshine and rain, can best be experienced by listening to the version of "Joy and Pain" on *Maze Live in New Orleans* (Capitol Records, 1981).

2. Posttraumatic growth is broadly defined as positive psychological change resulting from a struggle with highly challenging life circumstances (Tedeschi and Calhoun 2004, 1).

3. Apartheid ended in South Africa on April 27, 1994.

4. As a teachable moment, we should understand microaggressions to include the MACRO aspects of microaggressions or macroaggressions. The MACRO or macroaggression framework is threefold, based on time, scale, or time and scale. First, the accumulative effect as well as the legacy of a microaggression played out over generations has MACRO power or effect, thus creating a macroaggression over time. The second MACRO aspect is the microaggression based on scale. A large-scale or overt aggression that permeates and saturates at the societal level (i.e., on the national or global stage) would be considered a macroaggression.

5. "There are now reports in the literature of a very wide array of major life challenges that have acted as catalysts for posttraumatic growth. Many of the earlier research reports mentioned these growth outcomes in passing, but more recent investigations have been more specifically focused on these outcomes. Among the life crises that have produced reports of posttraumatic growth, at least in some form, are college students experiencing negative events" (Tedeschi and Calhoun 2004, 3)

6. One of the first to bring the notion of racial battle fatigue to LIS was Renate Chancellor, in "Racial Battle Fatigue: The Unspoken Burden of Black Women Faculty in LIS" (2019).

BIBLIOGRAPHY

Bell, Derrick A. 1980. "Brown v. Board of Education and the Interest-Convergence Dilemma." *Harvard Law Review* 93 (3): 518–533.

Beverly, Howard, lyricist. 1981. "Joy and Pain," by Frankie Beverly and Maze, on *Live in New Orleans*. Capital.

Chancellor, Renate L. 2019. "Racial Battle Fatigue: The Unspoken Burden of Black Women Faculty in LIS." *Journal of Education for Library and Information Science* 60 (3): 182–189.

Christian, Mark. 2002. "An African-Centered Perspective on White Supremacy." *Journal of Black Studies* 33 (2): 179–198.

Collins, Patricia Hill. 2009. *Another Kind of Public Education: Race, Schools, the Media and Democratic Possibilities*. Boston: Beacon Press.

Dunbar, Anthony W. 2006. "Introducing Critical Race Theory to Archival Discourse: Getting the Conversation Started." *Archival Science* 6 (1): 109–129.

Dunbar, Anthony W. 2008. "Critical Race Information Theory: Applying a CRITical Race Lens to Information Studies." PhD diss., University of California, Los Angeles.

Frey, William H. 2015. *Diversity Explosion: How New Racial Demographics Are Remaking America*. Washington, DC: Brookings Institution Press.

Gentle, Lenny. 2011. "Poverty and Social Movements." In *Zuma's Own Goal: Losing South Africa's "War on Poverty,"* edited by Brij Maharaj, Ashwin Desai, and Patrick Bond, 359–371. Trenton, NJ: Africa World Press.

Gibson, Campbell, and Kay Jung. 2002. "Historical Census Statistics on Population Totals by Race, 1790 to 1970, and by Hispanic Origin, 1970 to 1990 for the United States of America." US Census Bureau, Population Division working paper no. 76. February 2002.

History.com. 2010. "Apartheid." *History.com*, October 7, 2010. https://www.history.com/topics /africa/apartheid.

Jayawickreme, Eranda B., Laura E. R. Blackie. 2014. "Post-Traumatic Growth as Positive Personality Change: Evidence, Controversies and Future Directions." *European Journal of Personality* 28 (4): 312–331.

Krysan, Maria, and Kyle Crowder. 2017. *Cycle of Segregation: Social Processes and Residential Stratification*. New York: Russell Sage Foundation.

Laski, Harold Joseph. 1919. *Authority in the Modern State*. [Hamden, CT]: Archon Books.

Madlingozi, Tshepo. 2017. "Social Justice in a Time of Neo-apartheid Constitutionalism: Critiquing the Anti-Black Economy of Recognition, Incorporation and Distribution." *Stellenbosch Law Review* 28 (1): 123–147.

Malcom, Shirley M. 2019. "400 Years and (Re)counting." *Science* 365 (6459): 1221.

Massey, Douglas S., and Mary J. Fischer. 2003. "The Geography of Inequality in the United States, 1950–2000." *Brookings-Wharton Papers on Urban Affairs*, no. 4: 1–40. doi:10.1353/urb.2003.0012.

Rashid, Kamau. 2011. "'To Break Asunder along the Lesions of Race': The Critical Race Theory of W.E.B. Du Bois." *Race Ethnicity and Education* 14 (5): 585–602.

Roberts, Alasdair. 2020. "Bridging Levels of Public Administration: How Macro Shapes Meso and Micro." *Administration & Society* 52 (4): 631–656. doi:10.1177/0095399719877160.

Rodino-Colocino, Michelle. 2016. "Critical-Cultural Communication Activism Research Calls for Academic Solidarity." *International Journal of Communication* 10:4017–4026.

Rothstein, Richard. 2017. *The Color of Law: A Forgotten History of How Our Government Segregated America*. 1st ed. New York: Liveright Publishing.

Schaeffer, Katherine. 2019. "The Most Common Age among Whites in U.S. Is 58—More than Double That of Racial and Ethnic Minorities." Fact Tank: News in the Numbers. Pew Research Center. July 30, 2019. https://www.pewresearch.org/fact-tank/2019/07/30/most-common-age -among-us-racial-ethnic-groups/.

Smith, William A., Walter R. Allen, and Lynette L. Danley. 2007. "Assume the Position…You Fit the Description." *American Behavioral Scientist* 51 (4); 551–578.

Tedeschi, Richard G., and Lawrence G. Calhoun. 2004. "Posttraumatic Growth: Conceptual Foundations and Empirical Evidence." *Psychological Inquiry* 15 (1): 1–18.

"Unmasking Neo-apartheid." 1986. Editorial. *Third World Quarterly* 8 (3): ix–xii.

5

COUNTERSTORIED SPACES AND UNKNOWNS
A Queer South Asian Librarian Dreaming

Vani Natarajan

The minimal attention to QOCs across a number of scholarly discourses in educational literature speaks to a politics of knowledge production which, intentionally or not, has reproduced QOC invisibility. Naming and disrupting that politics will be essential if educational researchers truly want to make room for QOC critique.

—Ed Brockenbrough

For library workers of color, and especially for those of us who are trans, nonbinary, queer, and/or gender nonconforming, finding ourselves in the literature and discourse of librarianship can feel like a fruitless process. Maybe it's also an endlessly exciting quest. What happens when we name our truths and theorize them? I imagine the most generative aspects of this journeying in the ways we might find, see, hear, and hold space for each other as QTPOC—queer and trans People of Color. Our words for our identities, experiences, and communities move far beyond the legibility of that acronym. What new language can we find, and make, to name both our lived experiences and what we dream about?

In this essay, I am trying to address what Critical Race Theorist Edward Brockenbrough provokes us to consider in the opening quote (Brockenbrough 2016, 291). How do interpretive and analytical lenses of Critical Race Theory help me narrate and make meaning from my experiences as a queer South Asian American librarian? How can we use CRT as praxis, to center the experiences, lives, and futures of queer and trans People of Color in libraries?

I write this essay for People of Color. At the heart of it, I am holding space for queer, trans, and gender nonconforming People of Color. Readers, I have an agenda, a QTPOC agenda. I want my agenda to be responsive to and shaped by other QTPOC, regardless of our relationships with or connections to libraries. I want to be in conversation about the strategies we have used, or could use, that are what Edward Brockenbrough describes as both "self-making and space navigating" (2015, 32).

How do I situate myself? I am a South Asian American with US citizenship privilege, with parents who migrated from India to the United States. I am both a non-Black Person of Color and a settler of color. I name these positionalities, recognizing that the violent and oppressive histories and continuation into the present of settler colonialism and enslavement of Black people are foundational to racial formation in the United States. I come from a Tamil Indian family that, as *savarna* (caste-privileged) Hindus, has for many generations in their home country, as well as in the United States, benefitted from access to resources and power, at the expense of Dalit and other caste-oppressed people. Having savarna heritage protects me from being subjected to the anti-Muslim and anti-Dalit violence to which much of the South Asian population (diasporic and in the region) is vulnerable. I am queer, femme, and nonbinary, and my pronouns are they/them. I move through the world as someone who often gets read as a cis Brown woman.

I ground my use of personal narrative in Daniel Solórzano and Tara Yosso's method of counterstorytelling, defined by the authors as a practice of critical race methodology (2002). In order to practice counterstorytelling, we need to understand, and push back on, White Supremacist "master narratives" about People of Color. Among the forms these take are social scientific literature defining People of Color according to a set of perceived and presumed "deficits" (Solórzano and Yosso 2002, 30). Deficit narratives get used to justify inequality and forced assimilation of students of color into dominant, white, class-privileged culture. They keep us from accessing knowledge about our communities and histories in our schools—all in the name of "helping" People of Color, even "saving" us from ourselves.

What majoritarian stories about QTPOC circulate in film media, literature, and other forms? One is that we don't exist, or that our gender and sexual identities eclipse our racialized ones (or vice versa), rather than being intimately intertwined. So often, LGBTQ+ people are assumed as white, or mostly white. I also see a "sidekick" trope applied to many QTPOC, that we exist solely to affirm and uplift the white, cis, and/or straight people around us. Rarely do we get to see depictions of QTPOC in relationship with one another. I notice prevailing narratives that characterize

QTPOC lives as defined by suffering and abjection. As I mention this, I don't want to erase the ways that structural impacts of racism, homophobia, and transphobia leave QTPOC vulnerable to so much oppression and violence. Yet, I wonder what it means that QTPOC joy, collective resistance, and world making can so often get overlooked, especially in academia.

Solórzano and Yosso usefully outline three possible forms of counterstorytelling: personal stories or narratives; other people's stories or narratives; and composite stories. Their definition of personal stories resonates the most with what I hope to do: "Personal stories or narratives recount an individual's experiences with various forms of racism and sexism. Often, these personal counter-stories are autobiographical reflections of the author, juxtaposed with their critical race analysis of legal cases and within the context of a larger sociopolitical critique" (2002, 32). In the personal narrative counterstory that I share with you, I use my own memory and historical documents (from personal journal entries to official library policy text) as primary sources, to revisit my experiences as a queer Person of Color in higher education and academic libraries. In this counterstory, I employ several Critical Race Theory lenses to analyze my experiences in librarianship.

I organize my counterstory in two parts: first, an account of my experiences as an undergraduate student at a small liberal arts college library in the late 1990s; next, my experiences as an academic librarian decades later. I consider these "both sides," as someone who remembers navigating a college library as a student and later as a librarian. Following these narrative sections, I will move into interpretation, revisiting my own narrative using three CRT frameworks: community cultural wealth, intersectionality, and queer of color critique.

GETTING LOST IN SPACE: 1997–2001

In the fall of 1997, I begin attending Swarthmore College. At the Tri-College preorientation program for students of color, I spend days in the company of other students of color, developing language around identity, racism, whiteness, privilege, South Asianness. I can finally speak candidly about growing up Brown in majority-white schools. Once TriCo ends and the academic year at Swarthmore begins, I am thrown into dizzying and much less supportive terrain.

I don't have a map for navigating "coming out." No one in my family of origin, as far as I know yet, is queer. No one from the tight-knit Indian American community in Virginia where I have grown up, as far as I know, is queer. Thus far, only one book

I have read depicts a queer South Asian character: Karim Amir, the Pakistani British bisexual teenage narrator of Hanif Kureishi's *The Buddha of Suburbia*. I reread the novel many times from the age of sixteen onward. It becomes an important imaginative space, but its London setting feels so far away from the small southern Virginia town where I grow up.

For many college students, the library is a workspace. But for me, it is a space to wander, procrastinate, and seek inspiration outside of what has been prescribed. Roaming the stacks, I feel as though I am making up for lost time. I'm anxious to see myself reflected. Anxious because the promise of that reflection feels at once joyful and scary. Will my reflection be just as excited to greet me?

On one of the few occasions where I seek out the support of a librarian at the Swarthmore library (because I am usually too intimidated), I ask for research help. I am writing a paper on the Asian American student movement, for my history of social movements class. I connect to this history; learning about the Asian American movement from a close friend of mine, who grew up in NYC's Chinatown, I know that Asian American student activists organized in solidarity with Black, Latinx, and Indigenous students to bring about ethnic studies in California. The white librarian with whom I speak seems skeptical that I'll find much. They set me up at a workstation with a database. I can't remember what I type in. Later, my friend Lena, the one who taught me about the Asian American movement, suggests a book. Among this text and its citation trails, I find a strong web of sources.

My white professor, a historian of feminism, is not happy with my paper. She writes in her comments that there isn't enough material on the Asian American movement for a whole paper, and I should have picked a different topic. I am disheartened and frustrated. I wonder how people come to know the things they know. Is my professor correct? (So much later evidence proves her wrong.)

How might my experience have differed if I had gotten to talk with a queer librarian of color? Maybe they would have expressed excitement about my research and shared a story about their interest in Asian American and/or other BIPOC- and LGBTQ-led movements of the era and their mutual connections. Even if we found a dearth of sources, we could analyze the silences. Maybe I could have challenged my professor's dismissive response to my research.

In second semester, I take an English class on Asian American theater and performance studies. I can't believe I get to take this elective my first year (there are otherwise no Asian American studies classes in the English department). My professor is queer, Filipinx, and brilliant. He doesn't lecture at us; he poses questions. He asks us to split into groups and create questions for each other. We learn about racist tropes and stereotypes that Asian folks have navigated in the Americas for centuries. Asian American performance artists, filmmakers, and playwrights have counterappropriated dominant images to make a powerful statement and reclaim the gaze. We call out fetishization in art, and these conversations spill into dining hall talk. We go to the Asian Arts Initiative to watch Justin Chin perform spoken-word poetry. The rage, wit, and tenderness of Justin's voice and words stay with me long after the performance. I get my copy of *Bite Hard* signed.

As I reflect on my own navigation of space as a queer South Asian American college student in the late nineties and early aughts, I am struck by a through-line of getting lost. Private liberal arts colleges were not, and still are not, designed with the well-being of queer and trans People of Color in mind. This lack of support frequently left me feeling bewildered, and searching for support. Getting lost could also be a site of agency, in wandering outside of prescribed paths to find community. It's telling that the unforgettable Justin Chin reading I attended was off campus—certain feelings, experiences, and connections become more possible when we leave the limits of academia.

TRANSFORMING SPACE: LIBRARY PROGRAMS

When I am hired at Barnard College Library in 2011, I become the only librarian of color in an otherwise all-white unit. From 2011 to 2018, I remain the only librarian of color in the Personal Librarians division of Barnard Library. In my first year, I mention to a white colleague that Barnard needs to address the whiteness of its hiring. She responds by telling me, "I don't think you should say that. According to HR, you're not allowed to state a hiring preference on the basis of race."

When, in 2014, I organize a reading for two amazing Asian Canadian trans writers, Vivek Shraya and Elisha Lim, I share copies of the flyer, with author-designed artwork, at a staff meeting. A white coworker scoffs in distaste at the intricately designed drawings and text—"Well, that's very loud!" No one counteracts this response with anything like an affirmation. I try to make up for the apathy by owning all of my enthusiasm for this event I am working so hard to plan. I feel absurd and alone in my excitement, as if I am cheering at a wall. Later, I close my office door and let the tears fall. I imagine an alternate universe, where I could share with coworkers, unapologetically, the joy I feel about the projects I am pursuing. Instead of needing to find a campus event space outside the mandated quiet of the library, we would be able to take up space *inside* of it.

I text my partner, my friends, calling on the networks of support that exist outside of my job. They help me reconstruct the narrative. Yes, my white coworker may have meant to diminish the event and my work in promoting it as "loud," as clashing with the library and its appropriate tenor and atmosphere. Should I feel ashamed? I rejoice in the loudness—how powerful to take up space in these small but significant ways!

I wonder how I measure my "success" at centering QTPOC voices and lives in my work. If success could even be a measurable outcome. To whom am I accountable? Can this work truly be done if it's just one person doing it?

In October of that year, I connect with queer and trans groups on Barnard and Columbia campus, among them Barnard/Columbia Proud Colors, a group for QTPOC students. I run across campuses, posting flyers for Vivek and Elisha's reading wherever I can. The night of the event, October 21, 2014, I prepare a speech to introduce the authors. Those words later get published in a write-up on Lambda Literary's site:

Vivek and Elisha's new books make me want to do the impossible: go back in time so that they could have been a part of my life when I was a much younger queer South Asian girl dizzily searching the library stacks to find books that could tell me more, in images and words, about being queer and brown, histories of migration, myths passed down from generation to generation and communities: ones that are already so close to us, ones we wish for. (quoted in Kerr 2015)

The event is so much more than a reading: it features screenings of Elisha's drawings, Vivek's film, musical performance, and a table with books and artwork for sale. I recognize students, as well as other folks from beyond the colleges. Two queer South Asian youth show up right after the reading has ended, and Vivek gives them a personal mini-singing performance, a cappella, incorporating classical Indian and contemporary pop vocal styles in a gorgeous melody. The room bubbles with excitement as the night wraps up, with many lingering in conversation. Vivek and Elisha tell me that they have been invited to hang out with Proud Colors afterward. Hugging them, I say thanks for a beautiful night.

The audience did not fill all of the chairs. I estimate about twenty or so people attended. I reflect now that attendance numbers can't measure success. I also struggle with a lack of "evidence" of that gathering and its impact on people, the absence of impressive figures. What I do know: these events live in us, and become spaces we return to—not necessarily even geographical ones, but ones we co-create. They allow us to value the power of more intimate acts of community building. This has, in turn, helped me carve out space to build connections with my QTPOC colleagues at the library, and with QTPOC working at other libraries. Whether we are collaborating on a task or bonding over coffee off campus, these connections sustain me.

CLAIMING SPACE: COLLECTIONS

Along with dynamic and memorable spaces created through programs and events, I engage with library space every day through the development of collections. The responsibility entrusted to librarians, to select books that students and other library visitors will turn to for research and inquiry, shapes and reshapes library space in pronounced ways. Decades and decades of collection development preceded me as I entered my role as primary selector for humanities and global studies at the Barnard College Library. The legacy of those decisions still leaves traces in rows of book stacks, organized within the framework of the Library of Congress Classification system. That system, itself in service to the US government, bolsters a nation-state founded in the ongoing theft of Indigenous land, violence against Black people, Indigenous people, and People of Color, xenophobia, and imperialism. In 2011, my first year of work at the Barnard College Library, the library's general statement on its collections, then reflected on the website, began:

The approximate 300,000 volume circulating book collection is intended to serve the Barnard College curriculum. With strength in women's studies, dance, art, and literature, the collections are built and actively managed in collaboration with the Barnard faculty. Books are arranged according to the Library of Congress classification system and are located on the second and third floors of the library. (Barnard Library 2011)

This language set the tone for the collection, and it obscured a lot. A close read of these sentences uncovers some telling patterns.

First, there is a glaring absence of the active voice. The statement lists many verbs (serve, managed, built, arranged) without subjects. Who is building and maintaining the collection? On one hand, librarians select titles for the collection. But theirs is just one part of the labor that goes into building and maintaining it. Circulation and operations workers—among them, access specialists, reserves coordinators, and student circulation desk workers—do essential, daily collections work. Most of Barnard Library's staff of color have worked in these areas. They also get no recognition in the above statement for their work. The statement names library faculty as collaborators, but it leaves out the library staff, who field requests, respond to student needs, and improvise solutions for challenges to access. Solórzano and Yosso's framework of community cultural wealth illuminates an erasure of the knowledges, skills, and agency of library workers of color in manifesting what we come to know as the collection. The concept of navigational capital can illuminate what is unwritten in the collections policy—namely, "skills of maneuvering through social institutions.

Historically, this infers the ability to maneuver through institutions not created with Communities of Color in mind" (Solórzano and Yosso 2002, 80).

The statement also opens by expressing an intent to "serve the Barnard College curriculum." This doesn't tell us how collections uphold dominant knowledges. That the receiver of the service is defined as a curriculum and not *people* should truly give us pause. By privileging the curriculum of the college over people's needs, especially the needs of People of Color, including QTPOC, the library upholds the college's White Supremacist structures. The library makes plain its priorities by refusing to name and challenge racism.

We may ask what constitutes a "strength" in "women's studies, dance, art, and literature." What materials make a collection "strong"? The canonical history of an academic library collection that historically centered white, cis, heteronormative, patriarchal knowledge is not accounted for. The statement does not identify the lingering persistence of these hegemonic ways of knowing. By quantifying "strength" in numbers of volumes and lists of disciplines, the library boasts its riches without telling much about their content. This solidifies the academic library's investment in whiteness as property, which Cheryl Harris defines as characterized by the "unconstrained right to exclude" (1993, 1780). What might happen if we could read a shadow statement that drew out the negative space of the collection? What if we could learn about the voices and knowledges that did not make their way to the collection, or even to print, that were passed up in favor of the "needs of the curriculum"?

In my role as a librarian at Barnard, I have found myself in the unique space of being tasked with both collecting books to "support" the Barnard College curriculum, and being able to make space to collect books that challenge it. Within the past year, I have been able to make clear to a new director of collections strategy that my assigned task of collecting young adult fiction with LGBTQ protagonists has limited me, when I want to amplify and carve out space in the collection for work by QTPOC writing for a range of audience ages. So far, this has meant being able to access a specific allocation of funds for selecting QTPOC work, and drawing from other subject area funds to select more QTPOC work (for instance, in Africana studies or in Palestine studies). We are also in the early stages of discussing what it would take to create and apply a cataloging term to work in our library's collection that is by and about QTPOC.

This has expanded the possibilities for my own work, but I wonder: What could it mean to ask *my colleagues* to try to center a QTPOC agenda in their collection work, too? Why have I hesitated to make this ask, given that to do this work and to do it well would require more than one person? As I write this, I am forced to confront that I have perhaps too easily accepted the politics of knowledge production that Brockenbrough calls out, and this is because I have so often been made to feel that I have no other choice. The radio silence that too frequently greeted me at work when I talked about projects that advanced a QTPOC agenda had led me to believe that I was on my own.

INTERPRETING MY COUNTERSTORY WITH CRT FRAMEWORKS

Through Critical Race Theorizing, I hope to extend my conversation. Using counter-story, I have tried to make sense of my experiences as a queer librarian of color. In Critical Race Theory, I find not only methodological tools like counterstory, but also theoretical tools that bridge gaps between lived experience and broader, institutional dimensions of power. How could CRT prise loose the tightly interlocked structures of racist oppression that I don't yet have language for, so that I can better see them? How can CRT help to unlock strategies of resistance and transformation?

I will focus here on three frameworks of CRT: community cultural wealth, intersectionality, and Queer of Color Critique. I look to these frameworks to interpret my experience and open up strategies for resistance. I start with community cultural wealth, which teaches me to look for the spaces and strategies QTPOC have already been creating, or are on the verge of creating, that can foster abundance for ourselves. Intersectionality helps me to locate myself with greater attention so that I can develop better practices of solidarity. The work of Kimberlé Crenshaw and subsequent readings and practices of her theory of intersectionality teach me to pay attention to differences in positionality and the different contextual workings of oppression, always—this even includes moments when I am considering a more specific intersection of identity like QTPOC. Queer of Color Critique reminds me that the interplay between naming oppression and resisting it is a perpetual dance queer and trans People of Color do, in libraries and all the other spaces we move through, and that resistance involves imagining and building new possibilities for how we share and take up space.

COMMUNITY CULTURAL WEALTH

As cultural work, librarianship deeply intertwines questions of power and value. Community cultural wealth, a Critical Race Theory framework developed by Tara Yosso, challenges the deficit view of culture. The deficit view, a lens through which social scientists and other researchers on communities of color have examined their "subjects," reproduces itself ad nauseum—researchers find the deficits they search for and perpetuate deficit master narratives. In contrast, community cultural wealth gives us the tools to recognize what Yosso outlines as at least six forms of "capital" developed and sustained by communities of color. Briefly, these include aspirational, linguistic, social, navigational, resistant, and familial capital (Yosso 2005). For the purposes of my analysis, I am going to replace the word *capital* with *abundance*; for me, these qualities challenge capitalism's logics of scarcity and competition. I see queer and trans People of Color accessing and sharing all six of these forms of community cultural abundance. Two feel especially salient to me in the academic library context that I engage: familial abundance and resistant abundance.

On familial capital, Yosso writes about "those cultural knowledges nurtured among *familia* (kin) that carry a sense of community history, memory and cultural intuition" (2005, 79). Yosso explicitly acknowledges that familia can extend beyond "racialized, classed and heterosexualized inferences that comprise traditional understandings of 'family'" (2005, 79). This capacious understanding of the familial resonates with how I have experienced myself as a queer person of color and how I've learned from other QTPOC. The idea of chosen family means a lot to many queer and trans folks of color, as the intersecting forces of racism, homophobia, and transphobia can make certain connections with families of origin difficult, or prompt us to redefine family by gifting us family not solely determined by genetic or marriage ties.

QTPOC sustain familial abundance in many social spaces I nurture and am nurtured by, including library spaces. This nurturing unfolds in myriad ways, such as how we speak up in support of each other at meetings (often when no one else does), the times we share experiences and advice over tea, the uniquely delightful ways we affirm each other's sense of style and fashion, the sense of relief we can sometimes feel opening up about our relationships and families, the ease of not having to do so much explaining and contextualizing to be mutually understood. These networks are intergenerational. How we navigate social forces, our own identities, and language changes over time. I have found that I learn so much from younger QTPOC that I don't see myself as the older provider of "wisdom," but rather as part of an exchange of knowledges and strategies for survival.

For Yosso, resistant capital "refers to those knowledges and behaviors fostered through oppositional behavior that challenges inequality" (2005, 80). I believe that QTPOC always already practice forms of resistant abundance by being who we are. QTPOC resistant abundance can emerge from the resistance we must practice at multiple levels, including when we find ourselves in largely white queer spaces, or among other folks of color perpetuating homophobia and transphobia against us, or when navigating the host of brutal systems that render QTPOC life vulnerable. This resistant abundance has allowed me to sustain myself through projects like developing QTPOC-created collections—this work has also, in turn, been supported by the familial abundance I feel from friendships with QTPOC in and outside the library, many of them writers and artists themselves. The strategies to navigate those layers of oppression and to push back on them are often subtle, often bold.

I have also had to call on my own resistant abundance to help remind my white colleagues of connections between axes of oppression that they may imagine as separate. I learn from my QTPOC colleagues here, as they are constantly doing this work, too. As an example, in the past few years, I have been working with a small but growing group of coworkers to push for more gender-inclusive bathrooms in the newly opened (as of fall 2019) Barnard Library building. I have noticed that while it's promising that many agree on the importance of access to gender-inclusive bathrooms, it is very hard for white people to acknowledge why this is *especially* important for People of Color. Maybe the mental images white coworkers have of trans and gender nonconforming people default to white. Or maybe they imagine racism and transphobia as discrete issues, never connecting.

For People of Color in academia, who are all too familiar with the violences of exclusion and the way that colleges inflict surveillance on People of Color, the resonance is not a stretch. Access to gender-inclusive bathrooms is always already a racial justice issue. Perhaps a vital sign of our community cultural abundance is when we can recognize that struggles for justice are never isolated—and that we don't need to operate on a model of scarcity in imagining a more just world. How might QTPOC community cultural abundance allow us to make more space for each other? How might we find more ways to care for ourselves and each other as we enact resistance?

INTERSECTIONALITY

Intersectionality theory extends my thinking about my work as a queer South Asian American librarian by forcing me to be mindful of my positionality in relation to larger structures of power. It is the desire not to flatten or oversimplify QTPOC identity that leads me here, even as I have intersectionality theory to thank for the acronym QTPOC. Kimberlé Crenshaw introduced intersectionality in her writing and has, over the years, developed the term in her work as a lawyer, legal scholar, and activist. In her 1991 piece "Mapping the Margins," she calls out the limits of identity politics, not to get rid of it, but to demand better from the ways we politicize identity: "The problem with identity politics is not that it fails to transcend difference, as some critics charge, but rather the opposite—that it frequently conflates or ignores intragroup differences....Contemporary feminist and anti-racist discourses have failed to consider intersectional identities such as women of color" (1991, 1242). Crenshaw outlines three categories of intersectionality: structural, political, and representational. Structural intersectionality considers lived experience at the intersection of social structures that are oppressive. In other words, how does a person's specific social location with regard to class, gender, sexuality, race, and religion, among other categories by which power is distributed, structure their experiences differently (1991, 1245)? Crenshaw uses these categories to think through multiple dimensions of violence against women of color. Since the early years of CRT, Crenshaw's influence has meant that intersectionality—as a term, a theory, a method, and sometimes a misapplied catchphrase—has traveled far and wide. The gift of Crenshaw's thinking has been that intersectionality theory deepens both analysis of and action against racist oppression. Crenshaw has attentively followed the circuits her own theorizing has taken, and she continues to share that reflection, writing in 2015: "Intersectionality was a lived reality before it became a term. Today, nearly three decades after I first put a name to the concept, the term seems to be everywhere. But if women and girls of color continue to be left in the shadows, something vital to the understanding of intersectionality has been lost."

As I read those words, I reflect on the moment at which I write. June 2019 is Pride Month and the fiftieth anniversary of the Stonewall uprisings, a historic moment, among many, of resistance led by Black and Latinx trans and queer people in opposition to police violence against their communities. As we witness and participate in the joy of some Pride celebrations, my friends and I notice corporations and the police capitalizing on Pride to present a false rainbow-painted image of themselves as LGBTQ-friendly. While these images and events unfold, there is yet another layer: the ongoing and horrific violence perpetuated against trans People of Color, and in particular against Black trans women, that continues unabated. More recently, the first weekend of June 2019 saw the death of Layleen Cubilette-Polanco Xtravaganza, a 27-year-old Afro-Latina trans woman held in solitary confinement in Rikers Island jail (Willis 2019)—I remember that news of Layleen's death at the hands of a violent carceral system emerged the same day as Brooklyn Pride.

At first glance, it may seem that my last paragraph has a tangential relationship to academic libraries. Festivals in street spaces and bars, commemorating uprisings in streets and bars, cops encroaching on all of it, and then the violence of incarceration—what do these have to do with the academic library? With intersectionality in mind, everything.

Using Crenshaw's framework, I want to look particularly at the structural. That is to say, the locations of queer and trans People of Color at the intersections of race, gender, and sexual oppressions would make our experiences of academic libraries different from that of white people (including LGBTQ+ white people), and also *different among ourselves*. The library functions in ways that are parallel to other social institutions, like the educational system, like prisons, like systems that administer (and fail to administer) health care. Crenshaw crucially confronts how even institutions that have a stated purpose of "helping," that are designed to offset harm, can compound injustice, focusing on the example of shelters for immigrant women surviving abuse. She writes, "Intersectional subordination need not be intentionally produced; in fact, it is frequently the consequence of the imposition of one burden that interacts with preexisting vulnerabilities to create yet another dimension of dis-empowerment" (1991, 1249). So what might seem like support and affirmation for a group might actually harm people in the group living at the intersections, because of an unrecognized dimension of their social location. What might be positioned as "safety for women" might engage tactics that have historically targeted People of Color, thereby being unsafe for POC and specifically women of color.

Like so many higher education institutions in the United States, Barnard College, and the Library building, have historically functioned as sites of racist surveillance, violence, and exclusion. Founded in 1889 as a private women's college in New York City, Barnard, like Columbia University (with which it's affiliated), occupies the land of the Lenape people, and it was built with the labor of enslaved Black people. With a current student body of less than 3,000, Barnard defines itself through its mission statement: "As a college for women, Barnard embraces its responsibility to address issues of gender in all of their complexity and urgency and to help students achieve the personal strength that will enable them to meet the challenges they will encoun-ter throughout their lives" (Barnard College n.d.-a).

Barnard's carefully curated image as a college that supports, broadly, "women," contradicts the realities students of color face. An assault by security guards on a Black Columbia student in the spring of 2019 spurred a campus dialogue on what many Barnard students of color, especially Black students, have known and experienced frequently: racist harassment, surveillance, and violence (Saharan 2019). The sur-veillance of gender operates in intersection with racist surveillance. Barnard College has failed to put forth an admissions policy truly inclusive of trans students—a 2015 policy update that some have claimed as more trans-inclusive still requires applicants to "consistently live and identify as women" (Barnard College n.d.-b), a clause that disrespects gender self-determination. Restrooms that are designated gender-inclusive remain few and far between, with only one per floor in the new library building, despite advocacy efforts from students and staff.

What does this mean for me as a queer South Asian American librarian? In my QTPOC agenda, I need to take Crenshaw's cue of paying attention to the differences in positionality inherent in a coalitional term like *QTPOC*. We must work toward not just centering experiences and identities that mirror our own, but asking who even gets to be in the room. How might my privileges of class and caste status, from being a non-Black settler of color with US citizenship, from being read as a cis woman, make it easier for me to be "out" as queer at work and somewhat outspoken in my politics? How are my QTPOC colleagues, and other QTPOC working in the school, navigating different hurdles? How do QTPOC I am connected to in other parts of my life (friendship, creative worlds, and activism) experience the space of the library? How do social structures like incarceration create barriers and limit the possibilities of connection between QTPOC?

Listening and acting in solidarity with POC and especially QTPOC students, staff, and faculty, especially those most directly impacted by forces of anti-Blackness, colonialism, homophobia, ableism, and transphobia, is vital. We must think beyond what we see in front of us, imagine what we can't see, and imagine possibilities. Working toward ending harm against QTPOC in the library, how could we reach further, beyond those walls? Our lives extend into so many spaces. How could we, as QTPOC library workers, work toward a world without prisons, a world where education is free and not a commodity, a world where accessibility is centered and not seen as optional?

QUEER OF COLOR CRITIQUE

Building off of intersectionality theory, I take up the work of Queer of Color Critique because of what it offers to the specific intersectional locations of queer and trans People of Color in libraries. It analyzes how things are and strategizes how we could make them different. While Roderick Ferguson introduced the phrase "queer of color critique" in his book *Aberrations in Black*, Edward Brockenbrough's writing has applied Queer of Color Critique to the constellation of Critical Race Theory with a focus on education. Brockenbrough writes, "A 'QOC critique' indexes an interdisciplinary corpus of scholarship on the dialectics between hegemony and resistance that shape the lives of queer People of Color across local, national, and transnational contexts" (2016, 286). Brockenbrough offers a working model of what queer of color analysis entails: giving language and context to marginalization, and developing strategies of resistance. Brockenbrough writes about the complex ways that QTPOC navigate identity, including invisibility as a strategy.

I see a beautiful and inspiring practice of the Queer of Color Critique in the collectively authored piece "Queer of Color Space-Making in and beyond the Academic Industrial Complex." Here, the authors use "we" to refer to a specific collective gathering of QTPOC and to gesture more broadly to QTPOC as a larger group. They write, "But beyond studying oppressed peoples' spatial, political, and historic interventions, we were deeply committed to finding better ways of making and sharing space with each other. Our experiences and how we make and share space together are indexes of power and viable categories of theoretical analysis" (Bacchetta et al. 2018, 44). This intentional, collective, resistant making of space together as QTPOC strikes me as a praxis that takes Queer of Color Critique into the everyday. Critique is just as much about generating and making new ways of being together as it is about necessarily breaking down oppressive structures. How might this transport into libraries?

To start to engage this question, I turn to the work of queer librarians and archivists of color. Though not an archivist myself, I see my work as adjacent to, and frequently overlapping with, archival practice. In "Queering the Archive: Transforming the Archival Process," Lizeth Zepeda (2018) takes up Queer of Color Critique as a lens to employ in the processing of archival collections, with the specific example of the Sarah Valencia Collection at the Arizona Historical Society. Zepeda's writing challenges us to consider the word *queer* itself as a verb and a theoretical framework, and reminds us that "queerness is complex and is often not expressed explicitly in communities of color or in general" (94). Zepeda's work in interpreting, imagining, and describing photographs dwells in spaces of potentiality, rather than the need to label and fix identity. Zepeda pursues a fluid and dynamic reading of the photographs of Sarah Valencia, writing, "The possibility that Valencia may very well have been a lesbian is not necessarily important in this sense. Rather, what is important here is reading her life as open to the possibility of queerness without presuming an identity" (98). Zepeda later speaks of the strategy of adding access points in description, to open it to interpretation.

In gratitude to Zepeda's archival theorizing, I want to open up my understanding of QTPOC space in libraries. If we were to use the lenses of Queer of Color Critique, we might hold open a space of unknowing, of "the *possibility* of queerness with-out presuming an identity" (Zepeda 2018, 98; emphasis mine), as we think about *all* People of Color. I know, of course, that there are limits to this—I am not particularly invested in convincing People of Color who don't self-identify at this moment as queer, that they somehow must. However, what would it mean to hold open the possibility that for all of us, as People of Color, the ways we live, feel, and name our genders and sexualities might change, might grow, might dismantle normative structures? What languages (beyond the categories we are used to) would feel important to us in recog-nizing this? How could we be more generous with each other, by each admitting what we don't know?

CONCLUSION

The generative unknowingness that Queer of Color Critique brings to my analysis of my counterstory as a queer South Asian American librarian suggests new places where I hope to extend my thinking. In what directions could it go? I reflect on what remains undertheorized and untheorized in my writing here. The categories I rely on, so US-ian in context, don't reflect a much larger world of people whose identities exist outside the dominant. How would my counterstory look different if I analyzed it in terms of caste and a commitment to dismantling caste? How would QTPOC librarianship that foregrounded decolonization be practiced? What would it mean to sustain library spaces that are inclusive of sex workers? What if the very institutions that we rely on for the infrastructure of the library, like academia, did not exist (or at least not as the privatized spaces that they now are)? I can't help but think of the opening lines of José Esteban Muñoz's *Cruising Utopia: The Then and There of Queer Futurity*, where he wrote, "We are not yet queer. we may never touch queerness, but we can feel it as the warm illumination of a horizon imbued with potentiality. We have never been queer, yet queerness exists for us as an ideality that can be distilled from the past and used to imagine a future" (2009, 1). These words take me beyond the present and into pasts and futures that always keep me moving, searching. I hope we can meet each other then and there.

BIBLIOGRAPHY

Bacchetta, Paola, Fatima El-Tayeb, Jin Haritaworn, Jillian Hernandez, SA Smythe, Vanessa E. Thompson, and Tiffany Willoughby-Herard. 2018. "Queer of Color Space-Making in and beyond the Academic Industrial Complex." *Critical Ethnic Studies* 4 (1): 44–63.

Barnard College. n.d.-a. "The College and Its Mission." Barnard College (website). Accessed August 10, 2020. https://barnard.edu/college-and-its-mission.

Barnard College. n.d.-b. "Transgender Policy." Barnard College (website). Accessed August 10, 2020. https://barnard.edu/transgender-policy.

Barnard Library. 2011. "The Collections." Barnard College Library (website). 2011. Archived at https://web.archive.org/web/20111110215502/http://library.barnard.edu/about-the-library/collections.

Brockenbrough, Edward. 2015. "Queer of Color Agency in Educational Contexts: Analytic Frameworks from a Queer of Color Critique." *Educational Studies* 51 (1): 28–44.

Brockenbrough, Edward. 2016. "Queer of Color Critique." In *Critical Concepts in Queer Studies and Education*, edited by Nelson M. Rodriguez, Wayne J. Martino, Jennifer C. Ingrey, and Edward Brockenbrough, 285–297. New York: Palgrave Macmillan.

Crenshaw, Kimberlé. 1991. "Mapping the Margins: Intersectionality, Identity Politics, and Violence against Women of Color." *Stanford Law Review* 43 (6): 1241–1299.

Crenshaw, Kimberlé. 2015. "Why Intersectionality Can't Wait: Intersectionality Was Meant to Help People Understand Each Other, Not to Divide Them." *Washington Post* blog, September 24, 2015. http://www.washingtonpost.com/news/in-theory/wp/2015/09/24/why-intersectionality-cant-wait.

Harris, Cheryl I. 1993. "Whiteness as Property." *Harvard Law Review* 106 (8): 1707–1791.

Kerr, Theodore. 2015. "Writers Vivek Shraya and Elisha Lim Talk Craft, Race, Identity, and Getting Compensated for Your Work." Lambda Literary (website), March 21, 2015. Accessed August 10, 2020. https://www.lambdaliterary.org/2015/03/writers-vivek-shraya-and-elisha-lim-talk-craft-race-identity-and-getting-compensated-for-your-work/.

Muñoz, José Esteban. 2009. *Cruising Utopia: The Then and There of Queer Futurity*. New York: New York University Press.

Saharan, Shubham. 2019. "Conversations on Institutional Racism, Campus Safety Take Center Stage in Classrooms following Barnard Public Safety Incident." *Columbia Daily Spectator*, April 30, 2019. http://www.columbiaspectator.com/news/2019/04/30/conversations-on-institutional-racism-campus-safety-take-center-stage-in-classrooms-following-barnard-public-safety-incident/.

Solórzano, Daniel G., and Tara J. Yosso. 2002. "Critical Race Methodology: Counter-Storytelling as an Analytical Framework for Education Research." *Qualitative Inquiry* 8 (1): 23–44.

Willis, Raquel. 2019. "Layleen Cubilette-Polanco Died in the System, but Her Fight Lives On." *Out*, November 20, 2019. https://www.out.com/print/2019/11/20/layleen-cubilette-polanco-died-system-her-fight-lives.

Yosso, Tara J. 2005. "Whose Culture Has Capital? A Critical Race Theory Discussion of Community Cultural Wealth." *Race Ethnicity and Education* 8 (1): 69–91.

Zepeda, Lizeth. 2018. "Queering the Archive: Transforming the Archival Process." *DisClosure: A Journal of Social Theory* 27 (1): 94–102.

6

ANN ALLEN SHOCKLEY
An Activist-Librarian for Black Special Collections

Shaundra Walker

In 1961 Paul M. Smith Jr., associate professor of education at North Carolina College at Durham (now North Carolina Central University), authored an article on special collections in Negro college libraries. He expressed concern that a review of the American Library Directory (1960) revealed that only nearly half of the libraries indicated the existence of a special Negro collection. Smith felt that most of the collections lacked the uniqueness that historically defined such collections (Randall and Goodrich 1936, 150). He was particularly critical of the ability of small Black college libraries to successfully maintain special collections, with their limited funds, staff, and facilities. Smith posited, "Does not such conditions raise questions as to the validity and meaning of special collections on the Negro in small colleges?" (1961, 151).

The "small Black colleges" Smith spoke of were likely those not as large or as well-known as schools like Howard University, Fisk University, and Atlanta University. His critique implies that outside of a few special institutions, Black colleges were generally ill-equipped to host and manage special collections. The definition that Smith used is limiting and fails to consider the possibility that such collections at smaller Black colleges could serve a different, yet equally significant purpose.

This chapter will argue that special collections in both large and small Black college libraries and those serving Black studies programs indeed have a unique meaning, one that is closely tied to the mission of historically Black colleges and universities and Black studies' to meet the needs of Black communities. Smith's definition of special collections focuses on attributes such as "comprehensiveness, quantity and worthwhileness"; as compared to collections at other libraries, Black special collections and Black studies collections often are special as they relate to the main collections in their libraries. In Black colleges, the development of these collections represents an attempt to push back against collections that were often imposed on Black libraries. Their development and maintenance speak to the deficiencies in cataloging and classification systems that traditionally have served to obliterate the experiences and accomplishments of Black people.

To shed light on Smith's question, this chapter will highlight the work of Ann Allen Shockley, a Black activist-librarian who wrote extensively on the purpose and function of Black special collections. Shockley, who was a part of a continuum of Black activist-librarians, was extraordinary in that she raised important questions about the need for special collections in libraries serving HBCUs, their function in support of Black studies programs on predominantly white campuses, and the roles of librarians and publishers in developing and supporting such collections.

COUNTERNARRATIVE/CRT DEFINITION

Black special collections serve a special function within the libraries of Black colleges and in libraries serving Black studies programs. Historical evidence confirms that there is a long tradition in the Black community of collecting and preserving information that describes the experience of Black people (Albritton 1998). Beginning in the early 1800s, free Blacks established literary and historical societies, with a focus on social uplift through the reading and discussion of literature. In cities throughout the eastern United States, "large circles of bibliophiles" developed, evolving into the Negro Book Collectors Exchange in 1915 (Wesley 1990). Prominent members included Henry Proctor Slaughter, Arthur Alfonzo Schomburg, Rev. Charles Douglass Martin, and John Edward Bruce.

These organizations and their bibliophile members and founders were the forerunners of today's Black special collections. Their materials functioned as a revisionist history for the race and "provided irrefutable proof that African Americans could achieve" (Albritton 1998, 38). Donations from collectors such as Schomburg, Jesse E. Moreland, and Slaughter enriched the libraries at Fisk University, Howard University, and Atlanta University, respectively. Their collections established Black intellectual legacies that persist into the present day.

Little attention has been paid to the role of Black librarians to advance the cause of highlighting the history and achievements of Black people. While bibliophiles such

as Schomburg, Moreland, and Slaughter collected materials, the ongoing responsibility of arranging and making collections widely available to researchers fell to librarians working in Black libraries (Battle 1990).

The building and maintenance of Black special collections is consistent with the
counternarrative tool that is often invoked in applications of Critical Race Theory
(CRT). CRT has recently been invoked in the literature of library science. In general,
CRT analyses in library and information science (LIS) critique the image of the library
as a neutral, objective, apolitical institution (Honma 2005). Seen through the lens of
CRT, these claims become masks for hiding the many ways that the library has been
used as a tool by dominant groups to maintain power and privilege. With the LIS
field, the framework has been used to critique cataloging and classification systems
(Adler and Harper 2018; Furner 2007; Higgins 2016), reference services (Brook, Ellenwood, and Lazzaro 2015; Hall 2012), and the recruitment and promotion of library
personnel (Hathcock 2015; Griffin 2013), among other topics. As demonstrated in
scholarship by Mabbott (2017), it is also is an appropriate framework for analyzing
the inherent power in collection development.

Several tenets of CRT will be engaged in this chapter, including an appreciation
for the lived experience of People of Color, a critique of liberalism, and an interrogation of institutionalized racism, particularly as it functions in cataloging and classification systems and library collections. Within the tenet that values the experiential
knowledge of People of Color, the counternarrative, one that challenges existing narratives, emerges as a particularly useful tool. Through the work of Ann Allen Shockley,
this chapter will present the idea that Black special collections, developed by Black
librarians and others concerned with the plight of Black people, have operated as
counternarratives within larger library collections. The traditional library collection
functions as a "master narrative," or single story, one that presents an often distorted, deficient narrative of Black people. CRT allows the Black special collection to
emerge as a liberating tool for advancing social justice.

Black activist-librarians have played a particular role in countering racial stereotypes, partnering with Black bibliophiles, intellectuals, and organizations to challenge
the embedded, persistent nature of racism in society and written knowledge. Such
collaborations have required activist librarians to wholeheartedly reject notions of the
library as a neutral, color-blind, apolitical institution. They have used their agency
to curate materials by and about Black people as a bold testament against prevailing
sentiments. The Black special collection is not just a mere assemblage of books and
manuscripts, but a weapon in a centuries-old war for recognition of Black humanity.

ABOUT HISTORICALLY BLACK COLLEGES AND UNIVERSITIES

For several reasons, it is critical to situate Ann Allen Shockley's life and work within the context of the historically Black college/university (HBCU). She received her undergraduate education from Fisk University, a private liberal arts HBCU. All of her experience working as a librarian was in libraries on HBCU campuses. Relatedly, her writings about libraries primarily center on working with Black special collections, initially in HBCUs and later in predominantly white institutions (PWIs) with Black studies programs. Collectively, these decisions suggest that Shockley was intentional about her praxis.

According to the Higher Education Act of 1965, HBCUs are "any historically black college or university that was established prior to 1964, whose principal mission was, and is, the education of black Americans, and that is accredited by a nationally recognized accrediting agency or association…or is, according to such an agency or association, making reasonable progress toward accreditation" (White House Initiative on HBCUs, n.d.). Today there are 107 of these institutions, primarily located in the southern United States.

HBCUs were founded to provide higher education to African Americans at a time when most colleges and universities denied such opportunities to them. Established by formerly enslaved men and women, Black church denominations such as the African Methodist Episcopal Church, and northern white missionary societies, these institutions endeavored to equip African Americans with the necessary skills to fully participate in American life.

Historically, HBCUs have faced significant challenges in areas ranging from enrollment to finances to leadership. Similarly, and relatedly, the libraries of HBCUs have faced problems related to their collections, staffing, technology, and funding. Despite the circumstances, Black librarians working in HBCUs have traditionally maintained separate collections of books and other materials about the Black experience. While several critiques of HBCU libraries exist in the literature, of note is a 1942 study of Black higher education, which compared libraries at Black colleges to their counterparts at PWIs. HBCU libraries were found to have larger collections of Black books and other resources than their counterparts (Brown et al. 1942).

It is worth noting that libraries at HBCUs have been the beneficiaries of white philanthropy, expressed through donations of funds to erect library buildings, to enhance collections, and to support the education of Black librarians. Foundations such as the Julius Rosenwald Fund donated collections of "well-balanced books" and appear to have had great influence over the development of library collections at

HBCUs (Smith 1940, 51). Within this context, attempts to build Black special collections at HBCUs, however meager, take on additional significance.

BLACK LIBRARIANS AS ACTIVISTS

According to Beilin (2018), "the ideology of library neutrality, still a structuring feature of librarianship in North America, has served to obscure, minimize, or even deny the many ways in which librarians in the past were activists, both inside and outside of their libraries" (21). This is especially true for Black librarians, who when faced with the consequences of dual, segregated, and unequal education systems, have long fulfilled the role of activists, both on their campuses and in the larger society. Realizing the power of information, these librarians have been advocates for establishing and maintaining library collections for Black communities and for full and equal participation by Black librarians within the library profession.

One such early activist-librarian was Ruby Elizabeth Stutts Lyells, whose work in HBCU libraries took place at two Mississippi HBCUs, Jackson State College (now University) and Alcorn Agricultural and Mining College (now Alcorn State University). Valedictorian of the Alcorn class of 1929 (BS history) and the Hampton Institute Library School (BS), she was the first Black Mississippian to earn a professional library degree when she graduated from the University of Chicago in 1942 (Posey 1994).

Lyells's educational achievements are noteworthy on several fronts. She was one of only 183 graduates of the Hampton Institute Library School, a ten-year Carnegie Foundation–funded experiment in segregated library education that provided bachelor-level training. She endeavored to obtain advanced librarianship training at a time when options for graduate education for Black students were limited. According to Curtis (1935), between 1900 and 1934, only two African Americans earned master's degrees. It was not until the library education program at historically Black Atlanta University was established in 1941 that Black students in the southeastern United States gained wider access to master's-level training. Prior to that date, those who aspired to obtain credentials beyond the bachelors of library science, like Lyells, were forced to attend library education programs in PWIs, where they were likely to encounter hostile conditions. For example, in response to a 1939 survey question on the performance of Black students in northern library schools, one school responded as follows:

While we have every sympathy for the Negro woman student of course no prejudice, we discourage them for trying to enter the ____ School for Library Science or indeed any department of the University, because there is literally no satisfactory place for them to live in ____. We have had, therefore, no Negro graduates since 1936. (Barker and Jackson 1939, 41)

It is worth noting that despite the passage of eighty years, the experience reflected in the quote above closely mirrors that of some contemporary library students of color who endeavor to gain master's-level education. The lack of progress in this area confirms the embedded persistent nature of racism in American society and the library profession, as CRT points out.

Lyells was an outspoken advocate for civil rights and libraries, both public libraries and those serving Black land grant institutions, such as Alcorn. At a time when the Mississippi Library Association denied membership to African Americans, she worked to establish a library division of the Mississippi Teachers Association, the state professional association for Black teachers who could not join the white Mississippi Association of Teachers (Carey 2018). She was also an active member of the Mississippi Republican Party and the Negro Federation of State Women's Club. A fiery orator, she understood the importance of collecting materials by and about Blacks, stating that "if a man can learn to look at himself through the perspective of history and of things to come, in whatever narrow category he may find himself acting at any given time, the immediate goals which he sets for himself will have direction and meaning" (Lyells, 1949, 660). While speaking at the 1944 Emancipation Day at the Jackson YMCA, Lyells connected the study of one's history to their liberation: "For when we study our past and contemplate our heroes, we fortify ourselves against a tendency to apologize for our racial identity. By frequently reviewing our history we come to know the heart and spirit of our race; we get a sense of our heritage; we get perspective and inspiration" (349–350).

Her graduate thesis evaluated the Negro special collection of the George C. Hall branch of the Chicago Public Library. She also wrote articles in various library and education journals, including *Library Journal*, *Library Quarterly*, and the *Journal of Negro Education*. Like the Black bibliophiles who came before her, Lyells engaged in efforts to document the history of African Americans. She authored a book titled *Understanding the Negro (Revised): A List of Books by and about the Negro, Selected to Give a Background for Understanding What the Negro Thinks in the Present Crisis*, a bibliography developed from reviews in *Book Review Digest*.

E. J. Josey is perhaps the best-known Black activist-librarian. Born in Norfolk, Virginia, in 1924, Josey served in the United States Army from 1943 to 1946. Once discharged, he enrolled at Howard University, a private HBCU in Washington, D.C., where he studied music and graduated in 1949. Josey would go on to earn an MS degree in history from Columbia University, an experience which led to a job in the university's journalism library. Encouraged to attend library school by a colleague, he received a master's in library science from the State University of New York at Albany in 1953, the second African American to earn an MLS from the school. After a brief stint at the Free Library of Philadelphia, he was employed at the library at Delaware State College (the 1890 land grant college for African Americans) before moving on to serve as director of the library at Savannah State College (Abdullahi 1992).

While working at Savannah State, Josey applied to join the Georgia Library Association (GLA), but was denied membership due to his race. GLA, like other southern library associations, denied membership to Black librarians well into the 1960s. Josey was strategic in calling for the American Library Association to deny membership to state organizations that excluded Black librarians from joining. His activism forced the GLA to integrate, and in 1964 he became the first Black member of the organization; other state library associations quickly followed suit, leading to a trickle-down effect that integrated virtually all of the southern state library associations. As African American librarians and other librarians of color continue to report discriminatory experiences in the profession, it is interesting to note that most southern library associations integrated less than sixty years ago.

Josey would go on to a long and prolific career in the profession. Among his many publications are *The Black Librarian in America* (1970), *What Black Librarians Are Saying* (1972), and *Handbook of Black Librarianship* (1977), the latter which was coauthored by Shockley. Lyells, Josey, and Shockley share several common experiences. Each of them received their undergraduate training in HBCUs. Favors (2013) argues that historically Black colleges and universities provided a "second curriculum" to their students, one that "ensconced students in racial consciousness, gave them political motive, and presented Black youth with a blueprint for how to tackle the hypocrisies embedded in American culture" (92). As students at Fisk, Howard, and Alcorn, respectively, Shockley, Josey, and Lyells were educated in this tradition. For example, while attending Fisk, Shockley wrote for the *Fisk Herald*, which described itself as "an outlet for the creative efforts of the Fisk student litterati [*sic*] and endeavors to make the student body more aware of the intellectual and social environment in which it finds itself today" (Fisk University 1948). Lyells served as associate manager for the *Alcornite*, Alcorn's yearbook.

Although educated in southern HBCUs, Lyells, Josey, and Shockley faced limited opportunities to obtain master's-level library training in the southeastern United States. As noted previously, it was not until 1941, when the library education program at Atlanta University opened, that southern African Americans gained wider access to master's-level preparation in their geographic region. Only two HBCUs,

Atlanta University and North Carolina Central University, ever offered an ALA-accredited master's of library science degree. Lyells, Josey, and Shockley all obtained advanced degrees at library education programs in PWIs.

Despite or perhaps because of their collective experiences, they all returned to service in HBCU libraries and, most importantly, served as activist-librarians in their own right. Of the three, Shockley is the only one whose library career took place exclusively in HBCUs.

ANN ALLEN SHOCKLEY

Ann Allen Shockley was born to Henry and Bessie Lucas Allen on June 21, 1927, in Louisville, Kentucky. In 1948 she graduated from Fisk University, a historically Black liberal arts university in Nashville, Tennessee. She went on to earn a master's of library science degree from Western Reserve University (now Case Western Reserve University) in 1959. Shockley began her career as a journalist, writing primarily for the *Louisville Defender*, the newspaper of her hometown (Dandridge 1987).

She is best known for her literary works centering the lives of Black lesbians. Her novels *Loving Her* (1974), *The Black and White of It* (1980), *Say Jesus and Come to Me* (1982), and *Celebrating Hotchlaw* (2005) illuminate the lives of an overlooked demographic. Her writing exemplifies the very type of work that Black special collections endeavor to preserve and make available, ones that illuminate experiences that might otherwise be unnoticed and undervalued by other collections. In addition to her literary works, she also authored *Afro-American Women Writers, 1746–1933: An Anthology and Critical Guide* (1988). Reportedly, the reference work was a labor of love for her, as she received no grant or clerical support, and she began assembling it in 1978, using extra time on holidays and over summers. In describing her inspiration for the work, she stated, "I shared a personal empathy with many of those women whose problems mirrored my own and those of women writers throughout the centuries" (Foster 1990, 151).

Between the time she worked as a journalist and when she authored her acclaimed novels, she was employed as a librarian in several libraries serving historically Black colleges and universities (HBCUs), including Delaware State College (now Delaware State University) in 1959 to 1960 and Maryland State College (now the University of Maryland Eastern Shore) in 1960 to 1969. She returned to her alma mater, Fisk University, in 1969, retiring as special collections librarian in 1988 (Bucher 2008, 184).

With the exception of recent scholarship by Pollock and Haley (2018), Shockley's writing on library issues and career as a librarian, and particularly her work as an activist-librarian, have received little more than passing references. This is particularly interesting when one considers that Shockley was a contemporary of E. J. Josey, who is well-known throughout the library profession. Their paths likely crossed on multiple occasions, as both worked at Delaware State College, the state's 1890 Black land grant institution. Relatedly, both were involved in the Black Caucus of the American Library Association, the oldest of the American Library Association's five ethnic caucuses. A decade after their paths crossed at Delaware State, Shockley and Josey collaborated on *The Black Librarian in America* (1970).

SHOCKLEY'S WRITINGS ON BLACK COLLECTIONS

Between 1961 and 1977, Shockley authored a series of articles and book chapters dealing with Black special collections. She first tackled the question of the proper place for books by and about Black people in a 1961 *Library Journal* article. At that time, Shockey was employed as circulation librarian at Maryland State College, where some students had questioned the library staff about why books by and about Black people were separated from the rest of the library collection. The topic appears to have also been discussed among librarians at Black colleges (Shockley 1961).

To address the question of the need for special Negro collections in the Negro college library, Shockley surveyed twelve Black colleges for their thoughts on the "nature, feasibility, and practicality" of such collections (1961, 2049). Of the twelve, only two lacked a Negro collection. Josey justified such collections this way: "Because of the progress of the Negro, he will be of increasing research interest" (Shockley 1961, 2049). At Hampton Institute, the respondent saw the collection as "a source of information as well as inspiration for its students" (Shockley 1961, 2049). At Fisk University, another advantage was advanced: the benefits of such a collection to the surrounding community.

Shockley (1961) seemed to favor Negro special collections, arguing that such collections needed "special housing, special staff supervision, special acquisition policies, special usage" (2050). She concluded that "the collection should be interpreted as a source of pride, dignity, and worth" (2050). The question of the appropriateness of Black special collections was not settled by Shockley's article. Black librarians and historians continued to debate the question.

For example, from October 21 to 23, 1965, the Atlanta University School of Library Service collaborated with the Association for the Study of Negro Life and History (ASNLH; now the Association for the Study of African American Life and History, or ASAALH) to deliver an institute called "Materials by and about American Negroes."

Sponsored by the Rockefeller Foundation, the institute featured librarians and historians concerned with available information on the Black experience. Atlanta University, where W. E. B. Du Bois wrote *The Souls of Black Folk*, edited the Atlanta University Studies, and established *Phylon*, among other accomplishments, was a fitting location for such a discussion. Ninety-six people including librarians and scholars attended (not including the historians), representing twenty-one states and the District of Columbia (Phinazee 1967).

This gathering of librarians and historians highlights the historical relationship between Black librarians and the professional association that birthed Negro History Week (now Black History Month) and published journals such as the *Journal of Negro History* and the *Negro History Bulletin*.

Of note was a panel titled, "Negro Collections vs. Negro Materials," which featured a series of librarians who shared their opinions on the efficacy of Black special collections. The first panelist was Dorothy Briscoe, librarian at Texas Southern University, the state's HBCU land grant institution. Briscoe affirmed the place and importance of Black special collections, stating,

College libraries, especially those that are predominately Negro and will undoubtedly remain that way for a number of years to come, more than ever before, are in need of collections for the study of Negro history. The Negro, for the most part, has been somewhat ignored and omitted from the history of the United States and much of what has been recorded has a one-sided orientation. For that reason, Negroes themselves know very little of their history and heritage and what is worse still, are inclined to be somewhat uninterested in their history. (Phinazee 1967, 6)

She suggested that a special collection was indeed beneficial. According to Briscoe,

The separateness of this type of collection is not based solely on the fact that material included is on the Negro. Rather, this type of special collection (made available through the gathering of books and other materials) allows for a more comprehensive consideration and treatment of a certain phase of history long neglected and misinterpreted, which by necessity must be studied, examined, and researched in order to provide the missing link in the history of a people and the history of a nation. (Phinazee 1967, 6)

Here we see a bold statement that alludes to the deficiencies of cataloging and classification systems that have historically marginalized nonwhite, non-Western materials. Black special collections then can be seen to have a liberating, emancipating function. Such collections, rather than relegating materials about the experiences of Black people to a subordinate status, instead elevate them to a level that is at least on par with libraries' primary or main collections.

Virginia Lacey Jones, dean of the library school at Atlanta University, agreed with Briscoe. "It seems important that as we [Negroes] move into the mainstream of American life that we do not lose track of our background and our contributions to American life," stated Jones (Phinazee 1967, 1–2). Speaking on the special role of librarians, she continued,

We need to make every effort to develop well-organized collections of materials by and about Negroes. We owe this to ourselves as a group and to society as a whole. It is our responsibility to collect and preserve the materials to document the story of our contributions, our struggles, our problems and our achievements. Collections of materials by and about American Negroes are vital to Negroes to help them to know the facts and to develop pride in their racial heritage. Such collections are just as important for members of other racial groups so that they can learn the truth and develop greater appreciation and understanding of the Negro. (Phinazee 1967, 1–2)

Jones's challenge to other librarians requires them to take on the role of a storyteller through their collection work, to correct the injustices of past collection development efforts toward a goal of both educating and informing Black people about their history, but also to inform those of other races. Her use of the word *truth* implies that there is a need to correct past injustices, to offer a counterstory to correct one that is lacking.

John E. Scott, librarian at West Virginia State College and former president of the West Virginia Library Association, argued against Black special collections. He was generally opposed to separate special collections in small and medium-sized college libraries, regardless of the subject. Like Smith (1961) before him, Scott was critical of the capacity of the "majority of Negro colleges" to develop collections of quantity or quality that would constitute a special collection (Phinazee 1967, 9). He offered that "all libraries should be saturated with excellent collections of good books by and about Negroes; however, I would not like to see these books separated or segregated from other books. They should take their rightful place on the shelves" (Phinazee 1967, 10).

The different perspectives on the place of Black special collections illustrate the range of opinions among librarians working in Black colleges. Briscoe's and Jones's positions represent a more aggressive approach to addressing the marginalization created by traditional cataloging and classification systems. Scott, while not in total agreement with his colleagues, indirectly emphasizes the problem, as he articulates that all libraries should contain an abundance of books by Black authors and about Black experiences. It is interesting to note that while West Virginia State College was founded prior to the Civil Rights Act of 1964 and meets the established criteria for designation as an HBCU, unlike Atlanta University and Texas Southern University, its student population transformed from a majority Black population to a majority-white, commuter, adult demographic. At the time that John E. Scott attended the conference, the college he represented was not necessarily representative of Black colleges of the day and likely had different needs and objectives.

The question of the relevancy of Black special collections does not appear to have been resolved at the meeting. Although Shockley's name is not among the list of attendees, she continued to write and speak on the topic. By 1969, she was head of special collections at her alma mater, Fisk University. Although she was working in an HBCU, she remained interested in Black collections in general, particularly the mushrooming collections designed to support burgeoning Black studies programs at PWIs.

The genesis of the discipline of Black studies is often traced back to pressures and demands from students at several colleges in California in the late 1960s. The period saw an influx of students of color on white campuses, students who "confronted the false notions that scholarly investigations were objective and unbiased explorations of the range of human knowledge, history, creativity, artistry and scientific discovery" (Bobo, Hudley, and Michel 2004, 2). With this in mind, students at San Francisco State College (now University) began pushing for a more socially relevant education. For example, the Black Student Union began pressuring the administration to create a free-standing Black studies program. Similarly, at the University of California Santa Barbara (USCB), students took over the computer center and outlined several demands, including the creation of a Black studies department and a Black studies center and support for library resources to support the curriculum, among other demands. The Black studies Department and the Center for Black Studies were established at USCB in the fall of 1969 (Bobo, Hudley, and Michel 2004).

While the programs at San Francisco State College and the University of California Santa Barbara are often seen as the first Black studies programs, several scholars (Warren 2011; White 2011) credit the field's beginnings to groundbreaking work earlier in the twentieth century by Black intellectuals such as Carter G. Woodson and W. E. B. Du Bois. Woodson's work in establishing the ASNLH and Negro History Week and his editorship of the *Journal of Negro History* and creation of the *Negro History Bulletin*, along with Du Bois's Atlanta University Conferences and related research reports, arguably laid the "conceptual origins" for Black studies (White 2011, 70). From this standpoint, the argument can be made that Black studies "emerged from the segregated and self-determined spaces" such as HBCUs and independent associations like ASNLH (White 2011, 70). If this stance is accepted, it should not surprise that Shockley's expanded interest in Black special collections coincided with the discipline's growth from within "segregated and self-determined spaces" to the establishment of autonomous programs and centers at PWIs. A close reading of her scholarship, both her writing and her speaking, supports this position.

Following her 1961 article on Black special collections in HBCUs, Shockley wrote numerous articles, served as an instructor at professional development conferences on Black special collections, and spoke on the topic. Her *Handbook for the Administration of Special Black Collections*, a rich collection of resources and activities, was used as a resource for four Black studies librarianship training programs hosted by Fisk in 1970, 1971, 1972, and 1974.

In her writing, she provided guidance on a wide range of topics related to Black special collections. She was keen to acknowledge the contributions of the forerunners of Black special collections, including HBCUs such as Howard, Fisk, Tuskegee, and Atlanta University, as well as the Schomburg Collection of the New York Public Library. According to Shockley (1971), those "libraries perceived the need for collecting and preserving materials on the black man as a truly visible force in the progress of mankind long before the black 'explosion'" (1).

She was openly critical of hastily assembled collections to support Black studies programs, noting that many were "staffed by librarians who know nothing about black history, black books, or black people" (1971, 1). In Shockley's view, librarians supporting Black collections "should be sensitive to the role of the Black man's experience in America and with that understanding, try to help interpret black people, black thoughts, and above all black feelings through books" (1971, 2). She understood the relationship between librarians and publishers, realizing that useful Black books would be overlooked if they were not reviewed in mainstream review publications. Black librarians in particular were encouraged to review Black books. Shockley lamented the lack of diversity among book reviewers; she advised concerned librarians to "take a cursory glance at the names of *Library Journal*'s reviews and see how many black ones you recognize" (10).

Her criticism was not limited to librarians; she also chastised publishers for putting out reprints of little value and charging high prices for original editions of books by and about African Americans (Shockley 1974b). Her writing offered advice on collection development and evaluation related to Black special collections, often including lists of useful bibliographies for consultation. She encouraged librarians to become familiar with obscure Black publishers such as Broadside Press, Third World Press, Black Academy Press, and others (Shockley 1974a).

Shockley advocated for faculty and staff participation in decisions about the development of Black special collections. She also saw a role for students in building collections, stating that "students, particularly black students, should also be enlisted to aid in selection. They should be made to feel that the establishing of a good collection that is indicative of the struggles, hopes and dreams of black people is *their* thing too!" (Shockley 1971, 4). She understood the value of the experiential knowledge of People of Color, an understanding that resonates with CRT as well as the Black studies discipline.

Shockley (1974a) also understood the embedded, persistent nature of racism and envisioned that Black special collections would always be needed:

As long as there is a need to study the black man's past and record the present for posterity—and this will always be—there will be the need for Special Black Collections. The academic world cannot afford to repeat its pattern of making the black man invisible. By refusing to recognize this visibility in the past, a great blight has been inflicted upon the ethical and creditable scholarship of the academic world. As a constant reminder of foregone inequities, Special Black Collections should stand out as resource testimonials to the history of the black man, for here is where the true information is housed. (ii)

Years before the development of CRT as an analytical framework, Shockley understood the potential for librarianship to be used as a tool to advance racial justice. Not only did she use her knowledge, as shared through her writing, teaching, and speaking, but also her career trajectory serves as an example to present-day librarians on how they can use their vocation to challenge assumptions about the history and achievements of Black people. Rejecting beliefs about the library as a neutral, apolitical institution, Shockley recognized the power and potential of library collections to dispute the validity of stereotypes.

While working at Fisk University, Ann Allen Shockley interviewed acclaimed author and Jackson State University professor Margaret Alexander Walker, who stated, "I personally believe that black people need to preach in their work, but to preach so subtly that you don't think of it as preaching" (Alexander 1973). Shockley's career as an activist-librarian personifies Walker's statement. While she was not viewed as an activist-librarian during her library career, viewing Shockley's accomplishments through the lens of CRT allows one to reveal, expand, and acknowledge her activism in new ways. Her advocacy for the proper administration of Black special collections, whether on HBCU or PWI campuses, can be seen as not only leadership in the profession but also social justice work. CRT provides an opportunity for collection development to become a subversive, political activity, one with the potential to create a revisionist collective history, a counternarrative to the prevailing stories about Black people that exist in many academic library collections.

BIBLIOGRAPHY

Abdullahi, Ismail. 1992. *E. J. Josey: An Activist Librarian*. Metuchen, NJ: Scarecrow Press.

Adler, Melissa, and Lindsey M. Harper. 2018. "Race and Ethnicity in Classification Systems: Teaching Knowledge Organization from a Social Justice Perspective." *Library Trends* 67 (1): 52–73. https://doi.org/10.1353/lib.2018.0025.

Albritton, Rosie L. 1998. "The Founding and Prevalence of African-American Social Libraries and Historical Societies, 1828–1918: Gatekeepers of Early Black History, Collections, and Literature." In *Untold Stories: Civil Rights, Libraries, and Black Librarianship*, edited by John Mark Tucker, 23–46. Champaign, IL: Publications Office, Graduate School of Library and Information Science.

Alexander, Margaret Walker. 1973. Interview by Ann Allen Shockley. Nashville, TN, July 18, 1973.

Barker, Tommie Dora, and Evalene Parsons. 1939. *Memorandum on the Need in the South for a Library School or Schools for Negroes*. Chicago, IL: American Library Association, Board of Education for Librarianship.

Battle, Thomas C. 1990. "Introduction." In *Black Bibliophiles and Collectors: Preservers of Black History*, edited by Elinor Des Verny Sinnette, W. Paul Coates, and Thomas C. Battle, xiii–xix. Washington, DC: Howard University Press.

Beilin, Ian. 2018. "Introduction: Reference and Justice, Past and Present." In *Reference Librarianship and Justice*, edited by Kate Adler, Ian Beilin, and Eamon Tewell, 19–22. Sacramento, CA: Library Juice Press.

Bobo, Jacqueline, Cynthia Hudley, and Claudine Michel, eds. 2004. *The Black Studies Reader*. London: Routledge.

Brook, Freeda, Dave Ellenwood, and Althea Eannace Lazzaro. 2015. "In Pursuit of Antiracist Social Justice: Denaturalizing Whiteness in the Academic Library." *Library Trends* 64 (2): 246–284.

Brown, Ina Corinne, Lloyd E. Blauch, Martin David Jenkins, and Ambrose Caliver. 1942. *National Survey of the Higher Education of Negroes. United States*. Office of Education. Washington, DC: Government Printing Office.

Bucher, Christina G. 2008. "Ann Allen Shockley." In *African American National Biography*, edited by Henry Louis Gates Jr. and Evelyn Brooks Higginbotham. Oxford University Press.

Carey, Thomas John. 2018. "Ruby Stutts Lyells." Mississippi Encyclopedia, Center for Study of Southern Culture. Updated April 14, 2018. https://mississippiencyclopedia.org/entries/ruby-elizabeth-stutts-lyells/.

Curtis, Florence R. 1935. "Librarianship as a Field for Negroes." *Journal of Negro Education* 4 (1): 94–98.

Dandridge, Rita B. 1987. "Gathering Pieces: A Selected Bibliography of Ann Allen Shockley." *Black American Forum* 21 (1–2): 133–146.

Fisk University. 1948. *Fisk Herald*.

Foster, Frances Smith. 1990. "Reviews." *Black American Literature Forum* 24 (1): 151–160.

Furner, Jonathan. 2007. "Dewey Deracialized: A Critical Race-Theoretic Perspective." *Knowledge Organization* 34 (3): 144–168. https://doi.org/10.5771/0943-7444-2007-3-144.

Griffin, Karin L. 2013. "Pursuing Tenure and Promotion in the Academy: A Librarian's Cautionary Tale." *Negro Educational Review* 64 (1–4): 77–96.

Hall, Tracie D. 2012. "The Black Body at the Reference Desk: Critical Race Theory and Black Librarianship." In *The 21st-Century Black Librarian in America: Issues and Challenges*, edited by Andrew P. Jackson, Julius C. Jefferson, and Akilah S. Nosakhere, 197–202. Lanham, MD: Scarecrow Press.

Hathcock, April. 2015. "White Librarianship in Blackface: Diversity Initiatives in LIS." *In the Library with the Lead Pipe*, October 7. http://www.inthelibrarywiththeleadpipe.org/2015/lis-diversity/.

Higgins, Molly. 2016. "Totally Invisible: Asian American Representation in the *Dewey Decimal Classification*, 1876–1996." *Knowledge Organization* 43 (8): 609–621. https://doi.org/10.5771/0943-7444-2016-8-609.

Honma, Todd. 2005. "Trippin' over the Color Line: The Invisibility of Race in Library and Information Studies." *InterActions: UCLA Journal of Education and Information Studies* 1 (2): 1–24.

Irby, Beverly J., Genevieve Brown, Rafael Lara-Alecio, and Shirley Jackson. 2013. *The Handbook of Educational Theories*. Charlotte, NC: Information Age Publishing.

Ladson-Billings, Gloria. 1998. "Just What Is Critical Race Theory and What's It Doing in a Nice Field Like Education?" *International Journal of Qualitative Studies in Education* 11 (1): 7–24. https://doi.org/10.1080/095183998236863.

Lyells, Ruby E. Stutts. 1944. "The New Emancipation: Responsibilities of the Negro." Speech delivered at Emancipation Day Exercises, Vicksburg, MS, January 3, 1944.

Lyells, Ruby E. Stutts. 1949. "A Look Ahead: What the Negro Wants." Speech delivered at the 20th Reunion of the Class of 1929, Alcorn A&M College, Alcorn, MS, May 15, 1949.

Mabbott, Cass. 2017. "The We Need Diverse Books Campaign and Critical Race Theory: Charlemae Rollins and the Call for Diverse Children's Books." *Library Trends* 65 (4): 508–522. https://doi.org/10.1353/lib.2017.0015.

Owens, Irene. 2001. "Stories Told but Yet Unfinished: Challenges Facing African-American Libraries and Special Collections in Historically Black Colleges and Universities." *Journal of Library Administration* 33 (3–4): 165–181. https://doi.org/10.1300/J111v33n03_01.

Phinazee, Annette L., ed. 1967. *Materials by and about American Negroes: Papers Presented at an Institute*. Atlanta: School of Library Science, Atlanta University.

Pollock, Caitlin M. J., and Shelley P. Haley. 2018. "'When I Enter': Black Women and Disruption of the White, Heteronormative Narrative of Librarianship." In *Pushing the Margins: Women of Color and Intersectionality in LIS,* edited by Rose L. Chou and Annie Pho, 15–59. Sacramento, CA: Library Juice Press.

Posey, Josephine McCann. 1994. *Against Great Odds: The History of Alcorn State University*. Jackson: University Press of Mississippi.

Randall, William M., and Francis Lee Dewey Goodrich. 1936. *Principles of College Library Administration*. Chicago: American Library Association and University of Chicago Press.

Sewell, George A., and Margaret L. Dwight. 1984. "Ruby Stutts Lyells: Mississippi's First Black Professional Librarian." In *Mississippi Black History Makers*, 238–239. Jackson: University Press of Mississippi. http://www.jstor.org/stable/j.ctt2tvh56.100.

Shockley, Ann Allen. 1961. "Does the Negro College Library Need a Special Negro Collection?" *Library Journal* 86:2049–2050.

Shockley, Ann Allen. 1970. *A Handbook for the Administration of Special Negro Collections*. Nashville, TN: Fisk University.

Shockley, Ann Allen. 1971. "Establishing Black Collections for Black Studies." *College Library Notes* 11:1–4.

Shockley, Ann Allen. 1974a. "Black Book Collections: Quality versus Quantity." Paper presented to the Colloquia Graduate School of Library Science, the University of Texas at Austin, November 25, 1974.

Shockley, Ann Allen. 1974b. "Black Book Reviewing: A Case for Library Action." *College and Research Libraries* 35 (1): 16–20.

Sinnette, Elinor Des Verny, W. Paul Coates, and Thomas C. Battle, eds. 1990. *Black Bibliophiles and Collectors: Preservers of Black History*. Washington, DC: Howard University Press.

Smith, Paul M., Jr. 1961. "A Critical Interpretation of Special Collections: Negro." *Journal of Negro Education* 30 (2): 150–152.

Smith, Samuel Leonard. 1940. "The Passing of the Hampton Library School." *Journal of Negro Education* 9 (1): 51–58.

Warren, Nagueyalti. 2011. *Grandfather of Black Studies: W. E. B. Du Bois*. Trenton, NJ: Africa World Press.

Wesley, Dorothy Porter. 1990. "Black Antiquarians and Bibliophiles Revisited, with a Glance at Today's Lovers of Books and Memorabilia." In *Black Bibliophiles and Collectors: Preservers of Black History*, edited by Elinor Des Verny Sinnette, W. Paul Coates, and Thomas C. Battle, 3–22. Washington, DC: Howard University Press.

West Virginia State University. n.d. "Our History Runs Deep." West Virginia State University. Accessed June 24, 2020. http://www.wvstateu.edu/About/History-and-Traditions.aspx.

White, Derrick E. 2011. "An Independent Approach to Black Studies: The Institute of the Black World (IBW) and Its Evaluation and Support of Black Studies." *Journal of African American Studies* 16 (1): 70–88. https://doi.org/10.1007/s12111-011-9166-1.

White House Initiative on HBCUs. n.d. "What Is an HBCU?" White House Initiative on HBCUs, US Dept. of Education. Accessed July 4, 2020. https://sites.ed.gov/whhbcu/one-hundred-and-five-historically-black-colleges-and-universities/.

7

THE DEVELOPMENT OF US CHILDREN'S LIBRARIANSHIP AND CHALLENGING WHITE DOMINANT NARRATIVES

Sujei Lugo Vázquez

While educators, library workers, authors, and youth continuously challenge racial, ethnic, and tribal (mis)representation in US children's literature by, for example, writing about anti-Blackness and Orientalism in Dr. Seuss's body of work (Ishizuka and Stephens 2019) or studying the representation of anthropomorphic apes in picture books (Campbell 2018), there is, relatedly, a need for an examination of how library service to children enacts, replicates, and maintains the inequities of a white hegemonic society. The establishment of children's librarianship was tied not only to the development of reading habits in children, but also to the shaping of their worldviews, their assimilation to White Supremacist "norms," and their guidance toward "piety, purity, and knowledge" (Garrison 1972–1973).

As a first-generation, college-educated, Brown Puerto Rican children's librarian, I'm aligning myself with the critical work done around whiteness, power, and racial identity in children's librarianship. Through my work, and the work of Indigenous, Black, and People of Color (IBPOC) library workers such as Augusta Braxston Baker, Pura T. Belpré, Charlemae Hill Rollins, Effie Lee Morris, and Lotsee Patterson, we want to recognize and provide a revisionist history to center and affirm the lives and identities of Indigenous children and children of color and Indigenous librarians and librarians of color. Racial equity in library and information science (LIS) is an ongoing process, commitment, and work, and this chapter aims to examine, using a Critical Race Theory (CRT) lens, the history of US children's librarianship and past and present collection development practices, as well as to provide recommendations on how to reimagine these practices.

The incorporation of CRT into the analysis of children's librarianship gives me and the IBPOC women discussed in this chapter the opportunity to challenge white dominant narratives and center our voices in the "retelling" of US children's librarianship. As IBPOC in a predominantly white field, our "experiences lead to different understandings of racism" (Matsuda et al. 1993) and its impact on our work, our field, and its history that it is constantly whitewashed, distorted, and sanitized. There's a need to bring collective IBPOC historical accounts and experiences to the landscape of the field.

CRITICAL RACE THEORY AND WHAT IT HAS TO DO WITH A "NICE" AND "CUTE" FIELD LIKE CHILDREN'S LIBRARIANSHIP[1]

CRT analyzes the role racism plays in perpetuating inequities and oppressions in society. It is a tool of analysis that is not often discussed or integrated into coursework for current and future children's library workers. It was through my independent studies, experiential knowledge (Cappiccie et al. 2012), and a school of social work graduate course that I was exposed to CRT, and I subsequently made my own connections to use it to expose and deconstruct white dominant and oppressive perspectives in children's librarianship.

One of the basic tenets of CRT is the notion of the permanence of racism, that it is embedded in the fabric of US society and social structures. It suggests that "racist hierarchical structures govern all political, economic, and social domains" (DeCuir and Dixson 2004), which include social institutions like the US public library system. Given the persistence and permanence of racism and how it is produced, replicated, and challenged in social systems, Patricia Hill Collins proposes the *domains of power framework* to think of racism as a system of power with four domains (Collins 2009). Each domain is defined below, and I present each one's racial analysis, context area, and power dynamics. At the same time, I incorporate how public libraries, where the majority of children's collections are based, are represented in the four domains, which will provide the framework of analysis for this essay.

The *structural domain* is the first domain of power, and it shows how racial inequities are organized through social institutions such as schools, hospitals, and government agencies. Collins describes it as "the structure of how racism as a system of power is set up, and how it is organized without anybody doing anything" (Collins

2009, 53). The US public library system and buildings as a social institution are clearly situated in this domain of power.

The *disciplinary domain* is the second domain of power, where "people use the rules and regulations of everyday life to uphold the racial hierarchy or to challenge it" (Collins 2009, 53). This includes the chastising, surveillance, and filtering practices of organizations. Library policies and guidelines are designed and established to control and regulate access to and usage of library buildings, services, collections, and materials.

The *cultural domain* is the third domain of power, which manufactures and replicates the ideas and views that justify racial inequities. This domain is increasingly significant in constructing representations, ideas, and stories about race and racism as a *system of power*, particularly through the media (Collins 2009, 53). This is done through works such as texts, illustrations, films, TV, music, toys, and memorabilia. Contemporarily, children are exposed to problematic cultural artifacts and racist ideologies from birth, and school curriculum and library materials are not exempt from these unequal representations. Library collections mimic this *cultural domain*, and collection development processes play a role in upholding or questioning racial inequities in materials available.

The *interpersonal domain* is the fourth and last domain of power, which shapes and enacts race relations among individuals, among themselves, and in one-on-one encounters, and it "involves ordinary social interactions where people accept and/or resist racial inequality in their everyday lives" (Collins 2009, 54). This domain also encompasses relationships between organizations, institutions, and communities. In a public library setting, this domain is represented through library worker–library worker (management, supervisors, colleagues), library worker–library user (adults, teens, children, teachers, caregivers), library worker–library stakeholders (publishers, vendors, community groups, and organizations), and library user–library user interactions. All, individually and collectively, represent, produce, and resist racial power dynamics impacted by their identities and social systems.

Within and across each domain of power presented by Patricia Hill Collins's framework, racism is produced, replicated, and resisted, and all are necessary for the ability of racism to function as a system of power. US public libraries mirror each domain, and throughout this discussion of US children's librarianship, I will pay particular attention to the *structural domain* (public library) and *cultural domain* (children's collections).

Collections portray and carry the past, present, and future of white hegemonic structures and racial inequities of society and libraries. While library workers and those in charge of developing the collection come and go, collections are steadier and are more representative of society's ideologies. The *cultural domain* in children's library rooms, which are spaces in public libraries created for children's materials, services, and programs, is represented by books and other cultural products that are part of their collections. What do children's collections represent to our community, children, and field? Collections mirror the racist past and present, reflecting whose lives are deemed valuable, meaningful, and worth remembering. Although a library collection has the capacity for representation, validation, and possibility, it also harms, invalidates, misrepresents, and offers distorted images to our children. Adults whose charge is to select, acquire, and incorporate books into library children's collections hold a great amount of power over the stories available to children (Aggleton 2018), as does the content and ideas we are reproducing and transmitting to them.

But then, what are the racial, ethnic, and tribal identities, ideologies, and biases of the children's library workers in charge of developing the collections? What are the ideologies expressed and portrayed in the evaluation, acquisition, and selection tools used by these library workers? How are White Supremacy and racist ideologies over-represented through the different areas of children's collection development? This is why positioning a CRT framework and lens in children's librarianship is intrinsic to critiquing and disrupting racial oppressive ideas and conditions in our "nice" and "cute" field. But it can also present possibilities and actions for change and it can be used to "propose radical solutions for addressing it" (Ladson-Billings 1999, 27). The inclusion of collection development practices and resources in this chapter aims to provide a base in helping reimagine racial equity and justice in children's librarianship and the much-needed commitment to CRT's social justice element in children's collections.

THE "PURE" HISTORY OF US CHILDREN'S LIBRARIANSHIP: THE EARLY YEARS (1785–1938)

From the beginning, children's library services were establishing and replicating whiteness and social control within the *structural domain* and *cultural domain*. The earliest accounts of book collections and library services to children in the US are through Sunday school libraries dating back to 1785. Christian churches, especially those located in the North and West (Harris 1984), kept small collections of books for their Sunday schools in an attempt to "reduce crime and illiteracy and in general to improve some of the moral and social conditions of [white] children in the late eighteenth century" (López 1976, 318).

In 1803, white Boston teacher Caleb Bingham presented a collection of 150 books to the town of Salisbury, Connecticut, establishing the Bingham Library of Youth (López 1976, 317). This library was for the use of white children ages nine to sixteen and is generally considered to be the first US library for children. Several public libraries that are often mentioned among the claims of the earliest children's collections and services include the Town Library (1834) in Peterborough, New Hampshire; the Arlington Public Library (1835) in Arlington, Massachusetts; Aguilar Free Library (1886) of New York; and the Public Library of Brookline (1890) in Brookline, Massachusetts (Jenkins 2000; Jordan 1913; Rose 1954). Although the beginnings of print materials and resources for children in libraries are located in New England states, other schools and libraries in the Northeast and Midwest and on the West Coast were relevant in this early history. Along with expanding library services and sharing books with children, they were also guilty of inculcating White Supremacist ideologies into youth.

One of the most renowned and harmful spaces for the instruction and "education" of Indigenous children was the Carlisle Indian Industrial School in Pennsylvania. Since its establishment in 1879, the school's stated purpose was to assimilate and "destroy" Indigenous children through its teaching and punishments. The school's *cultural domains*, represented by the curriculum and reading rooms, included materials that presented Euro-American worldviews and "conduct of life," vocational education, religious doctrine, stories of American Indians who adopted "American" lifestyles, and titles that encouraged children's cultural assimilation (Lear 2015). The library purposely avoided titles that challenged white racial ideologies or recounted harsh discipline and violence toward Native Americans. Children's book collections in residential schools are vivid examples of integrating and replicating the *structural, disciplinary,* and *cultural domains,* and "helped implement both cultural and biological forms of racism" (Lear 2015, 180).

The history of public libraries in the United States is a racialized and gendered one, and as Gina Schlesselman-Tarango emphasizes, when we talk about the development of early librarianship and early library workers, we are likely referring to white women (Schlesselman-Tarango 2016). The roles of domesticity and mothering historically imposed on women, along with the elitist, altruistic, and "niceness" notions surrounding libraries and children, are worth accentuating, as a reminder that children's library collections were created and shaped by "educated" middle- and upper-class white women who focused on reproducing White Supremacy. Since its inception, children's librarianship has been hiding behind the idea of neutrality and purity, avoiding conversations regarding library workers' racial, ethnic, and tribal identities and white privilege and their impact on children's collections.

Some of the "educated" white women who played a role in the early years of the field were Caroline M. Hewins from Hartford (Connecticut) Public Library, Alice M. Jordan from the Boston Public Library, Clara Whitehill Hunt from Brooklyn Public Library, and Anne Carroll Moore from the New York Public Library, four white librarians who are known as the "founders" and developers of specialized collections and library services to children. They guided other library workers to design "children's rooms and services such as storytelling and became cultural authorities in the rapidly growing area of children's publishing" (Pawley 2015, 14).

The creation of separate areas for children, which can be seen as another layer within the *structural domain*, became a major focus of public libraries that rapidly spread around the United States due to the public's embracing of this new white women–dominated field and their work with children, their "kindly material guidance" to lead children, and their goal to focus on the guidance of the minds and morals of the future citizens (Garrison 1979, 224). White children's librarians hiding behind the idea of "progressive ideology of literacy and readership," "shaping a better tomorrow by guiding a child's reading," and recommending books to develop "educated and well-behaved citizens" were simply manufacturing, replicating, and inculcating white hegemonic ideologies to children through *cultural domains* (Hand 2012, 37; Kimball 2014, 502n).

Many of these early white children's librarians were establishing themselves as leaders and tastemakers of the field, and their biggest goal and purpose was to "get good books to children" (Vandergrift 1996, 690), fueling them to develop booklists, work as book reviewers, and work closely with publishers and booksellers to impact (control) selection tools and collection development practices used in children's librarianship. As more children's rooms were developing, library workers turned to other librarians and professional groups as "authorities" in guiding them to select books for their collections.

Among the first children's librarians to develop recommended booklists for children was Caroline M. Hewins, whose lists focused on "classics" and "quality" literature for youth (Vandergrift 1996). Her first booklist, *Books for the Young*, was published in 1882 and generally included books with a white Westernized view and entertaining "but never trashy" topics (Eaton 2014, 41). Later on, the list was edited and published by the American Library Association (ALA) in 1897 as *Books for Boys and Girls: A Selected List*, and in its preface Hewins lays out a clear vision of whose children (white, of course) she was targeting the list to and which stories were worth including and omitting.

Another booklist created by white children's librarians was *The Bookshelf for Boys and Girls: From Nursery Rhyme to Grown-Up Time*. In the introduction they write, "We include stories of boys and girls who have good times at home and at school, on the farm and in the city" (Hunt, Fletcher, and Mathiews 1919, 13). When describing the selection of picture books, they demand, "Do not allow little children to see ugly and vulgar pictures" (3). This invites one to ask which children they are envisioning as readers. Which children are they "protecting" by creating a false sense of reality and superiority? How would IBPOC library workers and children read and internalize reading the following annotations created by white library workers?

At the turn of the twentieth century, the H. W. Wilson Company was establishing itself as a children's collection development resources provider, with the publication of their *Children's Catalog*. First published in 1909, the *Children's Catalog: A Guide to the Best Reading for Young People Based on Twenty-Four Selected Library Lists* opened the market of commercially produced catalogs of recommended children's books for libraries (Bush 1996). Still in print today, retitled *Children's Core Collection*, this catalog was, and still is, included as a required resource for library school courses focused on children's and school librarianship. Lists created by Caroline M. Hewins, Alice M. Jordan, and Anne Carroll Moore were among those incorporated in the 1916 *Children's Catalog*, demonstrating the influence and power the white children's librarians who had "founded" children's rooms in US public libraries had over children's collections in all libraries. They were interlocking and integrating the *structural, cultural, and interpersonal domains* within systems of power of the subfield of US children's librarianship.

Throughout the years, US children's librarianship kept expanding and situating itself as a professional field and a powerhouse working along with the children's literature world. Within the oldest US library association, the American Library Association (ALA), several milestones of the field were established. In 1895, ALA formally recognized "children's librarian" as a job title and specialization of librarianship (Hand 2012), and a couple of years later, at the 1900 ALA convention in Montréal, Canada, the Club of Children's Librarians was formed by eight children's librarians, including Anne Carroll Moore and Caroline M. Hewins (Bush 1996). This "informal club" became the official Section of Children's Librarians within ALA, currently known as the Association for Library Service to Children (ALSC). This new section that focused on children's librarianship was also commended with the responsibility of two children's book award that would shape what was envisioned to be considered "distinguished" and "high quality" books within US children's literature: the John Newbery Award (1922) and the Randolph Caldecott Award (1938) (Association for Library Service to Children, n.d.-a, n.d.-b).

Certainly, the early years of the development of children's rooms, collections, and librarianship as a field portrayed the role US public libraries had in enacting, replicating, and maintaining inequities. White women, with their leading roles in the field, were creating the base of the canon of US children's literature and must-have titles for children's libraries. Collection development tools and practices presented the power of the *cultural domain* in sustaining and supporting the *structural domain* in the white hegemonic systems of power. But children's librarianship and public librarianship were also the setting for early library worker leaders and activists who would recognize and confront the White Supremacist ideologies of cultural works, the field, and society.

CHALLENGING PATTERNS AND NARRATIVES IN CHILDREN'S LIBRARIANSHIP

In US children's librarianship, between the years 1921 and 1972, there were prominent IBPOC children's librarians whose lives and work ran parallel to (or appeared soon after) the white children's librarian "founders" of the field; who experienced racial injustice at the personal and professional levels; and whose careers, lives, and work intertwined with their commitment to their communities and the humanity and experiences of IBPOC children in the US, and in children's books.

While in New York we had Augusta Braxston Baker and Pura T. Belpré, the Midwest had Charlemae Hill Rollins and Effie Lee Morris, and Lotsee Patterson was all around Indian Country, resisting racial inequities and challenging different domains of power through their lives and work. These IBPOC children's library workers present a unique voice, where their stories, experiences, and work are counternarratives in our field. In contrast to their white counterparts, Baker, Belpré, Hill Rollins, Morris, and Patterson were explicitly supporting and mentoring each other and centering the life and humanity of the IBPOC children they worked with, and constantly challenging the *interpersonal domain* (by confronting their white peers' racism) and the *disciplinary domain* (by "breaking" segregating library and lending rules). They dedicated their work and voice to disrupting white dominant ideologies through the *cultural* and *structural domains* by expanding, creating, and critiquing children's cultural works, children's literature, and children's collections. Their impact is still felt today.

Augusta Braxston Baker was an African American children's librarian and storyteller at the New York Public Library, and a bridge between the early white children's librarians and early and contemporary IBPOC children's librarians (Vandergrift 1996). Experiencing segregation as a child, and then the continuous racial inequities in the field, Baker set out to create and increase the children's collections at the New

York Public Library with an emphasis on books about the African American experience. She worked closely with Arturo A. Schomburg and community members in Harlem to establish and develop the James Weldon Johnson Memorial Collection for children (Vandergrift 1996).

Baker, aware of the power of *cultural domains*, was concerned about the children's books with racist and harmful texts and images of African Americans that were included on the lists and given to all children. She went on to create a set of criteria to evaluate the illustrations, plots, and storylines of children's books and their representations of African American characters, and also provided her own list of recommended titles. In 1938, the first list of her publication *Books about Negro Life for Children* was printed, and revised editions were subsequently published throughout the years, later as *The Black Experience in Children's Books* (Smith 1995). Her list not only assisted children in locating books in the library, but also was distributed, sold, and consulted by children's librarians, children's literature editors and authors, and caregivers.

Augusta Braxston Baker, through the *interpersonal domain*, challenged other children's librarians and their attitudes toward IBPOC children in their libraries. She encouraged them to "inform themselves about prejudice, human relations, and intercultural activities" (Vandergrift 1996) and purposely evaluate the barriers they were replicating through *structural, disciplinary, and interpersonal domains* in their children's rooms. In her 1955 article published in *Top of the News*, Baker does the emotional labor and addresses directly her fellow (white) children's librarians: "Your attitude toward minority groups has an important bearing on the attitudes of your children. Therefore, it is your primary duty to improve your own human relations" (Baker 1955, 40). Baker later expands and focuses on the *cultural domain* through the library's collections: "Now think about your room. Are there books on the shelves which will hurt and alienate your newcomers while at the same time they perpetuate stereotyped ideas in the minds of your regular library users?" (Baker 1995, 41). Augusta Braxston Baker challenged the benevolent notion of the early years of US children's librarianship and provides concrete examples of how children's librarians can disrupt white dominant narratives.

Another IBPOC library counterstoryteller who played a founding role in US children's librarianship was Pura T. Belpré, an Afro–Puerto Rican bilingual children's librarian, storyteller, and puppeteer. She began her long career with the New York Public Library in 1921 and focused her work on challenging *cultural and interpersonal domains* along library services to Spanish-speaking children, mainly Puerto Ricans arriving to New York in the first decades of the twentieth century. Believing that "reading always enhances children's understanding of both themselves and the world" (Sánchez González 2013, 15), she went on to write Puerto Rican stories missing from library shelves; working and providing children's library services in her language; and disrupting the "traditional" US library services to children in public libraries. Later on, in a new position as the Spanish children's specialist of the New York Public Library, she went around the library system evaluating children's collections and updating their Spanish-language titles and resources, breaking and disrupting the *structural domain.*

Belpré created Spanish-language children's booklists to be distributed among libraries, community centers, and organizations that work with children. Through her work, she was also critical of lists and books that "demean African American children" and wrote about racism and children's books and lists. In *Fragment on Racism and Children's Fiction*, Belpré writes,

In evaluating Black and biracial books for pre-school through grade levels, a major criterion was that no book would be listed if it was considered likely to communicate any *racist concept* or *cliché* about Blacks to either a Black or a white child, or if it failed to provide some strong characters to serve as role models. (Sánchez González 2013, 50; emphasis added)

In creating lists of recommended titles for children, Belpré was intentional in centering the humanity of IBPOC children, principally Black children, and the possible impact of the presence of White Supremacist ideologies in children's books on the lives and worldviews of all children. Additionally, she interrogated the role these children's books play in replicating racial inequities and the messages they send with their very presence in children's collections.

Moving away from the Northeast, Charlemae Hill Rollins, an African American children's librarian at the Chicago Public Library (1926–1963), was also playing a role in disrupting white dominant narratives. For three decades she held her position as head of the children's department at a Chicago Public Library branch located in a predominantly African American neighborhood. Throughout her career she was a powerful counterstoryteller and strongly advocated for library services in African American communities and for respectful depictions of African Americans in the *cultural domain* of children's books. She not only focused on accurate and respectful representation in cultural works for the sake of African American children themselves, but also aimed "to create a more equitable and democratic world for everyone" (Mabbott 2017, 521).

Using her position and voice, she turned her concerns about White Supremacist ideologies in children's books and libraries' booklists into action. She constantly voiced complaints, through the *interpersonal domain*, about the children's books included on the Chicago Public Library buying lists that portrayed stereotypical and damaging representations of African Americans, and also wrote letters and reached out to publishers about the lack of appropriate books for African American children (Tolson 1998). In 1941, she published her seminal work, *We Build Together: A Reader's Guide to Negro Life and Literature for Elementary and High School Use*, which included a guide to aid teachers and children's librarians in evaluating and selecting the best children's books for their collections. Several editions were published throughout the years and were widely consulted for children's collection development; the book's publication exalted Rollins's status as an expert in children's literature, a children's librarianship advocate, and a leader in the field (Willet 2001).

Charlemae Hill Rollins was actively involved in professional organizations such as the ALA and its Children's Services Division, becoming in 1957 the first African American librarian to serve as president of the children's librarians section (Willet 2001). She also served on the Newbery-Caldecott Award Committee and other children's award book committees. Her leadership skills were apparent not only in her community, the library system, and professional organizations, but also in the network of IBPOC children's librarians, where she served as mentor, advocate, and supporter of their work, critically expanding her commitment to social justice.

African American children's librarian Effie Lee Morris was another of the IBPOC early leaders of the development of racially inclusive library collections for children. She made contributions to different library systems across the US and professional organizations, expanding her impact through different *structural domains*. Morris started her career at the Cleveland Public Library in 1946, focusing her work on library services for African American children and establishing the first Negro History Week celebration for children at her library (Garner 2009). Nine years later, she moved to the New York Public Library, where in 1958 she started library services for visually impaired children, serving as the children's specialist at the NYPL's Library for the Blind. Later, in 1963, she arrived in California and became the first coordinator of children's services at San Francisco Public Library, where she remained for the rest of her children's librarian career.

At the San Francisco Public Library, Effie Lee Morris established the Children's Historical and Research Collection, a collection focused on out-of-print children's books "that depict the changing portrayal of ethnic and culturally diverse groups over time" (California Library Association, n.d.). She was also vocal about the harmful and stereotypical representations of African Americans in children's books and the lack of high-quality titles included in children's collections. In an interview for *American Libraries*, Morris commented on the lack of accessibility and dearth of African American children's literature. In the 1983 piece she argues,

> Meanwhile many books that have presented the truths of black heritage and black culture are no longer in print. Did not the Civil Rights Movement offer any lasting insights into the Black quests for humanity and dignity? Have we rolled back so far from the knowledge gained in the 60's? The increasing instances of repression against minorities are reported daily. History repeating itself. (Brandehoff 1983, 132)

"History repeating itself"—a statement that still resonates today in children's librarianship, with the (mis)representations (or lack) of IBPOC characters in children's books and its inclusion/exclusion of children's collections. Effie Lee Morris would continue to discuss her work and experiences in library services to children and with critical literacy at conferences, gatherings, committee meetings, and local and international events. Within professional organizations that work with children's library services and literature, Morris was an active member of the ALA, ALSC, Public Library Association (PLA), and the Black Caucus of the American Library Association (BCALA), and served as the first chair of the Coretta Scott King Book Awards Committee and chair of the Newbery Book Award and the Caldecott Book Award committees. Throughout her career, she valued and supported children's book awards like the Pura Belpré Award, Coretta Scott King Book Awards, the Newbery and Caldecott, and understood their impact on children's collection development (Orange 2012).

Comanche counterstoryteller, librarian, and educator Lotsee Patterson was one of the first to take a leading role in tribal librarianship and library services to Native children. In 1959, she started her career as a teacher at a public school in the town of Boone in Oklahoma. Her students, who were Apache, Comanche, and Kiowa, didn't have a library at their school and didn't have reading materials at home (Biggs 2000). The experience drove Patterson to commit her life to Native American library services. She reached out to school administration to train teachers and recruit Native Americans to be trained in basic library skills to develop school library collections. Later, this initiative developed into grant-supported projects for training in the creation, selection, and maintenance of library collections and services for Native children and communities.

Patterson touched on *interpersonal*, *cultural*, and *structural domains* and dedicated her research to write about the lack of American Indian librarians, collection development for Indigenous materials, and how current collection development selection resources, like book reviewing magazines, "lack expertise or extensive knowledge of the topic of American Indians" (Hogan 2011, 90). She created several bibliographies and collection development tools, such as *A Core Collection for an Indian Community Library* (Biggs 2000), which is one of the widely used unpublished bibliographies in libraries.

Like many of the previously mentioned IBPOC women librarians, Patterson was also active in professional library organizations. In a meeting at the 1972 ALA conference, she expressed her frustration at the lack of support for tribal libraries and library services for Native Americans. Along with several colleagues, she helped establish the ALA Subcommittee on Library Services to Native Americans, which later became the American Indian Library Association, which Patterson cofounded (Sampson, n.d.).

This brief historical overview (1921–1972) presents the life and work of IBPOC children's library workers, highlighting their labor in positioning themselves in the history of US children's librarianship and doing the work to disrupt the white dominant voices in children's collections. Their social/racial justice work continues to directly influence the collection development processes practiced by children's librarians and the cultural works that are handed out to children. The presence and impact of the different *cultural domains*—bibliographies, book awards, selection tools, and literary works—on collection development is still felt to this day.

REIMAGINING OUR PAST: TOWARD RACIALLY INCLUSIVE COLLECTION DEVELOPMENT PRACTICES

Evaluating and situating US children's librarianship in the present day, what can we learn and unlearn from the early years of US children's librarianship and the work of white and IBPOC children's librarians? How can *we all* work to dismantle whiteness and dominant narratives reflected in our work and children's collections? In this section, I would like us to reimagine the early years of the field, and what a racially just and inclusive field looks like for all library workers and children. I point out areas that library workers in the children's librarianship field should center in their work to take steps toward disrupting the root of white dominant ideologies that have been controlling and molding our libraries, collections, and practices. It is only through an action-based commitment to social justice and racial equity that we can work toward the eradication of all forms of oppression in the field.

- *Acknowledge the humanity of ALL children.* Part of our work is to enrich and support the life and existence of children through cultural works. Valuing and centering the humanity of historically marginalized IBPOC identities and critiquing the impact of harmful representations in the materials we incorporate in our collections would move us toward true racially inclusive children's collections.

- *STEP BACK, support, and value IBPOC children's library workers in the field.* The work of Augusta Braxston Baker, Pura T. Belpré, Charlemae Hill Rollins, and many other IBPOC children's librarians was central to providing tools and practices to disrupt white dominant ideologies. As for librarianship itself, children's librarianship is overwhelmingly white (Association for Library Service to Children, n.d.-c) and there's a need to bring and value IBPOC library workers into the field to continue the work of the early leaders. The work of past leaders also inspires current and future generations of IBPOC children's librarians, and hiring, mentoring, retaining, and supporting IBPOC library workers to develop children's collections and work with children would continue to pave the way toward racial inclusivity.
- *Be INTENTIONAL in challenging white dominant narratives in children's collections.* When creating and expanding a collection, evaluate the quantity and quality of cultural works by and about IBPOC. Some libraries undergo a "diversity audit" (Jensen 2018) as a first step toward evaluating their current collections, and its results serve to identify the gaps in their libraries. Incorporate a clause in your library's collection development policies that intentionally advocates for the selection and inclusion of materials by and about IBPOC in the children's collections.
- *LEARN about, AMPLIFY, and USE collection development tools and resources by and about IBPOC communities.* Book reviews in major publishing journals continue to be the go-to place for children's librarians to learn about new titles to include in their library collections. A 2015 "Diversity Baseline Survey" (Low 2016) in which eight review journals participated shows that 89 percent of book reviewers are white, which will have an impact on how they read, critique, and evaluate children's books. We need to look at reviewers outside mainstream sources, in outlets created by librarians such as *American Indians in Children's Literature*, the *CrazyQuiltEdi* blog, and *Hijabi Librarians* to center the perspectives and representations of IBPOC communities. Look for small and independent publishers that historically have published children's books by and about IBPOC marginalized voices and experiences, and include their titles in libraries.
- *CENTER and UPLIFT the work done by IBPOC children's librarians.* Professional library organizations were created to provide safer places for IBPOC librarians to organize, mentor, support, and do work for and about the IBPOC communities they represent and work with. Organizations like the American Indian Library Association (AILA), the Asian/Pacific American Librarians Association (APALA), the Black Caucus of the American Library Association (BCALA), the Chinese American Librarians Association (CALA), and the National Association to Promote

Library and Information Services to Latinos and the Spanish-Speaking (REFORMA) offer subcommittees, working groups, and spaces for IBPOC children's librarians. Along with other colleagues, they also produce reading lists and book award lists and promote the work of IBPOC creators. All of these serve as selection tools for children's collections.

- *Critically QUESTION and CHALLENGE the children's literature publishing industry.* Just as Augusta Braxston Baker and Charlemae Hill Rollins addressed publishers and editors of children's books directly to challenge and call out the harmful representations they keep propagating, current children's librarians need to continue that pattern to disrupt the narratives that dominate children's books and, hence, children's collections. Through social media, in professional conferences' exhibit halls, and in campaigns such as *#StepUpScholastic*, librarians, along with teachers, caregivers, authors, illustrators, and children themselves, can raise concerns about the representations and misrepresentations of IBPOC communities and children in children's cultural works to those in leadership roles in children's publishing.
- *LEARN and UNLEARN about bias, internalized oppressions, and White Supremacist ideologies in ourselves and our structures, and about its impact on our work.* White allies and IBPOC librarians continue to create tools and provide resources and analyses to teach and challenge White Supremacist ideologies in our field, and to suggest ways to promote and support the ongoing process of learning and unlearning oppression that impacts our collection development practices. Resources like Simmons University's "Anti-oppression LibGuide" (Simmons University 2020) and the "Guide for Selecting Anti-bias [*sic*] Children's Books" (Derman-Sparks 2016) are essential professional development tools for our work as children's librarians. *Reading While White* also serves as a relevant resource to evaluate and challenge whiteness in children's librarianship. It is a blog created by white children's librarians that discusses how allyship, white privilege, and solidarity could be used to amplify IBPOC voices.

Bringing a CRT lens to US children's librarianship helps situate it within the larger conversations and works about CRT in library and information science more broadly, and about who is constantly left out as an area of critical analysis and scholarly work. Collins's domains of power framework (2009) is just one of the CRT frameworks and tools that provide opportunities to center race and whiteness in children's librarianship and to expose and challenge white dominant narratives in the field and collections. Nostalgia, niceness, and "purity," sentiments and ideas historically tied to childhood and children's literature, have the effect of erasing and avoiding the critique of how racism, whiteness, and oppression impact the experiences and lives of children and works written for children. As library workers whose role and work directly impacts children, we need to constantly evaluate our identities, white hegemonic structures, and the structural and cultural domains that shape, influence, and celebrate whose humanity, selves, and existences we center in our collections and world.

NOTE

1. Title inspired by Gloria Ladson-Billings's article "Just What Is Critical Race Theory and What's It Doing in a Nice Field Like Education?"

BIBLIOGRAPHY

Aggleton, Jen. 2018. "Where Are the Children in Children's Collections? An Exploration of Ethical Principles and Practical Concerns surrounding Children's Participation in Collection Development." *New Review of Children's Literature and Librarianship* 24 (1): 1–17.

Association for Library Service to Children. n.d.-a. "The John Newbery Medal." Association for Library Service to Children. Accessed June 1, 2019. http://w1ww.ala.org/alsc/awardsgrants /bookmedia/newberymedal/aboutnewbery/aboutnewbery.

Association for Library Service to Children. n.d.-b. "The Randolph Caldecott Medal." Association for Library Service to Children. Accessed June 1, 2019. http://www.ala.org/alsc/awardsgrants /bookmedia/caldecottmedal/aboutcaldecott/aboutcaldecott.

Association for Library Service to Children. n.d.-c. "Diversity within the Children's Library Service Profession: A 2016 Survey by the ALSC Equity, Diversity, and Inclusion Task Force." Association for Library Service to Children. Accessed June 15, 2019. http://www.ala.org/alsc/sites/ala.org .alsc/files/content/aboutalsc/alsc-diversity-survey-results.pdf.

Baker, Augusta. 1955. "The Children's Librarian in a Changing Neighborhood." *Top of the News* 10 (March): 40–41.

Biggs, Bonnie. 2000. "Bright Child of Oklahoma: Lotsee Patterson and the Development of America's Tribal Libraries." *American Indian Culture and Research Journal* 24 (4): 55–67.

Brandehoff, Susan E. 1983. "Jake and Honeybunch Go to Heaven: Children's Book Fans Smoldering Debate." *American Libraries* 14 (March): 130–132.

Bush, Margaret. 1996. "New England Book Women: Their Increasing Influence." *Library Trends* 44 (4): 7–19.

California Library Association. n.d. "California Library Hall of Fame: Effie Lee Morris." California Library Association. Accessed June 3, 2019. https://www.cla-net.org/page/1033.

Campbell, Edith. 2018. "On Negroes, Monkeys, and Apes." *CrazyQuiltEdi* (blog), Last modified April 27, 2018. https://crazyquiltedi.blog/2018/04/26/on-negroes-monkeys-and-apes/.

Cappiccie, Amy, Janice Chadha, Muh Bi Lin, and Frank Snyder. 2012. "Using Critical Race Theory to Analyze How Disney Constructs Diversity: A Construct for the Baccalaureate Human Behavior in the Social Environment Curriculum." *Journal of Teaching in Social Work* 32 (1): 46–61.

Collins, Patricia Hill. 2009. *Another Kind of Public Education: Race, Schools, the Media and Democratic Possibilities*. Boston: Beacon Press.

DeCuir, Jessica T., and Adrienne D. Dixson. 2004. "'So When It Comes Out, They Aren't That Surprised That It Is There': Using Critical Race Theory as a Tool of Analysis of Race and Racism in Education." *Educational Researcher* 33 (5): 26–31.

Derman-Sparks, Louise. 2016. "Guide for Selecting Anti-bias Children's Books." *Social Justice Books: A Teaching for Change Project*. https://socialjusticebooks.org/guide-for-selecting-anti-bias -childrens-books/.

Eaton, Gale. 2014. *The Education of Alice M. Jordan: Navigating a Career in Children's Librarianship*. Lanham, MD: Rowman & Littlefield.

Garner, Carla. 2009. "Effie Lee Morris (1921–2009)." *Blackpast*, February 26, 2009. https://www .blackpast.org/african-american-history/morris-effie-lee-1921/.

Garrison, Dee. 1972–1973. "The Tender Technicians: The Feminization of Public Librarianship, 1876–1905." *Journal of Social History* 6 (2): 131–159.

Garrison, Dee. 1979. *Apostles of Culture: The Public Librarian and American Society, 1876–1920*. New York: The Free Press.

Hand, Shane. 2012. "Transmitting Whiteness: Librarians, Children, and Race, 1900–1930s." *Progressive Librarians* 38–39 (Spring): 34–63.

Harris, Michael H. 1984. *History of Libraries in the Western World*. Metuchen, NJ: Scarecrow Press.

Hewins, Caroline M. 1897. *Books for Boys and Girls: A Selected List*. Boston: ALA Publishing Section.

Hogan, Kristen. 2011. "Tribal Libraries as the Future of Librarianship: Independent Collection Development as a Tool for Social Justice." In *Tribal Libraries, Archives, and Museums: Preserving our Language, Memory, and Lifeways*, edited by Loriene Roy, Anjali Bhasin, and Sarah K. Arriaga, 81–103. Lanham, MD: Scarecrow Press.

Hunt, Clara Whitehill, Sheldon Fletcher, and Franklin K. Mathiews. 1919. *The Bookshelf for Boys and Girls: From Nursery Rhymes to Grown-Up Time*. https://catalog.hathitrust.org/Record/006751905.

Ishizuka, Katie, and Ramón Stephens. 2019. "The Cat Is Out of the Bag: Orientalism, Anti-Blackness, and White Supremacy in Dr. Seuss's Children's Books." *Research on Diversity in Youth Literature* 1 (2). https://sophia.stkate.edu/cgi/viewcontent.cgi?article=1050&context=rdyl.

Jenkins, Christine A. 2000. "The History of Youth Services Librarianship: A Review of the Research Literature." *Libraries and Culture* 35 (1): 103–140.

Jensen, Karen. 2018. "Diversity Auditing 101: How to Evaluate Your Collection." *School Library Journal*, October 22, 2018. https://www.slj.com/?detailStory=diversity-auditing-101-how-to-evalu ate-collection.

Jordan, Alice M. 1913. "A Chapter in Children's Libraries." *Library Journal* 38 (1): 20–21.

Kimball, Melanie A. 2014. "A Home-Like Atmosphere: The Advent of Children's Rooms at St. Louis Public Library, 1906–1912." *Library Trends* 62 (3): 489–503.

Ladson-Billings, Gloria. 1999. "Just What Is Critical Race Theory, and What's It Doing in a Nice Field Like Education?" In *Race Is…Race Isn't: Critical Race Theory and Qualitative Studies in Education*, edited by Laurence Parker, Donna Deyhle, and Sofia Villenas, 7–22. Boulder, CO: Westview Press.

Lear, Bernadette A. 2015. "Libraries and Reading Culture at the Carlisle Indian Industrial School, 1879–1918." *Book History* 18:166–196.

López, Manuel D. 1976. "Children's Libraries: Nineteenth-Century American Origins." *Journal of Library History* 11 (4): 316–342.

Low, Jason T. 2016. "Where Is the Diversity in Publishing? The 2015 Diversity Baseline Survey Results." Lee & Low Books, *The Open Book Blog*, January 26, 2016. https://blog.leeandlow.com /2016/01/26/where-is-the-diversity-in-publishing-the-2015-diversity-baseline-survey-results/.

Mabbott, Cass. 2017. "The We Need Diverse Books Campaign and Critical Race Theory: Charlemae Rollins and the Call for Diverse Children's Books." *Library Trends* 65 (4): 508–522.

Matsuda, Mari J., Charles Lawrence III, Richard Delgado, and Kimberlé Williams Crenshaw. 1993. *Words That Wound: Critical Race Theory, Assaultive Speech, and the First Amendment*. Boulder, CO: Westview Press.

Orange, Satia Marshall. 2012. "Pay It Forward for Effie Lee Morris: A Tribute." In *The 21st-Century Black Librarian in America: Issues and Challenges*, edited by Andrew P. Jackson, Julius C. Jefferson Jr., and Akilah S. Nosakhere, 253–256. Lanham, MD: Scarecrow Press.

Pawley, Christine. 2015. "Libraries and Information Organizations: Two Centuries of Experience." In *Information Services Today: An Introduction*, edited by Sandra Hirsh, 14–25. Lanham, MD: Rowman & Littlefield.

Reading While White (blog). n.d. Accessed June 15, 2019. http://readingwhilewhite.blogspot.com/.

Rose, Ernestine. 1954. *The Public Library in American Life*. New York: Columbia University Press.

Sampson, Zora. n.d. "An Interview with Dr. Lotsee Patterson, a Founding Member of AILA." American Indian Library Association. Accessed June 5, 2019. https://ailanet.org/35-anniversary -lotsee-patterson/.

Sánchez González, Lisa. 2013. *The Stories I Read to the Children: The Life and Writing of Pura Belpré, the Legendary Storyteller, Children's Author, and New York Public Librarian*. New York: Center for Puerto Rican Studies.

Schlesselman-Tarango, Gina. 2016. "The Legacy of Lady Bountiful: White Women in the Library." *Library Trends* 64 (4): 667–686.

Simmons University. 2020. "Anti-oppression LibGuide." Simmons University. Last updated June 8, 2020. https://simmons.libguides.com/anti-oppression.

Smith, Henrietta M. 1995. "An Interview with Augusta Baker." *Horn Book Magazine*, March 1, 1995. https://www.hbook.com/1995/03/authors-illustrators/interviews/an-interview-with-augusta-baker/.

Step Up Scholastic. n.d. Tumblr blog. Accessed June 15, 2019. https://stepupscholastic.tumblr.com/.

Tolson, Nancy. 1998. "Making Books Available: The Role of Early Libraries, Librarians, and Booksellers in the Promotion of African American Children's Literature." *African American Review* 32 (1): 9–16.

Vandergrift, Kay E. 1996. "Female Advocacy and Harmonious Voices: A History of Public Library Services and Publishing for Children in the United States." *Library Trends* 44 (4): 683–718.

Willet, Holly G. 2001. "Rifles for Watie: Rollins, Riley, and Racism." *Libraries a Culture* 36, no. 4 (Fall): 487–505.

8

RELEGATED TO THE MARGINS

Faculty of Color, the Scholarly Record, and the Necessity
of Antiracist Library Disruptions

Harrison W. Inefuku

Knowledge, as it has been shaped in the United States, is grounded in whiteness. Academic publishing, and scholarly communication more broadly, have been shaped by professions that are overwhelmingly white—academia, publishing, and librarianship. These professions have developed a scholarly communication system comprised of policies, practices, and beliefs that marginalize contributions by and about communities of color.

Scholarly communication is "the system through which research and other scholarly writings are created, evaluated for quality, disseminated to the scholarly community, and preserved for future use" (ACRL Scholarly Communications Committee 2003). A core tenet of Critical Race Theory (CRT) is that racism is ordinary and pervasive in societal structures—scholarly communication is no exception. It is marked by a series of gatekeepers that judge the admissibility of research into the scholarly record, sending messages to People of Color that they do not belong in academia and their research is not valuable. The inequities in publishing are representative of racial power dynamics in greater society, reflecting and reinscribing White Supremacy over the construction of knowledge.

Academic publishing, the publication of the products of scholarly research, is the primary means through which knowledge is validated and entered into the scholarly record. In order to get published, research products typically undergo editorial and peer review, through which decisions are made as to whether these products are valid and significant enough for publication. Critique of liberalism is a tenet of

CRT—an analysis of academic publishing through this lens reveals that the standards of validity and significance are neither objective nor meritocratic, but work to buttress whiteness in the construction of knowledge.

This chapter is a consideration of the role of race and power in the construction of knowledge, employing a CRT lens. Engaging with the CRT tenets that racism is ordinary and pervasive, and the critique of liberalism, I analyze four gatekeeping processes that impact the creation and acceptance of knowledge—the selection of research topics and methodologies; peer review; knowledge dissemination; and faculty evaluation, promotion, and tenure. Through these processes, academic publishing in the United States creates a body of knowledge that privileges a white worldview and marginalizes the perspectives, experiences, and contributions of communities of color. I close the chapter with a call for academic librarians, libraries, and our professional organizations to engage in social justice work to center research by and about communities of color in the scholarly record.

GATEKEEPING IN ACADEMIC PUBLISHING

The pervasiveness of White Supremacy and racism in the United States presents barriers to scholars of color at numerous points in their education and careers, impacting the construction of knowledge. It begins early, with biased textbooks and curricula and messaging that tells women and People of Color that they don't belong in science and technology. It continues through college and university admissions, government and nonprofit funding priorities, grant-making decisions, and hiring and promotion, among many other points. Through gatekeeping practices, academic publishing deprives communities of color of representation in many spheres of society beyond academia, and of knowledge necessary to advance an antiracist and antioppressive agenda.

THE GATEKEEPERS: ACADEMICS, PUBLISHERS, AND LIBRARIANS

Academic publishing is located at the intersection of three professions—academia, publishing, and librarianship, with each having gatekeeping roles at various points in the research and publication cycle (Inefuku and Roh 2016). Academia provides the pool of authors, editors, and reviewers; publishing determines whose voices are included in the scholarly record; and librarians play a large role in disseminating knowledge and helping scholars locate scholarly resources.

The demographics of these professions are overwhelmingly white. Faculty of color in the United States comprise 24 percent of the professoriate (McFarland et al. 2019), significantly less than their number in the American population at large, of which 39 percent identified as Hispanic or Latinx, a racial category other than white, and/ or multiracial (US Census Bureau, n.d.). Publishing and librarianship are even more homogenous. A study of demographics of professionals working in scholarly publishing found that 90.67 percent of respondents identified as white or Caucasian (Greco, Wharton, and Brand 2016). The American Library Association's (2012) "Diversity Counts" study found that 86.1 percent of credential librarians in higher education were white.

These demographics speak to the obstacles People of Color face in entering and thriving in these professions and to their absence in shaping the policies and practices that have shaped the scholarly record. The norms of academic publishing have been constructed from a perspective of whiteness, with limited to no input from communities of color. Systemic biases manifest in the cultures and practices of all three professions that contribute to the academic publishing endeavor, working in concert to uphold a master narrative that centers knowledge that adheres to dominant (white) topics of inquiry and methodologies.

RESEARCH TOPICS AND METHODOLOGY

Academic publishing serves to define the limits of "legitimate" knowledge. Higher education professor Christine Stanley (2007, 14) argues, "There is a master narrative operating in academia that often defines and limits what is valued as scholarship and who is entitled to create scholarship. This is problematic, because the dominant group in academia writes most research and, more often than not, they are White men." Similarly, Dolores Delgado Bernal and Octavio Villalpando (2002, 177) propose that "by marginalizing the knowledge of faculty of color, higher education has created an apartheid of knowledge where the dominant European epistemology is believed to produce 'legitimate' knowledge, in contrast to the 'illegitimate' knowledge that is created by all other epistemological perspectives."

White Americans are uncomfortable talking about race and the impact of racism on People of Color in the United States (DiAngelo 2018). This discomfort erects barriers to publishing for scholars who conduct research on race and racism or employ activist perspectives and methodologies. In discussing the experiences of four LIS faculty of color, Nicole A. Cooke and Joe O. Sánchez (2019) write, "All of the authors have previously had their work and personal experience dismissed, minimized, and ignored because these experiences raised upsetting questions or conclusions about how the field and the professoriate treat people of color" (169). The pressure on scholars of race to adopt mainstream (white) subjects and methodologies serves to highlight the prevalence of white fragility in academia.

The methodological norms of a discipline can also hinder research on communities of color. In psychology, for example, studies of underrepresented populations may be considered methodologically flawed if they do not have a white control group, whereas studies of whites are never required to include African American control groups (Korchin 1980). Psychology professor Stanley Sue (1999, 1073) states that psychological research often assumes universality of research, and "the burden of proof is placed on researchers concerned about race, ethnicity, and bias to show that there are ethnic differences." Such attitudes toward race in science reinforce the construction of whiteness as the default and standard, with scholars researching communities of color having to push against the pervasiveness of color-blind attitudes.

Scholars with a social justice orientation and others who conduct research on communities of color often receive feedback that their work is too narrow, biased, activist, descriptive, and/or lacking intellectual or scientific rigor (Sue 1999). Thus, faculty of color with an interest in social justice scholarship may be dissuaded from taking an activist approach, and instead utilize mainstream methodologies or focus on nonracial forms of oppression (such as gender) (Simpson 2010). CRT's focus on intersectionality, however, stresses that scholars do not have to choose between researching race, gender, or other forms of oppression, because these forms of oppression are interlinked and overlapping.

When scholars of color interested in researching race and racism succumb to this pressure and avoid race-based research, they give up a part of their identity and purpose (Del Carmen Salazar and Rios 2016). This approach is assimilationist and implies that faculty of color are unable to develop their own research agendas (Stanley and Lincoln 2005). Within our field of library and information science (LIS), faculty of color have shared experiences that they are expected to be experts in diversity-related issues, while being dissuaded from pursuing research agendas in diversity to avoid being "pigeonholed" (Ceja Alcalá et al. 2017).

The pressures to adhere to dominant research topics and methodologies work to uphold White Supremacy in the formation of knowledge. Color-blind attitudes toward research negate the reality of White Supremacy in American society and give scholars and institutions a pass on confronting their complicity in systems of racial oppression.

PEER REVIEW

When an article is submitted to a journal, it is first reviewed by an editor who does an initial review. The editor then assigns the article to peer reviewers. Most peer reviews are either single-anonymous, in which the identities of the reviewers are hidden from the author, but the reviewers are aware of the author's identity; or double-anonymous, in which the identities of the authors and reviewers are hidden from each other.[1] The peer reviewers make recommendations on whether to accept or reject a submission or request revisions, with the final decision lying with the editor. Viewing peer review through CRT's critique of liberalism helps us see that peer review does not result in objective evaluations of scholarship.

By making the identity of authors available to reviewers, single-anonymous review opens the process to biases held by reviewers. In describing the history of peer review for the Royal Society, Aileen Fyfe (2018) writes, "Certain surnames could conjure up stereotypes about, for example, Indian or Japanese researchers and there was never any doubt about which authors were female, thanks to the allegedly chivalrous insistence upon giving the first names (and/or gender specific titles, such as 'Mrs') of female authors." Although double-anonymous peer review is designed to protect a work from reviewer bias, neither process protects the work from any biases that may be held by an editor. Triple-anonymous reviews, in which the identity of the author is also hidden from editors, and open peer review, in which the identities of reviewers are made available to authors, have been proposed as more equitable approaches to peer review.

While research on the impact of gender on peer review has generated mixed results (Darling 2014), the journal *Behavioral Ecology* noted a significant increase in female authors after switching to double-anonymous peer review in 2001 (Budden et al. 2008). This finding has been cited by other journals that have switched to double-anonymous reviews. While the literature lacks studies on the impact of race and ethnicity on peer review, peer review is not immune to the biases that exist in society that disadvantage communities of color. Economics professors Marianne Bertrand and Sendhil Mullainathan (2004) found that job applicants with Black-sounding names were less likely to receive callbacks from job applications than applicants with white-sounding names. Authors with Black-, Latinx-, or Asian-sounding names may similarly be impacted by systemic biases in peer review.

In addition to bias toward authors of color, there is also significant bias toward research on race and racism, as noted in the previous section. Communications scholar Jennifer Lyn Simpson (2010) points out that "authors who push the boundaries of the discipline may both disrupt foundational assumptions that undergird the field and challenge people's core beliefs about their identity. Meritocratic review holds up poorly in these circumstances" (151).

When receiving submissions or publications for review about communities of color, there is no guarantee that the editor will try to send the submission to reviewers who are engaged in, knowledgeable about, or even receptive to studies of race and racism. There is also nothing stopping those who are unfamiliar with studying race and racism from accepting invitations to review articles on the subject. Katherine Grace Hendrix (2002, 161) frames her analysis of peer reviews that question the legitimacy of methodologies used by scholars of color in terms of "(a) a lack of knowledge regarding validity and reliability issues for scholars of color and (b) the power to judge the merit of research by scholars of color versus the ability to do so."

Indeed, there are examples of editors assigning publications to reviewers with histories of supporting racist theories and views. In 2017, the *American Historical Review* published a book review of Ansley T. Erickson's *Making the Unequal Metropolis: School Desegregation and Its Limits*. The author of the review, known for publishing in white nationalist venues, included a critique that Erickson doesn't mention sociobiology—widely discredited for naturalizing racism and justifying racist viewpoints—in her work (Jaschik 2017). Readers without prior knowledge of sociology may be led to believe Erickson failed to include an important methodological approach in her work. Biased reviews can lead to poor evaluations of research in tenure and promotion decisions or lead librarians to decide to not purchase the book for their library's collection, limiting the scholar's career trajectory and readers' access to the work.

Part of the issue is that the pool of potential editors and reviewers (i.e., the professoriate) is not diverse—a direct result of the pervasive role of systemic racism in academia. A demographic survey of editorial board members of ACRL publications demonstrates how the lack of diversity within a field (in this case, academic librarianship) impacts the diversity of editorial boards who make decisions on what content gets published. The survey found that the demographics of editorial board members is closely aligned with the demographics of librarianship, as measured in the ALA's "Diversity Counts" survey, with 88 percent of respondents identifying as white (Ford, Kaspar, and Seiden 2017). Increasing representation, however, is not the only answer. As Stanley (2007) argues, editors and reviewers need to educate themselves on the ways privilege and oppression manifest in the review process and to recuse themselves from reviewing scholarship that they are unfamiliar with. Simpson (2010) stresses the importance of not overburdening the limited pool of experts conducting race-related research, writing:

Editors might choose to have manuscripts reviewed by scholars outside the discipline of communication who specialize in race-related research and should expect reviewers within the discipline who have expertise germane to some but not all of the content to follow-up and review citations that complement their existing knowledge. (157)

These calls place the burden of work on editors and peer reviewers to educate themselves on systems of white privilege and racial oppression when reviewing works on race. It is not the role of scholars of color to educate their editors and reviewers on theories and methodologies that underpin research on race and racism (beyond what is outlined in an article's methodology section), which places on these researchers additional expectations that are not shared by white scholars.

KNOWLEDGE DISSEMINATION

Many publishers are driven by market forces, with the selection of books or journals to publish determined in part by the perceived market for publications and the alignment of the publications with the mission of the press. This can make it hard for scholars conducting research on communities of color or other marginalized communities to find a publisher—these topics may be considered to be too "niche" or specialized by publishers who are concerned with recouping publishing costs and turning a profit.

Once faculty of color are published, the ability of their publication to reach readers is heavily dependent on libraries. The collection-building policies and practices and discovery tools employed by libraries has a significant impact on whether the research will be read and used. The selection of titles to add to a library's collection may impact citations, with articles published in journals carried by a library cited more often by the library's users (Corby 2003). Past and present library policies and practices in collection development, description, and cataloging have made libraries complicit in the development of a scholarly record that privileges white voices, perspectives, and experiences.

Once publications enter a library's collection, the ability for researchers to find the publications is impacted by metadata, cataloging, and descriptive standards and the discovery tools offered by the library. Research has shown that the algorithms behind the search engines, library discovery tools, and social media sites that drive today's information seeking reflect societal biases (Bozdag 2013; Noble 2018; Reidsma 2016; Reidsma 2019). Although technological solutions are often viewed as objective, they retain the biases of their human creators, and through machine learning, they can inherit the biases of their users. The controlled vocabularies applied by librarians to organize information reflects societal biases, making it difficult to locate resources on marginalized populations (Olson 2001). In describing the three predominant indexing and classification systems used in law, critical race scholars Richard Delgado and Jean Stefancic (2000) note: "The systems function rather like molecular biology's double helix: They replicate preexisting ideas, thoughts, and approaches. Within the bounds of the three systems, moderate, incremental reform remains quite possible, but the systems make foundational, transformative innovation difficult" (217).

Our classifications systems are slow to change—efficient at finding existing and dominant knowledge but slow to incorporate new ideas, theories, methodologies, and vocabularies. As Hathcock notes, this chapter would be challenging to find using the Library of Congress Subject Headings, as "there is a heading for *White Supremacy Movements* but not *White Supremacy* (as an ideology) or *White Privilege*" (2016; emphasis in original). Likewise, there is no heading for Critical Race Theory. Hathcock points to the bias present in the available terms around whiteness—by including White Supremacy movements and omitting White Supremacy and white privilege, the headings adhere to the notion that racism consists of individual acts, instead of a structural norm in American society. The lack of a heading for Critical Race Theory also illustrates the slowness of change in classification systems, as the framework has been in existence for over thirty years. Although today's library discovery systems are built on standards and technology, these systems are neither universal nor unbiased, and they help to contribute to the invisibility of research by scholars of color, limiting their ability to be read and cited.

FACULTY EVALUATION, PROMOTION, AND TENURE

In addition to research and scholarship, faculty are also expected to perform other duties, including teaching and service. Teaching and service, however, are not weighted as heavily in faculty evaluations. Research has shown that faculty of color spend more of their time on service, which is given little value in making promotion and tenure decisions. Education professor Amado Padilla (1994) developed the term *cultural taxation* to name the increased expectations placed on faculty for service, especially service around issues of diversity and climate. A study of faculty at the University of Oregon found that nonmarginalized assistant professors were able to dedicate *four times* the mean of marginalized assistant professors (including faculty of color, sexual minorities, and those from disadvantaged class backgrounds) of their awake time on research (Social Sciences Feminist Network Research Interest Group 2017). With more time dedicated to research, white faculty have an advantage in the publication numbers-counting game in consideration for tenure and promotion.

Measures have been built into the faculty evaluation process with the intention of increasing the objectivity of evaluations, including providing criteria and standards for evaluators for qualitative approaches and using multiple data sources for quantitative approaches (Whitman and Weiss 1982). The reliance on quantitative data, such as citation counts, however, is not objective, as such data reflect the biases inherent in academic publishing (Reece and Hardy 2017; Jensenius et al. 2018). Meritocracy "negates the importance of raced experience and holds everyone to a standard originally and primarily defined by Whites and biased in favor of the status quo" (Simpson 2010, 151). Thus, tenure and promotion, processes that are allegedly based on merit, instead work to uphold White Supremacy in academia.

With the growth of open-access publishing and library publishing programs, there has been a growth of opportunities to create journals dedicated to publishing subjects and methodologies that are ignored by the dominant publications. These journals can help to build communities of researchers and practitioners and provide publishing opportunities for emerging scholars. Yet, "while providing essential outlets for new perspectives and developing areas of research, publications in these journals may be devalued in standard decision-making processes for moving faculty up the career ladder" (Turner 2003, 118). The growth of library publishing provides our profession with an opportunity to reenvision and implement new modes of publishing that center communities of color.

With a faculty member's promotion and tenure dependent largely on their research productivity and publication output, the obstacles scholars of color face in publishing at each step of the career ladder and research life cycle accumulate to form a significant barrier. Promotion and tenure data from the University of Southern California demonstrates the challenge facing faculty of color—while 81 percent of white junior faculty were awarded tenure between 1998 and 2012, only 47.6 percent of junior faculty of color received tenure (Junn 2016). As English professor Patricia A. Matthew (2016) writes, "Even though personal processes are inherently subjective at every level, those who are part of those processes deploy the language of meritocracy in the belief they are being objective" (9). Standards, criteria, and procedures are claimed to be objective and meritocratic, but a CRT lens tell us that claims to liberalism allows systems to ignore and perpetuate past and current injustices. Edward Taylor (1998) notes, "By relying on merit criteria or standards, the dominant group can justify its exclusion of blacks to positions of power, believing in its own neutrality" (123). Concepts such as "best" as "qualified" have been constructed in a white worldview, and the perspectives, approaches, and knowledge of scholars of color are marginalized and devalued. The result is a professoriate that continues to lag behind society and a student body that is increasingly diverse.

THE LIBRARY'S ROLE IN PROMOTING ANTIRACISM

With the increase in critical approaches to librarianship, there has been a growing call for librarians to adopt a social justice mindset and actively embrace their agency to make library collections and services more inclusive, serving as agents of change (Morales, Knowles, and Bourg 2014; Inefuku and Roh 2016). As experts in information, librarians are in a prime position to challenge the systemic biases in academia that hinder the careers of faculty of color.

This section draws on the CRT commitment to social justice tenet, identifying ways libraries can partner with campus stakeholders, dismantle White Supremacist policies and practices in our libraries and across campus, and create systems of knowledge that values and centers the stories, experiences, and perspectives of communities of color. These recommendations require a deep commitment to antiracism and antioppression, not just on the part of individual librarians, but in a system-wide effort that includes our institutions, organizations, and educators.

ANTIRACIST COLLECTIONS AND SYSTEMS

One of the significant sources of power a library holds is its collections budget—as stated earlier, collections decisions not only influence the market for academic publications, but also can also impact citations. "The decisions made about…what books and journals to buy are inevitably biased, based as they are on some combination of judgments and interests of individual libraries and librarians and on those same librarians' sense of the tastes and needs of patrons" (Morales, Knowles, and Bourg 2014, 446). Libraries must ensure that their collections include the voices of scholars of color.

The shape of library collections must be reenvisioned to include and highlight the breadth of knowledge of communities of color. Libraries should develop clear definitions and goals for diversity, and staff engaged in collection development should be trained to understand the importance of diversity to collections (Ciszek and Young 2010). Understanding the role libraries play in upholding white privilege in knowledge production, and learning strategies for disrupting it, should be part of the education and training of library workers. Audits should be conducted to identify gaps in the collection, and librarians should work with vendors to develop purchasing programs that proactively identify titles by authors of color to add to the collection. Journal cancellation and weeding projects should employ data points beyond circulation and usage statistics, including qualitative measures and subject expertise, to ensure titles by authors of color are not further erased in library collections (Baildon et al. 2017).

Antiracism must be included in library collection development policies that explicitly state that works by authors of color and those that center their perspectives and experiences are to be added to the collection. By doing this, libraries can begin to rectify the propagation of work that libels our communities, creating and perpetuating damaging stereotypes. In chapter 4 of this volume, Miranda Belarde-Lewis and Sarah R. Kostelecky describe information projects that respect and center Zuni knowledge systems, in contrast to scholarship on Indigenous communities written by outsiders that violates the norms and ethics of Indigenous communities.

As I illustrated in the previous section, the descriptive and discovery systems employed by libraries—our controlled vocabularies and indexes—are slow to change, and reflect the biases of our society. Our reliance on standards and technology, which have been created by dominant groups, and Library of Congress Subject Headings in particular, which are subject to political influence, renders the work by and about communities of color invisible. In chapter 5, Vani Natarajan describes encounters with white librarians and professors who have minimized scholarship on Asian Americans, and their efforts to engage in collection development that centers QTPOC authors. Sujei Lugo Vázquez in chapter 7 provides action items libraries can use to build racially inclusive children's collections—these action items can easily be applied to collection development in academic libraries, too.

In addition to building collections that are inclusive of authors of color, we have technology available in libraries, including LibGuides, publishing platforms, and social media, that enable us to increase the visibility of scholarship about communities of color. These platforms also allow us to respond quickly to current events and provide access to sources that counter the misinformation spread by talking heads and foreign bots. The Charleston Syllabus is a prime example of how social media has been deployed to promote the spread of race-related knowledge in response to contemporary events. Williams, Williams, and Blain (2016) recount how, following the 2015 Charleston church shooting, in which African Americans attending bible study were murdered by a white extremist, the #CharlestonSyllabus hashtag was used on Twitter to point to resources about the shooting and its historical context. They describe the engagement of librarians Cecily Walker, Ryan P. Randall, Melissa Morrone, and Elliot Brandow, who organized and linked the list of titles generated by the hashtag to WorldCat and created tags in WorldCat to enhance their discoverability (3–4).

ENGAGING LIBRARY PUBLISHING

As libraries move into the publishing arena, librarians have gained the power to directly insert the voices of faculty of color, as well as communities of color outside academia, in the published record. As part of the effort to transform scholarly communication, academic libraries have started establishing programs that publish journals, conference proceedings, and books on behalf of faculty and students. These programs often focus on open-access titles and publications that would be considered unprofitable by commercial publishers and university presses.

The Library Publishing Coalition's *An Ethical Framework for Library Publishing* (2018) calls on library publishing programs to "intervene and reduce the impact of bias in content selection and create hospitable environments for a diversity of identities, viewpoints, and approaches" (35), by providing publishing opportunities for authors from underrepresented backgrounds and supporting efforts to make metadata and indexing standards and practices more inclusive. In regards to traditional publishing, Paul Royster (2008) notes, publication decisions are made in the self-interest and preservation of the publisher, with the scholarship they publish forming salable units in the bookselling business. As many library publishing programs operate without a profit motive, they present an opportunity to publish scholarship that commercial publishers have considered too niche to be marketable.

Library publishing programs are an ideal platform for the publication of scholarship that resists dominant white ideology and uplifts the knowledge and experiences of communities of color. By virtue of being connected to academic libraries, these programs lend the reputations of their host libraries and universities to these publications and can help to increase the perceived legitimacy of the scholarship.

These programs can also create a pipeline of emerging scholars of color who understand the processes, politics, and power dynamics of academic publishing. Academic libraries with library publishing programs can leverage their programs to help socialize students of color in academic publishing by providing them with hands-on experience. Library publishing programs can provide paid assistantships for graduate students of color to serve as managing editors of journals and teach all student assistants best practices to minimize the impact of bias and center voices of color in publishing. The provision of managing editors can also support faculty of color who want to launch new journals but lack the funding to hire assistants and the time to manage the projects. By providing emerging scholars of color with experience in academic publishing, library publishing programs can give them a foundation to challenge and opportunities to disrupt White Supremacy in publishing.

VALUING SCHOLARSHIP BY AND ABOUT COMMUNITIES OF COLOR

Where academic publishing silences research on race and racism, CRT places value on the experiential knowledge of communities of color and embraces counterstory-telling as a methodology. Through counterstorytelling, communities of color share their experiences with oppression. This is an important intervention, "because of their different histories and experiences with oppression, black, American Indian, Asian, and Latino writers and thinkers may be able to communicate to their white counterparts matters that the whites are unlikely to know" (Delgado and Stefancic 2017, 11). CRT also promotes interdisciplinarity and draws from ethnic studies, gender studies, history, law, and other disciplines to understand race and power and to challenge systems of oppression (Solorzano and Yosso 2001). By promoting interdisciplinary approaches and uplifting the experiential knowledge of communities of color, CRT creates space for perspectives and methodologies that challenge the white-dominated worldview privileged in academic publishing. Libraries must join the call to uplift the knowledge of communities of color.

Awe (2006) argues that "to help remove the marginalization and the devaluation of African American faculty research, departments should publicize the academic and scholarly achievements of African American scholars" (48). Academic libraries can help to spearhead this effort. Many academic libraries already pursue initiatives to recognize and celebrate faculty authors, from building bibliographies and databases of faculty publications to holding receptions and other celebratory events (Bonnet, Alvarez, and Cordell 2014; Stringfellow and Armstrong 2012). Libraries can host similar events to specifically celebrate the publishing accomplishments of faculty of color, raising their visibility on campus.

Because research on race and racism is often dismissed and devalued, libraries must leverage these events to demonstrate the value in this type of scholarship. In examining the changing roles of academic libraries, Wegner and Zemsky (2007) assert that library professions must have "the ability to educate faculty members, helping them to understand the power and applicability of resources and modes of inquiry that have come about since the time of a professor's own graduate training."

These events can demonstrate the value of approaches utilized by those studying race and racism, such as counterstorytelling. Hosting a panel of local faculty and students who can share their reactions to an article on microaggressions in the classroom, for example, can bring a close, human connection to the scholarship. Likewise, for faculty whose scholarship is based on community engagement, members of the community can be invited to share the impact the work of faculty has had on their communities, providing evidence of research impact that can't be captured by citation counts and journal impact factors.

These can be done in partnership with the university's diversity and inclusion office, as well as the provost's office. These events can help boost the visibility of scholarship of faculty of color and normalize the theories and methodologies they employ and the perspectives they bring to the scholarly record. Libraries can play a significant role in reinforcing the message that faculty of color, and researchers studying race and racism are productive and their work and methodologies are legitimate and valuable.

LEVERAGING LIBRARIAN EXPERTISE AND AGENCY

Education has been a central role of libraries, through the offering of information literacy courses, computer literacy sessions, and workshops on all aspects of information, knowledge, and learning. Libraries can expand their offerings through workshops on academic publishing, targeted to students and faculty from marginalized groups (Baildon et al. 2017). Charlotte Roh (2016) hosts brown bag lunches for graduate students of color where she provides an overview of the publication process and describes the lack of diversity in academic publishing, helping to socialize these students in the publishing endeavor should they choose to pursue careers in academia. At Iowa State University, I led a workshop for undergraduate male students of color where we discussed the lack of representation of People of Color in the media and stressed the importance of telling one's stories. These workshops can also help address the lack of mentorship for students and junior faculty of color by providing an alternate avenue to receive information on how to successfully navigate the publishing process.

Libraries should also educate faculty on campus tasked with evaluating scholarship—whether as editors, peer-reviewers, university administrators, or members of tenure and promotion committees—on the implications of White Supremacy and bias in academic publishing and the value of critical approaches to scholarship. As Stanley (2007) argues, the publication of nonmainstream approaches requires work on the part of reviewers, "includ[ing] deep reflection on understanding White privilege, including uncovering taken-for-granted assumptions, premises, and values of Whiteness in higher education and voice" (22). Such education can help decision makers understand the choice of research topic, methodology, and publication venue, instead of relying on metrics and concept of "high-impact" publications that privilege researchers who adopt dominant approaches.

Libraries should actively engage faculty of color as allies with expertise in the creation and dissemination of knowledge. In chapter 6 about Ann Allen Shockley, Shaundra Walker provides an example of an important librarian who engaged with faculty and students to build collections that captured the Black experience. The Association of College and Research Libraries recommends that libraries should work with faculty and administrators to educate them on the limitations of research metrics and advocate for more inclusive tenure assessments (ACRL Research Planning and Review Committee 2019). Libraries can help faculty of color and white faculty interrogate existing journal rankings used in faculty evaluations; identify alternative methods for demonstrating research impact, including leveraging institutional repository metrics and providing testimonials; and explain the significance of journals with diversity and social justice orientations and the limitations of "mainstream" journals. In doing so, libraries can contribute to CRT's rejection of liberalism, illuminating how faculty evaluation systems are neither color-blind nor objective and helping to build new antiracist and antioppressive structures.

CONCLUSION

A recent study indicates that there has been little progress in diversifying the professoriate. Between 2013 and 2017, the percentage of tenured white faculty members at doctoral-granting institutions has decreased 3.17 percent. However, this decrease is not matched by an equivalent increase of faculty of color—the number of tenured Black faculty members increased by only 0.10 percent and tenured Hispanic/Latino faculty increased by 0.65 percent. The number of tenured American Indian/Alaska Native faculty *decreased* by 0.01 percent (Vasquez Heilig et al. 2019). The inability of scholars of color to secure a place, persist, and thrive in academia is due, in part, to the significant barriers they face in academic publishing. With publishing a central determinant of a scholar's ability to progress in careers in academia, the persistence of racism in the process creates a negative feedback loop that suppresses the number of faculty of color, resulting in a scholarly record that continues to be dominated by whiteness.

The construction of knowledge that privileges white experiences, methodologies, and perspectives has far-reaching effects. The perpetuation of a body of knowledge in which communities of color are marginalized means that our communities are not represented in our textbooks, curricula, media, public policy, and in many other spheres of society.

Libraries must recognize their role in upholding White Supremacist structures in academic publishing and scholarly communication and adopt a CRT lens in developing antiracist policies and practices. In discussing the changing roles of academic libraries in the twenty-first century, Wegner and Zemsky argue that libraries "have a major role in ensuring that they and their home institutions remain vital players in the changing terrain of information and education" (2007). Academic libraries can leverage their role in collecting, preserving, and providing access to knowledge to help advocate for and advance an antiracist agenda on their campus by ensuring that their collections and systems reflect a world of knowledge that centers the voices of communities of color and their publishing programs provide spaces for new and critical voices and perspectives; to educate the campus on how current policies and practices uphold institutional racism; and to promote antiracist alternatives.

NOTE

1. While the terms *single-blind*, *double-blind*, and *triple-blind* are the predominant phrases used to describe peer review, I use the terms *single-anonymous*, *double-anonymous*, and *triple-anonymous* in this chapter and my practice, in rejection of ableist language.

BIBLIOGRAPHY

ACRL Research Planning and Review Committee. 2019. "Environmental Scan 2019." Association of College and Research Libraries white paper. http://www.ala.org/acrl/sites/ala.org.acrl/files/content/publications/whitepapers/EnvironmentalScan2019.pdf.

ACRL Scholarly Communications Committee. 2003. "Principles and Strategies for the Reform of Scholarly Communication." Association of College and Research Libraries white paper. http://www.ala.org/acrl/publications/whitepapers/principlesstrategies.

American Library Association. 2012. "Diversity Counts: 2012 Tables." American Library Association. http://www.ala.org/aboutala/sites/ala.org.aboutala/files/content/diversity/diversitycounts/diversitycountstables2012.pdf.

Awe, Clara. 2006. "Retention of African American Faculty in Research Universities." *Metropolitan Universities* 17 (2): 33–57.

Baildon, Michelle, Dana Hamlin, Czeslaw Jankowski, Rhonda Kauffman, Julia Lanigan, Michelle Miller, Jessica Venlet, and Ann Marie Willer. 2017. "Creating a Social Justice Mindset: Diversity,

Inclusion, and Social Justice in the Collections Directorate of the MIT Libraries." MIT Libraries DISJ Task Force report. September 2, 2017. https://hdl.handle.net/1721.1/108771.

Bertrand, Marianne, and Sendhil Mullainathan. 2004. "Are Emily and Greg More Employable than Lakisha and Jamal? A Field Experiment on Labor Market Discrimination." *American Economic Review* 94 (4): 991–1013. http://www.jstor.org/stable/3592802?origin=JSTOR-pdf.

Bonnett, Jennifer, Barbara Alvarez, and Sigrid Anderson Cordell. 2014. "Let's Get This Party Started: Celebrating Faculty Authors in the Library." *College and Research Library News* 75 (10): 550–559. https://doi.org/10.5860/crln.75.10.9210.

Bozdag, Engin. 2013. "Bias in Algorithmic Filtering and Personalization." *Ethics and Information Technology* 15 (3): 209–227. https://doi.org/10.1007/s10676-013-9321-6.

Budden, Amber E., Tom Tregenza, Lonnie W. Aarsen, Julia Koricheva, Roosa Leimu, and Christopher J. Lortie. 2008. "Double-Blind Review Favours Increased Representation of Female Authors." *Trends in Ecology and Evolution* 23 (1): 4–6. https://doi.org/10.1016/j.tree.2007.07.008.

Ceja Alcalá, Janet, Mónica Colón-Aguirre, Nicole A. Cooke, and Brenton Stewart. 2017. "A Critical Dialogue: Faculty of Color in Library and Information Science." *InterActions: UCLA Journal of Education and Information Studies* 13 (2). https://escholarship.org/uc/item/1gq2s8q5.

Ciszek, Matthew P., and Courtney L. Young. 2010. "Diversity Collection Assessment in Large Academic Libraries." *Collection Building* 29 (4): 154–161. https://doi.org/10.1108/01604951011088899.

Cooke, Nicole A., and Joe O. Sánchez. 2019. "Getting It on the Record: Faculty of Color in Library and Information Science." *Journal of Education for Library and Information Science* 60 (3): 169–181. https://doi.org/10.3138/jelis.60.3.01.

Corby, Katherine. 2003. "Constructing Core Journal Lists: Mixing Science and Alchemy." *portal: Libraries and the Academy* 3 (2): 207–217. https://doi.org/10.1353/pla.2003.0029.

Darling, E. S. 2014. "Use of Double-Blind Peer Review to Increase Author Diversity." *Conservation Biology* 29 (1): 297–299. https://doi.org/10.1111/cobi.12333.

Del Carmen Salazar, Maria, and Francisco Rios. 2016. "Just Scholarship! Publishing Academic Research with a Social Justice Focus." *Multicultural Perspectives* 18 (1): 3–11. https://doi.org/10.1080/15210960.2016.1127073.

Delgado, Richard, and Jean Stefancic. 2000. "Why Do We Tell the Same Stories? Law Reform, Critical Librarianship, and the Triple Helix Dilemma." Reprint in *Critical Race Theory: The Cutting Edge*, edited by Richard Delgado and Jean Stefancic, 214–224. 2nd ed. Philadelphia: Temple University Press.

Delgado, Richard, and Jean Stefancic. 2017. *Critical Race Theory: An Introduction*. 3rd ed. New York: New York University Press.

Delgado Bernal, Dolores, and Octavio Villalpando. 2002. "An Apartheid of Knowledge in Academia: The Struggle over the 'Legitimate' Knowledge of Faculty of Color." *Equity and Excellence in Education* 35 (2): 169–180. https://doi.org/10.1080/713845282

DiAngelo, Robin. 2018. *White Fragility*. Boston: Beacon Press.

Ford, Emily, Wendi Arant Kaspar, and Peggy Seiden. 2017. "Diversity of ACRL Publications, Editorial Board Demographics." *College and Research Libraries News* 78 (10): 548. https://doi.org/10.5860/crln.78.10.548.

Fyfe, Aileen. 2018. "Then and Now—Exploring Diversity in Peer Review at the Royal Society." Publishing blog, the Royal Society. September 10, 2018. https://blogs.royalsociety.org/publishing/peer-review-at-the-royal-society/.

Greco, Albert N., Robert M. Wharton, and Amy Brand. 2016. "Demographics of Scholarly Publishing and Communication Professionals." *Learned Publishing* 29 (2): 97–101. https://doi.org/10.1002/leap.1017.

Hathcock, April. 2016. "Open but Not Equal: Open Scholarship for Social Justice." *At the Intersection* (blog), February 8, 2016. https://aprilhathcock.wordpress.com/2016/02/08/open-but-not-equal-open-scholarship-for-social-justice/.

Hendrix, Katherine Grace. 2002. "'Did Being Black Introduce Bias into Your Study?': Attempting to Mute the Race-Related Research of Black Scholars." *Howard Journal of Communications* 13:153–171. https://doi.org/10.1080/10646170290089935.

Inefuku, Harrison W., and Charlotte Roh. 2016. "Agents of Diversity and Social Justice: Librarians and Scholarly Communication." In *Open Access and the Future of Scholarly Communication: Policy and Infrastructure*, edited by Kevin L. Smith and Katherine A. Dickson, 107–128. Lanham, MD: Rowman & Littlefield.

Jaschik, Scott. 2017. "The Wrong Reviewer." *Inside Higher Ed,* April 18, 2107. https://www.insidehighered.com/news/2017/04/18/history-journal-apologizes-assigning-review-book-urban-education-and-inequality.

Jensenius, Francesca R., Mala Htun, David J. Samuels, David A. Singer, Adria Lawrence, and Michael Chwe. 2018. "Benefits and Pitfalls of Google Scholar." *PS: Political Science and Politics* 21 (3): 820–824. https://doi.org/10.1017/S104909651800094X.

Junn, Jane. 2016. "Memorandum re: Analysis of Data on Tenure at USC Dornsife." In *Written/Unwritten: Diversity and the Unhidden Truths of Tenure*, edited by Patricia A. Matthew, 271–275. Chapel Hill: University of North Carolina Press.

Korchin, Sheldon J. 1980. "Clinical Psychology and Minority Problems." *American Psychologist* 35 (3): 262–269. https://doi.org/10.1037/0003-066X.35.3.262.

Library Publishing Coalition. 2018. *An Ethical Framework for Library Publishing, Version 1.0.* San Francisco: Educopia. http://dx.doi.org/10.5703/1288284316777.

Matthew, Patricia A. 2016. *Written/Unwritten: Diversity and the Hidden Truths of Tenure.* Chapel Hill: University of North Carolina Press.

McFarland, Joel, Bill Hussar, Jijun Zhang, Xiaolei Wang, Ke Wang, Sarah Hein, Melissa Diliberti, Emily Forrest Cataldi, Farrah Bullock Mann, and Amy Barmer. 2019. "The Condition of Education 2019." NCES 2019–144, National Center for Education Statistics, Institute of Education Sciences, US Department of Education. https://nces.ed.gov/pubsearch/pubsinfo.asp?pubid=2019144.

Morales, Myrna, Em Claire Knowles, and Chris Bourg. 2014. "Diversity, Social Justice, and the Future of Libraries.2 *portal: Libraries and the Academy* 14 (3): 439–451. https://doi.org/10.1353/pla .2014.0017.

Noble, Safiya. 2018. *Algorithms of Oppression: How Search Engines Reinforce Racism.* New York: New York University Press.

Olson, Hope A. 2001. "The Power to Name: Representation in Library Catalogs." *Signs* 26 (3): 639–668. https://doi.org/10.1086/495624.

Padilla, Amado M. 1994. "Ethnic Minority Scholars, Research, and Mentoring: Current and Future Issues." *Educational Researcher* 23 (4): 24–27. https://doi.org/10.3102%2F0013189X023004024.

Reece, Robert L., and Margaret C. Hardy. 2017. "Moving beyond Metrics: A Primer in Hiring and Promoting a Diverse Workforce in Entomology and Other Natural Sciences." *Annals of the Entomological Society of America* 110 (5): 484–491. https://doi.org/10.1093/aesa/sax059.

Reidsma, Matthew. 2016. "Algorithmic Bias in Library Discovery Systems." *Matthew Reidsma* (personal blog), March 11, 2016. https://matthew.reidsrow.com/articles/173.

Reidsma, Matthew. 2019. *Masked by Trust: Bias in Library Discovery.* Sacramento, CA: Library Juice Press.

Roh, Charlotte. 2016. "Inequities in Publishing." *Urban Library Journal* 22 (2). https://academicworks .cuny.edu/ulj/vol22/iss2/2/.

Royster, Paul. 2008. "Publishing Original Content in an Institutional Repository." *Serials Review* 34 (1): 27–30.

Simpson, Jennifer Lyn. 2010. "Blinded by the White: Challenging the Notion of a Color-Blind Meritocracy in the Academy." *Southern Communication Journal* 75 (2): 150–159. https://doi.org/10 .1080/10417941003613248.

Social Sciences Feminist Network Research Interest Group. 2017. "The Burden of Invisible Work in Academia: Social Inequalities and Time Use in Five University Departments." *Humboldt Journal of Social Relations* 39:228–245. https://digitalcommons.humboldt.edu/hjsr/vol1/iss39/21/.

Solorzano, Daniel G., and Tara J. Yosso. 2001. "Critical Race and LatCrit Theory and Method: Counter-storytelling." *Qualitative Studies in Education* 14 (4): 471–495. https://doi.org/10.1080 /09518390110063365.

Stanley, Christine A. 2007. "When Counter Narratives Meet Master Narratives in the Journal Editorial-Review Process." *Educational Researcher* 36 (1): 14–24.https://doi.org/10.3102/0013189X06298008.

Stanley, Christine A., and Yvonna S. Lincoln. 2005. "Cross-Race Faculty Mentoring." *Change: The Magazine of Higher Learning* 37 (2): 44–50. https://doi.org/10.3200/CHNG.37.2.44-50.

Stringfellow, Julia, and Michelle Armstrong. 2012. "The University Authors Recognition Reception at Boise State University: A Celebration of Scholarship." *Idaho Librarian,* May 9, 2012. https:// theidaholibrarian.wordpress.com/2012/05/09/the-university-authors-recognition-reception-at -boise-state-university-a-celebration-of-scholarship/.

Sue, Stanley. 1999. "Science, Ethnicity, and Bias: Where Have We Gone Wrong?" *American Psychologist* 54 (12): 1070–1077. http://dx.doi.org/10.1037/0003-066X.54.12.1070.

Taylor, Edward. 1998. "A Primer on Critical Race Theory." *Journal of Blacks in Higher Education* 19:122–124. http://www.jstor.org/stable/2998940.

Turner, Caroline S. 2003. "Incorporation and Marginalization in the Academy: From Border toward Center for Faculty of Color?" *Journal of Black Studies* 34 (1): 112–125. https://doi.org/10.1177/0021934703253689.

US Census Bureau. n.d. "ACS Demographic and Housing Estimates: 2013–2017 American Community Survey 5-Year Estimates." American FactFinder, US Census Bureau. Accessed June 5, 2019. https://factfinder.census.gov/faces/tableservices/jsf/pages/productview.xhtml?src=CF.

Vasquez Heilig, Julian, Isabell Wong Flores, Alicia Eileen Barros Souza, Joseph Carlton Barry, and Selene Barceló Monroy. 2019. "Considering the Ethnoracial and Gender Diversity of Faculty in the United States College and University Intellectual Communities." *South Texas College of Law Houston Hispanic Journal of Law and Policy* 2019:1–31.

Wegner, Gregory, and Robert Zemsky. 2007. "Changing Roles of Academic and Research Libraries." Association of College and Research Libraries. http://www.ala.org/acrl/issues/value/changingroles.

Whitman, Neal, and Elaine Weiss. 1982. "Faculty Evaluation: The Use of Explicit Criteria for Promotion, Retention, and Tenure." AM-LE-ERIC/Higher Education Research Report no. 2, American Association for Higher Education.

Williams, Chad, Kidada E. Williams, and Keisha N. Blain. 2016. "Introduction." In *Charleston Syllabus: Readings on Race, Racism, and Racial Violence*, edited by Chad Williams, Kidada E. Williams, and Keisha N. Blain, 1–8. Athens: University of Georgia Press.

RADICAL COLLECTIVE IMAGINATIONS TOWARD LIBERATION

With editing by contributors Jennifer Brown, Isabel Espinal, Harrison W. Inefuku, Sarah R. Kostelecky, Kafi Kumasi, and Marisa Méndez-Brady

INTRODUCTION TO PART III:
FREEDOM STORIES

Tonia Sutherland

My first awareness of a substantive articulation in library and information studies that I understood as a critique of race and racism in the profession was through a chance encounter with the words of E. J. Josey, the second Black American to earn a master's degree in librarianship and also the second Black president of the American Library Association (the first, Clara Jones, held the office in 1976). I earned my own master's in library and information sciences (MLIS) at the University of Pittsburgh, where Josey had long served as a member of the LIS faculty. Wandering the halls one afternoon before I began my graduate program, I found a tiny exhibit dedicated to a Black man who had worked at the Free Library of Philadelphia, just miles from where I worked in Bucks County, Pennsylvania. In the corner of the exhibit, barely visible and written on a sticky note—a postscript left by another wanderer—was the quote: "Support the humanity of Black people."

I would later learn to attribute this sticky note quote to Josey, and I would also learn why this note had been left as a passerby's plea. With those six words, Josey had articulated a need, and that need told me more about my future positionality within the LIS profession than any syllabus, lecture, or assignment I would encounter. With those six words, Josey had named the conditions of possibility for liberation, he had told a six-word freedom story. So, too, was his edited volume, *The Black Librarian in America*, a freedom story: in it, Josey offered the field a groundbreaking collection of essays—and the first book focused entirely on the Black American experience in the library profession. Josey's very existence in the profession as a Black man and scholar and even more so as an activist devoted to human and civil rights showed us what was possible. His own story solidified for me—and for many Black library and archives professionals of my generation—that liberatory and emancipatory practices can be cornerstones of our professional work. Today, for many Black, Indigenous, and other librarians and archivists of color, working toward liberation remains at the core of our approach to both professional practice and theoretical discourse.

Research on "diversity and inclusion" in the LIS professional literature (and here I am speaking of diversity and inclusion research *not* conducted by Black, Indigenous, and other LIS professionals of color) has too often attended to the rhetorics of diversity and inclusion, and practical recommendations from the literature for diversity and inclusion initiatives are frequently anemic and ineffective. Rather than challenge the actual practices of privilege, whiteness, racism, and colonialism in libraries and archives and among librarians and archivists, the research historically undertaken and questions posed around diversity and inclusion have remained largely the same: they have centered on "pipeline" concerns, the purported benefits of meritocracies, individual successes, and notions of diversity so broadly conceived as to be deleterious acts of erasure for Black, Indigenous, and other librarians and archivists of color. Moreover, the unique ways Black, Indigenous, and other People of Color (BIPOC) actually approach the *practice* of librarianship and archivy are too often rendered invisible: centering communities and their unique voices, needs, and practices; expanding how information professionals understand context to challenge the idea that context is always bounded and easily knowable; challenging the limits of our roles as librarians and archivists to make visible the possibilities inherent in our practical and theoretical interventions; developing practices with an intentional eye toward harm reduction; and, perhaps most importantly, intentionally crafting of freedom stories.

Critical race theory (CRT) has many tenets and can be employed in many ways. One of the most compelling aspects of CRT is its dedication to narrative and counternarrative as liberatory frames. Using storytelling to animate CRT often serves to illuminate and explore experiences of racialized oppression while also envisioning more liberatory and emancipatory futures. Each of the chapters in this section takes storytelling, narrative, and counternarrative as starting places, engaging the very heart of Critical Race Theory's ability to light the way toward liberation, toward freedom. In "Dewhitening Librarianship: A Policy Proposal for Libraries," Isabel Espinal, April M. Hathcock, and Maria Rios examine how historical racial stratification and economic oppression are keeping People of Color from choosing professions such as librarianship, further deepening disparities in financial circumstances between

BIPOC librarians and their non-BIPOC counterparts. Beginning and ending with narrative possibility and interweaving their own stories throughout, the authors examine the intersections of race, gender, and class and call for an acknowledgement that systemic change does not happen in isolation. This carefully crafted piece makes tangible and actionable suggestions for bringing more BIPOC into the library and archives professions. Through sharing their own stories, these three authors issue a call to action, one that encourages us to challenge existing institutional narratives—particularly those that are weaponized against BIPOC such as pipeline shortages and resource scarcity—where questions of equity and inclusion as steps toward liberation are concerned.

Authors Torie Quiñonez, Lalitha Nataraj, and Antonia Olivas challenge claims of objectivity, meritocracy, and neutrality in their chapter, "The Praxis of Relation, Validation, and Motivation: Articulating LIS Collegiality through a CRT Lens." Informed by their own experiences of—and active resistance to—racism and other forms of oppression, these authors work to privilege experiential knowledge and the lived experiences of those who have been marginalized, often through storytelling and counternarrative. This work brings with it an explicit act of refusal, one powerful way to imagine a more liberatory future. Quiñonez, Nataraj, and Olivas refuse a deficit framework, choosing instead to put validation theory in conversation with Critical Race Theory (and Black and Indigenous feminist epistemologies of refusal). From this work, we can envision a liberatory future in which librarians and archivists use, as Quiñonez, Nataraj, and Olivas suggest, validation and community cultural wealth as frameworks for relational mentoring.

Authors Anne Cong-Huyen and Kush Patel further our thinking around precarity and feminist ethics of care in their thoughtful piece, "Precarious Labor and Radical Care in Libraries and Digital Humanities." This chapter speaks to how libraries have come to depend on workflows that have created conditions ideal for exploiting emerging professionals. The authors argue that such conditions have relied on the perception of library work as feminine and predominantly white, and, echoing the discussion above, they note that diversity and inclusion work is often thought of as belonging to People of Color. From narratives crafted from their own experiences as immigrant and migrant librarians of color, Cong-Huyen and Patel push us to challenge expectations that normalize invisible labor, precarious lives, and undercompensated labor as a rite of passage in librarianship, and they argue that the profession must undertake this work in a more just and equitable manner as a step toward more liberatory praxis.

In presenting an argument for critical race praxis in archival work, Rachel E. Winston asserts that Critical Race Theory offers one way to begin systematically addressing White Supremacy and the colonial thumbprint in archival repositories. In "Praxis for the People: Critical Race Theory and Archival Practice," Winton argues that for a more liberatory future, we must engage voices that have previously been pushed to the margins and allow them to lead, noting that a feminist ethic of care challenges us to refashion the role of archivist to that of a caregiver, honoring webs of responsibility to the records themselves and the communities documented within them. Winton challenges us to be disruptive and responsive, our plans to be actionable, our praxis to be informed and caring. Bringing together aspects present in each of the other chapters, Winton offers narrative, counternarrative, and an action plan as a roadmap and a guide—a gift to archivists and librarians looking for concrete ways to effect change in their everyday practice.

I close this introduction with remarks on Kafi Kumasi's "'Getting InFLOmation': A Critical Race Theory Tale from the School Library," in large part because Kumasi's piece is LIS storytelling at its finest. Although it is tempting to retell the tale here, I will not ruin the joy of it for you, reader. I will only say that this brightly woven story shines light on the places where diversity and inclusion initiatives fail, where unchecked privilege and whiteness do harm to everyone touched by them, where inequality ruins lives, and where libraries might be spaces of hope and possibility. Kumasi's Critical Race Theory tale is rhythm, rhyme, and remix. It is the best kind of story—a story we might follow all the way to freedom.

9

DEWHITENING LIBRARIANSHIP
A Policy Proposal for Libraries

Isabel Espinal, April M. Hathcock, and Maria Rios

LET'S BEGIN WITH A CRT IN LIS STORY[1]

What a morning! LaTonya Lan has spent it reading and answering emails, texts, and social media messages congratulating her on becoming Dean of Libraries at So and So University. The messages came from all over, but she noticed that only the librarians from the ethnic affiliate professional library groups had mentioned that she was in fact the first woman of color to lead a major academic research library in her state, not to mention her entire region of the country. LaTonya was not surprised by this because her white colleagues, though very nice people, had always been very uncomfortable talking about race.

That's why one of the emails she received particularly caught her attention. It came from her friend Janice, a white library dean at XYZ University, who wasn't afraid to talk about race: "Congratulations LaTonya! I remember that wonderful chat we had at that last big conference. You're now the first library dean I know who I've ever had a conversation with about Critical Race Theory! Speaking of which, a friend of mine shared a CRT-based proposal she has coauthored with two other librarians. With their permission, I am sharing with you. Would love to hear your thoughts as a new dean. Is this something that you could get behind?"

INTRODUCTION

Diversity is a core value of the largest library professional association, the American Library Association (ALA), and of its higher education library affiliate, the Association of College and Research Libraries (ACRL) (American Library Association 2010;

Association of College and Research Libraries 2018). But how are libraries and their administrators and trustees showing that this is indeed an important value? How are we putting our stated commitment to racial diversity in library and information science (LIS) into practice? In assessing the success of libraries' diversity work when it comes to race, we should not just look for the presence of the word *diversity* in mission statements; rather, we should look at the numbers of librarians of color in the profession. In assessing just how serious libraries are in their stated mission of diversifying the profession, we should look at how much of library budgets have been allocated to racial diversity and to recruiting, retaining, supporting, and promoting librarians of color.

Thinking from a place of personal and professional experience, solidarity, frustration, and optimism, the authors join together here to share a proposal one author, Isabel, made to her own library, the University of Massachusetts Amherst (UMass), as a case study and a case in point. While the initial proposal was grounded in the culture and circumstances of UMass, an academic library in the northeastern United States, the proposal itself is really for *all libraries*. It has thus been shared with the greater community of academic libraries through conferences and other presentations in New England and throughout the United States (Espinal, Freedman, and Smith 2018; Alburo et al. 2018).

In this chapter, we not only present this proposal but also ground it in Critical Race Theory (CRT), a form of critical approach to social issues of power disparity and oppression that centers examinations of race, racism, and whiteness (Delgado and Stefancic 2001). We use CRT to examine some of the causes for the persistent lack of racial diversity in the library profession and to thus tie in our proposal as a potential practical and structure-based solution addressing those causes. Our proposal, aimed at redirecting library budgets toward the recruitment and training of librarians of color, consists of the creation of postbaccalaureate library positions that include full funding for MLIS degrees targeted toward People of Color. Adopting a CRT lens allows us to examine the ways in which historical racial stratification and economic oppression are keeping People of Color from choosing professions such as librarianship, further deepening disparities in financial circumstances between People of Color and whites. In order to achieve racial parity and equity, libraries need to allocate large influxes of financial resources to help People of Color become librarians, resources that historically have been diverted to other projects. What we suggest is essentially a racial equity project that consists of "dewhitening" the LIS profession.

DIVERSITY STORY AND COUNTERSTORY IN LIS

The origin story of our proposal to dewhiten librarianship is tied to the story of diversity in LIS. In particular, it is tied to the dominant narratives of diversity in LIS and the growing counternarratives that have arisen in response.

Currently, the racial composition of librarianship at our institutions and in the librarian profession at large is woefully unrepresentative of the United States' population, just as it was years ago (Howland 1998; Adkins and Espinal 2004). Despite numerous analyses of this problem over the past decades, the demographics have remained stagnant, unaffected by previous efforts to improve racial diversity and representation. For example, for many years, UMass Amherst did not have a single Black/African American librarian on staff; it now only has one Black/African American librarian with permanent status, and one temporary Black/African American librarian (a library resident with a term of two to three years). We focus on UMass as a site for infiltrating the status quo and turning its whiteness on its head, using the Critical Race Theory method of counternarrative, "opening a window onto ignored or alternative realities" (Delgado and Stefancic 2001, 46).

In the twenty-two years Isabel has been at UMass, the lack of Black/African American librarians has been salient in her experience. The same can be said for April and Maria and their experiences of racial homogeneity in their library careers. Unfortunately, the official narratives of the library make no mention of this aspect of our experiences. Instead, the dominant narrative results in protecting and preserving whiteness in the profession; this protection of the white status quo extends even to the initiatives and efforts ostensibly used to create more diversity (Hathcock 2015; Espinal 2001). Well-meaning white librarians and administrators create and participate in diversity and inclusion committees and include diversity, inclusion, and equity language in their mission statements and strategic plans, but they almost always stop short of enacting real, transformational change.

This dominant narrative of whiteness is ubiquitous and insidious, hiding behind seemingly innocuous values such as "color blindness" and "meritocracy" (Delgado and Stefancic 2001, 37–42) and even "diversity" (Hudson 2017). "Diversity" was essentially invented as a way for the courts to elide the question of affirmative action for racial redress while still allowing race as a factor in college admissions (Carr 2018, 205–207). But diversity as a substitute for affirmative action has come at the expense of students of color (Martinez-Watts 2013, 52, 62). *Diversity* as a term has been diluted over time within the LIS profession to serve as a buzzword, or more dangerously, a performative placeholder for actual transformative change. To advocate for an expansion of Black, Indigenous, Latinx, Asian American, and Pacific Islander librarian-credentialed professional presence in historically white spaces, we need a shared vocabulary to engage with the discourse. Rooting and anchoring the activist tenet of CRT (decentering whiteness) is why we introduce the verb *dewhiten* as a way to name what is often simply called diversifying. We make the case for an effective race-conscious affirmative action proposal with the goal of dewhitening librarianship and changing the skewed demographics of our field.

At times it's been extremely difficult for us as female-identified People of Color in this profession to live with our "counterreality" in the face of the dominant narrative of whiteness. CRT helps us relax and understand that it's not us, it's the racialized system that creates an ontological dissonance. We can attest that CRT does indeed give us what Delgado called "psychic self-preservation" and "healing" (Delgado 1989, 2437). It also provides a theoretical framework to help us see the validity of our stories and the importance of centering our perspectives. Indeed, CRT started in the legal profession as a means of introducing the power of new voices and perspectives into the dominant narrative:

A final element concerns the notion of a unique voice of color....The voice-of-color thesis holds that because of their different histories and experiences with oppression, black, Indian, Asian, and Latino/a writers and thinkers may be able to communicate to their white counterparts matters that the whites are unlikely to know. (Delgado and Stefancic 2001, 9)

The legal origins of CRT are of particular importance to one of our authors, April, who began her professional life, and her work in diversity activism, as a practicing attorney. Finding power in her unique voice of color and legal, now library, storytelling has helped April to engage with the profession's whiteness and move toward making it better.

Thus, for all of us, CRT empowers our voices as women of color in the profession and proposes that our perspectives be at the center, rather than the margins, of our profession's discourse. Critical race theory also encourages us that, although we come from groups that have been deemed "minority," our minority status is far from what we are and what we have to offer, even if in our day-to-day interactions in this overwhelmingly white profession, we often feel like a lone voice. What's wonderful is when we are able to join forces with fellow librarians of color via projects like the very writing of this chapter, and know that we are not alone.

RACIAL DEMOGRAPHICS IN LIS

Of course, and unfortunately, our stories are not unique, and neither are the numbers unique to the libraries where we work. The demographics of the profession nationally, as outlined in figures 9.1 and 9.2, do not bode much better than at our respective institutions.

The Institute of Museum and Library Services (IMLS) in November 2017 tweeted the graph depicted in figure 9.2.

The AFL-CIO's Department for Professional Employees reports that in 2018, only 6.8 percent of librarians identified as Black or African American, 8.6 percent as Hispanic or Latino, and 4.6 percent as Asian American or Pacific Islander, and that the "librarian profession suffers from a persistent lack of racial and ethnic diversity that shows few signs of abating" (AFL-CIO 2019, 3). The ALA's "Diversity Counts" notes a persistent lack of racial and ethnic diversity in library workers at all levels, and it ties this lack to an increased rate of attrition for library workers of color, connected in significant part to lack of leadership and professional advancement opportunities (Davis and Hall 2007, 11; Moore and Estrellado 2018, 351). In 2014, Chris Bourg, director of libraries at Massachusetts Institute of Technology (MIT), used racial demographic comparisons to show the difference between reality and representativeness of LIS (figure 9.3) and asked the profession to consider a ten-year plan to diversify. Even pretending that the US population would wait for us to catch up (i.e., if the racial composition of the US stayed steady), we would need to replace nearly 3,000 white

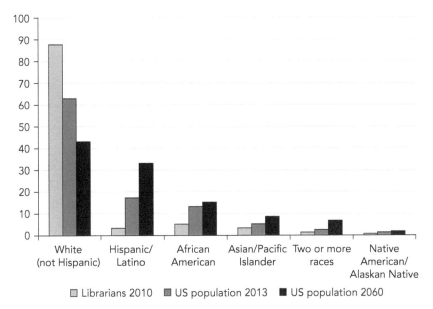

9.1 Racial composition of librarians 2010 versus US population (2013 and projected 2060) (Bourg 2014).

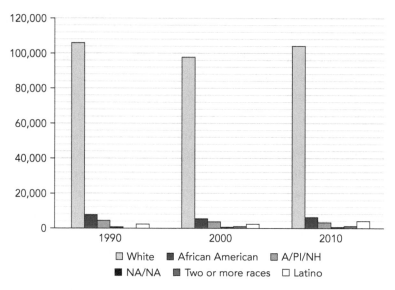

9.2 Credentialed librarians by race/ethnicity (IMLS 2017).

	Actual number of librarians	Target number based on racial representation (2013)	Difference between reality and representativeness
White	104,392	74,760	−29,632
African American	6,160	17,800	11,640
Latino/a	3,661	20,173	16,512
Asian/Pacific Islander	3,260	6,289	3,029
Two or more races	1,008	2,848	1,840
Native American (including Alaskan Native)	185	1,424	1,239

9.3 Target racial demographics for LIS (Bourg 2014).

librarians every year with over 1,000 African American librarians, 1,650 Latino/a librarians, 300 Asian/Pacific Islander librarians, 180 multiracial, and 120 Native American/Alaskan Native librarians. A five-year plan would require double those numbers (Bourg 2014). Yet to date, we have not seen any plan on a large scale to address these racial imbalances that have now been well documented. Even as some library leaders acknowledge the need to diversify librarianship, the demographics persist to weigh in favor of whiteness across institutions, including at the authors' libraries, UMass Amherst and NYU, and at MIT, Bourg's institution. We hope that our proposal below would be a cornerstone of such a plan.

INTERSECTIONS OF RACE AND CLASS AND ECONOMIC DISPARITIES IN LIS

No true narrative about race in LIS, nor any attempt to dewhiten the profession, would be complete without an examination of how race intersects and interacts with class. Indeed, one of the areas that CRT concerns itself with is this intersection of race with issues of class and socioeconomic status. It's important to note, however, that CRT focuses on the *intersections* and *interplay* of race and class and does not substitute class as a proxy for racialized oppression (Delgado and Stefancic 2001, 107–111). The issues that arise from this interplay between race and class are crucial to any efforts to dewhiten librarianship. While it is clear from the statistics presented above that librarianship has a whiteness problem, those data do not present the whole picture. Evidently, librarianship also has a class problem as well, which operates to complicate the racialized oppression at work in our professional demographics. In his 2000 survey of US labor statistics, Keith Curry Lance found that while the number of librarians from racial and ethnic minority groups fell far below those groups' respective representations in the overall population, the number of paraprofessional library assistants ran much closer to population demographics for most groups (Lance 2005, 42).

These data highlight the fallacy of many arguments for the status quo that claim that People of Color have no interest in engaging in library work. It is clear that many of us do, and in numbers more representative of our group demographics in larger society. However, we are often found almost exclusively in paraprofessional positions and, for those of us wishing to advance, we encounter a seemingly insurmountable *white ceiling* preventing our advancement.

This class dimension affecting the advancement of library workers of color is nothing new to the authors of this chapter; we observe the microcosmic representations of the macrocosmic interplay of race and class in our workplaces and throughout our institutions. Moreover, library literature suggests that these issues can be easily observed in virtually any academic library setting. In their article critiquing the use of binary demarcations between *professional* and *paraprofessional* library work, Jones and Stivers use racialized language, without referencing race directly, to describe the class distinctions at work in library workplaces: they refer to paraprofessionals as "the help" and describe their work as following a trajectory rooted in "separate but equal" philosophy (Jones and Stivers 2004, 92). This racialized intervention of class politics was highlighted during a 2018 ACRL/NY Symposium panel discussion on the experiences of professional academic librarians who began their careers as non-MLIS library staff (Binnie et. al. 2018). Speaking from their identities as cisgender women of color, Alyssa Brissett, Kenya Flash, and Diana Moronta surfaced the ways in which racism, sexism, and classism intersected in their workplaces to present barriers to their advancement, more so than was the case for their white counterparts on the panel and in their professional spheres. They described the lack of support, and sometimes explicit discouragement, they received when looking to advance their library careers, particularly through obtaining the master's of library information science (MLIS).[2]

When People of Color *do* express an interest in pursuing the MLIS, and a long-term career in the field, lack of financial support and resources often is a significant barrier to professional entry (Kim and Sin 2006, 168–169). A CRT lens shows that these financial barriers are not random, but a result of the historical economic conditions that produced racial stratification in the first place, often concealed behind color-blind policies. There are a number of historically rooted material and economic conditions experienced by librarians of color and potential librarians of color that prevent them from staying in, advancing in, or even joining the profession in the first place. One of those conditions that LIS must acknowledge is the racial wealth disparity between whites and nonwhites. In 2020, amid the heightened Black Lives Matter protests and antiracism statements by many organizations, including libraries, the *New York Times* published an article which stated that "economic inequity…serves as the backdrop" of "the power imbalance involved in the deaths of George Floyd and too many others like him," and showed that "at nearly every stage of their lives, black Americans have less than whites" (Lieber and Siegel Bernard 2020).

Even when white and nonwhite individuals have the *same level of education and income*, they continue to have *vastly different levels* of *wealth* (Asante-Muhammad 2018; Thompson 2018; Zaw et al. 2017). Katherine Richard (2014) explains that wealth is not the same as income; it's "what we own minus what we owe." Wealth includes inherited assets, bank accounts, home or vehicle ownership, stocks, and bonds. The racial disparities are astounding, as Richard reports: "In 2007, White women had a median wealth of $45,400, while African American women and Latinas had a median wealth of $100 and $120, respectively." The starkest contrast in wealth is between white persons and Black and Latinx persons, as Asante-Muhammad's (2018) report shows (see figure 9.4), with patterns very similar to the racial demographic charts of librarianship.

Although the financial statistics above focus on Blacks and Latinx vis-à-vis whites, disparities show up for other racialized groups as well, as other studies have demonstrated. For example, Martinez, Jiménez-Castellanos, and Begay use Critical Race

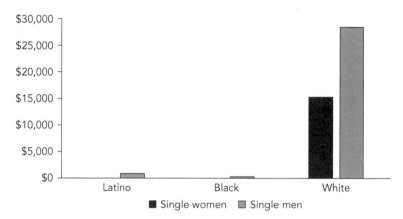

9.4 Median wealth of single persons by race, Latinx identity, and gender (Asante-Muhammad 2018).

Theory and Tribal Critical Theory to link poverty levels, school funding levels, and Navajo school achievement and participation (2019).

These facts and consequences have a huge impact on librarians of color and on our recruitment and retention, as Minter and Chamblee-Smith (2018) observe:

Income disparities in the LIS field are not unique to WOC. However, because many communities of color have been prevented from accumulating wealth, hardships that arise from obtaining advanced degrees and pressure to work in under- or un-compensated jobs as new professionals have a unique impact on those from lower to low-middle income backgrounds. (238)

Compounding this problem is the fact that student loan debt is stunningly higher for college graduates of color. The Brookings Institution reports, "The moment they earn their bachelor's degrees, black college graduates owe $7,400 more on average than their white peers ($23,400 versus $16,000)." But over time, "differences in interest accrual and graduate school borrowing lead to black graduates holding nearly $53,000 in student loan debt four years after graduation—almost twice as much as their white counterparts" (Li and Scott-Clayton 2016). Other studies have found that students with higher debts are less likely to choose occupations in fields in which salaries are low, notably such as education or librarianship, thereby affecting the career choices of graduates and color and creating a lack of diversity in these fields (Rothstein and Rouse 2007; Fiddiman, Campbell, and Partelow 2019).

Any library dewhitening initiative worth its salt would have to address these huge divides in wealth and acknowledge that People of Color who are qualified to get the MLIS degree (i.e., who have a college degree) may already be in huge debt and do not have a fraction of the assets that our white counterparts have. Libraries committed to equity and diversity have to act on these disparities in a meaningful and effective way. CRT scholar Charles R. P. Pouncy notes:

If we believe that the roots of the ideologies of subordination lie in the structures used to maintain particular distributions of assets, resources, and opportunities, ... then we recognize that the processes by which these distributions are maintained will become the battle lines and boundaries that circumscribe and limit our ability to achieve praxis—for those boundaries protect the financial claims that flow to people with white skin as a consequence of the ideologies and white privilege and white superiority. (2002, 842)

For LIS, the message is clear: providing substantial funding for obtaining the library credential, the MLIS, is imperative in any true dewhitening agenda. To neglect to do so would mean continuing to maintain the unequal distribution of assets by racial subordination embedded in our society, thus maintaining white privilege in LIS and keeping the demographics of our profession white as well. Providing the needed funding was the impetus for Elizabeth Martínez to introduce the Spectrum Scholarship Program in the late 1990s (Martínez 2018). But Spectrum and the American Library Association alone cannot accomplish the huge task that is dewhitening librarianship. As Teresa Neely and Lorna Peterson (2007) assert, we need a "comprehensive, collaborative (among all stakeholders) recruitment and public awareness campaign for recruitment purposes" (6), and we need to identify and implement the most effective recruitment, retention, and promotion strategies (12).

CHANGING THE NARRATIVE: DEWHITENING LIBRARIANSHIP

It is clear that we need new approaches. It is not enough to continuously demonstrate and bemoan the state of affairs; we need to take action, another tenet of CRT. Delgado and Stefancic point out that the CRT movement comprises both activists *and* scholars committed to both studying *and* "transforming the relationship among race, racism, and power," and that CRT "not only tries to understand our social situation, but to change it; it sets out not only to ascertain how society organizes itself along racial lines and hierarchies, but to transform it for the better" (2001, 2–3). This action-oriented dimension of CRT informs our approach and budget-driven proposal.

With this in mind, one of our authors, Isabel, while writing an update to a conceptual essay about whiteness in librarianship (Espinal, Sutherland, and Roh 2018), decided to come up with a strategy and policy proposal to change the demographics, which she would actually bring to her library. She suggested to her library administration that her institution could take the lead with an innovative approach that could be replicated across the country, and if replicated, it could significantly increase the numbers of librarians of color. Imagine if every large academic and public library in the country did this! Let's just look at academic libraries. According to the National Center for Education Statistics, in 2012 there were 1,770 academic libraries in the US with expenditures above $500,000 (Phan et al. 2014). Following Bourg's logic, if each of these libraries were to support two new People of Color each year to attain their MLIS, we could increase the number of librarians of color by 3,478 per year (Bourg 2014). If we added large public library systems to this equation, we would achieve even better results.

The time is ripe: librarianship is at a turning point, when many librarians hired in the 1970s, 1980s, and 1990s are retiring, although many are working longer than previous generations (Long and Sheehan 2015, 746). Retirements are likely to continue as the age of librarians is much higher than the general population: 31.5 percent of librarians are over the age of fifty-five, as compared to only 19 percent of the general workforce (AFL-CIO 2019, 3). Diverting a portion of the cost savings from retirements to a diversity recruitment and retention program will have a large return on investment, bringing highly qualified candidates into the field who otherwise might never consider librarianship because of its historic whiteness. Over the course of the past fifteen years or so, libraries have used salary savings from retirements as a way to further strategic priorities related to technology and innovation or to budget for organizational change. As one library administrator notes, "Related to organizational change is the reallocation of resources to hire in key areas, which are either of emerging importance to research libraries or are gaps that we just didn't have" (Meier 2016, 273–274). It is time to use this managerial strategy to achieve the strategic goals of increasing and enhancing diversity, inclusion, and equity, addressing this key area of LIS to dewhiten the profession. If racial equity is to have any meaning, it must be backed by substantial funding, and when no additional funds are coming to libraries, libraries must take it upon themselves to reorganize their existing budgets to be able to allocate funds for dewhitening projects. If not, LIS will likely continue to be just as white as ever.

ONE PROPOSAL: POSTBACCALAUREATE FELLOWSHIP POSITIONS

The essence of this concrete proposal is this: to create postbaccalaureate fellowship positions in libraries that financially support, and thus attract new library science students of color. In their 2018 article on decentering whiteness in librarianship, Espinal, Sutherland, and Roh suggested that libraries can pay employees of color to obtain the MLS on the job, and can create jobs specific to this purpose (157). This proposal fleshes that idea out with more detailed terms. In particular, our proposal puts accountability on the library from the onset, bringing it home, as opposed to relying solely on the professional associations such as the ALA, ACRL, or ARL.

The participants of the proposed LIS postbacs would have their tuition and educational expenses fully covered by this program; libraries themselves would bear the costs by allocating funds for the program in their budgets, cutting from other areas of the budget as needed or using savings from retirements as available. The aim is to recruit People of Color into the field of librarianship, thus increasing the pool of librarians of color both at specific libraries and in the profession at large, by removing the financial barrier of the cost of attaining a graduate degree in library and information studies.

A sample breakdown of the budget for the program's components would look as follows, based on information from a proposal to UMass Amherst in 2017. The goal is to each year fund two part-time positions that include part-time tuition at an accredited library school program. The salaries for the two fellow positions are at 50 percent of an entry-level, non-MLIS salary grade, plus benefits. Reimbursement for part-time tuition cost would vary, but two representative examples include $6,606 for one year of part-time tuition at one library school and $22,140 at another.[3] To fund a fellow in each institution would cost a total of $28,746. In addition, we envision covering other key outreach and development costs to provide a complete professional and educational experience for the fellows (see table 9.1). We estimate those total costs at $4,400 for the first year. Altogether, the estimated cost for the first year of the program would be $70,014 (see table 9.2). In subsequent years this would increase, as two new fellows would be added each year, as two fellows would graduate.

Table 9.1 Outreach and professional development expenses

Receptions and social gatherings	$500
Application materials and fees	$200
Outreach	$500
Professional travel: $1,500 per fellow	$3,000 in year, $6,000 in subsequent years
Miscellaneous (unexpected expenses)	$200
Total	$4,400 in year, $7,400 in subsequent years

Table 9.2 Full costs of implementation

Year one costs		Year two & subsequent years costs	
Salaries for fellows (2 part-time staff)	$36,868	Salaries for fellows (4 part-time staff)	$73,736
Tuition reimbursement	$28,746	Tuition reimbursement	$57,492
Outreach and professional development	$4,400	Outreach and professional development	$7,400
TOTAL year one	$70,014	TOTAL subsequent years	$138,628

It is important to note what is different about this particular proposal as compared to other residency programs already in existence in some libraries: a postbaccalaureate fellowship is NOT a residency. Many academic libraries have instituted diversity residencies as an answer (and sometimes, problematically, the only answer) to the question of how to bring diversity to the librarian ranks. Diversity residencies are usually construed as entry-level positions for librarians of color who have just received their MLIS degrees. While they may help bring diversity to the libraries that have these positions, they do not increase the numbers of People of Color who obtain the MLS. Therefore, they do not increase the overall number of librarians of color. A postbaccalaureate fellowship, constructed in such a way as to recruit college graduates of color who might not have entered a library studies master's program, most likely will increase the numbers of People of Color who become librarians because it may bring people into the profession who would not have done so otherwise.

CONCLUSION

We are trying to be realistic and optimistic. Realistically, we doubt that any library will actually use the term *dewhitening*. This term is introduced in the service of articulating a speculative vocabulary for antiracist efforts within LIS that is both unambiguous and palpable for flipping whiteness on its head. Yet, our collective lived experience in the profession has cautioned us to not expect real change in the racial diversity (i.e., dewhitening) of library staff and management unless each library as an organization acknowledges that systemic change does not happen in isolation. We need policies, not platitudes—broad budget allocations in addition to inclusive mission statements. Critical Race Theory can lead us to concrete solutions for tackling the profession's demographics problem, which is persistently skewed toward whiteness. Critical Race Theorists Delgado and Stefancic argue that "traditional civil rights" has reached its limits due to "incrementalism and step-by-step progress"— the same can be said of traditional LIS diversity initiatives. By applying CRT, we can see that traditional diversity efforts are marginal to the fundamental problems of systemic racism that are embedded in our institutions.

CRT helps us understand why this approach has not been used in libraries and helps us move forward in removing the racial, historical, and structural biases and barriers that have held us back from taking effective measures to truly "diversify" librarianship. Just as there is an "education debt," as explained by CRT scholar Ladson-Billings, there is a "library professional debt" owed to POC; this dewhitening proposal conceptualizes that debt and aims to pay it back. The postbac proposal is part and parcel to dewhitening librarianship but is not meant to replace current initiatives, such as diversity residences for entry-level librarians. The postbac crafts the capacity for marginalized groups to enter librarianship as credentialed professionals without ancillary financial burden. The ultimate goal is that, through such a direct challenge to the systems of oppression designed and maintained by white values, we can expand the hegemonic library landscape to exemplify and empower underrepresented groups. Knowledge production for collective liberatory practices has been percolating on the fringes; our proposal serves as a vehicle for cultural accountability that is sustainable in the service of disrupting and dismantling oppression.

MOVING THE NARRATIVE FORWARD

LaTonya was energized. "Janice!" she wrote back. "This is the best congratulations message I've gotten all day. I know you probably don't like the word *dewhiten*, but I got to tell you I really vibed on it. What say you and I be the first deans to get on board with this proposal? Let's get this done!"

NOTES

1. Storytelling is a CRT technique used extensively in fields such as law and education (Delgado 1989, 2418–2434; Solórzano and Yosso 2000, 43–59, 156–164). We use this technique, presenting Dean LaTonya Lan, a fictional character made up of very real experiences, to set a context where we imagine how a library dean or director of color might read a proposal such as ours.

2. The librarian master's degree can be an MLIS, MLS, or MS. For consistency we will use MLIS.

3. At University of Alabama and Simmons College, respectively (2017 costs).

BIBLIOGRAPHY

Adkins, Denice, and Isabel Espinal. 2004. "The Diversity Mandate." *Library Journal* 129 (7): 52–54.

AFL-CIO Department for Professional Employees. 2019. "Library Professionals: Facts and Figures. 2019 Fact Sheet." AFL-CIO Department for Professional Employees. https://static1.squarespace .com/static/5d10ef48024ce300010f0f0c/t/5d1bb02b4942c60001ba93ea/1562095659756/Library +Workers+Facts++Figures+2019.pdf.

Alburo, Jade, Eugenia Beh, Eileen K. Bosch, Joanna Chen Cham, Isabel Espinal, Nikhat J. Ghouse, Regina Gong, and Del Hornbuckle. 2018. "Developing an Inclusive Workplace for Librarians of Color by Librarians of Color." Preconference workshop at the Third National Joint Conference of Librarians of Color (JCLC), Albuquerque, NM, September 26–30, 2018.

American Library Association. 2010. "B.1 Core Values, Ethics, and CoreCompetencies." *ALA Policy Manual*. Chicago: American Library Association. http://www.ala.org/aboutala/governance /policymanual/updatedpolicymanual/section2/40corevalues.

Asante-Muhammad, Dedrick. 2018. "Racial Wealth Divide Snapshot: Women and the Racial Wealth Divide." *Prosperity Now*, March 29, 2018. https://prosperitynow.org/blog/racial-wealth-divide -snapshot-women-and-racial-wealth-divide.

Association of College and Research Libraries. 2018. "ACRL Plan for Excellence." Association of College and Research Libraries. http://www.ala.org/acrl/aboutacrl/strategicplan/stratplan.

Binnie, Naomi, Alyssa Brissett, Kenya Flash, Kelleen Maluski, and Diana Moronta. 2018. "Can We Reach the White Tower? Barriers to Staff Promotion and Retention in Libraries." Panel presentation at the ACRL/NY Symposium 2018, New York, NY, December 7, 2018.

Bourg, Chris. 2014. "The Unbearable Whiteness of Librarianship." *Feral Librarian* (blog), March 3, 2014. https://chrisbourg.wordpress.com/2014/03/03/the-unbearable-whiteness-of-librarianship/.

Carr, M. Kelly. 2018. *The Rhetorical Invention of Diversity: Supreme Court Opinions, Public Argument, and Affirmative Action*. East Lansing: Michigan State University Press.

Davis, Denise M., and Tracie D. Hall. 2007. *Diversity Counts*. Chicago: American Library Association.

Delgado, Richard. 1989. "Storytelling for Oppositionists and Others: A Plea for Narrative." *Michigan Law Review* 87 (8): 2411–2441. https://doi.org/10.2307/1289308.

Delgado, Richard, and Jean Stefancic. 2001. *Critical Race Theory: An Introduction*. New York: New York University Press.

Espinal, Isabel. 2001. "A New Vocabulary for Inclusive Librarianship: Applying Whiteness Theory to Our Profession." In *The Power of Language—El Poder de la Palabra: Selected Papers from the Second REFORMA National Conference*, edited by Lillian Castillo-Speed, 131–149. Englewood, CO: Libraries Unlimited.

Espinal, Isabel. 2003. "Wanted: Latino Librarians." *Críticas* 3 (5): 19–24.

Espinal, Isabel, Kate Freedman, and Pete Smith. 2018. "We've Failed at Diversifying Our Librarian Ranks, Now What? A Plan for Addressing the 'Pipeline' Problem." Presentation at the Association of College and Research Libraries New England Chapter (ACRL NEC) Annual Conference, Plymouth, MA, May 4, 2018.

Espinal, Isabel, Tonia Sutherland, and Charlotte Roh. 2018. "A Holistic Approach for Inclusive Librarianship: Decentering Whiteness in Our Profession." *Library Trends 67* (1): 147–62. https://doi.org/10.1353/lib.2018.0030.

Ettarh, Fobazi. 2018. "Vocational Awe and Librarianship: The Lies We Tell Ourselves." *In the Library with the Lead Pipe*, January 10, 2018. http://www.inthelibrarywiththeleadpipe.org/2018/vocational-awe.

Fiddiman, Bayliss, Colleen Campbell, and Lisette Partelow. 2019. "Student Debt: An Overlooked Barrier to Increasing Teacher Diversity." Center for American Progress. July 9, 2019. https://www.americanprogress.org/issues/education-postsecondary/reports/2019/07/09/471850/student-debt-overlooked-barrier-increasing-teacher-diversity/.

Hathcock, April M. 2015. "White Librarianship in Blackface: Diversity Initiatives in LIS." *In the Library with the Lead Pipe*, October 7, 2015. http://www.inthelibrarywiththeleadpipe.org/2015/lis-diversity/.

Hines, Samantha. 2019. "Leadership Development for Academic Librarians: Maintaining the Status Quo?" *Canadian Journal of Academic Librarianship* 4 (February): 1–19. https://doi.org/10.33137/cjal-rcbu.v4.29311.

Howland, Joan. 1998 "Diversity Deferred." *Law Library Journal* 90 (4): 561–575 https://scholarship.law.umn.edu/faculty_articles/462.

Hudson, David James. 2017. "On 'Diversity' as Anti-Racism in Library and Information Studies: A Critique." *Journal of Critical Library and Information Studies* 1 (1). https://doi.org/10.24242/jclis.v1i1.6.

Institute of Museum and Library Services (IMLS). 2017. "Today, We're Talking about Diversity in the #library Workforce—Here's a Breakdown. #LB21." Tweet. @US_IMLS. November 7, 2017. https://twitter.com/US_IMLS/status/927922066896146432.

Jones, Phillip J., and James Stivers. 2004. "Good Fences Make Bad Libraries: Rethinking Binary Constructions of Employment in Academic Libraries." *portal: Libraries and the Academy* 4 (1): 85–104. https://doi.org/10.1353/pla.2004.0011.

Kim, Kyung-Su, and Sei-Ching Sin. 2006. "Recruiting and Retaining Students of Color in LIS Programs: Perspectives of Library and Information Professionals." *Journal of Education for Library and Information Science* 47 (2): 153–177.

Ladson-Billings, Gloria. 2006. "From the Achievement Gap to the Education Debt: Understanding Achievement in U.S. Schools." *Educational Researcher* 35 (7): 3–12.

Lance, Keith Curry. 2005. "Racial and Ethnic Diversity of U.S. Library Workers." *American Libraries* 36 (5): 41–43.

Li, Jing, and Judith Scott-Clayton. 2016. "Black-White Disparity in Student Loan Debt More Than Triples after Graduation." The Brookings Institution. October 20, 2016. https://www.brookings.edu/research/black-white-disparity-in-student-loan-debt-more-than-triples-after-graduation/.

Lieber, Ron, and Tara Siegel Bernard. "The Stark Racial Inequity of Personal Finances in America." *New York Times*, June 9, 2020. https://www.nytimes.com/2020/06/09/your-money/race-income -equality.html.

Long, Valeria, and Lynn Sheehan. 2015. "Sustaining Library Faculty: The Elephant Is Big and Gray and Is in the Library." In *Creating Sustainable Community: The Proceedings of the ACRL 2015 Conference*, edited by Dawn M. Mueller, 746–756. Chicago: Association of College and Research Libraries. https:// works.bepress.com/valeria_long/4.

Martinez, David G., Oscar Jiménez-Castellanos, and Victor H. Begay. 2019. "Understanding Navajo K–12 Public School Finance in Arizona through Tribal Critical Theory." *Teachers College Record* 121 (5).

Martínez, Elizabeth. 2018. "Spectrum Scholarship Program: A Long Time Coming," American Library Association. May 31, 2018. http://www.ala.org/advocacy/spectrum/long-time-coming.

Martinez-Watts, Lena. 2013. "Reforming Diversity: Finding Our Way to a More Inclusive Affirmative Action Jurisprudence." *Georgetown Journal of Law and Modern Critical Race Perspectives* 5 (1): 51–76.

McKenzie, Lindsay. 2017. "The White Face of Library Leadership," *Inside Higher Ed*, August 30, 2017. https://www.insidehighered.com/news/2017/08/30/survey-reveals-overwhelmingly-white -face-leadership-research-libraries.

Meier, John J. 2016. "The Future of Academic Libraries: Conversations with Today's Leaders about Tomorrow." *Portal: Libraries and the Academy* 16 (2): 263–288. https://muse.jhu.edu/article /613842.

Minter, Alyse, and Genevia M. Chamblee-Smith. 2018. "'Sister, You've Been on My Mind': Experiences of Women of Color in the Library and Information Science Profession." In *Pushing the Margins: Women of Color and Intersectionality in LIS*, edited by Rose L. Chou and Annie Pho, 197– 251. Sacramento, CA: Library Juice Press.

Moore, Alanna Aiko, and Jan Estrellado. 2018. "Identity, Activism, Self-Care, and Women of Color Librarians." In *Pushing the Margins: Women of Color and Intersectionality in LIS*, edited by Rose L. Chou and Annie Pho, 349–389. Sacramento, CA: Library Juice Press.

Neely, Teresa Y., and Lorna Peterson. 2007. "Achieving Racial and Ethnic Diversity among Academic and Research Librarians: The Recruitment, Retention, and Advancement of Librarians of Color." Association of College and Research Libraries. http://www.ala.org/acrl/sites/ala.org.acrl /files/content/publications/whitepapers/ACRL_AchievingRacial.pdf.

Phan, Tai, Laura Hardesty, Jamie Hug, and Cindy Sheckells. 2014. "Academic Libraries: 2012. First Look." NCES 2014–038, National Center for Education Statistics, US Department of Education, https://nces.ed.gov/pubs2014/2014038.pdf.

Pouncy, Charles R. P. 2002. "Institutional Economics and Critical Race/LatCrit Theory: The Need for a Critical Raced Economics." *Rutgers Law Review* 54 (4): 841–852.

Richard, Katherine. 2014. "The Wealth Gap for Women of Color." Fact Sheet. Center for Global Policy Solutions. http://www.globalpolicysolutions.org/wp-content/uploads/2014/10/Wealth-Gap -for-Women-of-Color.pdf.

Rosa, Kathy, and Kelsey Henke. 2017. "2017 ALA Demographic Study." Office of Research and Statistics, American Library Association. http://www.ala.org/tools/sites/ala.org.tools/files/content /Draft%20of%20Member%20Demographics%20Survey%2001-11-2017.pdf.

Rothstein, Jesse, and Cecilia Elena Rouse. 2007. "Constrained after College: Student Loans and Early Career Occupational Choices." NBER Working Paper 13117, National Bureau of Economic Research. May 2007. https://doi.org/10.3386/w13117.

Solórzano, Daniel, and Tara Yosso. 2000. "Toward a Critical Race Theory of Chicana and Chicano Education." *Charting New Terrains of Chicana(o)/Latina(o) Education*, edited by Carlos Tejeda, Corinne Martínez, and Zeus Leonardo, 35–65. New York: Hampton Press.

Solórzano, Daniel G., and Tara J. Yosso. 2002. "A Critical Race Counterstory of Race, Racism, and Affirmative Action." *Equity and Excellence in Education* 35 (2): 155–168.

Thompson, Brian. 2018. "The Racial Wealth Gap: Addressing America's Most Pressing Epidemic." *Forbes*, February 18, 2018. https://www.forbes.com/sites/brianthompson1/2018/02/18/the-racial -wealth-gap-addressing-americas-most-pressing-epidemic/.

Zaw, Khaing, Jhumpa Bhattacharya, Anne Price, Darrick Hamilton, and William Darity Jr. 2017. "Women, Race and Wealth" Research Brief Series vol. 1, Samuel DuBois Cook Center on Social Equity and Insight Center for Community Economic Development. January 2017. https:// insightcced.org/wp-content/uploads/2017/01/January2017_ResearchBriefSeries_WomenRace Wealth-Volume1-Pages-1.pdf.

10

THE PRAXIS OF RELATION, VALIDATION, AND MOTIVATION
Articulating LIS Collegiality through a CRT Lens

Torie Quiñonez, Lalitha Nataraj, and Antonia Olivas

In this chapter, we use Critical Race Theory (CRT) to demonstrate how our critical raced/gendered epistemologies are supported by validation theory within a relational-cultural mentoring framework, and how they work to empower both students and librarians to assert their rightful places as scholars and members of a larger academic community. We also borrow from Latina/o Critical Theory (Lat-Crit), which, in concert with CRT, emerged as a theoretical framework from legal studies, to theorize issues particular to the Latinx identities shared by many of our students, such as language, immigration and citizenship status, and identity. A Lat-Crit analysis is especially valuable now, in a place and time where students and their families are literally criminalized and targeted for deportation. For ourselves and for our students, the axis of citizenship/legal status intersects with language, class, and phenotype to articulate a specific raced subjectivity that is politically targeted. All of these intersections impact both our worldview and the ways we are perceived by our students and colleagues. We see our professional practice, including teaching, research, and service, in alignment with Solórzano's five defining elements of CRT in educational research:

- Our perspective is *informed by the experience of racism and other forms of oppression*, and of our active resistance to the same.
- Our work *challenges claims of objectivity, meritocracy, and neutrality*, which form the dominant ideology of higher education.

- We demonstrate our *commitment to social justice* with the specific goal of working for the empowerment of Black, Indigenous, and People of Color (BIPOC) and other marginalized groups.
- Our pedagogy and our research practices privilege experiential knowledge and the lived experiences of marginalized people, often expressed through counterstory-telling (narratives that are counter to the majoritarian "story").
- Our perspective is interdisciplinary, coming from the fields of ethnic studies, women's and gender studies, psychology, and education. (Solórzano 1997)

Drawing from the varying levels of experience, areas of professional inquiry, and individual experiences of its three authors, this chapter will apply a critical race analysis to explore the dynamic process by which we support each other's development of professional identity in a way that acknowledges, nurtures, and supports the long-term well-being and effectiveness of teacher-scholar-librarians of color. We do this by delving deeper into the concepts of validation theory and relational cultural theory and by sharing our counterstories.

In our professional practice, we are particularly interested in the work of challenging the dominant ideologies of neutrality and objectivity as they are valorized in information literacy pedagogy, and we will explain the ways we employ this particular element of CRT in our teaching and research. The same tools that we use to empower students help us to empower each other, as women of color librarians. Using a critical race analysis and validation theory to examine relational teaching and mentoring, we center the lived experiences of both students and teacher-librarians of color to understand how racism and other forms of oppression intersect to mediate our experiences of higher education.

Our place of work is a midsized, regional public university and designated Hispanic-Serving Institution located in Southern California, in the US-Mexico borderlands. Many of our students experience the specific forms of oppression that come with a militarized border and heightened policing of People of Color. In our relatively conservative region, long-standing xenophobia informs an expectation for Latinx people to "blend in" and assimilate in order to earn the right to live among "real" Americans, despite how long our families have been here. Nationalistic White Supremacy informs assumptions about Latinx people being unassimilable. This has a long history that is borne out in historical research of education policy in the United States. "Today, bilingualism often continues to be seen as 'un-American' and considered a deficit and an obstacle to learning" (Delgado Bernal 2002, 112). The assumption of resistance to assimilation has to do with the fact that Latinxs are always and forever seen as immigrants, owing to the historical amnesia around the fact that we are liv-ing on land colonized by multiple waves of ancestors who were here long before it was the United States. Counter to Eurocentrism is the Chicana feminist epistemol-ogy that values collective experiences and community memory, which is taught to youth through various modes of storytelling. "It is through culturally specific ways of teaching and learning that ancestors and elders share the knowledge of conquest, segregation, patriarchy, homophobia, assimilation, and resistance" (113). Learning the history we are not taught in schools, we learn survival skills—literally inform-ing the way we survive as a culture. "Within this framework, Chicanas and Chica-nos become agents of knowledge who participate in intellectual discourse that links experience, research, community, and social change" (113).

By centering the assets that our students bring to higher education, we refuse the deficit framework that prevented so many of us from believing that we had some-thing of value to say in an academic environment. We also resist the assumptions about our cultures that we've been told are implicitly at odds with university life. For example, there is an assumption that college marks a threshold across which a teenager moves in order to become an adult, and this usually means moving away from their families and establishing independence of belief, opinion, politics, and so on. While this independent sensibility is still present for our students who continue to live at home while attending college, remaining closely tied to their communities helps them maintain a sense of safety and belonging that college doesn't offer to out-siders. Putting aside the reality that it takes major economic resources to live inde-pendently anywhere in San Diego County, the fact that our Latinx students highly value family and community support makes their experience of college different from students who are mirroring their parents' experience of making this transition. It is important that we realize that the university community is not our students' only community, and it's not necessarily the most important one.

Faculty of color often come to academia with personal and scholarly commit-ments to social transformation and the uplift of marginalized people in our own and other communities. Our cultural resources inform all aspects of the work we do, whether or not we think this work will be rewarded or even highly regarded. "The cultural resources and epistemologies that many faculty of color bring to academia contribute to the goals of higher education and to the overall knowledge base in aca-demia, yet these resources and epistemologies are often unrecognized or devalued" (Delgado Bernal and Villalpando 2016, 88). The possession of these unique cultural resources is supposedly part of the reason we were hired in the first place, but the inability of promotion and tenure committees to adequately value the expertise and emotional labor required can mean that our contributions are minimized and often totally ignored. Mentoring by other faculty of color helps us to navigate these inequities on our respective career paths. In this chapter, we explain how we have used the same theories and frameworks—validation theory, community cultural wealth, and relational-cultural theory—that we use to build up our students, in order to create a bottom-up, radical grassroots mentoring formation among library faculty of color at our institution. The CRT imperatives to challenge notions of neutrality and objectivity, as well as the privileging of experiential knowledge, figure powerfully in both our pedagogy and community building.

For faculty who intentionally craft their pedagogy using culturally responsive methods, the shift from a Eurocentric epistemological perspective is often seen as not in conformity to the values we wish to instill in college students as future scholars. In an institution that promotes norms of neutrality, objectivity, and meritocracy, "alternative" epistemologies veer too far from the valorized evidence-based practice. Applying tenets of CRT that seek to challenge the limitations of official knowledge, Delgado Bernal and Villalpando (2016) write, "A Eurocentric epistemological perspective can subtly—and not so subtly—ignore and discredit the ways of knowing and understanding the world that faculty of color often bring to academia" (81). They call this an *apartheid of knowledge*, and go on to describe the assets that this form of apartheid ignores and excludes: "We believe that cultural resources include the knowledge, practices, beliefs, norms, and values that are derived from culturally specific lessons within the home and local communities of people who have been subordinated by dominant society" (2016, 81). Showing that we value these cultural resources runs counter to the academic insistence on an "objectivity" that privileges Eurocentric epistemologies.

Race and racism inform the experience of our work in academic librarianship in several ways. We often endure microaggressions that extend from white-dominant assumptions about what authority in higher education looks like, and that can come from both colleagues and the students with whom we work. We constantly negotiate power differentials in the classroom. Incorporating issues of racialized oppression in our teaching, a value that our social justice–focused campus espouses, lands in different ways depending on the racial makeup of the students in any given class. Despite socially progressive values, our campus's Western teaching and collegial practices are still firmly ensconced in norms of neutrality, objectivity, and meritocracy, and "alternative" epistemologies are seen as veering too far from valorized evidence-based methods. Our authority and expertise are questioned by students and faculty of record alike when we push up against sacrosanct academic values like objectivity and neutrality. Despite our positions of power in relation to our students, academic librarians' experiences of institutional hierarchies are especially complicated by the fact that our status as faculty is often contested.

Our small numbers in the academy as a whole, but especially in academic libraries, contribute to a lack of opportunities to mentor and be mentored by folks who share an understanding of life as a marginalized person. If we are mentored at all, we are often given advice that runs counter to our cultural values or are told that we have to cover or hide aspects of ourselves that don't conform to what a scholar or professional looks like. No mentorship in research and teaching means that our pedagogies, teaching identities, and research methodologies go unsupported.

RESISTING INSTITUTIONAL RACISM AND EUROCENTRIC PEDAGOGIES

VALIDATION THEORY

Validation theory (Rendón 1994) in its original higher educational context specifically defines validation as an "enabling, confirming and supportive process initiated by in- and out-of-class agents" (44) to support a student's academic and personal development. When a student is validated, they feel capable of learning, have higher self-worth, and feel that they bring something unique and valuable to the college experience. Validation is recommended for students from underrepresented backgrounds who come to higher education with high anxiety about belonging and succeeding. Students interviewed in Rendón's original research indicated that the reassurance and validation they received from any number of individuals helped them believe that they could be successful in college. "For many students, this was the first time someone had expressed care and concern and the first time someone made them feel that their prior life experiences and knowledge were valuable" (Rendón Linares and Muñoz 2011, 15). In counterpoint to these "nontraditional" students who are first in their family to attend college, traditional students can be defined as those whose families have a legacy of college attendance and hold an assumption that they, too, will attend and succeed in higher education. These expectations and attendant conversations are part of the culture of the family.

We have incorporated validating practices in our own teaching of first-year Latinx students participating in a grant-funded student success initiative. Many of our validating actions are achieved through individual interactions with students, but the vast majority of engagement is made in class. The main way is through the design of culturally relevant pedagogy, which Ladson-Billings defines as "a theoretical model that not only addresses student achievement but also helps students to accept and affirm their cultural identity while developing critical perspectives that challenge inequities that schools (and other institutions) perpetuate" (1995, 469). Framing the process of inquiry and the resulting scholarship around their own lives and communities (in which students have unique existing expertise) allows them to use their community circumstances as official knowledge, which allows for students to think critically about the conditions of their lives. For example, when students are encouraged to consider their home or social communities as sites of inquiry, they begin to understand that their experiences in these groups are valid and important forms of knowledge. A favorite, real-life illustration of this process comes from a group of students struggling to identify a common community that they felt was worthy of scholarly focus. After they were shown that their actual common affinity, skateboarding, has been the subject of scholarly inquiry in many disciplines, they were able to present their own wealth of knowledge. What they understood about the politics of public space, the limitations of city planning, and the impact of public skateparks on juvenile crime complemented the existing scholarship in urban studies and sociology. These students were able to see that their lived experience, rather than being illegitimate or unimportant, was actually a valuable addition to a scholarly conversation when they were given the chance to critically examine it.

COMMUNITY CULTURAL WEALTH AND CHICANA FEMINIST EPISTEMOLOGIES

Coming out of CRT as a way to challenge deficit thinking in education, community cultural wealth (Yosso 2005) is an alternative to Bourdieu's concept of cultural capital, which we see as centering white middle-class values and white privilege, and another example of white supremacy culture reflected in the values of higher education. "In other words," Yosso writes, "cultural capital is not just inherited or possessed by the middle class, but rather it refers to an accumulation of specific forms of knowledge, skills, and abilities that are *valued* by privileged groups in society" (76; emphasis in original). To counter, if not replace, these culturally specific and exclusionary ways of knowing and being, students of color often bring a wealth of knowledge and experience from their communities, families, and cultures of origin that higher education has not sought to value. Yosso names six forms of capital, and we've included an example for each:

1. Aspirational: the ability to maintain hopes and dreams for the future, even though you know you'll face significant challenges. Example: I know I'm going to have to pay for college myself, but I'm going to be the first in my family to graduate, and this will improve the upward mobility of my whole family.

2. Linguistic: the intellectual and social skills that come from being able to communicate in more than one language and/or style. Example: I can easily move from talking like "myself" to talking like an academic, because I have had to employ various forms of code-switching my whole life.

3. Familial: cultural knowledge nurtured among family members that "carr[ies] a sense of community history, memory and cultural intuition" (79). Example: I know where I come from, I know what my family members endured, I know how we are unique and how their stories inspire my own understanding of who I am. I know the history of Mexican American people in California and I know about the specific legacies of colonialism in the Southwest.

4. Social: networks of people and community resources. Example: I would not have been put on the road to college if Mom hadn't used her connections as an office worker for San Diego City Schools.

5. Navigational: having the resilience and the ability to move through spaces not created for your benefit (e.g., school). Example: I entered higher education through community college and the transfer process, which is something I had to negotiate on my own, as no one in my family had gone to college.

6. Resistant: the will and ability to participate in strategies and behaviors that challenge inequality. Example: Whether or not we are explicitly taught to resist oppression, we are part of a long line of people who fought to survive, to preserve our culture, and to resist the status quo, particularly in regard to race, gender, and class inequality.

By shedding the idea that our lived experiences don't belong in our pedagogies and other interactions with students, we might establish what Rendón calls a *familia* atmosphere in the classroom or at the reference desk. Because we self-disclose the fact that we are, variously, first-generation college graduates, immigrants, Spanish speakers, or working-class, students will seek us out even if we aren't their subject librarian. There is a shared vulnerability that garners a sense of safety for students when they know that some of us understand firsthand how hard it is to work full-time while trying to stay in school, or when we counsel students to care for themselves first when they or their families are facing a crisis. Connecting students to the right faculty members for advancing on their educational paths, or to social services when they are struggling in other ways, can be especially impactful when we can share our experiences of having been there, too. Even the practice of talking a student through selecting a research topic can benefit from acknowledging a standpoint that we can personally relate to but that might seem taboo to talk about with other faculty. A student who wanted to do research about why her working-class Mexican family didn't seem to value a college education in the way mainstream US culture does was surprised to find out that Torie's family also had no clear cultural expectation for her to achieve a college degree. Rather than accepting these beliefs as evidence of a backward and deficient culture, we were able to talk about the cultural and historical complexities that surround our families' relationships to hegemonic US institutions.

Chicana feminist epistemology (Delgado Bernal 1998) is a powerful mode of envisioning cultural wealth because personal experience also includes collective experience, community memory, and ancestral knowledge, all of which have been deployed in our communities as survival strategies. As information literacy librarians, we are especially interested in epistemological questions: What kinds of knowledge are valid or "authoritative"? Epistemologies are culturally informed, and we need to be transparent that the epistemologies that higher education privileges as objective or authoritative are culturally informed by Eurocentric, capitalist hegemony. Critical Race Theory challenges color blindness and meritocracy and shows how they work to disadvantage marginalized people to further advantage whiteness. Delgado Bernal (2002) points out what we might consider our main challenge within the hegemonic university: "In other words, they believe their stories are based on facts, and because Eurocentrism and white privilege are invisible, they fail to see how subjective their stories are" (120). We mustn't forget that the concept of neutrality has always been part of the core ethics of librarianship. In what ways might we break that concept apart in service to the reality that nothing is free of human values, and put deeper critical thinking about information at the forefront of our information literacy practice? When we identify the ways that we reproduce these Eurocentric, liberal values in our teaching and interactions with students, as well as within the organization of power in the university itself, we can begin to decenter whiteness.

When students can see their home knowledge, including their language, their immersion in two (or more) cultures, and their strong commitment to uplifting their communities as unique assets, we as educators also have an opportunity to see the worldview and community history that we share with our students as a site for connection.

VALIDATION AND COMMUNITY CULTURAL WEALTH
AS FRAMEWORKS FOR RELATIONAL MENTORING

First-generation college students experience the academic environment with the anxiety of not knowing whether they can or will succeed, with the stakes being earning a college diploma and gaining upward mobility and the status of being educated. It is a highly competitive milieu where they continue to be measured according to standards that privilege the epistemologies inherited by continuing-generation and mostly white students. The validating message we want to signal to these alienated students is, "You belong here." Community cultural wealth communicates, "Your unique cultural resources are valuable here." What if we extended that pedagogical strategy to our professional relationships?

In a profession with so few visible People of Color, where we are constantly measuring ourselves against white people who have been raised in the normative (Eurocentric) way of relating and competing with each other, while also trying, often in vain, to fit in and succeed, who will tell *us* we belong here? How might we use the concept of community cultural wealth in both our approaches to information literacy pedagogy and the development of our teacher identities? How can we apply validation theory in our professional role (in relation to our students), as well as in our approach to peer-mentoring relationships with other BIPOC librarians at our institutions and beyond? We suggest that relational-cultural theory (RCT), a feminist therapeutic practice developed in the late 1970s by psychiatrist Jean Baker Miller and the Stone Center Theory Group at Wellesley College, offers a framework through which we can concretize ways to create authentic, validating, and supportive mentoring relationships among colleagues of color.

RELATIONAL-CULTURAL THEORY AND FOSTERING
AUTHENTIC CONNECTION

A central goal of relational-cultural theory (RCT) is to create "power with" connections with colleagues and students, rather than imposing "power over" them. In "power over" relationships, "one person has the ability to decide the rules of discourse and the direction that the relationship will take" (Jordan 2004a, 35). A "power over" dynamic also prizes competitive individualism over "power with" cooperative connections such that gendered and raced meritocratic systems disenfranchise those who have never been afforded any power to begin with—namely, BIPOC, women, and queer and disabled communities (Jordan 2004c, 12). Critical Race Theory, then, provides a lens through which we may identify, critique, and specifically name those oppressive structures, particularly white supremacy, and attendant negative practices that facilitate and reify the disconnection marginalized folks experience in LIS. These structures include white supremacist institutions and discourses that privilege *objectivity* and *neutrality* over experiential knowledge and epistemologies grounded in non-Western identities. "Transformative social action in pursuit of social justice is a critical objective of the [CRT] paradigm" (Ortiz and Jani 2010, 190). Undergirding this paradigm is the analysis of social interactions across a range of subordinating identities that allows us to better understand multiple levels of privilege and oppression (190). RCT examines disconnection caused by systemic marginalization and oppression (Jordan 2009) and offers practical, relational approaches for actualizing CRT's social justice values that focus on challenging destructive systems and structures of domination in higher education.

As Latina, Chicana, Desi, female-identified, immigrant, *pocha*, of mixed-status family, bilingual, working-class, middle-class, parents, nonparents, white-passing, and visibly "Other," we don't always see our ways of knowing (or being) acknowledged, which complicates our ability to fully advocate for self-determination within the academy. The undercutting of our identities is tied to "power over" dynamics in academia that stratify racial and gender differences. "This stratification is the consequence of systematic miseducation that teaches that white is superior and black is inferior. The *stratification*, not the *difference*, constrains our capacity for authenticity and undermines our desire for connection" (Walker 2004, 93). Racial stratification leads to what Kendrick terms *deauthentication*, a cognitive shift requiring BIPOC to engage in intense emotional labor in order to navigate primarily white workplace environments (2018). To avoid macro- or microaggressions, we mask any detectable markers of ethnic, racial or cultural identities, including language, physical presentation, values, and traditions (Kendrick 2018). We not only suppress our full selves, we also must wear the mantle of whiteness in order to be regarded as legitimate contributors to the academy. Deauthentication is profoundly painful when you consider how BIPOC preempt shame and humiliation through performing whiteness in the workplace out of fear of appearing inadequate. Brown and Leung note the futility of this task, where no matter how much we "stuff down the parts of ourselves deemed too far from normative identities … the reality is that no amount of pretending or silence erases who we are, and it certainly doesn't stop us from being made hypervisible at will" (2018, 340–341).

We cannot inure ourselves to microaggressions from library users and colleagues that range from "Where are you *really* from?" to "Your English is impeccable!" These inquiries seem innocuous to non-BIPOC, but are actually emotionally debilitating reminders that we don't belong, despite how hard we try. Every moment spent on correcting such misperceptions reinforces our sense of shame over being viewed as Other. This shame is compounded when you happen to be the only faculty of color at your institution and you begin to feel "a sense of unworthiness to be in con-nection, an absence of hope that an empathic response will be forthcoming from another person" (Brown and Leung 2018, 340–341). When we publicly decry these microaggressions as symptoms of structural racism, we are met with skepticism or outright denial (macroaggression), which demoralizes and isolates us.

"Power with" relationships emphasize interdependence and have the potential to mitigate the trauma of shame and isolation through mutually empowering connec-tions (Fletcher 2004, 276). "Power with" culture also dismantles the notion of instru-mental competence, which has traditionally been defined as mastering a task and demonstrating measurable success in a competitive (read: capitalist) context (Jordan 2004c, 13). In the "power with" paradigm, we move instead toward relational compe-tence, which is the capacity to engender a sense of well-being in a relationship (15). Relational competence shifts us toward associations where vulnerability is perceived as a strength and a site of growth (15). In being open about our need for support and acceptance, our trio connected in meaningful, real ways, rather than uphold-ing a completely false barrier of neutrality, authority, and competitiveness. It is only through the guidance of our women of color (WOC) peers that we have been able to courageously bring our real selves into the classroom. We leverage our own vulner-abilities in material ways, including vocally supporting each other at instructional planning meetings and implementing learning objects in our first-year information literacy courses that explicitly address lived experiences of People of Color and mar-ginalized groups. As individuals, it can be intimidating to agitate for paradigm shifts, but collectively and visibly ("I've got your back, girl"), we are concretely changing teaching and learning departmental values, which has implications for greater insti-tutional change.

SURVIVING AND THRIVING IN SPACES NOT MADE FOR US

Our cultural resources (Delgado Bernal and Villalpando 2016, 81) connect us to our students and show them that we, too, have to learn how to survive in this space that was not made for us. As professionals having to perform on this putatively neutral ground, our cultures nurture and empower us. We can apply a relational lens to

Yosso's six forms of capital to survive and thrive in a professional environment in which we feel like outsiders, no matter how long we've worked there.

1. *Aspirational*: We intentionally envision, strategize, and sometimes enact a radically different form of higher education that puts equity first.
2. *Linguistic*: We freely code-switch in class or in a reference interaction, as well as with our colleagues.
3. *Familial*: We feel a responsibility to the larger community, which is why we focus our instruction on first-generation Latinx students.
4. *Social*: Librarians are the ultimate social network connectors for students who feel lost or out of place, or don't know what questions to ask. With our colleagues, too, our knowledge sharing connects and lifts us all up.
5. *Navigational*: As we learn "the ropes" and unspoken rules of academia (often the hard way), we share that knowledge with our colleagues.
6. *Resistant*: Our personal visions and professional missions almost always involve dismantling oppressive structures that harm our students and our colleagues. We form networks and strategies to this end.

Similarly, Rendón's (1994) elements of validation are acted out every day in our peer-mentoring cluster, and they truly keep us focused on why we belong here, why we must be here. They are:

1. The responsibility for initiating contact is on the institutional agents: the senior, tenured librarian approached the newly tenure-track librarian, the tenure-track librarian approached the new lecturer. No one had to formally ask for mentorship. We initially approached each other with invitations to team-teach and do research together, as well as to signal that we are "safe" to talk to.
2. We value each others' unique experiences and perspectives, especially as they apply to teaching and research.
3. Consistent validation by our colleagues helps us to feel more like we belong here, that there is a place for us in higher education and in librarianship.
4. Validation can occur in and out of class. The parallel to this is that validation by colleagues happens on a professional and a personal level. We commiserate, celebrate, grieve, rage, and strategize during walks on campus, in our offices with the doors closed, on Slack, through texts, and out in social spaces.
5. Validation nurtures us throughout all stages of our careers.
6. Validation is most critical when it is administered early. The first few weeks in a new position are when we need the most help and when we are looking for mentors but not sure if it's OK to ask.

How do we support each other to push our professional practice into a more courageous and honest one? We do this partly by sharing our stories with each other and validating each other's experiences. We foster supported vulnerability and validate each other's teacher identity by team teaching with each other and allowing each person to share their expertise in the classroom with our students. Instead of competing, we collaborate professionally (teaching, research), but we also care for each other personally (closing ranks, seeking safe harbor in each other). Unlike typical, top-down mentoring structures, our connection is formed through affinity rather than an institutional process. We get different things professionally out of our relationships with each other than we get with our non-WOC colleagues: real talk about being a WOC in academia versus real talk about academia. Both are helpful, but only one truly honors our authentic experiences. Part of those authentic experiences is sharing sometimes painful memories/experiences of our professional journeys without each other.

OUR COUNTERSTORIES

As a CRT strategy, counterstorytelling disrupts majoritarian narratives (Solórzano and Yosso 2002, 32; Cooke 2019, 223) and enhances the agency of oppressed populations by centering their stories and experiences (Ortiz and Jani 2010, 186). Far from simply being responses to the dominant narratives, counterstories have the power to further conversations and reform around institutional racism by illuminating, preserving, and strengthening social, political, and cultural survival, as well as resistance (Solórzano and Yosso 2002, 32).

We employ collaborative autoethnography (collaborative, autobiographical, and ethnographic) to share our counterstories (Chang, Ngunjiri, and Hernandez 2015, 17). Autoethnography focuses on self-interrogation and self-reflection, but when we shift toward a collaborative methodology, we are "building on each other's stories, gaining insight from group sharing, and providing various levels of support" (17). Cooke notes that counterstorytelling can be a cathartic but also emotionally exhausting process that requires the reliving of painful experiences (2019, 228). We eased some of this pain by creating an affinity group where we shared previously untold stories in an empathic, safe environment without feeling isolated or unsafe (Fedele 2004, 197). Here, we relate our individual stories and further examine how these experiences have critically shaped our trio relationship to the extent that we feel empowered to bring our authentic selves into our work.

TONI

When I first started my career in librarianship nearly twenty years ago, I was fortunate to be a part of Knowledge River and Spectrum, so I had strong support groups from other librarians of color both as colleagues and as mentors.[1] It wasn't until I moved into the real world of academic librarianship that I felt isolated. For the first time in a long time, I was one of "the only" in a sea of "the majority" and, although it was not always intentional, I was made to feel very much an "Other." Being the Other naturally means one does not fit in to the interdependent order of a society and is, therefore, disenfranchised in a sense. I will not go so far as to say I was completely ostracized from my library communities, because I certainly had friends and allies from various backgrounds. The times I did feel excluded (or disenfranchised), I had to learn how to navigate the climate of my institutions and quickly turn to my allies for help and support.

As an example, there were times earlier in my career when my ideas were quickly dismissed or simply ignored for reasons I did not fully understand. I came to realize it was the messenger these colleagues didn't like, not the ideas themselves. Unfortunately, I was the messenger, so I learned to be silent. Thankfully, I was able to navigate my way around this issue by asking close colleagues and allies (sometimes that included people from outside my institutions) to pitch these ideas as their own. And sure enough, the ideas were met with enthusiasm. I'm not proud of this silence and this dependency on colleagues to help further my ideas, but I was in a situation where even my research was not valued the same as that of my colleagues, who published works on more traditional library topics. Although I produced multiple articles, a dissertation, and even a book on topics of diversity in libraries, it felt as if it simply didn't matter. Either the topic of diversity was not valued or I was not valued, and I felt that hit more strongly when I decided to take the next step in my career.

When I decided to go up for tenure and full librarianship, I did not feel comfortable asking very many of the senior librarians for help. Instead, I looked to other senior faculty on and off campus (current and retired) to help me with my dossier. Although I successfully earned tenure and full librarian rank, there was still this feeling of "not good enough." Regardless of how many degrees, awards, or publications were under my belt, I still felt invalidated and rejected by many of my associates. Yet, I was celebrated outside my institution.

I am told by junior colleagues that I am a leader in their eyes, but I admit to not always feeling the part. I am not like other leaders in our institution (or even in our profession). I try not to accept the lie I've allowed myself to believe over the years—the lie that I am "not good enough," or that my ability to be authentic with these junior colleagues is not equal to traditional leadership styles. Instead, I am learning to understand that once we as librarians of color build the powerful structure of nontraditional leadership ourselves, we begin to build a critical mass within the profession itself. Amplifying ourselves as leaders to help bring other librarians of color up and empowering them as leaders as well is how we change not only how we view ourselves in this line of work but the profession itself.

TORIE

Toni was the only working-class Latina librarian in our place of work when I started on the tenure track. Coming from a nontraditional educational and career path, I never expected to feel comfortable in a professional environment. At the time I was hired, I received formal mentoring from various tenured librarians who could answer my questions about campus culture and internal politics, as well as expectations of new faculty regarding research, teaching, and service. Toni and I developed our friendship outside of this formal mechanism. We connected over family stories, shared cultural references, and the particular grief and rage that comes from loving people who are constantly fighting (and mostly losing) battles with addiction, violence, the criminal justice system, and the militarization of the US-Mexico border. Our perspectives on the things that really matter to us went far, far beyond our jobs. We were both committed to supporting our communities, and that included the Latinx students at our university. We knew what it meant, to them and to their families, to come to college—many of them were the first in their families ever to do so, after making it out of underfunded high schools and a lifetime of low expectations.

Toni invited me to team-teach with her, working with a cohort of students from migrant laborer backgrounds. I saw how powerful it was for her to speak of her own childhood in the fields and of her mixed-status family, to fluently switch between English and Spanish, and the way this seemed to put students at ease. The fact that she was sharing this with me felt intimate, like she was trusting me with this other, authentic self. We went on to design a culturally responsive information literacy curriculum together, and cotaught every semester until she went to work in another unit of the library. We continue to write and publish together, as she was the person who convinced me that my experiences, perspectives, and ideas needed to be out in the world. When I became an academic librarian, I never entertained the idea that I would research emerging technologies or assessment metrics. I was told that research that focused on cultural competence, social justice, or "diversity work" wouldn't be taken as seriously as more traditional library science topics. My motivation for doing the work of culturally responsive pedagogy in the information literacy classroom was and is to validate students and their communities as creators of knowledge and to affirm marginalized people as valuable members of the academic community.

Presenting my research in a way that shows my very personal connection to the work has been challenging. Finding my audience hasn't been easy, and learning how to write in a way that feels completely inauthentic to me but is the standard for my profession is a constant exercise in keeping my imposter syndrome at bay. Having a mentor like Toni, who believes in the importance of my work, assures me that I belong here, that what I am contributing to our students and to our field is worthwhile and unique. It is with this bolstered confidence that I can believe that I am a worthy mentor to both her and Lali. What Toni and I did in the classroom is akin to forging a space that didn't exist before. We gave each other room and permission to offer our authentic selves in the service of pedagogy, and now when Lali and I teach together, we're making that space even bigger.

LALITHA

Despite my firm goal of becoming an academic librarian, the first professional role I accepted was in a public library, a field in which I had virtually no experience beyond a handful of LIS classes. I knew within my first month on the job that I was not right for this institution and it was not right for me, but for the next four and a half years I proceeded to ignore red flags including lack of mentorship, minimal validation from my superiors, and a general lack of collegiality. My white supervisor advised me to "smile more" in order to appear more approachable to coworkers and the general public. Looking back, I recognize that this so-called feedback was a form of intersectional oppression, but I shrugged off my discomfort, choosing to see this microaggression as a form of genuine regard for my professional development. Considering how outgoingness and general sociability are typically coded as Western (read: white) traits (Matsumoto and Kudoh 1993, 223), my apparent lack of approachability signaled my Otherness. Over the years, these and similar interactions I endured (from colleagues and community users alike) in public libraries eroded my confidence to the point where I questioned my professional (and personal) value.

When I transitioned to full-time academic librarianship two years ago, I was a solid mid-career librarian, which should've made me feel secure in my expertise. But

I tentatively stepped into my lecturer role, feeling unsure and unwilling to take risks because I wanted to demonstrate off the bat that I was a cooperative and competent colleague who fit in. But according to what standards? Imagine my surprise when I stepped into a department that prioritized psychological safety and protection of its most vulnerable members—the lecturers and tenure-track librarians. I profoundly connected with Toni and Torie because, like me, they actively researched and reflected on topics related to cultural identity, institutional racism, and social justice, tying these ideas to our pedagogical practices and campus values. But more importantly, we had similar histories, being first-generation women of color in LIS. I often spoke with Toni and Torie about growing up with immigrant parents who didn't impart the social cues deemed necessary to navigate a society that privileges whiteness, and how that impacted my educational and professional experiences. These are stories that resonated not only with them, but also with our first-generation students who also understood the difficulties and the joys of navigating two different cultures.

Knowing my aspiration of becoming a tenure-track librarian, Toni and Torie were more than willing to take me under their wings and work together with me on writing projects. In championing my research potential, they were both validating my place, as well my ideas, in the academy. When a tenure-track position opened at our institution, Toni and Torie not only encouraged me to apply, they also advocated for showing realness during the application and interview process, which included calling out the inherent white supremacy in LIS and drawing on lived experiences to detail strategies for approaching pedagogical and research practices with an equity lens. Without their support, I could not have visualized myself in, let alone pursued, a tenure-track position.

OUR TRIO CONNECTION

In relating our counterstories and assessing them through a collective autoethnographic lens, we are trying to address the question, "How do we build up the librarian to do the critical work of validating our students?" Given the master narrative of whiteness that prevails in higher education, it is difficult for BIPOC to see their marginality as a site of strength and resistance; on an individual level, we have had to grapple with our positionality as teachers and how to create the spaces in scholarly *and* collegial conversations to raise up and legitimize our own lived experiences. Critical Race Theory gives us the language to identify the "intercentricity of racism and other forms of subordination" (Solórzano and Yosso 2002, 25) in higher education.

Informed by a CRT and LatCrit lens, we apply relational, validational, and community cultural wealth frameworks to create relationships that not only help us do good work, but also help us to acknowledge that we are our best selves when we can openly challenge and critique white hegemony.

Our trio relationship is premised on fostering connection, and we adhere to psychological safety, which is the idea that we can freely share ideas without fear of reprisal or shaming from each other (Edmondson 1999, 354). Too, we practice care for each other by engaging in relational practices that mitigate our emotional labor. These specifically include what Fletcher terms *mutual empowering* and *creating team* (2004, 272). As a senior-level librarian of color at our institution, Toni leverages her own power to lift up fellow BIPOC colleagues; by offering to publish and coteach with us, she is putting effort into increasing our (Torie's and Lali's) competence, self-confidence, and knowledge (Fletcher 2004, 275). Mutual empowerment is grounded in interdependence and fluid power relations (275); Toni's mentorship of Torie was instrumental to Torie's ability to mentor Lalitha. In *creating team*, Toni helped two librarians of color achieve tenure-track positions, which contributed to an institutional and professional legacy of inclusion.

CONCLUSION

The working theory of this chapter is that the same critical tools we use to build up our underrepresented students in order to help them claim their rightful sense of authority and belonging in higher education are the very same tools that librarians of color employ among ourselves for the same purposes. Chief among those tools is the liberatory act of sharing power that comes with forging human connection. Mutual empowerment is rooted in intentional actions designed to foster interdependent, productive relationships and minimize power differences (Fletcher 2004, 277). For example, by resisting the idea that effective pedagogy comes from a sense of authoritative neutrality, we build capacity for authentic participation in an ongoing relationship between student and teacher. Likewise, when librarians of color form a strong sense of relational bonding and are validated in the workplace for what we bring to the table, it has the potential to increase confidence and self-efficacy and to build trust. Through validation and relation, we may be seen as valued and respected contributors to the profession, increasing the potential for us to see ourselves as leaders who may inspire others.

When we are encouraged to voice our views and ideas in the workplace, we feel recognized and appreciated. Team-teaching creates a supportive environment where we can feel comfortable putting forward our ideas and questioning things openly without fear. It is vital to the psychological safety and well-being of each librarian in these relationships to have the ability to take risks and be vulnerable in front of our peers without fear of ridicule or perceived weakness. Using the lens of Critical Race Theory to understand how our epistemologies confront the accepted values of higher education in the US, we theorize that our direct resistance to hegemonic expectations built by centuries of white supremacy might force open a space for us, our colleagues, and the generations who come after. What would librarianship look like if we all felt strong, supported, and validated throughout our careers?

Library workers of color are currently engaged in this critical work through validating in-person and online spaces including Libraries We Here, WOC + Lib, and LOCLA.[2] But at our individual institutions, we must be intentional about voicing the need for change. The three of us acknowledge the uniqueness of the Teaching and Learning Department of the library, in that we have a significant amount of autonomy in how we experiment with and deploy our pedagogy. However, these values do not necessarily extend to the whole of the library or campus. For one of us, twenty years in academia has proven that we cannot rely solely on our white colleagues to consistently support our work and be dependable allies. We place our trust in each other because of our common experiences, and in doing so, we help build up the leadership capacity of other library workers of color. To challenge the macro-level institutional racism, we must call for what Brown, Cline, and Méndez-Brady eloquently refer to in chapter 3 of this volume as an "arable beginning," by collectively refusing to go along with inequitable labor practices. As they argue, we must ask our white colleagues to critically reflect on their own complicity in reinforcing dominant hierarchies that subjugate their colleagues of color, and we must also require fair compensation, demanding salary transparency at all levels of the job search. We lean on the relational bonds within our affinity group for one of the most difficult asks of our white colleagues: to use CRT to explicitly surface in their work (from administration to technical services to teaching) the historical failure of our profession to support our most vulnerable populations, including students and faculty of color, and to take concrete actions (rather than voice vague platitudes and promises) that are officially documented and shared publicly to create equitable and just working and learning environments. By articulating these material desiderata, we shape the world we want to live in now, which is the ultimate validation of each other's teaching, research, and identity as academic librarians.

NOTES

1. See University of Arizona Knowledge River, https://ischool.arizona.edu/knowledge-river; American Library Association Spectrum Program, http://www.ala.org/advocacy/spectrum.

2. See Libraries We Here, https://www.wehere.space/; WOC+Lib, https://www.wocandlib.org/; Librarians of Color–LA (LOCLA), https://www.instagram.com/librariansofcolor/.

BIBLIOGRAPHY

Brown, Jennifer, and Sofia Leung. 2018. "Authenticity vs. Professionalism: Being True to Ourselves at Work." In *Pushing the Margins: Women of Color and Intersectionality in LIS*, edited by Annie Pho and Rose L. Chou, 329–347. Sacramento, CA: Library Juice Press, 2018.

Canton, Cecil. 2013. "The 'Cultural Taxation' of Faculty of Color in the Academy." *California Faculty Magazine*, December 5, 2013.

Chang, Heewon, Faith Ngunjiri, and Kathy-Ann C. Hernandez. 2015. *Collective Autoethnography*. London: Taylor and Francis.

Cooke, Nicole A. 2019. "Impolite Hostilities and Vague Sympathies: Academia as a Site of Cyclical Abuse." *Journal of Education for Library and Information Science* 60 (3): 223–230.

Delgado Bernal, Dolores. 1998. "Using a Chicana Feminist Epistemology in Educational Research." *Harvard Educational Review* 68 (4): 555–582.

Delgado Bernal, Dolores. 2002. "Critical Race Theory, Latino Critical Theory, and Critical Raced-Gendered Epistemologies: Recognizing Students of Color as Holders and Creators of Knowledge." *Qualitative Inquiry* 8 (1): 105–125. https://doi.org/10.1177/107780040200800107.

Delgado Bernal, Dolores, and Octavio Villalpando. 2016. "An Apartheid of Knowledge in Academia: The Struggle over the 'Legitimate' Knowledge of Faculty of Color." In *Foundations of Critical Race Theory in Education*, edited by Edward Taylor, David Gillborn, and Gloria Ladson-Billings, 77–91. New York: Routledge.

Edmondson, Amy. 1999. "Psychological Safety." *Administrative Quarterly* 44:350–383.

Fedele, Nikki M. 2004. "Relationships in Groups: Connection, Resonance, and Paradox." In the *Complexity of Connection: Writings from the Stone Center's Jean Baker Training Institute*, edited by Judith V. Jordan, Maureen Walker, and Linda M. Hartling, 194–219. New York: Guilford Press.

Fletcher, Joyce K. 2004. "Relational Theory in the Workplace." In *The Complexity of Connection: Writings from the Stone Center's Jean Baker Miller Training Institute*, edited by Judith V. Jordan, Maureen Walker, and Linda M. Hartling, 270–298. New York: Guilford Press.

Herzberg, Frederick. 1964. "The Motivation-Hygiene Concept and Problems of Manpower." *Personnel Administration* 27 (1): 3–7.

Jordan, Judith V. 2004a. "Relational Resilience." In *The Complexity of Connection: Writings from the Stone Center's Jean Baker Miller Training Institute*, edited by Judith V. Jordan, Maureen Walker, and Linda M. Hartling, 28–46. New York: Guilford Press.

Jordan, Judith V. 2004b. "Shame and Humiliation: From Isolation to Relational Transformation." In *The Complexity of Connection: Writings from the Stone Center's Jean Baker Miller Training Institute*, edited by Judith V. Jordan, Maureen Walker, and Linda M. Hartling, 103–128. New York: Guilford Press.

Jordan, Judith V. 2004c. "Toward Competence and Connection." In *The Complexity of Connection: Writings from the Stone Center's Jean Baker Miller Training Institute*, edited by Judith V. Jordan, Maureen Walker, and Linda M. Hartling, 11–27. New York: Guilford Press.

Jordan, Judith V. 2009. *Relational-Cultural Therapy*. Kindle ed. Washington, DC: American Psychological Association.

Kendrick, Kaetrena. 2018. "Considering: Deauthenticity in the Workplace." *The Ink on the Page* (blog), February 5, 2018. https://theinkonthepageblog.wordpress.com/2018/02/05/considering-deauth enticity-in-the-workplace/.

Ladson-Billings, Gloria. 1995. "Toward a Theory of Culturally Relevant Pedagogy." *American Educational Research Journal* 32 (3): 465–491. https://www.jstor.org/stable/1163320.

Matsumoto, David, and Tsutomu Kudoh. 1993. "American-Japanese Cultural Differences in Attributions of Personality Based on Smiles." *Journal of Nonverbal Behavior* 17 (4): 231–243. https://doi .org/10.1007/BF00987239.

Olivas, Antonia. 2014. "Understanding Underrepresented Minority Academic Librarian's Motivation to Lead in Higher Education." EdD diss., University of California San Diego.

Olivas, Antonia P. 2017. "'Should I Stay or Should I Go?' The Motivation of Underrepresented Minority Librarians to Lead." Paper presented at the Association of College Research Libraries Conference, Baltimore, MD, March 22–25, 2017. http://www.ala.org/acrl/sites/ala.org.acrl/files /content/conferences/confsandpreconfs/2017/ShouldIStayorShouldIGo.pdf.

Ortiz, Larry, and Jayshree Jani. 2010. "Critical Race Theory: A Transformational Model for Teaching Diversity." *Journal of Social Work Education* 46 (2): 175–193.

Rendón, Laura I. 1994. "Validating Culturally Diverse Students: Toward a New Model of Learning and Student Development." *Innovative Higher Education* 19 (1): 33–51.

Rendón Linares, Laura I., and Susana M. Muñoz. 2011. "Revisiting Validation Theory: Theoretical Foundations, Applications, and Extensions." *Enrollment Management Journal* 2 (1): 12–31.

Solórzano, Daniel G. 1997. "Images and Words That Wound: Critical Race Theory, Racial Stereotyping, and Teacher Education." *Teacher Education Quarterly* 24 (3): 5–19.

Solórzano, Daniel G., and Tara J. Yosso. 2002. "Critical Race Methodology: Counter-storytelling as an Analytical Framework for Education Research." *Qualitative Inquiry* 8 (1): 23–44.

Walker, Maureen. 2004. "Race, Self, and Society: Relational Challenges." In *The Complexity of Connection: Writings from the Stone Center's Jean Baker Miller Training Institute*, edited by Judith V. Jordan, Maureen Walker, and Linda M. Hartling, 90–102. New York: Guilford Press.

Yosso, Tara J. 2005. "Whose Culture Has Capital? A Critical Race Theory Discussion of Community Cultural Wealth." *Race Ethnicity and Education* 8 (1): 69–91. http://dx.doi.org/10.1080 /1361332052000341006.

11

PRECARIOUS LABOR AND RADICAL CARE IN LIBRARIES AND DIGITAL HUMANITIES

Anne Cong-Huyen and Kush Patel

I want there to be a diversity of care tactics. And I want everyone to be able to create wildly intimate, healing relationships where your care needs are present in the room, not crammed in the garbage. I want everyone to have access to this joyful, dangerous, wide-open pleasure, because it's the vulnerable strength we all deserve.

—Leah Lakshmi Piepzna-Samarasinha

SETTING THE STAGE

Richard Delgado and Jean Stefancic write, "Unlike some academic disciplines, Critical Race Theory contains an activist dimension. It not only tries to understand our social situation, but to change it; it sets out not only to ascertain how society organizes itself along racial lines and hierarchies, but to transform it for the better" (2001, 3). In this chapter, we attempt to combine this activist mode of Critical Race Theory (CRT) with Third World feminisms and feminist antiracist praxis into a discussion of labor in academic libraries. In doing so, we are seeking to critique and unpack systemic structures to change them together. We want to effect change that is imbued with the "creativity, power, wit, and humanity of the voices speaking about ways to change that structure" (Harris 2001, xx). This is especially important when we consider that "librarianship has feigned political and social neutrality while exploiting the labor of those who exist outside the spectrum of white, able-bodied, cisgender, neurotypical-ness that so many working librarians occupy" (Brown et al. 2018, 163). To focus this chapter, we use digital humanities positions in academia as a case study to examine the systemic and structural issues that have led to the current state of precarious and contingent labor in libraries, especially for librarians of color. We focus here on digital humanities librarianship, providing extensive background on its more recent formations, the critiques that have emerged, and its corollaries, not only because of our own situatedness and proximity to the field, but because of the significance of the field, where we have seen increasing allocations of resources, space, and positions for the support of such work. The trends we see in digital humanities, we argue, portend troubling developments that reverberate across librarianship more broadly.

The trends we have identified that link digital humanities and librarianship include characterizations of both fields as inclusive, "nice," or "neutral," while they are targeted with critiques of whiteness perpetuated by exclusionary politics, policies, and daily practices. Efforts in both digital humanities and librarianship to address the issue of overwhelming whiteness have included a number of initiatives to diversify the fields, which have been largely unsuccessful and instead only revealed the prevalent homophily and consequent homogeneity in both domains. These efforts have included different kinds of competitive short-term appointments (resident librarians, fellowships, postdocs, among others), all instantiations of precarious labor, many of which, however, also remain limited to US citizens and permanent residents; efforts to increase the talent pipeline from graduate programs into the profession; and conferences or workshops that sometimes end up further segregating the profession (though some are specifically designed to establish safe spaces for dialogue and collectivism). In some cases, these programs have had complicated effects on individuals, and more broadly in the profession. Using the CRT method of storytelling and counterstorytelling to situate this chapter, we start with our own experiences in an attempt at a "working identity" within the space of an academic library as Brown digital humanities–adjacent librarians who have occupied a range of roles in and outside of libraries in support of digital humanities work (Carbado and Gulati 2000).[1] As Richard Delgado writes, "Stories told by underdogs" can be powerful because they "can shatter complacency and challenge the status quo" (1989, 2414). More importantly, counterstorytelling does this work by drawing attention to the "ridiculous, self-serving, or cruel," thereby deconstructing those structures, proposing alternatives, and helping us to "understand when it is time to reallocate power" (2415).

We write these words as librarians and faculty who have been beneficiaries of these same initiatives. Having suffered from job contingency, financial stresses, racial microaggressions, and the vagaries of the immigration system, we are very much aware of our own positionalities as South and Southeast Asian/American librarians. We're the Brown Asians whose identities are outside of the Black-white binary. Borrowing from Claire Jean Kim, we are triangulated and "Othered" as more inferior than white populations, less inferior than Black ones, and more foreign than both. Although we are outside of the neat Black-white binary, we are never outside of the structures determined by whiteness. We also came to librarianship via rather irregular trajectories as PhDs who intentionally chose to pursue academic careers that value knowledge making and community-centered service. Anne has a PhD in English, was a postdoctoral fellow in transnational cultural studies, and then coordinated a digital liberal arts program in an "alternative academic" or "alt-ac" (read: non–tenure-track faculty) position from within a library at a small liberal arts college. Kush holds a PhD in architecture, was a postdoctoral fellow in two humanities centers, and was a public humanities graduate fellow at a large R1 university. We both found ourselves working as academic librarians supporting digital scholarship and pedagogy at a prominent and historically white research university in the Midwest. Our distinct careers in digital and public humanities brought us together to collaboratively advance and sustain a bottom-up infrastructure for digital humanities scholarship at a massive resource-rich academic library.

Although our introduction to each other would be important to our own identity and community formation as immigrant South and Southeast Asian/American digital humanities–adjacent librarians, we also would come to encounter many obstacles that would test this newfound relationship, most importantly around an inflexible immigration system that is built on White Supremacist ideologies and structures. For us as feminist of color librarians committed to equitable labor, radical care, and social justice, this process has been a difficult one, filled with silences, absences, erasures, and quiet traumas that span a spectrum from forced leaves of absence to international displacement. These experiences are not unique, but they help us to reevaluate more critically what Sara Ahmed calls our "relationship to institutional worlds" (2012, 5). They are the intentional result of legacies of historically racist systems and structures meant to make it easier for certain populations to immigrate and enter the fold of the US body politic, and more difficult for others. This chapter attempts to focus attention on the intersectional complexities of race, gender, sexuality, and immigration status as they affect the lives of librarians with PhDs whose positions support digital humanities work. We draw parallels between libraries and the digital humanities as fields that have struggled with issues of diversity, equity, and inclusion, while also being characterized as "nice." We will utilize Ahmed's critique of diversity work to identify the paradoxes of doing and *being* diversity in digital humanities and libraries. We will close by highlighting alternative action, based on adrienne maree brown's *Pleasure Activism*, where she urges us "to learn how to practice love such that care—for ourselves and others—is understood as political resistance and cultivating resilience" (2019, 59), to help those in positions of power to support feminist anticolonial and antiracist praxis that is more inclusive, human-centered, equitable, and pleasurable, within their own libraries or digital humanities programs. We find that despite these difficult experiences brought on by our identities in White Supremacist structures, there is also the opportunity for positive things to emerge that can be made real only through our commitments to each other. As Gloria Ladson-Billings writes, "It is because of the meaning and value imputed to whiteness that CRT becomes an important intellectual and social tool for deconstruction, reconstruction, and construction: deconstruction of oppressive structures, reconstruction of human agency, and construction of equitable and socially just relations of power" (1998, 9). Based on this premise, we propose practical steps to reimagining labor in digital humanities and libraries that uplifts, rather than exhausts and excludes, librarians of color.

INTERSECTIONALITY AND JURIDICAL IDENTITIES

In recent decades, *intersectionality* has been somewhat of a popular buzzword taken up in feminist theory and applied to any number of analyses (Bilge 2013; Cooper 2015).[2] It would seem to be particularly applicable here as we write of being racialized bodies in libraries, spaces that have been documented as primarily white and female. As numerous studies, presentations, and publications have noted, "The library profession is amply aware that White librarians are over-represented among its workers" (Brook, Ellenwood, and Lazzarro 2015, 261). In a white paper published for the Association of College and Research Libraries in 2007, the authors contextualized current labor dynamics within a longer US history, writing, "Academic librarianship recruitment history cannot be divorced from the history of education and federal education policy in the United States," a history that included racism, segregation, discrimination, Indian schools, forced assimilation, and a litany of other injustices (Neely and Peterson 2007, 8). Likewise, we have seen similar questions being raised about the apparent whiteness of the smaller field of the digital humanities (DH). In 2012 Tara McPherson was moved to ask, "Why are the digital humanities so white?" in an attempt to explain the phenomenon through "lenticular logic," a "covert racial logic" of the mid-twentieth-century post–civil rights era that forces us to view the whole in terms of fragments or nodes that removes history, "relation and context" (2012, 144). In professions and fields that are overwhelmingly white, how might an intersectional approach help us to untangle the embodied, the legal, and the historical politics of digital humanities and librarianship work?

Brittney Cooper describes intersectionality as "an analytic frame capable of attending to the particular positionality of black women and other women of color both in civil rights law and within civil rights movements" (2015, 385). Cooper traces the genealogy of intersectionality as far back as the nineteenth century, to the writings of Black women like Anna Julia Cooper, who wrote of being victim to both the "woman question" and the "race problem," while likely "confronting crushing poverty too" (387). When Kimberlé Crenshaw theorized intersectionality, it was a deliberate move to, as Cooper describes, "[allow] for recognition of the black female subject within *juridical* structures of power, where she had heretofore remained invisible and illegible, and thus unable to obtain any kind of justice" (390; emphasis added). Most important, as Brittney Cooper points out, is the emphasis on "structural identities," or the ways in which laws and institutions determine peoples' identities, which are different from personal identities, a form of representation that has primarily been used in feminist theories as "traveling theories" (Cooper 2015, 387; Bilge 2013). For example, Anne identifies as a cisgender Vietnamese American feminist, the primary income earner in her family, a mother to rescue dogs and cats, an academic, a librarian, a digital humanist, and lover of genre fiction. The law determines her identity outside of these self-identifications, from categories assigned along juridical lines. According to the law, she is a naturalized citizen, a refugee arriving before 1995, a married woman who pays joint taxes in a certain tax bracket, and so on. If Anne were to have been caught forging checks in her youth, she could be detained and deported (Do 2018; Dunst 2018; Wiltz 2016). It doesn't matter how Anne identifies, unless it aligns with categories that matter to the state: nationality, legal status, tax bracket, criminal history.

This past year, these legal categories loomed as specters over our professional and personal lives, when Kush's visa status became indeterminate. Kush's yearlong appointment was accompanied by arduous, behind-the-scenes advocacy work, requiring them and those they valued as community to produce endless documentation to prove how their doctoral degree in architecture and related work in the digital and public humanities had prepared them for a career in digital pedagogy librarianship practice. Both of us were hired as digital pedagogy librarians because of our experiences practicing digital pedagogy in our own classes and supporting it in those of others. We met the qualifications outlined in the job: MLIS *or equivalent*. Neither had an MLIS degree, and that detail proved to be a complicating factor. Kush's lack of an MLIS, in addition to their foreign-born status, made them ineligible to continue in this role as per the books of our institution's international center. The experience of trying to meet shifting, incomprehensible bureaucratic expectations to prove educational and professional equivalency was alienating and exhausting to say the least, making all the more real the question of institutional erasures that many international candidates like Kush remain subjected to during and beyond their student and postdoctoral lives.

Throughout their appointment, Kush advanced a praxis of survival whilst trying to make sense of the recurring contingencies of a hybrid digital humanities career invested in public scholarship. They grappled with ways in which to collaboratively build digital pedagogy infrastructures to include those who are surviving institutional erasures. Following the words of queer scholar Keguro Macharia on the teachings of Audre Lorde (2017), Kush also found themself thinking about individuals who did not survive the injustices of historically white, upper-caste, patriarchal spaces, and still others whose labors might never survive these interconnected forces. For Kush—as a queer feminist scholar, writer, and teacher—their partnership with Anne was not merely academic or geographical but *against their hybridity*, and often deeply personal. With transitions in professional titles and therefore legal categories, the legibility of Kush's right to stay in the US was made precarious. Ultimately, Kush had to transition out of their academic role and move to India, their country of origin. It did not matter that Kush was a brilliant scholar, a hard-working employee, a top US university–trained academic, and a valuable librarian. Their doctoral credentials did not perfectly map onto the job category, and the institutions and structures that had the power to determine whether they were able to remain refused to act on their behalf. The result was heartbreaking.

In recounting these personal stories, we are not trying to elicit sympathy. Instead, we draw connections between the personal, the political, and the theoretical and ground them in the real and material, a prominent concern of CRT. We apply this lens to our work as academics and librarians whose identities are rooted in the Global South and the Third World, who write this chapter across time zones and borders, despite rolling blackouts and monsoons, and differential care duties. We are practicing what Third World feminist Chandra Mohanty describes as

"feminism without borders" ... to stress that our most expansive and inclusive visions of feminism need to be attentive to borders while learning to transcend them.... It acknowledges the fault lines, conflicts, differences, fears, and containment that borders represent.

It acknowledges that there is no one sense of a border, that the lines between and through nations, races, classes, secularities, religions, and disabilities are real—and that a feminism without borders must envision change and social justice work across these lines of demarcation and division. (2003, 2)

In our particular cases, our bodies literally marked diversity at our majority-white institution. That legible diversity and difference in itself was not enough to be held as valuable. Nor is diversity enough. We want to move beyond definitions of diversity as "benign variation" that "bypasses power as well as history to suggest a harmonious empty pluralism," and recognize the extensive labor that is involved in "doing diversity" (Mohanty 2003, 193). Extending Mohanty's analysis with a more thorough ethnographic study of diversity workers, Sarah Ahmed writes that the "responsibility for diversity and equality is unevenly distributed. It is also the case that the distribution of this work is political: if diversity and equality work is less valued by organizations, then to become responsible for this work can mean to inhabit institutional spaces that are less valued" (2012, 4). This is especially the case for People of Color, as "you *already* embody diversity by providing an institution of whiteness with color" (4; emphasis in original). We want to acknowledge that in addition to providing color, we also provide additional benefits in terms of expertise, critical perspective, and disciplinary training, and that these benefits also come with discomfort, as they make visible our politics and commitments to change making along deliberate structural lines.

LIBRARIES, DIGITAL HUMANITIES, AND IDEOLOGIES OF "NICENESS"

It is important to draw out the connections linking librarianship and digital humanities, which on the surface may seem incomparable outside the fact that digital humanities is present in various forms within academic libraries. One of the most striking parallels in librarianship and digital humanities is the prevalence of scholarship and subcommunities that have been important in critiquing the neutrality of the two fields, not unlike the emergence of CRT to incorporate the critical examination of race and power within legal studies. This trend amounts to rigorous systemic and structural critique that attempts to diagnose problems of whiteness and the rhetorics and ideologies of benignancy, niceness, collegiality, and neutrality. In librarianship, groups like #CritLib and #LibrariesWeHere in LIS, and in digital humanities, movements like #transformDH, #dhPoCo, #FemDh, #RaceDH, #QueerDH, #AnticolonialDH, and #OurDHIs, have been doing critical work to draw attention to inequities in practice and to structural and systemic racism, which informs the development of the fields, but they also have provided powerful arenas for community building and collectivity for marginal groups.

Unlike digital humanities—which is identified as a "big tent," an academic field, or a community of practice, depending on who you ask—librarianship is often attributed an ethos and a set of professional values as a vocation.[3] As Fobazi Ettarh writes, "Many librarians refer to the field of librarianship as a calling" (2018). This notion of a calling leads to her larger critique, wherein she names "vocational awe" as something that determines the general lack of critical reflection among librarians about librarianship. Ettarh defines "vocational awe" more clearly as "the set of ideas, values, and assumptions librarians have about themselves and the profession that result in beliefs that libraries as institutions are inherently good and sacred, and therefore beyond critique." These understandings of librarianship have had material consequences in the makeup of the profession, which is overwhelmingly white and female, a reification of the "Lady Bountiful," a Victorian archetype that represented white women as virtuous and philanthropic, performing "civilizing" work within a colonial context (Schlesselman-Tarango 2016).

Digital humanities, by comparison, is much younger as a field and would not be considered a profession with its own set of professional values or ethics, though there has been a preoccupation among some to identify such values. With "'This Is Why We Fight': Defining the Values of the Digital Humanities" (2013), Lisa Spiro became an early proponent of developing a core set of values for digital humanities in light of extensive debates occurring in the early 2000s, when humanities computing of the 1980s was evolving into the field we would come to know as digital humanities. Scholars, funding agencies, administrators, and others were struggling to define what "counted" as digital humanities and who had the right to call themselves a digital humanist.[4] Spiro intervened to argue that there were more important things to establish first and foremost: "Rather than debating who is in and who is out, the DH community needs to develop a keener sense of what it stands for and what is at stake in its work" (2013, 17). These statements suggest that regardless of its decades-long history, the digital humanities did not have a core set of values by which its scholars identified themselves or operated. In describing the process and significance of establishing a values statement, Spiro goes on to recommend example values documents, including the American Library Association's "Core Values of Librarianship." Spiro writes that "this list of eleven values emphasizes the civic role that libraries play in promoting access, confidentiality/privacy, democracy, diversity, education and lifelong learning, intellectual freedom, preservation, the public good, professionalism, service, and social responsibility" (21). She goes on to discuss the potential importance of a core set of values for digital humanities, as a field that bridges academic organizations and libraries: "Bridging these two communities, the digital humanities community brings together core scholarly values such as critical dialogue and free inquiry with an ethic focused on the democratic sharing of ideas" (21). It is notable that it is a white woman and LIS professional who is advocating for this, even though digital humanities itself has historically been white and male.[5]

The debate about the soul of DH took on a very different tenor and a much more public form in the *Los Angeles Review of Books* (*LARB*), where Daniel Allington, Sarah Brouillette, and David Golumbia warned us about the stakes of not establishing our values, arguing that the digital humanities had become complicit in the neoliberal "takeover" of the university (2016). Responses were swift and withering. One commenter described the article as "a shockingly one-sided, narrow, and insulting analysis," another stated it was "needlessly oversimplified polemicizing," while yet another described the tone of the article as one of "a deep and slightly paranoid sense of insecurity." For a field known for its niceness, criticism was not a pill easily swallowed.

In recent years, however, we have seen work in the digital humanities that has greatly diversified and become more inclusive. In addition to the plethora of projects and initiatives around Anglo, early American, and European authors and contexts, we now see projects like the Colored Conventions Project (CCP), which built a feminist collective and distributed community around a digital archive of the nineteenth-century Colored Conventions and the celebration of Douglass Day through transcribe-a-thons, and the Torn Apart/Separados project, which describes itself as "a rapidly deployed critical data & visualization intervention in the USA's 2018 'Zero Tolerance Policy' for asylum seekers at the US Ports of Entry and the humanitarian crisis that has followed" (Mobilized Humanities Collaboration 2018). These advances, however, are *in spite of*, not *because of* the evolution in digital humanities as a field. Title VI of the Civil Rights Act of 1964 would seemingly prevent discrimination in academic settings on "the basis of race, color, and national origin," based on the principle of equality, but the reality is a field rife with disparity in terms of funding, opportunities, and resources, all symptoms of institutional and structural racism. This is a reminder that there are material consequences that are evidently political, regardless of any discourse on niceness or neutrality. It is exceptional when projects receive the level of funding and support that CCP did, and it almost always involves the already overburdened faculty, students, and staff taking great risks in launching projects that later go on to receive public acclaim, as was the case with Torn Apart/Separados. Such work is not new to BIPOC folx in the academy, who are taking risks large and small, every day, to do our jobs, to improve our institutions, and to do good by our communities.

"WORKING IDENTITY" AND PRECARIOUS LABOR

Of the many incendiary claims made in the *LARB* piece by Allington, Brouillette, and Golumbia, one that really struck a chord with critics, was the argument that digital humanities promoted "the rebranding of insecure campus employment as an empowering 'alt-ac' career choice, and the redefinition of technical expertise as a form (indeed, the superior form) of humanist knowledge" (2016). One vocal critic responded in the comments by writing, "The implication that all academics who refer to themselves as 'alt ac' are there because they could not do 'better' (presumably, as TT academics) is insulting to everyone involved." At this point, it may be helpful to backtrack a bit and ask: What exactly is meant by the term *alt-ac*? What parallels do we see elsewhere in the academy? Why is the term so contentious? And what does this have to do with librarians of color?

Bethany Nowviskie and Jason Rhody (NEH Office of Digital Humanities) are credited with coining the term *alt-ac* in a series of tweets in 2009, "to describe the scholarly work performed by many of us in and in the orbit of the academy who do not hold traditional faculty jobs but do perform scholarly labor" (Rogers 2013; Posner 2013). In a report for the Scholarly Communication Institute, Katina Rogers wrote:

The changing nature of career paths for humanities scholars is an issue of particular concern to digital humanities practitioners, who have long been working in hybrid roles that combine elements of traditional scholarship, like research and teaching, with other elements, such as software development, librarianship, high-level administrative responsibilities, and more. (2013, 3)

Though some find the term problematic, following the economic crisis of 2008, these non-tenure-track academic positions seemed a godsend for humanities PhDs for whom there were dwindling job prospects. As Miriam Posner stated at the American Studies Association in 2013, "For many grad students, alt-ac has been a revelation. It's so important for Ph.D. students to know that you can, in fact, work as something other than a faculty member with your Ph.D. And you can love this work and feel that you're using what you're [*sic*] learned in your program, too." What became troubling, as Posner and others have noted, is that alt-ac as an additional career trajectory was quickly lauded "as a solution to the academic jobs crisis" (Posner 2013). The rise of the alt-ac, in an age of increasing contingency and economic retrenchment in the university, boded poorly for the future of humanities PhDs. As Posner noted in the same talk, in addition to the rewarding and challenging nature of the work, there are also many downsides to alt-ac jobs: these jobs tend to be insecure, have little to no representation in faculty governance, tend to be underpaid, are often short-term, and you don't own your work the way a faculty member might own her scholarly work.

These alt-ac, contingent, term appointments are also how we came to be in libraries. Anne, in 2014, accepted a position as a "digital scholar" at a small liberal arts college in Southern California. It was a position funded by a Mellon humanities grant, a collaboration between a faculty member and the library, which would provide funding to create a "digital liberal arts program" (essentially a digital humanities program at a liberal arts school). This grant would also provide bridge funding to transition the three-year appointment into a permanent position. She would become a full-time employee, neither librarian nor faculty, physically situated in the library and teaching courses among the faculty. At a small resource-poor institution, this position was designed to be the "lonely only" digital person on campus, the "miracle worker."[6] For Anne, she was the only Asian American in a library where all but one of the librarians were white. Faculty and staff were confused by her status: Was she a librarian? Was she faculty? Was she staff? Did she get a vote in faculty governance? What department did she teach in? Who evaluated her teaching? Which onboarding training did she attend as a new employee? These questions became increasingly difficult to wade through as the political climate changed on campus and as resources became more scarce. Her teaching load increased while her coordination, programming, and consultation work did not. And as the original three-year term came to a close, a change in administrators meant a change in institutional priorities and commitments. For those in the libraries, this kind of appointment will sound familiar, as it resembles temporary diversity residencies and newer library positions in emerging fields where institutions are unsure about making long-term commitments.

Toward the end of their doctoral education, Kush secured a yearlong postdoctoral fellowship at the humanities center of the same university where they completed their PhD. Building on an extensive set of experiences in arts and humanities program coordination, academic mentoring, public engagement, and undergraduate teaching, this role and its nontraditional focus on academic administration, research, and teaching were deeply transformative for Kush. The position enabled Kush to deepen cross-campus connections and meaningfully integrate them into thinking about the publics of engaged humanities work. This collaborative role allowed them to practice

new connections with academic librarians and members of the teaching and learning center around digital humanities pedagogy and research. In their postdoctoral
work, Kush also served as the codirector of the university's graduate teacher certificate
in digital media program, supporting the professional development of graduate students interested in developing critical pedagogy that engages in digital practice and
inquiry. Amid the center's leadership shift, Kush's yearlong appointment got extended
by another year, but the questions from human resources on how a PhD in architecture mapped onto an "alt-ac" public and digital humanities career remained. And
these questions were not without consequence. Like Anne, Kush was the only person
of color in an organization of otherwise all-white full-time staff. Additionally, as an
international candidate, Kush's advocacy around work sponsorship in an increasingly
anti-immigrant climate meant that the experience and labor of proving their intellectual worth in the face of recurring microaggressions were unique to them.

Such narratives are a common refrain for those of us who have been in and out
of alt-ac positions. We've been in libraries, in digital humanities centers, in research
clusters, in postdocs, in technologist and programmer positions, and fellowships.
Similar contingent positions are also prevalent in libraries in the form of internships,
residencies, fellowships, grant-funded positions, and other term appointments. Often,
these librarians are floating between departments, asked to learn about the operations
of new environments and to make substantive, structural change while essentially
being outsiders whose appointments have end dates. In many cases, the conditions of
precarity are made ever more uncertain by additional vectors of insecurity determined
by one's race, gender identity, religious identity, economic status, immigration status,
or family status. In our cases, we lacked what Harris calls "the property functions of
whiteness," which Ladson-Billings describes as "rights of disposition, rights to use and
enjoyment, reputation and status property, and the absolute right to exclude" (Harris
1993; Ladson Billings 1998, 59). Because we are not in possession of the "treasured
property" of whiteness, we become the ones who are excluded and whose security and
employment are always under threat, sometimes overtly. Of paramount importance
for many of these positions like ours is the burden placed on the individuals hired as
librarians or staff members of color (who may or may not also be burdened by student
loans, care responsibilities, the threat of deportation, and so on) who are, by virtue of
their very racially marked bodies, hired to be diversity workers and asked to address the
prevailing whiteness and homogeneity of libraries and digital humanities.

Though we do not have demographic data on digital humanists, the ALA has published data on libraries, citing that 86.7 percent of librarians identify as white and

81 percent identify as female (Rosa and Henke 2017).[7] Numerous studies and presentations in recent years have noted the impact of such white work environments on librarians and staff of color. As legal scholars Carbado and Gulati describe it, we librarians of color spend a good deal of our personal resources on "working identity," or negotiating and performing our identities to conform to or match the dominant expectations of our workplace culture (2013, 223). They go on to say that "performing identity consumes resources in the form of time and effort, which is one of the costs of discrimination" (229). As Brown and colleagues observed, "This demands learning about not only the organizational culture but also the white 'professional' culture, all in an attempt to 'fit' within our institution's boundaries of whiteness" (2018, 169–170). Performing our identities, molding ourselves to "fit" into our workplace, overcoming "vocational awe"—these are all enormous tasks of affective labor that take a toll on our physical and emotional health and well-being (Drake 2017; Ettarh 2018). And this only applies to those benign, "neutral," well-meaning workplaces, not those where fellow colleagues and supervisors are overtly hostile, unwelcoming, or abusive. Such daily experiences often lead to feelings of isolation and alienation, depression, burnout, and other more extreme symptoms of "low morale" among employees (Kendrick 2017; Brown et al. 2018).

As Sara Ahmed so poignantly reminds us, "If institutionalizing diversity is a goal for diversity workers, it does not necessarily mean it is the institution's goal" (2012, 22). Likewise, "diversity work is hard because it can involve doing within institutions what would not otherwise be done *by* them" (25). If anything, institutions, libraries and digital humanities spaces included, are designed to resist efforts to diversify and become inclusive, and those who are tasked with making long-term structural changes must "fight their way" (26). Is there potential, however, to make this fight more manageable, and the work more sustaining for those who are charged with or moved to do it?

RADICAL CARE, OR HOW TO DO BETTER

Perhaps it comes as no surprise that the changes we have seen in recent years in the digital humanities have not been spontaneous. Much of the progress has come after ample critique. In 2011, in response to the back-and-forth debates, the navelgazing, and the boundary setting that was happening in digital humanities, the #transformDH collective, a group of queer and BIPOC (Black, Indigenous, and People of Color) graduate students and postdocs, came together at the American Studies Association and issued a series of critical questions for digital humanists. Anne was among this collective, who identified itself somewhat facetiously as "an academic guerrilla movement seeking to (re)define capital-letter Digital Humanities as a force for transformative scholarship by collecting, sharing, and highlighting projects that push at its boundaries and work for social justice, accessibility, and inclusion" (#transformDH 2011; Bailey et al. 2016). Within a few weeks, we started to receive backlash. In one of the kinder critical blog responses, Roger Whitson wrote,

> Do we really need guerrilla movements? Are war metaphors, or concepts of overturning and redefining, truly the right kind of metaphors to use when talking about change in the digital humanities? It seems to me that the word "guerilla" reappropriates the collaborative good will of the digital humanities.... The digital humanities doesn't need to be changed. I can already see it changing the atmosphere of the MLA, making it easier for people to connect with each other, enjoy their time together, and conceptualize new and exciting work. (qtd. in Cecire 2012)

Whitson's use of the phrase "collaborative good will" to describe the beneficence of the field aligns with what some had termed its "niceness"—a pervasive and recurring issue in numerous fields and disciplines.

As #transformDH and others would point out, some found the DH brand of welcome more inviting than others, and this had much to do with one's embodied identity, one's marked or unmarked body. Natalia Cecire, in response to Whitson, critiqued this notion, writing,

> The valuation of the guerilla, the oppositional, the maroon, and the fugitive that characterizes #transformDH is, as I see it, clearly indebted to the legacies of queer theory and critical race studies.... This is not a language that comports very well with the dominant rhetorics of digital humanities, which emphasize openness, collaboration, and inclusiveness—which are, in short, liberal. (2012)

Again and again, the language of openness, of collaboration, of inclusiveness is reiterated in relation to the identity of digital humanities. As junior scholars of color on the receiving end of criticism from (often) senior scholars in the field, it did not feel welcome and inclusive to us. Indeed, Alexis Lothian would write, "People feel fannish about digital humanities and that digital humanities' networks operate like a fandom" (2018). For all its talk-friendly inclusivity, the debates that unfolded in this period were "shaped like fannish conflicts" (Lothian 2011).

In 2018, another group project and public performance called #OurDHIs at a summer digital humanities institute brought to life the continuities and collaborations within and beyond the #transformDH movement. #OurDhIs served as a call-for-action hashtag to extend the political origins of the previously successful #MyDHIs organizing into a community praxis around what DH pedagogy is and can be. Kush was part of this organizing effort, or "interruption," as it was referred to by a few nonparticipating members during the weeklong event. Collaboration was key to this class project, but so was critique—critique of the erasures and silencing of discourses on race, Indigenous studies, and social justice, and postcolonial, queer, and feminist scholarship in the practices of the capital-letter Digital Humanities. The participants' goal was not to reduce #OurDhIs to a singular moment, but rather to position it as a supportive, critical, and living framework that interconnects the layered histories, sites, and minoritized communities of digital humanities scholarship and pedagogy.

From our individual and collective work, we want to turn to the work of adrienne maree brown, who asks us to "begin to understand what is possible when a collective of humans is not afraid to feel life together" (2019, 273). Already, we see groups like We Here in LIS cohere would-be marginalized individuals into radical loving, caring communities that help underrepresented researchers, librarians, teachers, and activists to sustain each other through community building. For us, our ongoing work with our respective collectives—for Anne that includes #transformDH and the Situated Critical Race+Media (SCRAM) collective, and for Kush that means #OurDHIs and the Pedagogy of the Digitally Oppressed #AnticolonialDH—have been instrumental to our own academic activist work.

Most crucially, these collectives have provided space not only where we can come together as allies in struggle, but also where we can model and enact care to help the marginal survive academic or hostile spaces. In some spheres, this type of activity has been termed building "counterspaces" for peer mentorship. In the case of Pedagogy of the Digitally Oppressed, for instance, we call ourselves colearners and activists. In other spaces, as in the case of SCRAM, we call ourselves "kin" (SCRAM 2019). These counterspaces are made functional through programming, regular meetings, cowriting, professional mentorship, and informal relationships. We must recognize, however, that this kind of community building requires a substantial investment of added invisible labor that is seldom recognized or rewarded by our institutions. For some of us, though, this is pleasurable, life-sustaining labor. This is how we care for each other and ourselves. It is the kind of labor that keeps us in our jobs and as part of our professions. We are always reminded that the neoliberal academy will prioritize efficiency-centered interventions over lived and structurally transformative relationships. In spite of that, we nurture our relationships, even when they may slow down the system. It is relationships that will always serve as the organization's nurturing core.

CONCLUSION

Ultimately, we hope this chapter illuminates the complexities experienced by folx working at the intersection of libraries and digital humanities who are also inhabiting racialized or "Othered" identities. For these individuals, there is a pressure to "build" and "make" (programs, projects, relationships, among others), often while simultaneously being expected to bring an uncritical "diversity" to these programs. This practice results in erasing difference and excluding the valuable perspectives, experiences, and contributions such varied situated knowledge would bring to these contexts. This experience does not need to be the norm, however, and we have the opportunity to do better, to build the feminist, antiracist, and anticolonial digital humanities library spaces of our dreams. It is about more than simply bringing in people with different backgrounds or embodying different identity markers in white spaces. It's about recognizing the White Supremacist histories embedded within the institutions and systems where we work and live, and learning ways to resist and to build generative, nurturing relationships from within. It's about making each other feel *cared for*, *seen*, and *heard*. Those of us who have the power to shape our organizations must intentionally work toward making our workplaces spaces of love and growth, rather than oppression and extraction. As adrienne maree brown asks us to consider, "What would happen if we aligned with a pleasure politic, especially as people who are surviving long-term oppressive conditions?" (2019, 5). We live and work in oppressive structures that do not value us, yet want to take from us. We do not have to let this happen, though. We can take small steps toward change to help ourselves and others feel loved and cared for. We can also endeavor to change those structures, break them down, make them better.

NOTES

1. In general, we personally identify as "Brown" in the way that Carbado and Gulati (2000) describe as "sense of self" identity. Likewise, our workplaces and external institutions have also attributed racialized identities ("attributal" identity) to us because of our racialized names, our marked bodies, and our immigration statuses.

2. Intersectionality is a critical framework developed by Kimberlé Crenshaw in the late 1980s and early 1990s to explore the overlapping dimensions of Black women's identities that determine their experiences.

3. Though the "big tent" circus metaphor has been used by numerous people, here we cite Alan Liu, who both defines and historicizes the term and then calls for us to move away from it: "The 'big tent' metaphor, of course, comes down to us from old-timey showcases of mass experience

such as nineteenth-century tent revivals and big-top circuses. … Circuses, for example, were spectacles of variety. … We need new paradigms and *dispositifs* or, in computer-speak, *platforms* for diversity that move the modern democratic paradox of open and closed (inclusive and exclusive) beyond nineteenth- and early-twentieth-century paradigms of mass 'variety'" (2018). Laura Braunstein defines digital humanities as a "community of practice," meaning "lot of people doing a lot of different things" (Kim 2016).

4. There are numerous blogs, articles, and chapters that attempt to do this, including a series of articles published in the *Digital Humanities Quarterly*, numerous panels at the Modern Language Association annual meetings, and chapters such as Matthew Kirschenbaum's "What Is Digital Humanities and What's It Doing in English Departments?" where he points interested readers toward the Wikipedia article on the topic.

5. This has been changing in recent years, and it is made ever more visible with the efforts of groups like #transformDH and #BlackDH, but examples abound. Tara McPherson notes the whiteness of DH in "Why Are the Digital Humanities So White?" Bethany Nowviskie discussed this dynamic in her blog post "What Do Girls Dig?" (2012), which notes that the NEH-funded Digging into Data Challenge Conference included only two female speakers out of thirty-three, and in a follow-up tweet acknowledging, "I'm so used to being the only woman in the room." In 2015, in a talk at the International Digital Humanities Conference, Deb Verhoeven called out the "parade of patriarchs" and told the "blokes" in the auditorium, "You have made a world designed around ensuring your own personal comfort, but it's not comfortable for many, many other people. … This is not about issuing another policy advisory for 'inclusion.' This is not about developing a new checklist to mitigate your biases. And it's definitely not about inviting a token female speaker to join you—this actually needs to be about your plans to exit the stage" (2015). Often, the most striking example is the list of course offerings and instructors for the Digital Humanities Summer Institute (where we have both taught), where in any given year, more of the instructors are white men named John or Chris than women *or* People of Color. Notably, in the cases of McPherson and Nowviskie, at the time, one considered race and the other considered gender, but not both together.

6. As Paige Morgan describes it, in 2017 the Digital Libraries Federation announced a working group for "miracle workers," or "digital humanities and digital scholarship librarians who are often tasked with accomplishing monumental goals with minimal support" (Morgan 2017). Though it was meant to be playful, many took issue with the term, arguing that it obscures the deep expertise of these professionals and the very real challenges they face in their institutions.

7. With regard to demographic data on digital humanists, again, arguments about "who counts" as a digital humanist makes this kind of work impossible.

BIBLIOGRAPHY

Ahmed, Sara. 2012. *On Being Included: Racism and Diversity in Institutional Life*. Durham, NC: Duke University Press.

Allington, Daniel, Sarah Brouillette, and David Golumbia. 2016. "Neoliberal Tools (and Archives): A Political History of Digital Humanities." *Los Angeles Review of Books*, May 1, 2016. https://lareviewofbooks.org/article/neoliberal-tools-archives-political-history-digital-humanities/#.

Bailey, Moya, Anne Cong-Huyen, Alexis Lothian, and Amanda Phillips. 2016. "Reflections on a Movement: #transformDH Growing Up." In *Debates in the Digital Humanities 2016,* edited by Matthew K. Gold and Lauren Klein, 71–79. Minneapolis: University of Minnesota Press.

Bilge, Sirma. 2013. "Intersectionality Undone: Saving Intersectionality from Feminist Intersectionality Studies." *Du Bois Review* 10 (2): 405–424.

Boyles, Christina, Anne Cong-Huyen, Carrie Johnston, Jim McGrath, and Amanda Phillips. 2018. "Precarious Labor and the Digital Humanities." *American Quarterly* 70 (3): 693–700. https://doi.org /10.1353/aq.2018.0054.

Brook, Freeda, Dave Ellenwood, and Althea Eannace Lazzaro. 2015. "In Pursuit of Antiracist Social Justice: Denaturalizing Whiteness in the Academic Library." *Library Trends* 64 (2): 246–284. https:// doi.org/10.1353/lib.2015.0048.

brown, adrienne maree, ed. 2019. *Pleasure Activism: The Politics of Feeling Good.* Chico, CA: AK Press.

Brown, Jennifer, Jennifer Ferretti, Sofia Leung, and Marisa Méndez-Brady. 2018. "We Here: Speaking Our Truth." *Library Trends* 67 (1): 163–181. https://doi.org/10.1353/lib.2018.0031.

Carbado, Devon W., and Mitu Gulati. 2000. "Working Identity." *Cornell Law Review* 85 (5): 1259–1308.

Cecire, Natalia. 2012. "In Defense of Transforming DH." *Works Cited* (blog), January 8, 2012. https://nataliacecire.blogspot.com/2012/01/in-defense-of-transforming-dh.html.

Cooper, Brittney. 2015. "Intersectionality." In *The Oxford Handbook of Feminist Theory,* edited by Lisa Disch and Mary Hawkesworth. New York: Oxford University Press. https://doi.org/10.1093 /oxfordhb/9780199328581.013.20.

Delgado, Richard. 1989. "Storytelling for Oppositionists and Others: A Plea for Narrative." *Michigan Law Review* 87 (8): 2411–2441. https://doi.org/10.2307/1289308.

Delgado, Richard, and Jean Stefancic. 2001. *Critical Race Theory: An Introduction.* New York: New York University Press.

Digital Humanities Summer Institute. n.d. "Course Archive (2001–2019)." Digital Humanities Summer Institute, Electronic Textual Cultures Lab, University of Victoria. Accessed June 27, 2020. Archived at https://web.archive.org/web/20200818171028/https://dhsi.org/course-archive-2001 -2020/.

Do, Anh. 2018. "Vietnamese Americans Rally in Little Saigon against Trump Administration's Push to Deport Thousands of War Refugees." *Los Angeles Times,* December 15, 2018. https://www.latimes .com/local/lanow/la-me-ln-vietnamese-refugee-march-20181215-story.html.

Drake, Jarrett M. 2017. "I'm Leaving the Archival Profession: It's Better This Way." *Medium* (blog), June 26, 2017. https://medium.com/on-archivy/im-leaving-the-archival-profession-it-s-better-this -way-ed631c6d72fe.

Dunst, Charles. 2018. "Trump Administration Quietly Backs Off on Deporting Vietnamese Immigrants." *New York Times,* Nov. 22, 2018. https://www.nytimes.com/2018/11/22/world/asia /vietnam-trump-immigrants-deport.html.

Ettarh, Fobazi. 2018. "Vocational Awe and Librarianship: The Lies We Tell Ourselves." *In the Library with the Lead Pipe*, January 10, 2018. http://www.inthelibrarywiththeleadpipe.org/2018/vocational-awe/.

Gold, Matthew K., and Lauren Klein, eds. 2012. *Debates in the Digital Humanities*. Minneapolis: University of Minnesota Press.

Harris, Angela. 2001. "Foreword." In *Critical Race Theory: An Introduction*, by Richard Delgado and Jean Stefancic, xv–xx. New York: New York University Press.

Harris, Cheryl I. 1993. "Whiteness as Property." *Harvard Law Review* 106 (8): 1707–1791.

Kendrick, Kaetrena Davis. 2017. "The Low Morale Experience of Academic Librarians: A Phenomenological Study." *Journal of Library Administration* 57 (8): 846–878. https://doi.org/10.1080/01930826.2017.1368325.

Kim, Claire Jean. 1999. "The Racial Triangulation of Asian Americans." *Politics and Society* 27 (1): 105–138.

Kim, Joshua. 2016. "6 Questions for a Digital Humanities Librarian." *Inside Higher Ed*, August 17, 2016. https://www.insidehighered.com/blogs/technology-and-learning/6-questions-digital-humanities-librarian.

Ladson-Billings, Gloria. 1998. "Just What Is Critical Race Theory and What's It Doing in a Nice Field Like Education?" *International Journal of Qualitative Studies in Education* 11 (1): 7–24. https://doi.org/10.1080/095183998236863.

Liu, Alan. 2018. "Digital Humanities Diversity as Technical Problem." *Alan Liu* (personal blog), January 15, 2018. https://doi.org/10.21972/G21T07.

Lothian, Alexis. 2011. "Mixed Metaphors, Marked Bodies, and the Question of 'Theory.'" *HASTAC*, September 4, 2011. https://www.hastac.org/blogs/alexislothian/2011/11/04/mixed-metaphors-marked-bodies-and-question-theory.

Lothian, Alexis. 2018. "From Transformative Works to #transformDH: Digital Humanities as (Critical) Fandom." *American Quarterly* 70 (3): 371–393. doi:10.1353/aq.2018.0027.

Macharia, Keguro. 2017. "Survival in Audre Lorde." *The New Inquiry*, August 25, 2017. https://thenewinquiry.com/blog/survival-in-audre-lorde/.

McPherson, Tara. 2012. "Why Are the Digital Humanities So White? Or Thinking the Histories of Race and Computation." In *Debates in the Digital Humanities*, edited by Matthew K. Gold and Lauren Klein, 139–158. Minneapolis: University of Minnesota Press.

Mobilized Humanities Collaboration. 2018. "Torn Apart / Separados, Volume 1." Torn Apart / Separados. https://xpmethod.columbia.edu/torn-apart/volume/1/.

Mohanty, Chandra T. 2003. *Feminism without Borders*. Durham, NC: Duke University Press.

Morgan, Paige. 2017. "Please Don't Call Me a Miracle Worker." *Paige Morgan* (personal blog), December 17, 2017. http://blog.paigemorgan.net/articles/17/please-dont.html.

Neely, Teresa Y., and Lorna Peterson. 2007. "Achieving Racial and Ethnic Diversity among Academic and Research Librarians: The Recruitment, Retention, and Advancement of Librarians of Color." Association of College and Research Libraries white paper, July 2007. https://crln.acrl.org /index.php/crlnews/article/view/7869.

Nowviskie, Bethany. 2012. "What Do Girls Dig?" In *Debates in the Digital Humanities*, edited by Matthew K. Gold and Lauren Klein, 235–240. Minneapolis: University of Minnesota Press.

Pedagogy of the Digitally Oppressed. 2019. https://pedagogyofthedigitallyoppressed.hcommons.org.

Piepzna-Samarasinha, Leah Lakshmi. "Care as Pleasure." In *Pleasure Activism: The Politics of Feeling Good,* edited by adrienne maree brown, 313–315. Chico, CA: AK Press.

Posner, Miriam. 2013. "What Alt-Ac Can Do, and What It Can't." *Miriam Posner* (personal blog), November 25, 2013. https://miriamposner.com/blog/what-alt-ac-can-do-and-what-it-cant/.

Rogers, Katina. 2013. "Humanities Unbound: Supporting Humanities Careers and Scholarship beyond the Tenure Track." Scholars' Lab, University of Virginia Library. April 23, 2013. https://scholarslab.lib .virginia.edu/blog/humanities-unbound-careers-scholarship-beyond-the-tenure-track/.

Rosa, Kathy, and Kelsey Henke. 2017. *2017 ALA Demographic Study*. Chicago: American Library Association Office of Research and Statistics.

Schlesselman-Tarango, Gina. 2016. "The Legacy of Lady Bountiful: White Women in the Library." *Library Trends* 64 (4): 667–686. https://doi.org/10.1353/lib.2016.0015.

SCRAM. 2019. "Love Letters." Media Map. http://www.mediamaplab.com/#filter=.love-letters.

Spiro, Lisa. 2013. "'This Is Why We Fight': Defining the Values of the Digital Humanities." In *Debates in the Digital Humanities*, edited by Matthew K. Gold and Lauren Klein, 16–35. Minneapolis: University of Minnesota Press. http://dhdebates.gc.cuny.edu/debates/text/13.

#transformDH. n.d. "About #transformDH." TransformDH.org. Accessed July 10, 2020. http:// transformdh.org/about-transformdh/.

Verhoeven, Deb. 2015. "Has Anyone Seen A Woman?" Speech delivered at Digital Humanities Conference 2015, Sydney, July 2, Australia, 2015. https://figshare.com/articles/Be_More_Than _Binary/1529347.

Wiltz, Teresa. 2016. "What Crimes Are Eligible for Deportation?" Pew Charitable Trusts. December 21, 2016 https://www.pewtrusts.org/en/research-and-analysis/blogs/stateline/2016/12/21/what -crimes-are-eligible-for-deportation.

12

PRAXIS FOR THE PEOPLE
Critical Race Theory and Archival Practice

Rachel E. Winston

The archival profession is nearly 88 percent white, with Black archivists like me making up not even 3 percent of the population (Society of American Archivists 2005). To address the overwhelming demographic whiteness of the field, the Society of American Archivists (SAA) has established programs like the Harold T. Pinkett Student of Color Award, of which I am a past recipient, to help diversify the profession.[1] While participating in initiatives like the Pinkett have been instrumental in my training, I also credit my professional success to the network of librarians, archivists, and colleagues of color who provide consistent support and encouragement. Relationships formed through scholarship and leadership programs, community work, conferences, campus affiliation, and familial connections are invaluable. This nationwide network is crucial, as I find myself one of fewer than five Black professional staff and the sole Black archivist in an entire library system at one of the largest universities in the country. Added to that, I focus almost exclusively on collections documenting Black people across space and time. Though the lack of professional diversity is disappointing, it is not a deterrent—what I bring to this work, and what brought me to this work, is my identity as a Black woman. Any way you slice it, my work is interesting, challenging, exciting, and highly racialized.

As a member of the professional minority, I feel a great deal of responsibility to the people represented in collections, the donors whose collections I steward, and my fellow People of Color (POC) colleagues. I must use every bit of privilege my position affords to support and create space for my fellow POC. As "the diversity" in an institution, I also have a self-imposed mandate to do this work without being siloed, as a way to garner the greatest support for the collections I work with. This necessitates putting myself in spaces and conversations I do not always want to be in, and requires a great deal of emotional labor once there. I have to be intentional about not appearing angry, even when I have the right to be, and being excited to collaborate, even when collaboration tests my bandwidth (though it is easy to disregard invitations to collaborate that seem to come around only once a year, in February).

The dimensions of whiteness in archives are twofold—in the workplace and in the collections. I feel its oppressive presence when I walk into the library building and when I walk into the archival stacks. Working with records documenting Black populations, I confront on a regular basis global anti-Black racism—that is, discriminatory beliefs and practices against Black and Afro-descended people across the world.[2] There is no escaping racism and violence, considering the Black experiences commonly found in an imperial archive—I interact with documents related to slavery and Black communities existing under a legacy of colonial empire. Doing this work, I do not have the privilege of turning away or disengaging with present and historical traumas, both of which take their toll.[3] In a world where anti-Blackness is as pervasive as the weather (Sharpe 2016), my work must demonstrate my high regard for Black lives past and present, and dedication to preserving Black legacies. I want my professional contributions to be an act of counternarrative, and in that, a means by which to challenge the normalization of erasure surrounding Black death.[4]

As a Black woman archivist, I am deeply familiar with the silences that exist in documenting Black life, and specifically the lives of Black women. Effective silencing does not require a conspiracy, or even a political consensus—its roots are structural (Trouillot 1995, 106). Within the structure of contemporary society, the Black woman's world has been rooted in the periphery to those most likely to keep records of any kind, white men and women, making manuscript collections on Black women scarce (White 1987, 237). Systems of oppression, sexism, and global anti-Blackness have created an archival ecosystem where Black women are consistently underrepresented. Even as an experienced researcher and archivist, I encounter difficulty identifying Black women in collections with regularity. Too often, we are documented, if at all, with language that does not render us visible. Though troubling on its own, this also calls for us to refashion collection descriptions and carefully reconsider what constitutes a "Black collection." If we are difficult to locate in conventional collections, using accepted vocabularies, perhaps new definitions and language can provide alternate points of access. To quote Saidiya Hartman, "The loss of stories sharpens the hunger for them; it is tempting to fill in the gaps and to provide closure where there is none" (2008, 8).

The hunger for stories and noticeable representation gaps found in archival collections demonstrates further the need for greater diversity in the profession. As archivist Kellee Warren notes, "The relationship that Black women have to the archives in which they are treated as subjects make Black women archivists a unique, if rare group (because of the paucity of archival materials that represent the lived experiences of black women and the small number of black women in the archives profession)" (2016, 777). The sisterhood in this rare group and the community of Black, women of color, and nonbinary archivists is invaluable. Regularly, we serve as peer mentors to each other, providing emotional and professional support, sharing similar experiences, and talking through different challenges (Powell et al. 2018, 7). As we continue on, we must consider how we welcome new professionals into the field and collectively work to dismantle the systems that keep many of us from reaching our highest success. The wider archival community must recognize that "the unearthing of silences requires not only extra labor at the archives but is also a project linked to interpretation" (Trouillot 1995, 58). To do that work, we must bring in voices that have been pushed to the margins, and let them lead. It is in our collective best interest to not only train but also support professionals who understand and can speak directly to the nuances of collections documenting ethnic and historically marginalized communities. Even with attempted "objectivity," finding aids and descriptions created for archives of People of Color or ethnic communities and authored by someone from outside of that community are often discernable. The outside gaze reveals itself through language. Here, word choice creates barriers to access for those most likely to use and see themselves represented in a particular collection, and intentionality aside, the inclusion of problematic, offensive terminology or the exclusion of informed detail that leads to erasure is troubling. Archivists from diverse backgrounds offer an important and underutilized perspective in the field.

In my five years as a professional, I have come to understand the culture of archival repositories and the organization of archival records. I have also grown familiar with discomfort and the emotional labor required for success. As a researcher looking for records that provide a glimpse into the lives of the enslaved, I know well the game of chance that is played when requesting incriminating records from repositories staffed by white people, where those records are often hidden under layers of silence or questionable descriptions. Navigating racialized channels of information finding is quotidian. Like many archivists of color, the majority of my professional

skills—processing collections, creating and publishing finding aids, providing reference, working with donors, and so on—are utilized while in my institutional role,
where I am not solely responsible for determining my priorities. It is on my own time
outside of work where I am able to fully engage my expertise in justice-based and
community-centered archival work.[5] The professional tension(s) experienced as an
archivist of color provides an opportunity to consider Critical Race Theory (CRT) as a
framework to move our professional practice forward. Engaging CRT offers a way to
begin systematically addressing White Supremacy and the colonial thumbprint that
dominate archival repositories and consequently influence our work.

In the spirit of CRT and its central tenet of storytelling, this chapter began in
autobiographical form to offer my personal experience as a counternarrative. In sharing my positionality, I hope to give voice to some of the challenges Black women
archivists encounter while trying to be our best professional selves. In full transparency, this is uncomfortable for me—I tend to shy away from the spotlight, focusing
more on the work and its success than on the processes. However, in talking about
my experience, I aim to demonstrate the urgent need for greater considerations of
race and actionable methods to approach the legacy of structural racism in archives.

I begin my discussion of CRT in archival enterprise by reviewing previous scholarship on the topic. Attention is focused on CRT as a framework, with particular
emphasis on a branch of CRT that is action-oriented, critical race praxis (CRP). In
providing an example of how CRP has been applied in the field of education, I hope
to demonstrate how it is a viable methodology to employ in archives. I then consider
critical archival studies to explore how critical theory has been engaged within the
archival community, and how this scholarship works toward shared goals with CRT.
I conclude by fashioning what critical race praxis in archives might look like and
questioning how it may further conversations in the profession and help us achieve
tangible change. This process of change making is aligned with the idea of transformative librarianship, the application of TribalCrit, and the continuum of activist
librarians discussed in this volume.[6]

CRITICAL RACE THEORY IN ARCHIVES

Anthony Dunbar's 2006 article "Introducing Critical Race Theory into Archival Discourse: Getting the Conversation Started" is the first piece of literature to directly
engage CRT in the archival profession. As a framework, Dunbar offers CRT as a
systematic approach to address cultural and social issues documented in archival

records and impacting archivists working in repositories (2006, 110). Specifically, he examines how CRT's methodological concepts of counterstories, microaggressions, and social justice have presence in archival praxis. Engaging these concepts in archivy provides a method to create space for racially and nonracially marginalized voices to be elevated. Dunbar suggests CRT's usefulness not only in an administrative focus, but also as a tool for examining the historical focus of a record—including its content, context, and structure—which thereby emphasizes the social implications of archival discourse (2006, 119–122).

CRT provides a framework from which aspects of the archival profession can be evaluated and improved, including collections stewardship and the archival workforce. As pioneering archivist and archival scholar Harold T. Pinkett asserts, "American archival theory does not exist as a systematically formulated body of ideas. It is essentially an aggregation of ideas drawn from well-tested and widely accepted European archival principles, and of pragmatic concepts developed to meet special needs of American archival administration and democratic traditions" (1981, 222). As a practice-driven profession, junior to European archival enterprise, Western ideals lie at the foundation of our praxis. Indeed, whiteness exists as the terra firma of the archives profession in the United States and informs the very formation of its praxis (Ramirez 2015, 340). Considering the European roots of our profession and scholarship, a CRT approach allows for critical examination to be made in specific relation to making our praxis attend to difference. To push Dunbar's conversation further, I would like to engage critical race praxis as a method to better understand archival work and the role the archival community can play in transforming these understandings into reality.

CRITICAL RACE THEORY AND PRAXIS

CRT first emerged from the field of critical legal scholarship and radical feminism in the 1970s. One of its principal founders, Derrick A. Bell, offered CRT as a mechanism for theorists to strive for specifically, more egalitarian state of affairs, and further, as a way to empower the traditionally excluded views and see all-inclusiveness as the ideal, out of a belief in collective wisdom (1995, 901). At its core, CRT asserts that racism is normal and ordinary. A product of social thought, racism is deeply embedded in the ingrained social structures that govern and affect our daily lives. Because of this, it can be hard to address and eliminate, because it must first be acknowledged (Delgado and Stefancic 2017, 8). Through CRT, we emphasize our marginality and turn it toward advantageous perspective building and concrete advocacy on behalf of those oppressed by race and other interlocking factors of gender, economic class, and sexual orientation (Bell 1995, 902)

In the late 1990s, legal scholar and Critical Race Theorist Eric K. Yamamoto pushed forward critical race praxis (CRP) as a way to provide structure to justice practice— which, though grounded in the messy and conflictual racial realities of those who experience it, can be difficult to define in a purely theoretical sense (1997, 875– 876). CRP, as an action-based framework grounding racial justice in concrete situations, starts with inquiry into the experiences and perceptions of racial groups and frontline justice practitioners (Yamamoto 1997, 881). CRP provides a way to move theoretical and intellectual discourse into practical action, as informed by the communities and lived experiences of those at stake. Yamamoto proposes four tenets: the conceptual, the performative, the material, and the reflexive.

Conceptual: focuses on the particulars and the context of a controversy or relationship in conflict by examining the racialization, heterosexism, patriarchy, class, and each of their interconnecting influences (1997, 878; 1999, 130).

Performative: raises the questions of "What?" and "Who should act?" in response to specific claims—responses to these questions "perform" to the specific case and dismantle subordinating social structures to rectify justice (1999, 131).

Material: highlights the material conditions of racial oppression and supports the idea that change is material when it is social structural and representational (1997, 880; 1999, 132).

Reflexive: alerts theorists, lawyers, and activists to reintegrate experience into practice and continually rebuild theory in light of the experiences of racial groups engaged in racial and antiracist struggles (1997, 881; 1999, 132).

APPLIED CRITICAL RACE PRAXIS

CRT and education scholar David O. Stovall has taken CRP beyond legal scholarship and applied it specifically to education. As a growing body of scholarship, CRT in education has been evolving since the late twentieth century. CRT was first introduced in education in 1995 by Gloria Ladson-Billings and William F. Tate as a framework both to underscore the school curriculum as a cultural artifact that upholds White Supremacy and disenfranchises many, and to democratize the education system. Discussions within the field of CRT in education can be instructive to archival enterprise, as much of our work supports the educational processes of research and instruction. CRT in education is commonly used as a framework to better understand and articulate social relationships and power structures in direct relation to race and racism in schools across the United States. Pushing discussions of CRT in education further, Stovall has engaged CRP with education (2013; Stovall et al. 2009) to better realize how scholars may suspend expertise and substitute it with the process of listening to members of communities with whom we work, with the specific intent to address identified issues (2013, 290). CRP in education positions the researcher to continually question their practice with community stakeholders (Stovall 2013, 292).

Grounding his argument in Yamamoto's CRP tenets, Stovall integrates theoretical constructs from educational, anthropological, sociological, legal, and public health scholarship to formulate a framework for CRP in education:

Commitment to on-the-ground work: theory should deal less with abstract concepts and be rooted in a tangible commitment to the physical, social, and intellectual support of communities experiencing educational injustice;

Social justice as an experienced phenomenon: justice work requires a material commitment to work with communities in reaching tangible goals;

Utilization of interdisciplinary approaches: it requires a commitment to use theoretical and methodological approaches to specifically address the racial, social, political, and economic concerns of communities;

Training others to move beyond the intellectual exercise of challenging dominant ideologies: it is necessary to continually develop the capacity of up-and-coming CRT scholars to engage communities and groups working for educational justice;

Commitment to self-care: justice work in education can be extremely taxing to the mind and body—it is imperative to commit ourselves to physical, mental, and spiritual well-being. (Stovall 2013, 294)

CRITICAL ARCHIVAL STUDIES

Introducing a critical framework to archival discourse creates space for those who want to approach information tenets with a critical social consciousness (Dunbar 2006, 111). Critical archival studies is a relatively recent movement in the archival field, gaining prominence only within the last decade. First introduced by Ricky Punzalan in 2010, critical archival studies is a growing dimension of archival scholarship. In fact, a 2017 special issue of the *Journal of Critical Library and Informa-tion Studies* focused entirely on the topic (Caswell, Punzalan, and Sangwand 2017). Blending critical studies and archival theory, critical archival studies provides an approach to consider the role of power in record creation, archival functions, the establishment of archival institutions, archival outreach and use and advocacy, who becomes archivists and how and why, and how we define and teach and practice core concepts (Caswell 2016, 3). Using this approach, archivists and scholars are able to evaluate the field in new ways, reconstructing both archival practice and theory. Ultimately, critical archival studies is an emancipatory project that seeks to trans-form both archival practice and research, and further, to interrogate how records contribute to what is wrong with the world, how records can be used to change it, and by whom (Sutherland 2017, 3; Caswell 2016, 5; Caswell, Punzalan, and Sang-wand 2017, 2).

Embracing critical archival studies means recognizing that theory and practice are a false binary, and that theoretical and political assumptions will always underlie the work of archives and archivists (Caswell, Punzalan, and Sangwand 2017, 5). Moving archival thinking into a social realm, critical archival studies provides a way "to lib-erate, interrogate, and usher in a 'real democracy,' where power is distributed more equitably, where White Supremacy and patriarchy and heteronormativity and other forms of oppression are named and challenged, where different worlds and different ways of being in those worlds are acknowledged and imagined and enacted" (6).

Archival scholar Michelle Caswell proposes a three-point definition, suggesting that critical archival studies

(1) explains what is wrong with the current state of archival and recordkeeping prac-tice and research and identifies who can change it and how;
(2) posits achievable goals for how archives and recordkeeping practice and research in archival studies can and should change; and
(3) provides norms and strategies and mechanisms for forming such critique. (Cas-well 2016, 6)

TOWARD A CRITICAL RACE PRAXIS IN ARCHIVES

Considering Yamamoto's CRP framework, its application in the education field set forth by Stovall, and Caswell's definition of critical archival studies, I would like to suggest what a critical race praxis might look like, and mean, for the archival field. While each of these tenets are related, I believe they may exist, operate, and be enacted independently. Collectively, however, I believe they can bring attention to race and the implications of racism, and ultimately revolutionize the profession.

DISRUPTIVE: ACKNOWLEDGE SYSTEMS OF POWER, RACE/RACISM, AND PRIVILEGE PRESENT IN ALL ASPECTS OF ARCHIVAL WORK AND SUBVERT THE IDEA OF NEUTRALITY

In his now canonical 1971 SAA presidential address, Howard Zinn discussed the ongoing bias in archival work, arguing that archivists tend to perpetuate the political and economic status quo simply by going about ordinary business (Zinn 1977). The very acts of preserving and making archival records accessible directly reflects social distributions of wealth and power. Inextricable from conversations of wealth and power is the social embeddedness of racism. Over forty years later, it is time to move our discussions beyond debate by acknowledging the inherent politics of our work and the false presence of archival neutrality. For the first time in SAA history, presenters at the 2019 annual meeting were explicitly encouraged to consider their positionality and address power structures as they related to their presentation topics via a message included in all proposal notification messages—for proposals accepted, selected as alternates, and declined.[7] This change was implemented by conference cochairs, with the intent to raise awareness and encourage thoughtful dialogue at the annual meeting.[8] While the effects of promoting this kind of self-awareness during the session submission and acceptance process is yet to be seen, anecdotally, the cochairs received feedback from attendees stating that the 2019 conference had some of the greatest representational diversity in presenters and topics seen at an annual meeting. In what ways can we acknowledge the systemic power dynamics in our institutional practices and the harm caused by upholding them? What privileges do we possess, at both the individual and institutional levels, and how might we use said privilege(s) to transform systemic power dynamics? How can we document decisions and policies to provide greater transparency and accountability to prevent the continuation of harmful practices?

RESPONSIVE: ADDRESS CURRENT ISSUES IN BOTH THE ARCHIVAL COMMUNITY AND SOCIETY AT LARGE AND EMPOWER PRACTITIONERS AT ALL LEVELS TO ENACT CHANGE WITHIN THEIR INFLUENCE

A responsive approach supports practitioners addressing social issues—legacies found in archival collections and currently happening in contemporary society—and encourages an archival perspective in creating social change. This approach is not fixed in status quo, established protocol or organizational hierarchy. All archivists, not just those in decision-making positions or library administration, "have a professional obligation to work toward a more equitable future" (Punzalan and Caswell 2016, 27). Indeed, it is up to every librarian and archivist to disrupt the affective implications of whiteness (Espinal, Sutherland, and Roh 2018, 158). As custodians of records documenting society, we are responsible to individuals and communities whose records we steward. Operating out of an understanding that racism is ordinary and neutrality does not exist in archivy, "archivists need to be willing to take a public stand at times" (Jimerson 2009, 290), addressing issues that affect the profession and the communities where we live and work.

For me, responsive archival work includes establishing a paid undergraduate internship in collaboration with the university's Black studies department. I sought to begin this internship as a way to provide exposure to students of color, introducing them to archival work and encouraging them to see themselves in the archive—while also paying them for their labor. There was no model or precedent for a collaborative or even paid undergraduate internship program in my repository. Through an endowment in Black studies supplemented with collection development funds, recruitment through Black studies faculty and student listservs, and selection by a committee of representatives from both campus units, the internship program is now successfully in its third year. In addition to working directly with Black diaspora collections, the intern also participates in donor relations and programmatic activities throughout the academic year. In what aspects of our work can we improve, or create, equity? How can our collective archival training and individual positionalities be used to benefit society, address silences and erasure, or enact justice? What spaces or platforms are available to articulate and promote these ideas and support people doing this work?

ACTIONABLE: CENTER SOCIAL JUSTICE IN ARCHIVAL WORK, RECOGNIZING THE LARGER SOCIAL RESPONSIBILITY TO COMMUNITIES AND INDIVIDUALS, PAST AND PRESENT, WHILE PROVIDING GOALS FOR IMPLEMENTATION AND MEASURES FOR ACCOUNTABILITY

Social justice in CRT pushes scholars to actively engage in their communities by using their academic resources and intellect to foster tangible change (Chapman 2013, 103). In the archival context, social justice and actionable practice address how archives can be used to generate or support social change. An actionable approach may necessitate the reevaluation or modification of established theory and/or practice to better support records and communities at stake—those existing outside of the white, elitist origins of archival enterprise. Social justice through action, and reparative action in particular, is a change in the traditional praxis of the archival profession. Not only that, it is a conscientious effort to begin one's work with the philosophy of inclusion from the margins (Hughes-Watkins 2018, 5). An effective first actionable step for many collecting institutions is revisiting collection development policies. If guiding documentation articulates a commitment to justice work and representational collecting, some of the challenges that can present in the context of this work are mitigated. How can our community of archival practitioners begin, and even end, our practice and workflows by centering those who are underrepresented or disenfranchised? In what ways can our practice support justice and liberation work? What systemic barriers exist in archives, and how can they be broken?

INFORMED: INCLUDE PRACTICES AND KNOWLEDGE SYSTEMS OUTSIDE OF THE ESTABLISHED "TRADITION," INCORPORATING SELF-REFLECTIVE PRACTICE, CULTURAL COMPETENCE/HUMILITY, AND CRITIQUE AS NORMALIZED EXPECTATIONS OF ARCHIVAL WORK

An informed approach emphasizes the need for and the contributions of understanding, culturally competent archival professionals. However, these people alone cannot undo oppressive systems of race and power—in fact, focusing exclusively on interpersonal attributes can reduce racism to individual relations, obscuring analysis of broader structures of racial domination (Hudson 2017, 17). As an example, in 2018, the SAA adopted *Protocols for Native American Archival Materials* as the profession's guiding resource for working with culturally sensitive records of Native American communities. *Protocols* was first introduced to the SAA Council for endorsement in 2006; the twelve-year opposition to its endorsement was the result of "cultural insensitivity and white supremacy" present in the council (Society of American Archivists 2018). While the delayed endorsement of the *Protocols* demonstrates the embeddedness and influence of White Supremacy in our profession, it also proves the reality of its undoing. If our practice is not informed by the diverse members of our profession, the communities we collaborate with, and those represented in the collections found in our repositories, we are doing nothing but a disservice. We must not only embrace but also privilege counterstories and alternate ways of knowing and performing archival work, particularly when these ways of knowing come from groups historically oppressed. This will lead to strengthened practice, which in turn will impact (and improve) nearly every aspect of archivy—appraisal, description, documentation strategy, and community archives, just to begin. How are certain ways of knowing privileged in archives, and what can be done about that? How are we continuously improving our practice and providing support to those who contribute to the growth and evolvement of archival work? In what ways can thoughtful archival practice transform society?

CARING: OPERATE OUT OF A COMMITMENT TO MINIMIZE HARM AND PROVIDE CARE FOR BOTH COLLECTIONS AND PROFESSIONALS

Discussions of care in archival work most often engage feminist theory and the ethic of care (e.g., Caswell and Cifor 2016; Jules 2016; Punzalan and Caswell 2016). This discourse challenges us to refashion the role of archivist from enforcer to caregiver, honoring webs of responsibility to the records themselves and to the communities documented within them. While there has been less engagement with Black feminist theory in archival discourse, it too has a lot to offer, particularly in how care is conceptualized in the profession. The Black feminist ethic of caring centers the notion that ideas cannot be divorced from the individuals who create and share them. Enacting an ethic of caring includes providing space for individual expressiveness, the appropriateness of emotions, and the capacity for empathy (Collins 2000, 262–264). Inherent in this is recognizing the significance of different kinds of knowing and individual experiences, and the valuable contribution they make to archival endeavors. As stated by Powell and colleagues, as Black women archivists, "our professional practice demonstrates caring for people as evidence of capacity to care for materials" (2018, 8).

A caring approach can begin with simply acknowledging the labor of archivists processing and working with challenging or difficult material and being intentional about being in relationship with them, as a supervisor or colleague. Michelle Caswell and Marika Cifor (2016) outline a four-part framework for affective archival relationships, including (1) archivist and record creator, (2) archivist and subject or records, (3) archivist and user, and (4) archivist and the larger community. Building from this, archivists Holly Smith, Elvia Arroyo-Ramirez, Molly Brown, Shannon O'Neil, Dinah Handel, Jasmine Jones, Rachel Mattson, Giordana Mecagni, and Kelly Wooten have suggested a fifth affective relationship—archivist to archivist.[9] The value and importance of caring relationships in the archival setting are important, and the relationships among and between archivists should not be minimized. We must extend care beyond the boxes, folders, and server space in our repositories. How are we honoring the humanity of the people in our collections and the professionals providing archival labor to support them? In what ways can our archival relationship be improved? How do we care for staff who engage with records documenting trauma or violence? How is labor distributed, and how can those required to exert increased emotional labor while on the job—most often, archivists of color—be supported?

CONCLUSION

CRT and CRP have a lot to offer the archival profession. In this chapter, my goal has been to consider what enacting a CRP can do for archives—both the professionals that sustain them and the collections in our care. By proposing a CRP framework in archives, I hope to encourage additional conversation on the subject. In fact, I invite others to further these suggested tenets to better articulate and support the needs and diverse perspectives in the field. I look forward to the day when the discussions centering race and the professional mechanisms that exist to support racially and ethnically diverse archivists are more the norm than the exception. Though it is unclear when this day will come, being critical of our work and mindful of the implications of our praxis gets us closer.

NOTES

1. In 2018, the name of this award was changed from "Minority Student Award" to "Student of Color Award"; see Berry 2018. For more on the program, see Poole 2017.

2. João H. Costa Vargas (2018) posits, "Antiblack racism is a constitutive aspect of the social world of the Black diaspora, and can be conceptualized as a shared set of attitudes, and their assumptions, that translate into everyday practice and measurable results" (26–27).

3. "POC experience both individual and collective trauma in this country. We can't be expected to produce, produce, produce without any acknowledgement of the horrors that POC in general and librarians of color in particular are having to process on a bodily level" (Espinal, Sutherland, and Roh 2018, 157).

4. "By failing to consistently collect visual evidence as an intentional counternarrative, American archives have effectively created a master narrative of normativity around Black death" (Sutherland 2017, 13).

5. I co-curated the exhibition *Juntos/Together: Black and Brown Activism in Austin, 1970–1983* at the George Washington Carver Museum and Cultural Center in Austin, TX, in 2018.

6. See, e.g., chapters 2, 4, and 6 in this volume.

7. The positionality statement for accepted proposals read, in part: "As presenters at the Joint Annual Meeting, it is important to reflect and acknowledge your positionality as it relates to your chosen topics. At the basic level, this involves reflecting on and acknowledging power structures and

your social location (intersecting identities) as it relates to your topic. To not acknowledge the power structures that control our work reproduces that power and, depending on the topic of your presentation, erases the contributions and voices of historically marginalized people and communities."

8. The 2019 SAA Program co-chairs included myself, Joyce Gabiola, and Tanya Marshall.

9. As presented in the session "Radical Empathy in Archival Practice" at the 2017 SAA annual meeting, Portland, OR, July 28, 2017, https://archives2017.sched.com/event/ABGy/301-radical-empathy -in-archival-practice; and in the Society of California Archivists webinar, "Applying Radical Empathy Framework in Archival Practice," September 17, 2018, https://calarchivists.org/event-3034395.

BIBLIOGRAPHY

Bell, Derrick. 1995. "Who's Afraid of Critical Race Theory?" *University of Illinois Law Review* 4:893–910.

Berry, Dorothy. 2018. "Harold T. Pinkett Award Name Change." Agenda item II.E, Society of American Archivists Council Meeting, Chicago, IL, November 2–3, 2018. https://www2.archivists .org/sites/all/files/1118-II-E-PinkettAwardName.pdf.

Caswell, Michelle. 2016. "Owning Critical Archival Studies: A Plea." Paper presented at the Archival Education and Research Institute, Kent State University, Kent, OH, July 8–12, 2016. http:// escholarship.org/uc/item/75x090df.

Caswell, Michelle, and Marika Cifor. 2016. "From Human Rights to Feminist Ethics: Radical Empathy in the Archives." *Archivaria* 81 (1): 23–43.

Caswell, Michelle, Ricardo Punzalan, and T-Kay Sangwand, eds. 2017. "Critical Archival Studies: An Introduction." Special issue, *Journal of Critical Library and Information Studies* 1 (2).

Chapman, Thandeka K. 2013. "Origins of and Connections to Social Justice in Critical Race Theory in Education." In *Handbook of Critical Race Theory in Education*, edited by Marvin Lynn and Adrienne D. Dixson, 121–132. New York: Routledge.

Collins, Patricia Hill. 2000. *Black Feminist Thought: Knowledge, Consciousness, and the Politics of Empowerment.* New York: Routledge.

Delgado, Richard, and Jean Stefancic. 2017. *Critical Race Theory: An Introduction.* New York: New York University Press.

Dunbar, Anthony W. 2006. "Introducing Critical Race Theory to Archival Discourse: Getting the Conversation Started." *Archival Science* 6 (1): 109–129.

Espinal, Isabel, Tonia Sutherland, and Charlotte Roh. 2018. "A Holistic Approach for Inclusive Librarianship: Decentering Whiteness in Our Profession." *Library Trends* 67 (1): 147–162.

Hartman, Saidiya. 2008. "Venus in Two Acts." *Small Axe: A Caribbean Journal of Criticism* 12 (2): 1–14.

Hudson, David J. 2017. "On 'Diversity' as Anti-racism in Library and Information Studies: A Critique." *Journal of Critical Library and Information Studies* 1 (1).

Hughes-Watkins, Lae'L. 2018. "Moving toward a Reparative Archive: A Roadmap for a Holistic Approach to Disrupting Homogenous Histories in Academic Repositories and Creating Inclusive Spaces for Marginalized Voices." *Journal of Contemporary Archival Studies* 5 (1).

Jimerson, Randall C. 2009. *Archives Power: Memory, Accountability, and Social Justice*. Chicago: Society of American Archivists.

Jules, Bergis. 2016. "Confronting Our Failure of Care around the Legacies of Marginalized People in the Archives." *On Archivy*, November 11, 2016. https://medium.com/on-archivy/confronting -our-failure-of-care-around-the-legacies-of-marginalized-people-in-the-archives-dc4180397280.

Pinkett, Harold. 1981. "American Archival Theory: The State of the Art." *American Archivist* 44 (3): 217–222.

Poole, Alex H. 2017. "Pinkett's Charges: Recruiting, Retaining, and Mentoring Archivists of Color in the Twenty-First Century." *American Archivist* 80 (1): 103–134.

Powell, Chaitra, Holly Smith, Shanee' Murrain, and Skyla Hearn. 2018. "This [Black] Woman's Work: Exploring Archival Projects That Embrace the Identity of the Memory Worker." *KULA: Knowledge Creation, Dissemination, and Preservation Studies* 2 (1).

Punzalan, Ricardo L., and Michelle Caswell. 2016. "Critical Directions for Archival Approaches to Social Justice." *Library Quarterly* 86 (1): 25–42.

Ramirez, Mario H. 2015. "Being Assumed Not to Be: A Critique of Whiteness as an Archival Imperative." *American Archivist* 78 (2): 339–356.

Sharpe, Christina. 2016. *In the Wake: On Blackness and Being*. Durham, NC: Duke University Press.

Society of American Archivists. 2005. "A*CENSUS Diversity Report." Society of American Archivists. https://www2.archivists.org/sites/all/files/Banks-ACENSUS.pdf.

Society of American Archivists. 2018. "SAA Council Endorsement of *Protocols for Native American Archival Materials*." Society of American Archivists. September 14, 2018. https://www2.archivists .org/statements/saa-council-endorsement-of-protocols-for-native-american-archival-materials.

Stovall, David O. 2013. "'Fightin' the Devil 24/7': Context, Community, and Critical Race Praxis in Education." In *Handbook of Critical Race Theory in Education*, 309–321. New York: Routledge.

Stovall, David O., Marvin Lynn, Lynette Danley, and Danny Martin, eds. 2009. "Critical Race Praxis." Special issue, *Race, Ethnicity, and Education* 12 (1): 131–266.

Sutherland, Tonia. 2017. "Archival Amnesty: In Search of Black American Transitional and Restorative Justice." *Journal of Critical Library and Information Studies* 2:1–23.

Trouillot, Michel-Rolph. 1995. *Silencing the Past: Power and the Production of History*. Boston: Beacon Press.

Vargas, João H. Costa. 2018. *The Denial of Antiblackness: Multiracial Redemption and Black Suffering*. Minneapolis: University of Minnesota Press.

Warren, Kellee E. 2016. "We Need These Bodies, but Not Their Knowledge: Black Women in the Archival Science Professions and Their Connection to the Archives of Enslaved Black Women in the French Antilles." *Library Trends* 64 (4): 776–794.

White, Deborah Gray. 1987. "Mining the Forgotten: Manuscript Sources for Black Women's History." *Journal of American History* 74 (1): 237–242.

Yamamoto, Eric K. 1997. "Critical Race Praxis: Race Theory and Political Lawyering Practice in Post–Civil Rights America." *Michigan Law Review* 95 (4): 821–900.

Yamamoto, Eric K. 1999. *Interracial Justice: Conflict and Reconciliation in Post–Civil Rights America.* New York: New York University Press.

Zinn, Howard. 1977. "Secrecy, Archives, and the Public Interest." *Midwestern Archivist* 2 (2): 14–26.

13

"GETTING INFLOMATION"
A Critical Race Theory Tale from the School Library

Kafi Kumasi

APRIL 2, 2019

I usually never check the mail at home. There's nothing there for me except the occasional reminder for a dentist appointment or a few prospective student packets from colleges that are not even on my radar. All my real college mail comes as football recruitment letters that Coach Rettner gives me during seventh-hour Team Sports class. Today was different though. It was raining hard outside and I saw some mail sticking out of the mailbox getting all wet when I pulled up the driveway. I parked in the backyard and hurried to the back door with my practice shoes almost falling out of my backpack. I fumbled around for my keys. Once inside, I headed straight down the main hallway to the front door, stopping only to drop my wet bookbag by the back door. As I grabbed all the mail from inside the box, I noticed a large white envelope with a rubberband around it. My heart skipped a beat when I saw Harvard's crest emblem on the top right corner. I also noticed that my full name was on the mailing label, without the usual "To the parents of" prefix. I separated the letter from the rest of the mail and headed upstairs feeling very grown up.

April 14, 2019

Jamar's Acceptance Letter to Harvard

Dear Admission Committee,

I am writing to accept your early admission offer to pursue my undergraduate studies and my collegiate football career at Harvard University. As my application essay indicated, I would like to focus my "freshman focus" project on helping reform the college admissions standards in the country in ways that mediate against the effects of institutional racism on K–12 schools. My project is more than an affirmative action effort. My goal is for college admissions programs to create a questionnaire for prospective students to identify areas where they feel they have been either "miseducated" or "undereducated" in their K–12 education. I want to gather data on what areas the questionnaire should cover during freshman inquiry class. I have several family members and friends who are just as deserving to attend a place like Harvard, but who have not been able to surmount the racist structural barriers that make school curricula at our local public schools outdated, irrelevant, and biased towards Eurocentric knowledge and ways of viewing the world. Nor have they been able to find solid academic footing in a schooling context where urban schools get less state funding than their wealthier suburban counterparts, causing a ripple effect of instability, most notably in teachers taking better-paying positions in suburban school districts. It is my privilege and honor to represent the voices, culture, and concerns of my community as best I can during my matriculation at Harvard. Please find the completed documentation attached to this email. I look forward to making Cambridge my new home in the fall.

Sincerely,
Jamar Johnson
C/O 2019
Morningside Prep Academy
@OutsideTheLines

Later that evening, I read my acceptance letter aloud at my aunt Theresa's house where we gathered for Thanksgiving dinner. I love Thanksgiving not only because my aunts can throw down in the kitchen, but it's also the time when I get to see all my cousins take part in games and heated discussions; oh and I can't forget the dancing. One time, one of my cousins recorded my aunts doing the ballroom hustle in the kitchen and the video had over 1,000 views on Facebook. At that point I realized that our Thanksgiving traditions are pretty unique and that I am lucky to have such a close-knit family. This year was no different. My mom and aunts caucused around the kitchen island while cooking, dancing and discussing the latest hot-button issues over prosecco, mojitos, and garlic butter shrimp. I listened as they argued about the pros and cons of the SAT board's new environmental context dashboard. This new app allows students and parents the ability to access benchmark data about where they stand on any number of life indices such as neighborhood crime data, household income, etc. It was designed to measure the level of adversity people experience compared to others across different demographic backgrounds. On paper, they describe it as an effort to get more nuanced data on college applicants instead of the typical race, class, gender, and test data. This topic had been the subject of one of our recent family group chats. Even the younger cousins are in the chat, but they rarely respond unless they are asked a pointed question. They may acknowledge the text by hitting the like button on their iPhones, but even that minimal effort is rare for some of the "too cool for school" teens in the family. Usually the messages are lighthearted, containing memes, gifs, emojis, and pictures from recent family gatherings or outings. However, my mom in all her inquisitiveness broke from tradition and asked a more serious question.

April 11, 2019

Johnson Family Group Chat

> **MOM:** So I see the SAT board has changed the name of their new data dashboard from the "adversity index" to the "environmental landscape" dashboard? Ya'll know what that's all about, right?
>
> **AUNT TRACY:** Um no, but I have a sneaky suspicion you are about to write a dissertation to explain it. But go off, sis. I'm here for it.
>
> **MOM:** Ha! You know me well, sis. Basically, the SAT board is trying to get around collecting racial demographic data in their new "adversity" dashboard so that they can sidestep squarely dealing with the lingering effects of White Supremacist policies in America on students of color today. Initially, they caught heat about calling the new dashboard an adversity index. People saw through their attempt to use a benign term like "adversity," which virtually everyone can claim they've experienced at some point in their life, regardless of their circumstances of birth. It's like that other term whites love to use—"diversity." Both of the words are too broad to be meaningful when it comes to changing the status quo. It's simply a way to give an even greater leg up to the average working-class white kid whose parents feel threatened by the browning of America and losing their unearned privilege of white skin they have accrued for several centuries in America.
>
> It's like how whites prefer "diversity" and "multiculturalism" over "race," "power," and "privilege" because they are more polite terms that assuage their guilt from benefiting from a system that dehumanized and disenfranchised entire races of nonwhite people. Meanwhile, WE already know that the single most galvanizing factor that defines what adversity looks like for people in any given community in a neighborhood is race. There's no greater factor than racism and White Supremacy that can explain why concentrated poverty, poor schooling, and lack of viable housing and job opportunities disproportionately affects communities of color.

But they don't want to collect that data on race because that would mean they'd have to acknowledge that race is the most salient factor dictating the level of adversity a student experiences in the first place. If they DO collect data on a student's racial background, they might have to actually do something about the trends they see. They might not be able to ignore the elephant in the room. They might have to concede that affirmative action for Black and Latinx students in inner-city schools is necessary to give them a fairer shake in college admissions decisions. But that's not why they designed this SAT dashboard. It's not for US.

AUNT TRACY: I know that's right, sis.

MOM: Can you even imagine a majority-white community where the schools are failing? Where the houses are abandoned and there are liquor stores and marijuana shops on every corner? Or can you imagine such a thing as "Black flight," where we took our resources and fled the inner city for the suburbs, leaving a largely disenfranchised white community behind? Imagine if all the surrounding suburbs had Black mayors who spent decades bashing the inner-city residents by calling them "white trash" and coordinating policies that strategically black-ball the inner city from economic growth? If you can't imagine any of these things, it's because race and racism is so deeply enmeshed in the social fabric of our society that it seems normal. Seeing People of Color experience racism is normal. By contrast, it is difficult to imagine whites, the group that has received the most unearned benefits and social status in society, in a position as a permanent underclass striving to be treated equal to Blacks. It's unfathomable.

AUNT TRACY: Sis, I don't know why you get so worked up. You KNOW the SAT was never about leveling the playing field for people who look like us. They're in the business of making money. If they can get the growing number of white parents who feel left behind by capitalism to buy into this idea that naming hardship they've experienced (even if it's mostly at the hands of conservative and racist economic policies) will somehow give their kid a better chance to attend an elite college, they're all for it. It's affirmative action for white students by another name.

After a pregnant pause in the conversation, their eyes turned toward me. "Well let's hear from Mr. Harvard over there," Aunt Joyce said. "He's our new resident expert on all things politics and education." I felt like I was being initiated into a Black family's version of a rite of passage ceremony. A common refrain in Black families is that "kids are to be seen and not heard." At that moment I understood that I had successfully graduated from the kids' table and was entering the adult cipher— also known as the kitchen table.

As I approached the counter, I mustered up the kind of composure one might expect from a Harvard-bound sixteen-year-old. I cleared my throat and began, "Well, aside from the fact that standardized tests are really no indicator on how well college freshman perform academically, this is really about keeping the testing companies in business. It's a way for them to placate the growing number of working-class whites who want their kids to attend elite colleges but they cannot afford the high-priced tutors and private schools that will better ensure their kid does well on the SAT." I kept going. "The fact that they don't track for race in their new index shows that they are not interested in solving the tough problems that create such disparate life outcomes for People of Color in America. Whatever remedy they propose, you better believe whites will have to benefit from it somehow in order for us to see any relief at all. It's called interest convergence."

"Okay Mar Mar!" My mom said with a prideful tone. "Go on n' school your aunts on what interest convergence means, baby." Without hesitation, I said, "Derrick Bell, who is one of the great legal minds of the twentieth century, coined the term 'interest convergence' to explain racial developments in America. He argued that white self-interest is the main reason Blacks have received any relief from racial oppression throughout American history." There was a collective sense of exasperation in the room. That sober moment was quickly interrupted by Uncle Chace yelling at the TV. "You gotta dunk that, man! My bad, I forgot Staffman's a role player kind of guy. Shiiit, pay me 40 million. I'll play any role you want me to play!"

May 5, 2019

Morningside Heights School Board Meeting

Dear parents or guardians,

At their regular meeting, May 1st, the Board of Education voted on new open-enrollment policies aimed at addressing student capacity at the high school while maintaining its growing reputation for excellence in urban education. This is the culmination of a year-long process that included the following:

- A June 2018 resolution that passed unanimously the criteria that would be used to determine open-enrollment boundaries and class size limits.
- Enrollment data from the November 2018 confirming that criteria had been met to enforce new enrollment policy as of Fall 2019.
- 6 Urban Education Council meetings—all materials posted online.
- 15 Town Halls attended by 1976 community members.
- 4 listening sessions conducted by the State Board of Education's Urban School Office.
- A 6 yes, 1 no vote to implement the new open-enrollment policy in the Fall of 2019–20.
- A 5 yes, 2 no vote to draw new district lines for open enrollment as a means of balancing open enrollment between the two high schools in Morningside Heights.

Information on new out-of-district boundaries and open-enrollment caps will be coming out shortly, as will opportunities for parents, staff, and student participation. We thank everyone for their participation to date. This process has been difficult because our community loves its schools. This solution allows the district to focus limited funding on programs and people that make Morningside Heights an exemplar of urban education in the nation. Together we will continue our work to carry out our mission: Educational Excellence, Future Readiness, and Community Engagement.

> This message has been sent on behalf of the Morningside Heights School System.

May 17, 2019

District Letter to Parents about New Enrollment Caps

To the parent or guardian of: <u>Ryan Murphy</u>

Based on the new out-of-district residency policy, your child is no longer eligible to attend Morningside Heights based on the address listed in your child's most recent enrollment application. Please visit our new website for more information pertaining to our new residency enrollment policy.

> This message has been sent on behalf of the Morningside Heights School System.

May 17, 2019

Kathy Murphy and Katelyn Boll Text Message

Kathy

I got a letter saying Ryan can no longer attend Morningside! I've already inquired about the appeal process with the district. I've already spoke with my lawyer and discussed our legal options. He thinks we have an affirmative action case since Ryan is the only white student affected by this new policy. Maybe I will call Peggy and see if she can run a story about this on the local news. Do you have her cell number?

Katelyn

Wow, smh! You would think they would appreciate the book drive donation we gave them. I will hold off on getting Tom's company to donate their used computers until I hear back on your appeal outcome. We're all staying tuned to see how your urban experiment goes. I'll share Peggy's contact in a sec.

May 26, 2019

Channel 4 News Release

A mother from the Bridgepoint community is challenging the local urban school district's out-of-district policy on the grounds of affirmative action. Here the full interview with this local mother and her attorney live at 11 on Talk It Out.

May 27, 2019

Black Twitter Buzz

 Morningside Heights LIT center and 200 others liked

 KumariHill@RebelRootsED
Becky and Keisha both want their kids to attend a "better" school. They BOTH bend the rules by using a family members' address to get their kid into their school of choice. Keisha gets jail time. What do you think Becky gets?

 Ria/ the RN
She gets a half hour news segment complete with tears and white fragility.

 Celebrityblogger
A new car! Compliments of the Make American Great Again (MAGA) social justice fundraiser.

 Starambrosia
A commemorative t-shirt with the words: "All students matter" on the front and the back reads: "Sponsored by Bridgepoint Border Patrol and Enforcement Office."

 Channel 4 @TalkitOut 1d Affirmative Action or Entitlement? Viewers sound off about a suburban parent's appeal of a local urban school district's new open enrollment policy.

77 comments   11.5K retweets   30K loves

 Morningside Heights LIT center and 300 others liked

 Justin Smith@ Just-usmedia
A white mother expecting kudos for donating used books to an urban school that is literally known for its state-of the-art library is the epitome of having a white savior complex.

#whiteprivilege #whitefragility #whitenessstrikesback

Channel 4 @TalkitOut 1d
Affirmative Action or Entitlement? Viewers sound off about a suburban parent's
appeal of a local urban school districts new open enrollment policy.

77 comments   11.5K retweets   30K loves

That next day, during InFLOmation time in the library, Ms. Brooks brought the
Twitter debate about Ryan's mom front and center. Ms. Brooks calls InFLOmation
a hip hop–based learning process that describes how today's youth live and learn
through digital media. She says that the library media center is all about learning
how to learn, so she created an inquiry model that draws on Black culture as the basis
for learning in the school library.

When we enter the library, we can choose to work at one of three stations that
mirror the elements of hip hop, including Rhythm, Rhyme, and Remix. Where you
choose to work depends on the level of the learning task you are engaged in for that
day. You can usually find me at the Remix station. Ms. Brooks asked me if I wanted
to help work on a new metadata schema that would allow us to hyperlink hip hop
songs to the MARC records cataloging system using new access points that mirror
the way we talk and think outside of school. Traditionally, librarians have to use the
standard vocabulary and subject headings assigned by the Library of Congress (LOC)
to catalog and classify their books. However, not many kids my age talk the way
the majority-white middle-aged men and women who created the LOC system talk.
Therefore, most of my friends find out about books by word of mouth rather than by
searching the library catalog using its assigned subject headings or key words.

That's why I like getting InFLOmation. If a kid is heavily into music, this model
allows them to use that as the bridge to building more traditional literacies like reading and writing. Ms. Brooks also gives us the option to work on a hip hop book
classification project that allows us to assign a book a set of hashtags that get linked
directly its MARC record. There's also a new MARC field that allows us to embed
links to songs or artists whose work deals with the themes in the book itself. It's a
pretty complex set of projects, but if we do it right, it will be something that puts
Morningside on the map, besides our football program.

Most of the kids go to the Rhythm or Rhyme stations because they are more
free-flowing and exploratory. As long as you submit an exit slip before you leave the
library, stating your level of flow in the InFLOmation process you were working in

that day—Rhythm, Rhyme, or Remix—then you are good. Ms. Brooks says that you will know when you are in the peak stage of FLO because you will lose track of time. She says FLO occurs when your skill level and the challenge level of a task are at their highest. If you are bored, distracted, apathetic, anxious, relaxed, or worried while you are in the library, it's because you are not engaging in learning tasks or inquiry projects that create an optimal combination of skill and challenge levels. It's actually true. I've been in the school library when the atmosphere was zen-like because you could tell the majority of students were in their zone, just flowin'. Sometimes I like to go to the Rhyme station because it's an intermediate level where I can work a short task I want to accomplish that day. Today I used InFLOmation time to find new people to follow on the library's Twitter feed, based on the approved hashtags like #HipHopEd and #FutureReadyLibraries or autogenerated recommendations that come from Twitter based on common hashtags and topics mentioned. I like this task because I get to see new activity not only on the library's website, but in the hallways on digital library kiosks stationed outside our classrooms.

Today, Ms. Brooks was fired up about our library hashtag, #GetLIT, going viral after Ryan's mom was on the news. As we entered the LIT center, she asked us to get InFLOmation with her. This means we prepare to lose track of time and forget about our daily problems of life in the process of seeking and creating information because our interests and skills are both being challenged at peak levels. I went first and sat at the edge of the commons area near the smart screen, which was clearly set up for an activity. Ms. Brooks asked us to take out our cell phones and enter one word into the Socrates app on the screen to describe how we felt about the news clip last night and all the Twitter buzz afterward.

We always use Socrates to jumpstart our inquiry projects during InFLOmation time, but this time the aura seemed urgent. I think everyone was ready to speak their mind. Plus, Ms. Brooks has a way of really hearing us out and helping us turn our passions into legit research. She's a big reason I applied to Harvard and decided to research college admission policies in the first place. Ms. Brooks went to college with my aunts and was known for her involvement in progressive Black education circles such as the Black Student Union. I can still remember when she gave all the ninth grade English classes an orientation to the school library. She complimented me on my locks and asked me where I got them twisted. When I told her my aunt twisted them, we quickly learned that we had a lot of mutual family and friends, namely my aunt who she went to college with and who was known for her budding talents as a natural hairstylist.

She put the three-minute timer on to allow us time to open the app and complete the task. I probably typed my response in three seconds flat. I had been thinking about the whole ordeal since last night when it hit the news. The timer went off and with the click of a button, all the words appeared on the screen.

"I see a lot of words. I see ANGRY, CONFUSED...someone wrote BEFUDDLED. Someone wrote TENSE; I also see, SAD, NUMB, and even NOTHING. These are quite descriptive words, you all!" Ms. Brooks exclaimed. "Thank you for your honesty."

She kept on, "Let's start with this one right here—BEFUDDLED. Would anyone like to share their thoughts on why this information you saw or read made you feel befuddled?"

I raised my hand and she immediately acknowledged me. "How come when a Black mother tries to get her son into a better school in a white neighborhood, she is given jail time for using her relative's address, but a white mom rallies the entire media community behind her claim that her son is being denied an educational opportunity? *She's* the one who bent the admissions rules to experiment with sending her son to a predominantly Black urban high school."

I had already learned during last year's InFLOmation project that the answer had something to do with the way racism and White Supremacy function in America. My research on Critical Race Theory had given me the tools to dissect this scenario. People like Kathy Murphy would ordinarily oppose affirmative action measures meant to allow students from underresourced urban schools a chance to attend elite expensive universities, on the grounds that unqualified applicants are taking up spots that should be reserved for their more qualified (aka white) students. However, these same folks would quickly abandon cries that affirmative action is a form of reverse discrimination if they think they can benefit from a quota system. This kind of hubris and entitlement falls squarely in the realm of white privilege and interest convergence. Ms. Murphy enjoyed the privilege of escaping scrutiny about whether her son Ryan belonged at a school like Morningside Heights in the first place. She also enjoyed the privilege of not being questioned about whether Ryan was taking away a spot at an Ivy League school from a more deserving student at Morningside Heights who has attended an underresourced school their whole life—not just junior and senior year.

At that moment, Ms. Brooks invites other students to begin researching incidents to support my statement about Black parents getting jail time over out-of-district residency policies at majority-white public schools. She quickly creates a folder on the smart screen inside our LIT center Google account for us to upload the documents and websites of our search results. She asks us what we would like to name the folder. Without hesitation, I say, "Name it 'Whiteness as Property' and inside it put any evidence you find that demonstrates the property functions of whiteness. If y'all need a refresher, I got you." I offered to airdrop from my phone to Ms. Brook's laptop a picture that I had screenshot last night from a website. It outlined the four main elements of whiteness as property:

1. Rights of disposition;
2. Rights to use and enjoyment;
3. Reputation and status property;
4. The absolute right to exclude.

Ms. Brooks acknowledged my contribution with a proud smile. She asked me to elaborate on which of the four elements of whiteness as property I thought were at play in Ryan's mother's case. I said, "All of them, but numbers 3 and 4 apply directly. For number 3, the logic (or illogic) of White Supremacy relies on symbolic cultural capital or the status reputation that implies that having a majority-white student population makes a school automatically better than one where students of color are the majority. In this sense, whiteness has a kind of cultural currency that can be carried around and traded like material goods and property. For example, when whites fled inner cities in the 1950s and 1960s, they were making a strategic investment in the property value of whiteness. Collectively, they had to buy into the idea that People of Color moving into their community would literally make their property value go down. They did just that. If one too many families of color tipped the scale and moved into a white neighborhood during the 1960s, whites would then start to flee to suburban communities in direct proportion. This pattern of migration, called white flight, helped cement the idea that it was white people in and of themselves that carried currency, or property value. So, a white mother like Ryan's mom is more apt to receive empathy in her efforts to give her child a more 'diverse' (aka nonwhite, urban) educational experience because the status and reputation of a Black school does not have as much cultural capital as a predominantly white school—even though Morningside Heights is an exception," I said with a sly smile of arrogance.

"For number 4, ever since Jim Crow, the US government has given white people a sense of entitlement to claim public spaces as exclusively reserved for their use and enjoyment. That legacy still permeates the way police engage with Black people and other racialized groups in their everyday lives—suspecting that they don't belong in certain spaces even if they live there or are visiting a relative. Trayvon Martin was killed going to buy Skittles near his father's house, because a wannabe cop has seen countless police get off scot free for killing unarmed Black people. That's not even mentioning how comfortable whites feel moving in and taking over formerly Black and Brown urban city spaces in the name of gentrification."

Later that day, I left my seventh hour class and headed to football practice. It was time to let my hair down—which in my case means tying my locks up and putting on my helmet and pads and locking down anyone who comes my way.

It was my hair that actually brought Ryan and me closer together than I could have ever foreseen. One day Ryan asked for a ride home on the same day that I had planned to get my locks twisted by my aunt Kemba. Since Kemba is one of the top natural hairstylists in Morningside Heights, she does not play about being late or being a no-show. You will never be able to get another appointment if you flake or cancel on her. I was not about to be out here searching for someone to retwist my hair last minute, because I have too much going on for that. Besides, I am in the running for class hair thanks to Aunt Kemba's fly double-strand twists and elaborate parts for men's looks.

Ryan said he would ride with me to get my locks tightened. He said he wanted to see what all the fuss was about having "tight"' hairstyles, as we called it. The locker room was a place where you either got roasted or got props for any range of things about your looks. I mostly got props because of the way I rocked my hair. But I've also been fried for my share of stuff, too. When we got to Aunt Kemba's, I could tell Ryan was nervous. He should have been. My family has a reputation for interrogating anyone about anything—at any time. It didn't matter that there were several people waiting to get their hair done. When Ryan and I came down to the basement where the makeshift salon was, the room got quiet and all eyes turned toward him. Normally, there are any number of arguments about politics, sexuality, religion, white people, or similar hot topics going on simultaneously at Black salons and barbershops. This time, we apparently walked in on a conversation about the current occupant of the White House, a flagrantly racist, bigoted simpleton who has made a mockery of the office of the president.

I introduced Ryan to Kemba and she went straight IN on him. A trial by fire it was indeed. She goes, "Oh, you're Jamar's teammate from Bridgeponte, aren't you?' "Yes ma'am," Ryan politely replied. She fired off a litany of questions without giving him time to respond. "How'd you get into Morningside? Yo' momma and them voted for that idiot in the White House, didn't they? How could so many white women be so ignorant? You know people think you only got into Morningside because of your white privilege, don't you? Do you think that's true? What was the last book you read? Do you read, or just stare at your phone like the other kids your age?"

Ryan's face was red as a tomato. He just kept swaying side to side and running his fingers through his hair while his other hand was playing pocket pool. When she finally let up on her verbal spray of questions, Ryan chose to answer one of her questions. "I read *The Autobiography of Malcolm X*," he said matter-of-factly. "Oh wow, really? I know they didn't let y'all read that at Bridgepoint," she replied curiously. "Well, actually we just finished it here at Morningside. It's part of our American lit assigned reading." "I knew it. They probably think Malcolm X was a Black Panther who walked around shooting white people. They the ones that need to be reading it…real talk."

The whole time, Ryan gave only a few nods and smiles. He couldn't really get a word in edgewise anyways, so it's probably good he kept quiet. As I sat in my aunt's chair, I could feel Ryan's emotions swinging back and forth on a pendulum between fear and curiosity. When we got back into the car two hours later, Ryan began to question me about what just happened.

"Man, your aunt is the real deal!" Ryan said with exasperation. "I know, right? She don't play. But she means well. She just don't believe in faking the funk…for anyone, especially not for white people. And I'm glad you told her about reading Malcolm X. She went to an HBCU and loves to speak on a lot of Black history and culture topics." "Yeah," Ryan mumbled. "It's all good. I actually like people that act like her because in my family everyone talks one way in public but another way in private when it comes to race."

May 27, 2019

Jamar and Ryan Text Messages

> RYAN: Are you still able to drop me off after practice?
>
> JAMAR: Sure, I'm surprised you asked. Must be hard being the white guy everyone loves to hate then riding home with me, the Blacktivist. I do think you should hear what we discussed during InFLOmation today, though. I'm not gonna be fake. Gotta keep it 100.
>
> RYAN: Ok thanks, I heard some guys talking about it in the hall but yeah I'd love your take.

I like Ryan, but sometimes he just doesn't get it. I guess it's not his fault that his mother and father are walking contradictions of self-proclaimed color blind and conveniently conservative thoughts and actions. They strike me as the kind of white people who are good with equality so long as it doesn't infringe on any of their unearned privileges. For Ryan's part, I usually give him a pass on the clueless things he says because between his parents, the school curriculum, and the news media, he hasn't been taught a balanced story of the contributions Blacks have made in America and in society at large.

Ryan has enjoyed seeing plenty of images of people who look like him in superhero roles at the movies, as protagonists in the required readings at school, as executives in banks and government and just about every other industry in America. So it's no wonder he has such an optimistic view of America. I try to take into account that he's been taught a narrow and stereotypical understanding of Black history and culture that typically centers around their experience of being enslaved and/or fighting against the legacy of white racism.

Rarely do schools, even urban schools, teach the history of African Americans from the view of how their presence forced America to reckon with how to live up to its ideals of freedom and democracy. We rarely talk about slavery as the singular historical event that put the constitutional creed of "All men are created equal" to the test. Instead, slavery is taught in ways that focus on the hardships and cruelty Blacks endured instead of the ways it shaped virtually every modern institution in America today. Because of this miseducation, Ryan still doesn't understand why Black people, including me, have a problem with him saying the N-word but are okay with him listening to Black music that contains the word. He doesn't understand why that word carries a special stigma like no other word in the American lexicon. I tried to explain it to him by using the word "redneck" in a hypothetical scenario of reverse racism.

I asked him to imagine if Black people enslaved white people and used the word "redneck" to keep them in their subordinate place both literally and symbolically. Ryan says he wouldn't care if I called him a redneck if all the songs white people made 200 years later used the term and if white kids used it in everyday conversation like we do now. I think my analogy failed, but its failure is a clear example of how White Supremacy is normalized in our collective imagination.

Ryan could not imagine the legacy of pain that would come from seeing documentaries of white men who look like his father being called "boy" by other grown Black men, or being told to address Black men as "sir" and not look at Black women in the eyes or show any sign of romantic interest. There is no Emmett Till–like figure in the white community that would allow young white kids like Ryan to understand the pain and history of the N-word. The fact that Black people reclaimed the N-word for use among themselves doesn't remove the stigma it carries when someone white uses the word. It doesn't help matters that Black people are generally accepting when it comes to allowing others to enjoy Black culture and be a part of the community.

A white rapper like Eminem enjoys mass cross-cultural appeal in large part because he was welcomed into the underground scene of Black Detroit rappers. Ryan kind of reminds me of Eminem, only without the rap skills or the poor upbringing. When he came to our school, we welcomed him into our culture. I started offering him a ride home once he made the football team. At times I would share things about my upbringing and school him on the origins of hip hop. However, it seems sometimes that Ryan just wanted to take in and copy all the good elements of Black culture without offering anything in return. I would have expected him to give proper credit to our car ride conversations on the history of sampling in his senior InFLOmation project. Even Eminem credited his rap style to Masta Ace, who is well respected but never gained the stardom he deserved. I never felt Ryan brought the same level of sharing or education as I did to our friendship. I've heard some people describe this phenomenon as "culture vultures."

May 29, 2019

Black Twitter Strikes Back

> **InFLOmation Center**
> Intrigued by what our favorite Harvard-bound QB @OutsideTheLines is saying about Black-ness. Let's hear the #InFLOmationWarriors speak on it?
>
> **Jamar Johnson @OutsideTheLines**
> Everyone wants to be Black until it's actually time to be Black. Smh

"Everyone wants to be Black until it's time to actually be BLACK." Who's got receipts?

I should have known Ms. Brooks was going to retweet my post from the library's Twitter account. But before I knew it, the whole school—PLUS the Black Twitter community—had gotten hold of it and it was taking on a life of its own. For my part, I was just trying to call Ryan out on his white privilege and cultural appro-priation. He had the nerve to tell me that the police were just doing their job when they stopped and frisked me and muscled me to the curb with handcuffs. It was just moments after I dropped Ryan off at his house after football practice. Ryan said he heard that a few cars were stolen in the area recently and that I probably fit the profile of the perp they were looking for. "Nothing personal," he said. It pissed me off that he couldn't take himself out of his lily-white Bridgepoint view and see that a similar exchange would be unfathomable if he were dropping me off at my crib in

Morningside, or anywhere for that matter. His mom's little experiment with Black culture does not seem to be working.

Plus, he thought nothing of taking the playlist I shared with him and using it as the basis of his senior LIT project. He didn't know any of the rappers on my playlist before I played them on in my car on our rides home. But now he wants to chronicle the influence of jazz on hip hop music sampling for his project. Someone's probably gonna call him out on it with the quickness. Imma sit back and watch.

June 3, 2019

Jamar's Letter to Harvard's Academic Advising Office

> Dear Academic Advising,
>
> Per your recent request, I am writing to confirm the topic of my "freshman focus" project. A lot has transpired since I wrote my acceptance letter back in April. Specifically, there have been several racially charged incidents at my high school and in the surrounding community. In one instance, I was racially profiled and harassed by the police on my way home from football practice after dropping a teammate off. Another incident involved this same teammate's mother, Mrs. Murphy, being caught in a firestorm of controversy surrounding her appeal of our school's new residency policy and her own alleged malfeasance in falsifying records. In all this, I have gained more experiential knowledge about how race, power, and white privilege function and intersect in our everyday lives. That said, I am going to adjust my "freshman focus" project to center on urban education reform. More specifically, I plan to institute a new mandatory exchange program where urban schools are matched with a nearby suburban school for an exchange that occurs 2x per week. This reform will differ from previous methods used to desegregate schools in the 1950s and 60s. It will be more comprehensive than simply busing students from inner-city to suburban schools. It will require city government involvement in housing relocation incentives and mass transit solutions.
>
> My philosophy is that white families have to have as much skin in the game as families of color if school desegregation is to truly work this time. One of the major pitfalls of the previous school desegregation policies is that they put the burden mainly on Black families to be bused into suburban white school communities. However, this had a few negative effects. For one, it instantiated the idea that predominantly white schools were inherently better by virtue of their whiteness, as opposed to the discrepancies in resources and community stability with urban Black and Latino communities. Yet, it did help show that when all things were equal, Black students have the same—if not greater capacity—to learn and do well when they receive the same instruction and resources as their white counterparts. Secondly, it further destabilized urban communities of color by accelerating white flight and draining urban communities of the talent and tax base of middle-class Blacks who sought better housing and schooling options in the suburbs after busing ended. I look forward to partnering with the Center for Urban Schooling at Harvard to help realize my plans. I appreciate your support and cannot wait to make Harvard my new home in a few short months.

My senior year ended with a bang, literally. Ryan was shot on his way home from the football banquet. He got into a Twitter beef with some neighborhood guys about who owns Black music and culture. His mother Kathy was actually locked up the night of the banquet for her role in a widespread college admission scandal where wealthy (mostly white) parents were relinquishing their guardianship of their kids so that they could be considered legally independent when applying for financial aid. Turns out, most of the people convicted could have easily paid for college, and the grant fund they drained caused hundreds of students with actual financial need to have to take out loans.

I visited Ryan at the hospital and he did show some remorse for stealing my playlist. He also said he didn't feel right about claiming independence on his financial aid forms, but that his mom said the loophole was meant for people smart enough to take advantage of it. It wasn't lost on me that the subtle implication here was that working-class Black and Brown parents were being stereotyped as too dumb or lazy to take advantage of the system.

I look forward to coming back to my alma mater in the fall for the "Twitter take-over" day. Ms. Brooks invited me to take over the LIT center's Twitter page to engage in a Twitter chat about my freshman focus project at Harvard. I invited Ryan and his mother to the event so that they could redeem themselves in the eyes of the Morningside community. We'll see if the diversity, equity, and inclusion training that Mrs. Murphy was mandated to attend as part of her probation sentence will make any difference in how she participates. Black Twitter will surely be the judge of that.

CONCLUSION: AFTERWOR(L)DING TOWARD IMAGINATIVE DIMENSIONS

Sofia Y. Leung and Jorge R. López-McKnight

Scholarship—the formal production, identification, and organization of what will be called "knowledge"—is inevitably political.
—Crenshaw, Gotanda, Peller, and Thomas

IF NOT NOW, WHEN? IF NOT US, WHO?

At the time of this writing, late August 2019, people who look like us and the contributors to this book continue to be locked up and/or murdered, to be heavily impacted by climate change, and to face physical and mental health issues, all due to White Supremacy and racism. On top of its normal levels of structural racism, the US federal government is defunding public services to create prisons for Brown children and families; deporting naturalized citizens to countries where they have never lived or haven't lived since they were children; outlawing reproductive health care; and raiding people's homes and jobs in the name of protecting this country. When things like this are happening in the world, Black, Indigenous, and People of Color (BIPOC) are still expected to go to work, be "collegial" to their colleagues and cheerful to patrons, and meet regular deadlines. As George Lipsitz puts it, "White vanity is considered more valuable than Black humanity" (2020). We, and especially Black and Indigenous peoples, are asked to be superhuman while our communities are in danger, while white folx go on living their racially supremacist, everyday lives. To that we echo Vincent Harding's words, "We have no time for charades" (1970, 78). Do not tell us to be patient, calm, or civil. We cannot waste time, energy, or empathy on white folx unwilling to process or even comprehend their racial power and complicity in these oppressive systems, when our communities are in danger. We demand better for ourselves, our communities, our world(s).

It is from this demand that this collection emerges, and our critique is coming from a special place of care, responsibility, and concern for the profession, for the field, and more importantly, for our communities and each other. Building toward larger systemic change, these chapters, individually and collectively, are trying to share with you (us all, really) something very important: we must upend the relationship between library and information studies (LIS) and White Supremacy. There is no other way; this is not up for debate. There is no compromise. The profession has to *get to* race if long-standing, structured inequities are going to change.

We must return to the beginning, to demand that the humanity of BIPOC be centered, embraced, and loved, to decide what knowledge is, to envision what we want our libraries and archives to be, and to ask ourselves, what does it look like to NOT oppress another group of humans?[1] When we accept everyone's humanity and realize our responsibility toward one another, what kind of futures can we build together? Any futures we construct must take into account the experiences of all peoples, not just the most vocal, privileged, and visible. We need to remember that Critical Race Theory is a critique of a critique. Its very existence tells us that an intersectional perspective is necessary—otherwise, we are missing the point. As contributors Myrna E. Morales and Stacie Williams remind us, if we aren't centering low-income BIPOC's pain and struggle—and we would add, joy and pleasure—then we're doing it wrong, because systems of domination impact them the most.

Thus, in critiquing systems of repression, it is important to understand that the insights offered by Critical Race Theory (CRT) are more than an abstract framework of concepts and methodologies. As illustrated by the chapters in this collection, CRT can be and has been operationalized, and the authors locate CRT not as an ending but as a necessary, particular place of beginning. While CRT pushes to interrogate the relationship of race and power that underlies White Supremacy and how structures of domination (re)shape our teaching, informational spaces, recruitment and retention, collections, production of scholarship, and knowledge systems, as well as other areas and issues of LIS, CRT also holds space for BIPOC and their ways of being, thinking, and imagining that impact each other, our communities, and the field in sustaining, affirming, and loving ways.

As the chapters express, it is foundational to understanding the world and thus, by extension, the profession and its associated institutions, and how we move through and against them to change the conditions of the dispossessed, marginalized, and subjugated. LIS, as the contributors to this volume have illustrated, can be a site where CRT grows. But we will need to be careful. As highlighted in the introduction, this framework has been activated in archives and library scholarship for almost fifteen years. However, just because it has been utilized does not mean it has evolved or has a frequent presence. In that way, as an intellectual movement, CRT (and any other critical theorization focused on race) has not been taken seriously in our field, which speaks to the inability and unwillingness of the discipline and profession to critically confront, analyze, and fight White Supremacy and racism.

These last pages put forward critical elements that—hopefully and lovingly—point us toward new liberated landscapes of community, being, and knowledge. Specifically, in the following sections we offer, as collectively and holistically informed by the chapters, two central ideas of a Critical Race Theory *of* library and information studies that attend to the relationship of race, power, and knowledge. From there, through notions of refusal, what the chapters presented, and boundary setting for liberation projects in LIS, we construct paths and visions for future worlds of LIS that demand radical care, community, and love, which is guided by the work of writer-activist adrienne maree brown and disability justice activist Leah Lakshmi Piepzna-Samarasinha.

Following from that, in the final section, we articulate future trajectories for Critical Race Theory, the collection, and LIS.

COLLECTIVELY TOWARD A CRITICAL RACE THEORY OF LIBRARY AND INFORMATION STUDIES

As one of the main purposes of this collection is to position CRT more centrally in LIS, here, we would like to offer collectively, as expressed by the chapters in this book, two core ideas that a Critical Race Theory *of* library and information studies framework must involve: a commitment to justice-focused efforts and to forward and center the experiences and knowledge of BIPOC as valued and essential. This particular articulation and the relationship between those two CRT elements and LIS are important to establish in order to attend to the specificity of LIS as an institution, one that is a racially dominant location of knowledge production, holding, and indexing, while claiming justice as a priority. This is necessary because although White Supremacy is predictable, it manifests contextually across social institutions, locations, borders, and time. Below, we extend and bring the chapters together around knowledge, power, information, and race, while offering insight into the process of identifying and naming the problem, and then, following from that understanding, determining the action, with BIPOC knowledge informing the justice effort.

In this (re)imagining of a CRT of LIS, we imagine what LIS could be if it began with the foundational CRT principles of a commitment to social justice and a rooted centering that the experiences and knowledge of BIPOC are valid, vital, and life-giving. We want to expand on what Tiffany Loftin, the director of the NAACP Youth and College Division, called "an abundance agenda," or "freedom as a proactive frame of reference," on the *Brown Girls Guide to Politics* podcast (Gholar 2020), by which we understood Loftin to mean that we must reframe our fight as a struggle *for* rather than *against*, to prevent burnout. We can push for BIPOC knowledge without invalidating or rejecting other knowledge(s) or considering it less valuable in order to make our own knowledge more important. To do so would not only be using the master's tools (Lorde 2007), but also lead to fatigue in the long run. As we are committed to structurally transforming LIS to be more just, we must continue toward liberation for and with BIPOC by interrupting how White Supremacy continues to construct knowledge under the same guise as the law, "seen as neutral, objective, and apolitical," as noted in the introduction.

By validating what is and is not knowledge—through the scholarship LIS produces, collections we center and make space for, institutional arrangements, and classification systems—LIS plays a key role in (re)constructing whiteness, gender, and racial power. Because knowledge, as it exists in library and archival collections, is created predominantly by white, cisgendered, wealthy, nondisabled, heterosexual men, and in support of white hegemony, knowledge is considered objective, color evasive, and true. Any other ways of knowing are not valid knowledge and therefore do not belong in a library or archive. As both the contributions of Anastasia Chiu, Fobazi Ettarh, and Jennifer Ferretti, and Morales and Williams demonstrate, libraries have a long-rooted allegiance to White Supremacy, beyond collections. The chapters in this book go a long way toward deconstructing how dominant white racial knowledges have maintained their power and control in society and LIS (and the consequences of that), while also reclaiming the knowledges that we, as BIPOC, have had all along and which deserve to be valued and regarded as a vital, leading part of a movement toward social justice and the fundamental restructuring of power in LIS. Morales and Williams establish epistemic supremacy's chokehold in this country, stating, "It seeks to establish biased, racialized information as fact and gains legitimacy through widespread dissemination across all media platforms." This is a key idea—libraries and archives are used to legitimize harmful, racialized information as knowledge (here we gain insight into how information institutions are actively constructing race) and disseminate said knowledge, while erasing other forms of knowledge, particularly those created by BIPOC.

The majority of information about BIPOC and other marginalized communities is from the dominant (read: white, cisgendered, heterosexual, nondisabled male, etc.) cultural perspective. Miranda Belarde-Lewis (Zuni/Tlingit) and Sarah Kostelecky (Zuni Pueblo) make this very point in their chapter:

Research by outsiders has resulted in the publication and dissemination of ancient sacred knowledge, esoteric traditions, and religious practices—without free, prior, and informed consent of Zunis. The information and knowledge collected was not the author's information to share or the readers' to know. In addition, subsequent publications build on this unethical work and continue to depict us only as historic people, ignoring our contemporary lives, which are a mix of our traditional culture and modern conveniences.

They make clear the danger and destruction in having Zuni stories told only by non-Zuni peoples, as do Sujei Lugo Vázquez; Shaundra Walker; and Torie Quiñonez, Lalitha Nataraj, and Antonia Olivas, with regard to other Black, Indigenous, and Latinx communities of color. Having someone else tell and hold your story allows them to direct the public narrative and results in stereotypes, myths, dehumanization, a shallower understanding of the story, and worse. It allows whiteness to dictate who BIPOC are allowed to be and justifies punishment when BIPOC do not fall into their neat, little categories. Vani Natarajan emphasizes this point through the lens of academic library collections when they state,

Deficit narratives get used to justify inequality and forced assimilation of students of color into dominant, white, class-privileged culture. They keep us from accessing knowledge about our communities and histories in our schools—all in the name of "helping" People of Color, even "saving" us from ourselves.

Not only are BIPOC perspectives continually, systematically erased, or positioned as less-than and needing to move toward whiteness, but our own knowledge is restricted from us. Harrison Inefuku, in particular, illustrates the dangers inherent in allowing the racist status quo of the scholarly communication system to continue as it is. Both he and Quiñonez, Nataraj, and Olivas introduce the term "apartheid of knowledge," gifted to us by Dolores Delgado Bernal and Octavio Villalpando (2002), to help demonstrate how Eurocentric knowledge is set in opposition to all other epistemological viewpoints. Libraries and archives, as well as the other social institutions they are connected to, will need to reckon with our role in upholding this intentional apartheid of knowledge.

In many of the chapters in the collection, the authors layer their analysis and arguments by combining several schools of thought that further advance their project's racial justice focus, thus engaging CRT's interdisciplinary approach (Matsuda et al. 1993; Yosso et al. 2009). Even the idea that knowledge can be interdisciplinary and intertwined is one that can be hard to express with intentionally exclusionary classification systems like the Library of Congress Subject Headings (LCSHs), as Chiu, Ettarh and Ferretti demonstrate with their examples of how difficult it can be to change headings that dehumanize whole groups of racialized, undocumented immigrant peoples. Our current classification systems have difficulty with nuance and complexity (Drabinski 2013). These systems deracialize and omit headings that allow BIPOC knowledge to be discoverable, which Inefuku affirms by pointing out that "Critical Race Theory" is not a LCSH. How will this book be classified by Library of Congress catalogers when the main heading it should be under does not even exist? What purpose does that flawed representation fulfill, and how does the absence of that descriptor contribute to the white-dominant racial hierarchy? The chapters by Belarde-Lewis and Kostelecky, Natarajan, and Quiñonez, Nataraj, and Olivas utilized distinct racialized expressions of Critical Race Theory—TribalCrit, Queer Critique of Color, and LatCrit—to attend to the specificity of racial domination experienced by Indigenous peoples and communities, queer communities of color, and Latinx peoples, in relation to the US government and libraries. How will folx interested in and who are part of these specific racialized communities discover their work if they don't already know it exists and are intentionally missing as part of White Supremacy's project to keep BIPOC knowledge out of white institutions? Considering the above questions together, we see the US nation-state, rooted in coloniality and White Supremacy, shape race, power, and knowledge in ways that socially reproduce hegemonic information classification and catalog systems.

Returning to collections, libraries and archives have been entrusted with the responsibility of upholding and maintaining dominant white racial knowledge narratives that overwhelming disempower communities of BIPOC and sustain racial subordination. Because that knowledge is seen as *neutral*, these institutions must necessarily be considered *neutral*, which then extends to workers in libraries and archives. Chiu, Ettarh, and Ferretti illuminate the circular reasoning this results in: "Because the written word is considered sacred, librarians who organize and bring together printed works are sacred by extension, and furthermore, any assumptions that they make about which materials are good for the library's community are seen to be true." If librarians and archivists are neutral and good, the continuation of that logic is that what we select for the collections must also be neutral and good—concepts that have been synonymous with whiteness, as many of these chapters have shown. What we have also seen to be true is that library and archival collections are primarily filled with the work of white folx, men in particular, because that is the only knowledge considered to be valid, true, and of value. Library and archival collections have been employed, both historically and presently, to uphold whiteness, similarly to property laws, on which the US nation-state is founded. As explored by Chiu, Ettarh, and Ferretti, Natarajan, and Kafi Kumasi, Cheryl I. Harris's concept of whiteness as property is used to demonstrate the policing of library spaces, colleges, libraries and their collections, and K–12 schooling and higher education. Harris points out that "whiteness and property share a common premise—a conceptual nucleus—of a right to exclude" (1714). As Anne Cong-Huyen and Kush Patel note, these same conditions, operations, and mechanisms of whiteness (psychic and material) in libraries and archives have led to the exclusion of BIPOC from LIS as a profession and from the spaces themselves (Leung 2019). This sophisticated, purposeful omission and erasure of BIPOC is critical to further normalize and protect knowledge rooted in whiteness. Yet, locating and understanding this phenomenon in LIS provides possibilities for carving out meaningful, authentic space for knowledges from BIPOC communities.

One of the ways this book is attempting to intervene in these racist systems (the White Supremacy of it all) is by expanding what is considered knowledge and establishing the significance and worth of BIPOC knowledge and experiential knowledge, in particular. Natarajan; Quiñonez, Nataraj, and Olivas; Jennifer Brown, Nicholae Cline (Coharie), and Marisa Méndez-Brady; Kumasi; Cong-Huyen and Patel; and Rachel Winston all illustrate the collective power and courage of counterstorytelling, and Lugo Vázquez and Walker also add the additional element of revisionist history. As Cong-Huyen and Patel write, "In recounting these personal stories, we are not trying to elicit sympathy. Instead, we draw connections between the personal, the political, and the theoretical and ground them in the real and material, a prominent concern of CRT." BIPOC stories are necessary in the struggle for social justice. Developing new and more just systems requires understanding how the old systems (and current ones) harmed and marginalized entire populations. Experiential knowledge, which is excluded from the foundations of traditional education for not being scientific, objective, or data-driven, forms the backbone of this change. As the chapters in the collection demonstrate, (settler) colonialism and White Supremacy are pervasive, intentional, and predictable, and they manifest in particular forms on the ground and in communities. Because of this, it becomes critically important to not just grow

CRT in LIS, but to center and attend to the very real, precise difference(s) experienced by communities of color.

Using the tenets and methodologies of racism as ordinary, critique of liberalism, and action oriented toward social justice, Isabel Espinal, April Hathcock, and Maria Rios show the material effects of racism, challenge the dominant diversity initiative approaches, and put forward a concrete proposal that we believe should force upper-level administration to contend with, that *they must* contend with. Their intervention is radical and specific. In fact, through CRT storytelling, the authors already envision how it will play out and the necessary solidarity it will require. In Kimberlé Williams Crenshaw's (2011) article, "Twenty Years of Critical Race Theory: Looking Back to Move Forward," she directs us to consider revisiting the past to understand contemporary configurations of racial power and help imagine new directions and possibilities. Crenshaw argues that the "key to building a coherent counter-narrative about race in American society is gathering up and integrating energies that are locked behind disciplinary walls and colorblind traditions" (1349). Engaging Crenshaw's idea of "looking back," both Walker and Lugo Vázquez center and share the stories of Black, Indigenous, and Afro–Puerto Rican women librarians and educators to offer inspiration, as Walker puts it, "[to] provide an opportunity for collection development to become a subversive, political activity, one with potential to create a revisionist collective history, a counternarrative to the prevailing stories about Black people that exist in many academic library collections."

We must connect present-day conditions to the chapters by our contributors because their work accounts for those bodies on the ground—the ones that get up, the ones that do not. Their research, scholarship, pedagogy, work holds them, it *applies to them*. This work is asking this question: What abundant, emancipatory futures can happen when we, as the authors in this collection have done, unquestioningly and collectively affirm and establish BIPOC knowledge and wisdom as foundational to the social and racial justice we are trying to get to?

ABUNDANT LIBERATORY AND CARING RACIAL FUTURES

Critical Race Theory is a movement that flows from the intellectual to a practice that can transform. The chapters in this book offer a vision that pushes the profession in a particular CRT direction that evokes foundational change. As Espinal, Hathcock, and Rios write, "Knowledge production for collective liberatory practices has been percolating on the fringes," and we want to move it front and center. We understand

and believe that "every site of knowledge is also a site of liberation" (Lipsitz 2020); this collection holds that understanding close to its heart and spirit. How has the process in shaping this book transformed us, Jorge and Sofia? Being in community with each other, with the chapter authors, and with the ideas in this book revolutionized us, awakened and reawakened us. It helped us see and feel how we could, and why we should, value everyone's humanity, especially that of BIPOC (who have been denied too long), within our current systems and structures because we allowed ourselves to be held accountable by each other. We feel more hopeful, thoughtful, patient with each other, and impatient with the rest of LIS. This book helped to establish boundaries of what we will and won't do. We hope it offers ways to actualize and carry forward ideas, actions, and principles in our professional and academic spaces that we move through and against. We want you, your praxis, your library, and our profession to be changed by this book.

With this project, we, the editors, purposefully carved out and held space for Black, Indigenous, and People of Color working in LIS, who, even while enjoined in this collective effort, were actively fighting off erasure of themselves and the communities to which they are accountable. These pages are a testament to the continued strength, resilience, and magic BIPOC are able to manifest even while undergoing trauma, experiencing structural racism, grappling with the legacies of (settler) colonialism and White Supremacy, and managing regular life interruptions. We, as fellow People of Color, understand the complexity of these struggles and pushed ourselves to uphold a principle of radical care to ensure that our contributors felt validated, cared for, and fully seen. As the late, beloved Toni Morrison said in a speech at Portland State University in 1975, "The very serious function of racism … is distraction. It keeps you from doing your work. It keeps you explaining, over and over again, your reason for being" (Morrison 1975). Having experienced this for ourselves, we tried to build in time for the violent effects of racism, for us, and for our contributors.

For us as editors, knowing what was happening in the world meant that this project of justice had to incorporate the principle of radical care from the beginning. This was nonnegotiable. How can we envision justice for ourselves if we can't hold ourselves accountable to the same values and standards we are advocating for? We wanted the process for this book to model the future systems and structures that CRT demands we construct in the name of liberation. By building community with this book and holding space for the experiences and knowledges that our chapter authors were bringing, we yielded what power we had as editors to allow them to share their vulnerabilities and what sustained them. The counterstories that white people have denounced or claimed were untrue were the truest stories in our eyes. These are the voices we bear witness to, that you are now bearing witness to. We challenged our chapter authors to claim their own empowerment, to use the language that was previously denied to us because of white racial domination. We assumed, and meaningfully held, the humanity of our chapter authors and ourselves. With that assumption and understanding, we were able to imagine what was possible for this project, without restraint.

We were inspired and moved by notions of refusal, thinking and feeling about our praxis, and how we might actualize CRT in our (institutional, professional, and personal) lives and realities, as well as in the communities we claim and to which we are accountable. We took our cues from Tuck and Yang (2018), and from here on, we refuse racial and social justice projects that "require us to prove humanity or worth[,] … appeal to the people who abuse us" (8), hoard power, employ only one way of doing things, force us to convince people, or even worse, convert people's thinking, accept "perfection" or "objectivity," or use a false sense of urgency to ignore the very real harm we could cause with our "solution" (Jones and Okun 2001). What will you discard from your practice or praxis? What no longer serves the communities you claim to support? What will you refuse to be complicit in?

With all that we refuse, we open up space for "collective liberatory practices" that align with CRT's goal of eliminating all forms of oppression through social justice action. While CRT gives us the tools to dismantle structures of White Supremacy, it also opens up pathways for us to move toward more racially just futures. CRT lends itself to a theoretical, speculative imagination, as many of the contributors in this work demonstrate. In particular, Natarajan's chapter advances a Queer Critique of Color to dream a world-building and meaning-making future that defies structures, boundaries, containment. Held in those pages are lessons on solidarity, taking up less space, belonging, and becoming. Kumasi's contribution shows us how fiction can expand our thinking around possible futures that allow Black youth to use their experiential knowledge to change the systems perpetuating violence against them for just existing. The book's collective mind created a whole host of ways to engage with and build justice-driven practices and systems.

We want to also take Gloria Ladson-Billings's following warning to heart, though she is specifically referring to the field of education, as we have already seen misuse and misunderstanding of CRT in LIS:

If we are serious about solving these problems … we have to be serious about intense study and careful rethinking of race and education. Adopting and adapting CRT as a framework for educational equity means that we will have to expose racism in education *and* propose radical solutions for addressing it. We will have to take bold and sometimes unpopular positions…but I fear we may never assume the liminal position because of its dangers, its discomfort, and because we insist on thinking of ourselves as permanent residents in a *nice* field like education. (1998, 22)

LIS is in danger of falling into the same trap that Ladson-Billings describes, where vocational awe is holding us captive in White Supremacy's embrace. We have to recalibrate our understanding of the world and stop holding so tightly to the idea that our profession is nice, good, and neutral, as Lugo Vázquez and Cong-Huyen and Patel have pointed out. We have to stop causing harm through the privileged roles we hold in libraries and archives. Recognize where we have agency, where we have multiple, small powers in our proximity to the community. We must listen to Chiu, Ettarh, and Ferretti's demand "that libraries finally change, not only to meet the world that we currently live in but to meet the world that we are striving for." We can use interest convergence to push for the change we want to see—as Brown, Cline, and Méndez-Brady remind us, libraries and librarians, archives and archivists don't want to be seen as racist or bad. We can employ Morales and Williams's powerful new praxis to fight an equally powerful structure of domination: epistemic supremacy. To fundamentally change libraries, Morales and Williams show us that "transformative librarianship is a pathway that could allow us to fully lean into our purpose of transforming and upholding libraries as the cornerstone of democracy. But it can only be achieved by recognizing epistemic supremacy as a framework being used to dismantle working-class and poor communities of color. We need a commitment to dismantling that epistemic supremacy, and to challenging it and ourselves at every turn."

BIPOC are born racialized and have been pushing beyond the racial boundaries placed on us to envision who we could be. White people have had little practice thinking of themselves as racialized, even though they are. CRT demands that all of us, but especially white people, accept and understand that racialization and determine for ourselves how it will shape laws, institutions, and policies. Jonathan Metzl, in a conversation with the activist DeRay Mckesson on the podcast *Pod Save the People*, argues that white people need to (re)claim their whiteness and decide what they want it to be, how they want it to be defined (2019). Do you all want to be defined by White Supremacists and the so-called alt-right? Or, just as dangerous, by progressive left-liberal whiteness? Do you want to be defined as the people oppressing all other peoples? Or do you want to join BIPOC in "solidarity not charity" (Piepzna-Samarasinha 2018, 41), to move toward the justice we know can exist?

In the direction of justice, care, and community are two foundational elements of radical transformation that we believe are absolutely rooted in the very fabric of CRT, even though they are not explicitly outlined as tenets of the framework. To help us imagine liberatory racial futures full of caring and community, we extend Winston's framework's caring tenet that's grounded in a Black feminist ethic of caring, return to adrienne maree brown's *Emergent Strategy*, which begins with the assumption, "Existence is fractal—the health of the cell is the health of the species and the planet" (2017, 13), and engage the work of disability justice activist Leah Lakshmi Piepzna-Samarasinha. Both brown and Piepzna-Samarasinha employ intersectional, radical care as foundational to their work. All of our contributors demand and deserve a level of abundance and radical care with their chapters from you, the reader. By centering BIPOC counterstories and treating BIPOC knowledge and experience as vital and essential, they model the care, trust, and importance with which we must show BIPOC counterstories, knowledges, and experiences. As Cong-Huyen and Patel argue, "It's about making each other feel *cared for, seen,* and *heard.*" Natarajan's use of abundance instead of capital when unpacking Yosso's framework makes space for all of humanity and brings us in community with one another. To engage with justice work requires radical care from all of us; it is what will sustain us in this long revolution. When care is central to the work, it allows space for healing, for growing. We provided some examples of what this can look like in real time, but will now explore some of the underlying principles.

"There is always enough time for the right work." (brown 2017, 41)

Radical care, to us, means assuming the humanity of the most marginalized folx, extending empathy for the violence and lack of care they often experience, and offering solidarity, patience, and gratitude for sharing space, time, and energy with us. To do that, you must build in time, energy, and the expectation that your first reaction of impatience, fear, or anger needs to be smothered and ignored or sat with and interrogated. The right work is having care for the people you are engaged with in your projects of justice. Ask them what they need from you to do their work. Make time to engage one-on-one and in whole-group settings.

"Small is good, small is all … [and] what you pay attention to grows." (brown 2017, 41–42)

The small acts matter. How you get to a milestone, a goal, a dream matters more than getting there. Small-scale change leads to large-scale change. The big picture will reflect what happens in smaller instances, so it is important to attend to those moments. Decide what you want to pay attention to, what you want to grow.

"Trust the People. (If you trust the people, they become trustworthy.)" (brown 2017, 42)

Our question here is, why wouldn't you trust the people? If you can't trust the people you are engaged in justice work with, why are you working with them? In some cases, of course, you can't always choose who you work with, but by extending your trust and vulnerability first, you empower others to do the same.

"Move at the speed of trust. Focus on critical connections more than critical mass—build the resilience by building the relationships." (brown 2017, 42)

In the types of movements and justice projects we are involved in, building the relationships are vital to the work itself. We cannot move forward without trust in each other and the rest of the community engaged in this work. Ask yourself how you can develop trust with others. Again, make time to do this essential work. If something goes wrong, think about your own actions first and where you might have made a misstep before jumping to defensiveness or blaming the other person or group.

"Networks for care by and for us." (Piepzna-Samarasinha 2018, 33)

We created the community we needed for the book, a network of care by and for us. We don't all have the same needs, but we know that we all have needs and we have to communicate what they are to each other. Many of the chapters illustrate the same desire for building networks of care and mentorship, in particular those of Quiñonez, Nataraj, and Olivas; Winston; and Natarajan.

"A model of solidarity not charity—of showing up for each other in mutual aid and respect." (Piepzna-Samarasinha 2018, 41)

Instead of imagining that those with less privilege need your help or charity, imagine that you need their help equally, if not more so. The answers to a truly just world lie with those most impacted and if we don't demonstrate solidarity with one another, we will never know those answers. Natarajan asks us to consider these profound questions: "What would it mean to hold open the possibility that for all of us, as People of Color, the ways we live, feel, and name our genders and sexualities might change, might grow, might dismantle normative structures? What languages (beyond the categories we are used to) would feel important to us in recognizing this? How could we be more generous with each other, by each admitting what we don't know?"

CLAIM SPACE FOR JOY

All projects for justice must claim space for joy. How will we sustain ourselves for the long freedom struggle ahead? Throughout the journey of this justice project, we tried to generate, touch, and build on moments of joy. As Piepzna-Samarasinha writes, "Dream ways to access care deeply, in a way where we are in control, joyful, building community, loved, giving, and receiving, that doesn't burn anyone out or abuse or underpay anyone in the process" (2018, 33). This is the hardest principle to achieve, and the one that requires the most imagination. But, in the pages that have come before, it has been realized. It has happened. How gorgeous, strong, and magnificent it is that we find joy when we are surrounded on all sides by people, places, and organizations that continually harm us.

As we move toward just landscapes, we believe deeply that something brought you to these voices and words; we *know* you found more than you were hoping for. As the ancestor Grace Lee Boggs said, "We have to change ourselves in order to change the world" (Lee 2014). This book is meant to give you a starting point or midpoint on your journey of transformation. It is meant to empower you to build a community that "engages these questions [we've raised throughout] collectively with a certain intention" (Crenshaw 2011, 1351).

It is necessary to listen to Black, Indigenous, and People of Color—*we* are the scholars of our own liberation. We invite you to reflect on and respond to all of the questions asked in this book, individually, collectively, and holistically, for further engagement, collusion, and coalitions. We hope the work pushes CRT deeper in LIS, constructs new, imaginative ways of being and doing, and changes how we understand the purpose and role of LIS. It has to; it must. Locating the work at a necessary point of redirection in LIS, one of our chapter contributors, Myrna Morales, said it best: "Everything we are offering in this collection together [has] to be the sharpest, precise-est intervention." Here in this specific moment, together with Anastasia Chiu, Fobazi M. Ettarh, Jennifer A. Ferretti, Myrna E. Morales, Stacie Williams, Jennifer Brown, Nicholae Cline, Marisa Méndez-Brady, Miranda Belarde-Lewis, Sarah R. Kostelecky, Vani Natarajan, Sujei Lugo Vázquez, Shaundra Walker, Harrison W. Inefuku, Isabel Espinal, April M. Hathcock, Maria Rios, Torie Quiñonez, Lalitha Nataraj, Antonia Olivas, Anne Cong-Huyen, Kush Patel, Rachel E. Winston, Kafi Kumasi, Todd Honma, Anthony Dunbar, and Tonia Sutherland, we believe it is.

TRAJECTORIES ON THE HORIZON

As this collection is one project in the direction of building just sites in LIS, we believe it is necessary to hold space for the absences and silences observed through-out the shaping of this book. This allows for possible new movements and paths to emerge and form. With the collection guiding us, we turn away from it and look toward the horizon to offer ideas, insights, and suggestions for future directions of Critical Race Theory in and of LIS.

One of the central aims of the collection is to structurally transform libraries by examining the consequences of White Supremacy in LIS through a CRT lens. Yet, notably missing from that sentence is a specific geographical location. In previous sections above, we state that White Supremacy is a force that is widespread and does not recognize borders. In other words, it is a global phenomenon, as are information institutions. Though this collection focused entirely on White Supremacy and colo-nialism in the US nation-state, we hope this focus prompts calls for contributions to further the Critical Race Theory projects in LIS transnationally.

A meaningful voice not in this collection is that of BIPOC faculty members who are currently teaching Critical Race Theory in LIS programs. Though this topic has been addressed elsewhere in recent LIS scholarship (Cooke and Sweeney 2017), given the professions' increased (often misguided) focus on diversity, equity, and inclusion—which we noted in the introduction—and the current geopolitical moment, a CRT approach in the LIS classroom undoubtedly presents challenges, movements, and transformations. But not only just for the faculty members, but for the learners in that space as well. Just as significantly, current or recent, BIPOC LIS student perspectives are importantly needed to contribute new, critical, attentive ideas and critiques of not only White Supremacy in LIS through a CRT lens, but also deeply rooted imaginaries of knowing, being, community, and lifeways beyond LIS as an institution, beyond the nation-state. Finally, this collection lacked the voice of library and archive workers who do the necessary day-to-day labor (e.g., processing and shelving the collections, cleaning the spaces, opening and closing buildings) that often gets erased but is central to the running of these institutions. How would our libraries and archives be improved by including these voices, particularly as many of them are BIPOC?

We hope that this collection points toward a generative conversation of further estab-lishing a Critical Race Theory *of* library and information studies framework. Many of the authors—ourselves included—employ CRT from either law or education. This is not a limitation of the chapters or collection, but rather signals a need for a distinct, clearly defined framing specific to LIS. We also understand, as the CRT legal scholar Devon W. Carbado (2011) expresses, that establishing boundaries can fracture movements and that that inclusion-exclusion process is perhaps in contradiction to the justice aims of CRT projects (1602–1607), and we know borders are always already political. Educational Critical Race Theorists Adrienne D. Dixson and Celia K. Rousseau Anderson (2017) suggest that setting boundaries also provides "a way to determine what might be left to do" (34). With that in mind, we hope future thinking and writing sets clear boundaries, while understanding that the core ideas in a CRT of LIS are shifting, developing, and understood as not final, not complete. In this way, a deeper, richer, and more complex framework might inform theory and practice, pushing our fields, profession, and institutions in a particular direction to understand and, ultimately, destroy White Supremacy. We invite collective meditations to further shape a CRT of LIS.

Thinking and dreaming toward, and through, where we hope the collection goes, we are pulled to appeal and direct the work to professional associations: the American Library Association, the Association of College and Research Libraries, and the Society of American Archivists. We are supposed to hope the collection makes its way to institutional diversity, equity, and inclusion committees or task forces, and moves in on LIS research and curriculum, and all levels of administration. Yet, we refuse that appeal and expectation.

It would bring us joy if BIPOC information workers committed to liberation engaged, debated, and assessed these ideas. We hope the work opens up new pathways of hope, imagination, and community, reshaping our relationships to the world, each other, and ourselves. The work, we hope, is always already in motion, and in the same moment, already where it needs to be, right here with you.

NOTE

1. As the central framework of this collection is Critical Race Theory (CRT)—which guides our approaches, understandings, and questions—it, in general, does not take up land and non–human being oppression; however, we believe it is necessary to attend to those relations in justice projects as we reimagine a new social order.

BIBLIOGRAPHY

brown, adrienne maree. 2017. *Emergent Strategy—Shaping Change, Changing Worlds*. Chico, CA: AK Press.

Carbado, Devon W. 2011. "Critical What What?" *Connecticut Law Review* 43 (5): 1593–1643. https://docs.wixstatic.com/ugd/17f3ef_2a72b27f3371460aad375c8b55d40a4b.pdf.

Cooke, Nicole A., and Miriam E. Sweeney, eds. 2017. *Teaching for Justice: Implementing Social Justice in the LIS Classroom*. Sacramento, CA: Library Juice Press.

Crenshaw, Kimberlé W. 2011. "Twenty Years of Critical Race Theory: Looking Back to Move Forward." *Connecticut Law Review* 43 (5): 1253–1353. https://docs.wixstatic.com/ugd/17f3ef_73ef859 9d44d44fd9433c46399b96928.pdf.

Delgado Bernal, Dolores, and Octavio Villalpando. 2016. "An Apartheid of Knowledge in Academia: The Struggle over the 'Legitimate' Knowledge of Faculty of Color." In *Foundations of Critical Race Theory in Education*, edited by Edward Taylor, David Gillborn, and Gloria Ladson-Billings, 77–91. New York: Routledge.

Dixson, Adrienne D., and Celia K. Rousseau Anderson. 2017. "And We Are Still Not Saved: 20 Years of CRT and Education." In *Critical Race Theory in Education: All God's Children Got a Song*, edited by Adrienne D. Dixson, Celia K. Rousseau Anderson, and Jamel K. Donnor, 34–38. 2nd ed. New York: Routledge.

Drabinski, Emily. 2013. "Queering the Catalog: Queer Theory and the Politics of Correction." *Library Quarterly* 83 (2): 94–111. https://doi.org/10.1086/669547.

Gholar, A'shanti F. 2020. "What Can We Expect in 2020?" *The Brown Girls Guide to Politics* (podcast). February 3, 2020. https://www.thebggguide.com/the-bgg-podcast/episode/d1f796e3/what -can-we-expect-in-2020.

Harding, Vincent. 1970. "Black Students and the Impossible Revolution." *Journal of Black Studies* 1 (1): 75–100.

Harris, Cheryl I. 1995. "Whiteness as Property." In *Critical Race Theory: The Key Writings That Formed the Movement*, edited by Kimberlé Crenshaw, Neil Gotanda, Gary Peller, and Kendall Thomas, 276–292. New York: The New Press.

Jones, Kenneth, and Tema Okun. 2001. "The Characteristics of White Supremacy Culture." In *Dismantling Racism: A Work*. ChangeWork. https://www.showingupforracialjustice.org/white -supremacy-culture-characteristics.html.

Ladson-Billings, Gloria. 1998. "Just What Is Critical Race Theory and What's It Doing in a Nice Field like Education?" *International Journal of Qualitative Studies in Education* 11 (1): 7–24. https:// doi.org/10.1080/095183998236863.

Lee, Grace, dir. 2014. *American Revolutionary: The Evolution of Grace Lee Boggs*. Documentary. San Francisco: Center for Asian American Media.

Leung, Sofia. 2019. "Whiteness as Collections." Accessed September 1, 2019. https://www .sofiayleung.com/thoughts/whiteness-as-collections.

Lipsitz, George. 2020. "Contesting Colorblindness; Decolonizing Knowledge." Lecture/Discussion, Critical Race Theory & Intersectionality: Key Concepts in the Fight against Anti-Black Racism. African American Policy Forum Summer School, July 28, 2020.

Lorde, Audre. 2007. "The Master's Tools Will Never Dismantle the Master's House." In *Sister Outsider: Essays and Speeches*, 110–14. Berkeley, CA: Crossing Press.

Matsuda, Mari, Charles R. Lawrence III, Richard Delgado, and Kimberlé Williams Crenshaw, eds. 1993. *Words That Wound: Critical Race Theory, Assaultive Speech and the First Amendment.* Boulder, CO: Westview Press.

Mckesson, DeRay, Clint Smith, Brittany Packnett, and Samuel Sinyangwe. 2019. "Walk into Your Gifts." *Pod Save the People* (podcast), August 13, 2019. https://crooked.com/podcast/walk-into -your-gifts/.

Morrison, Toni. 1975. "A Humanist View." Speech delivered at Portland State University, Portland, OR, May 30, 1975. https://www.mackenzian.com/wp-content/uploads/2014/07/Transcript _PortlandState_TMorrison.pdf.

Piepzna-Samarasinha, Leah Lakshmi. 2018. *Care Work: Dreaming Disability Justice.* Vancouver, BC: Arsenal Pulp Press.

Tuck, Eve, and K. Wayne Yang, eds. 2018. *Toward What Justice?* New York: Routledge.

Yosso, Tara, William Smith, Miguel Ceja, and Daniel Solórzano. 2009. "Critical Race Theory, Racial Microaggressions, and Campus Racial Climate for Latina/o Undergraduates." *Harvard Educational Review* 79 (4): 659–691. https://doi.org/10.17763/haer.79.4.m6867014157m7071.

CONTRIBUTOR BIOGRAPHIES

Miranda H. Belarde-Lewis (Zuni/Tlingit) is an Assistant Professor in the Information School at the University of Washington. Indigenous knowledge systems are central to her work as she examines the role of the arts in protecting, documenting, and perpetuating Native information and knowledge. She has worked with tribal, city, state, and federal museums to create Native-focused educational programming, publications, and exhibitions. She holds an MA in Museology and a PhD in Information Science, both from the University of Washington.

Jennifer Brown is an Undergraduate Learning and Research Librarian at the University of California, Berkeley, where she employs critical pedagogies such as Critical Race Theory (CRT), visionary fiction, and speculative futuring as part of her reference and instructional approaches. She received her MS in Information from the University of Michigan and her BA in Media Studies from UC Berkeley. Her research and creative interests include understanding how labor inequities permeate the academy, examining institutional diversity work through the lens of performativity, conducting close readings of media through the lens of blackness, queerness, and disability, and writing SFF short stories and novels.

Anastasia Chiu is a first-generation Chinese American and works as a Scholarly Communications Librarian at New York University. They are a former Cataloging and Metadata Librarian. They are interested in interrogating White Supremacy in library institutional work cultures, applying relational cultural approaches to library work, and educating about rights and copyright in digital collections. Anastasia received their MSLIS from St. John's University.

Nicholae Cline (Coharie) is the Scholarly Services Librarian at Indiana University Libraries, where they serve as subject liaison to the Media School and Gender Studies and Philosophy departments. They received their MLS from Indiana University's School of Library and Information Science (SLIS). Their research interests include ethics and epistemology; critical theory; animal liberation; queerness and gender studies; feminism; critical race and ethnic studies (particularly

Indigenous history and mixed-race identity); diversity, equity, and inclusion in higher education; and activism and social justice. Nicholae identifies as mixed-race, Indigenous, nonbinary, and queer, among probably many other things, depending on the day.

Anne Cong-Huyen is the Digital Scholarship Strategist at the University of Michigan Library. She was previously the Digital Pedagogy Librarian, and prior to that was the Digital Scholar and Coordinator of the Digital Liberal Arts Program at Whittier College, and a Mellon Visiting Assistant Professor of Asian American Studies at the University of California, Los Angeles. She holds a PhD in English from the University of California, Santa Barbara. She is a cofounder of #transformDH, serves on the steering committee of HASTAC, and is a director of the Situated Critical Race + Media collective of FemTechNet.

Anthony W. Dunbar is a thought leader in the areas of equity, inclusion, diversity (EID) and social justice, has experience as a project manager, EID consultant, adjunct professor, and has served as both an academic and public librarian. He received his PhD in Information Studies and MLIS from UCLA.

Isabel Espinal is the Research Services Librarian for Afro American Studies; Latin American, Caribbean, and Latinx Studies; Native American and Indigenous Studies; Spanish and Portuguese; and Women, Gender and Sexuality Studies at the University of Massachusetts Amherst. She is a past president of REFORMA, the National Association to Promote Library and Information Services to Latinos and the Spanish-Speaking, and has written and given presentations on whiteness and diversity in librarianship, Latinx information literacy, the climate crisis and libraries, Latinx literature, and Dominican women and transnationalism, among other topics. She has a PhD in American Studies (2018) from the University of Massachusetts Amherst. In 2003, she was named a Mover & Shaker by *Library Journal.*

Fobazi M. Ettarh is currently the Undergraduate Success Librarian at Rutgers University, Newark. A school librarian by training, she specializes in information literacy instruction, K–12 pedagogy, and co-curricular outreach. Creator of the concept "vocational awe," her research is concerned with the relationships and tensions between the espoused values of librarianship and the realities present in the experiences of marginalized librarians and users. She is also the creator of the open-access video game *Killing Me Softly: A Game about Microaggressions*, which leads the user through the personal and professional effects of ongoing microaggressions. She is a 2020 *Library Journal* Mover & Shaker and author of the blog *WTF Is a Radical Librarian?*, which examines the intersections of librarianship, labor, identity, and diversity. You can find her on twitter at @Fobettarh.

Jennifer A. Ferretti is an artist and Digital Initiatives Librarian at the Maryland Institute College of Art on Piscataway Land (Baltimore, Maryland). She is a first-generation American Latina/Mestiza whose librarianship is guided by critical praxis, not neutrality. With a firm belief that art is information, she is interested in the knowledge making and research methodologies of artists and non-Western forms of knowledge making and sharing. Recognizing the impact of the overwhelming whiteness of the library and information science profession, in 2016 she started the online community We Here specifically for people who identify as Black, Indigenous, and People of Color working in libraries and archives. Twitter: @citythatreads.

April M. Hathcock is the Director of Scholarly Communications and Information Policy at New York University on Mannahatta, an ancestral island of the Lenni Lenape. Her work involves educating the campus community on issues of ownership, access, and rights in the research life cycle. She has a JD and LLM in International and Comparative Law from Duke University School of Law and, before entering librarianship, practiced intellectual property and antitrust law for a global private firm. Her research interests include antiracism and anti-oppression in librarianship and higher education, cultural creation and exchange, and the ways in which social and legal infrastructures benefit the works of certain groups over others. She was named a *Library Journal* Mover & Shaker in 2018. April identifies as queer, femme, Black, and Indigenous and is the author of the article "White Librarianship in Blackface: Diversity Initiatives in LIS." She also writes the blog *At the Intersection*, which examines issues at the intersection of feminism, libraries, social justice, and the law.

Todd Honma is an Associate Professor of Asian American Studies at Pitzer College. His research focuses on race and social justice in LIS, Asian American popular culture, body modification, and zines and independent publishing. His work has been published in journals such as *InterActions: UCLA Journal of Education and Information Studies*, *Amerasia*, *AAPI Nexus*, *Radical Teacher*, and *Continuum: Journal of Media and Cultural Studies*.

Harrison W. Inefuku is the Scholarly Publishing Services Librarian at Iowa State University. He launched Iowa State University's institutional repository in 2012 and oversaw the development of a rapidly growing repository with high levels of faculty engagement across campus. More recently, he has worked to launch the Iowa State University Digital Press, Iowa State's library publishing program with a commitment to open-access publishing and the diversification of the scholarly record. Harrison advocates for diversity, inclusion, and social justice in libraries and archives and has published and presented on systemic biases in academic publishing. He received the Library Publishing Coalition's 2017 Award for Outstanding Scholarship in Library Publishing with his coauthor Charlotte Roh for their chapter, "Agents of Diversity and Social Justice: Librarians and Scholarly Communication."

Sarah R. Kostelecky (Zuni Pueblo) is an Associate Professor and the Director of Digital Initiatives and Scholarly Communication (DISC) at the University of New Mexico's College of University Libraries and Learning Sciences. Previously she served as the Subject Librarian for the College of Education and was part of the Indigenous Nations Library Program, also at UNM. In her prior position she was the Library Director at the Institute of American Indian Arts in Santa Fe, New Mexico. Sarah earned both her BA and MLS from the University of Arizona and was a 2002 Spectrum Scholar and in the Knowledge River first cohort. Her research interests include Indigenous representation in library collections and Indigenous language revitalization strategies.

Kafi Kumasi is an Associate Professor in the School of Information Sciences at Wayne State University. As a native Detroiter and former K–12 teacher and school librarian, her scholarly interests center around issues of young adult literacy, library education, diversity and inclusion, and hip hop culture. She recently developed a model using hip hop to explore youth's information creation behaviors, called InFLOmation. She has held numerous leadership positions, including editorial board member of the *International Journal for Information Diversity and Inclusion* (*IJIDI*);

executive board member of the Young Adult Library Services Association (YALSA); and mentor for the LILEAD Project, a professional development program for school library leaders. Her publications have appeared in top-ranked journals such as *Library and Information Science Research*, *School Library Research*, and *Library Trends*. She currently oversees the experimental School Library Media Certificate Program (15hr) at Wayne State.

Sofia Y. Leung is a librarian, facilitator, and educator in the Boston area. She is a first-generation Chinese American, originally from Brooklyn, New York. Her website is available at sofiayleung.com and her Twitter handle is @sofiayleung.

Jorge R. López-McKnight is a community college library worker. He currently lives in Austin, Texas.

Sujei Lugo Vázquez, a former elementary school librarian in Puerto Rico, is a children's librarian at the Boston Public Library. She holds an MLIS from the University of Puerto Rico, Río Piedras Campus, and is currently a doctoral candidate at Simmons University, focusing on race and children's librarianship. She is an active member of REFORMA (National Association to Promote Library and Information Services to Latinos and the Spanish-Speaking) and ALSC (Association for Library Service to Children), as well as the We Are Kid Lit Collective. Her body, mind, and solidarity constantly travel between Puerto Rico and Boston. Twitter: @sujeilugo

Marisa Méndez-Brady is an academic librarian currently living in Los Angeles. She received her Master's of Science in Information Studies (MSIS) at the University of Texas at Austin, has a graduate certificate in Instructional Design from the University of Maine, and holds a BA in History from Haverford College. Marisa is a 2012 ALA Spectrum Scholar, a 2017 NEH—Global Book Histories Scholar, and a 2019 *Library Journal* Mover & Shaker. Born in the Dominican Republic and raised in New York, Marisa identifies as Latina. You can find her on Twitter @msmendezbrady.

Myrna E. Morales is currently running communications for the Massachusetts Coalition of Domestic Workers and is a PhD candidate in Library and Information Science at the University of Illinois iSchool. She was Program and Communications Director for Community Change, an organization dedicated to organizing white people to combat structural racism. She has an MA in Teaching from Brown University, an MS in Library and Information Science from Simmons College, and a BA in Urban Studies from Bates College. She spent some years studying medicine and socialism at the Latin American School of Medicine in Havana, Cuba, and working as a public school educator in Newark and Boston before working in research data ethics and technology management for the National Network of Libraries of Medicine, New England Region. A longtime activist and organizer, Myrna fights for social change across a spectrum of different social causes. Her rich background in medical education, education, library and information science, and political activism has helped her understand that information is not only a tool that enables, permits, and creates injustices, but also a tool that can guide us toward collective liberation.

Lalitha Nataraj is the Social Sciences Librarian at California State University San Marcos. She holds an MLIS from UCLA and a BA in English Literature and Women's Studies from UC Berkeley. Her research interests include feminist pedagogy, relational-cultural theory in LIS, South Asian Americans in librarianship, and the intersection of sartorial representation and teacher and student-scholar identities.

Vani Natarajan is a queer femme South Asian American librarian living in Brooklyn, New York. Their interests include writing poetry and lyric essays, making pottery, 35mm photography, and enjoying time with friends and chosen family.

Antonia Olivas is the Engagement and Inclusion Librarian at California State University San Marcos. She earned her doctorate in Educational Leadership from the joint doctoral program of UCSD and CSUSM in 2014 and earned her master's in Library Science from the University of Arizona in 2003. She is a Knowledge River Scholar (first cohort) and an ALA Spectrum Scholar (2002).

Kush Patel is currently Associate Professor of Architecture and the Humanities at Avani Institute of Design in Kerala, India. They were previously Associate Librarian of Digital Pedagogy at the University of Michigan, where they partnered with colleagues in the Library and on-campus units to address the challenges and potentials of community-engaged learning and public humanities work in the digital age around such methods as digital storytelling and community archiving. Prior to joining the Library, Kush was a Postdoctoral Fellow at the Institute for the Humanities and the Michigan Humanities Collaboratory. Kush received their PhD in Architecture from U-M Taubman College of Architecture and Urban Planning, and they colead Pedagogy of the Digitally Oppressed collective with scholars at the University of Toronto, Canada.

Torie Quiñonez is the Arts and Humanities Librarian at California State University San Marcos. She holds an MLIS from Pratt Institute and a BA in American Studies from UC Santa Cruz. As a first-generation college graduate and Chicana, her professional interest in critical pedagogy and information literacy intersects with personal investment in the transitional experiences of Latinx and first-generation college students as they negotiate multiple identities.

Maria Rios is an academic librarian at the University of Massachusetts Amherst who is committed to dismantling all forms of oppression while centering and amplifying historically marginalized voices. Her research interests explore the intersection of critical, creative, and contemplative pedagogies with a library and information science lens. Recognized as an Association of Research Libraries Kaleidoscope Scholar 2016–2018 cohort, she is also a member of the fourth class of Library Freedom Institute, a Library Freedom Project initiative. She earned her MLIS from the University of South Carolina and identifies as Black, Puerto Rican, queer, and femme.

Lori Salmon is the Head of the Institute of Fine Arts Library at New York University, where she administers the Stephen Chan Library of Fine Arts and the Conservation Center Library through the Division of Libraries. Lori has published and presented on the topics of artists' books, artists' writing, and critical librarianship. Her current research questions structures of library associations and library management. She earned her Master of Library Science degree from Queens College, City University of New York, and holds a Master of Arts degree in Art History and Criticism from Stony Brook, State University of New York.

Tonia Sutherland is an Assistant Professor of Archival Studies in the Library and Information Science Program at the University of Hawai'i at Mānoa. Sutherland holds a PhD and an MLIS from the University of Pittsburgh's School of Computing and Information (formerly the School of Information Studies). Global in scope, Sutherland's research focuses on entanglements of records, technology, and culture. She is particularly interested in critical and liberatory work in the fields of archival studies, digital culture studies, and science and technology studies (STS).

Shaundra Walker serves as Associate Director of Instruction and Research Services/Associate Professor at Georgia College in Milledgeville, Georgia. She holds a BA in History (United States and African American History), MSLS from Clark Atlanta University, and PhD (Educational Leadership) from Mercer University. Her research interests include the recruitment, retention, and development of librarians of color, and critical information literacy.

Stacie Williams is the inaugural director of the Center for Digital Scholarship at the University of Chicago Libraries, and a member of the Chicago-based Blackivist archivist collective, which works with individuals and organizations to preserve Black Chicagoland memory and culture. Williams was previously an advisory archivist for *A People's Archive of Police Violence in Cleveland*, a 2015 oral history project that documented people's experiences with police violence and harassment in the Cleveland metropolitan area, and was a journalist for more than ten years. Her first book, *Bizarro Worlds* (Fiction Advocate), a bibliomemoir about race and gentrification, was released in 2018. She is a 2010 Spectrum Scholar.

Rachel E. Winston is the inaugural Black Diaspora Archivist at the University of Texas at Austin, where her work promotes research and study on the Black Diaspora through primary source material, curated exhibitions, and archival activism. Rachel holds a degree in anthropology with a minor in French from Davidson College. She is an alumna of the Coro Fellows Program in Public Affairs, and received her MSIS with a graduate portfolio in museum studies from the University of Texas School of Information.

INDEX